barcode P9-EDV-220

TCHAIKOVSKY
A Self-portrait

VLADIMIR VOLKOFF

Tchaikovsky

A SELF-PORTRAIT

BOSTON
CRESCENDO PUBLISHING COMPANY

LONDON
ROBERT HALE & COMPANY

1·5·76

Library of Congress Catalog Card Number 73-84133

ISBN 0 87597 088 5

Published simultaneously in Great Britain by
Robert Hale & Company
Clerkenwell House
45–47 Clerkenwell Green
London EC1R 0HT

ISBN 0 7091 4976 X

Printed in Great Britain by
Clarke, Doble & Brendon Ltd.,
Plymouth

TO THE MEMORY OF
MY KINSMAN
PETER ILICH TCHAIKOVSKY
APOLOGETICALLY
DEDICATED
V.V.

Contents

Author's Foreword

This book is based on 1,621 direct or indirect quotations. To give all the references would have made it look like a bibliography in itself. The following solution was adopted. Quotations from Tchaikovsky's own writings are given in quote marks, but without reference; most of them have been translated by the author from the original; some translations have been borrowed from Western sources, after careful checking of their quality. Quotations from biographers and critics are footnoted; the footnote indicates simply the name of the source; complete identification will be found in the bibliography at the end of the book; pages from which the quotations are borrowed are not indicated, so as not to overwhelm the text. Double quotes indicate a direct quotation; single quotes, either a phrase borrowed from a sentence, or a sentence which had to be slightly modified (for instance by replacing a first person by a third person pronoun).

It is always a problem to spell Russian names in any other alphabet. There are now excellent scientific systems of transliteration but it is doubtful whether the reader would easily recognize Tchaikovsky and Tchekhov in Chajkovskij and Chexov. And then think about Christian names, which can be transliterated, transcribed phonetically, or translated, not counting, of course, their numberless diminutives. It must be confessed that no systematic rendition has been adopted here; tradition, pronunciation, spelling, onomastics have been curbed into a more or less peaceful coexistence.

As for the calendar, the Soviet system has been adopted. For events which take place in Russia, the date is given in the Julian calendar; for events outside Russia, in the usual Gregorian calendar. Add twelve days to the Julian date to obtain the Gregorian one.

V.V.

Acknowledgments

Acknowledgments to:

Mr G. A. Shamkin, Director of the Tchaikovsky Archives and Museum in Klin, U.S.S.R., for valuable documentary help.

Mr P. Schorokhov, for the use of the Tchaikovsky coat of arms.

Agnes Scott College, Decatur, Ga, U.S.A., for technical and documentary help.

The Novosti press-agency, for photographic material,

and, for permission to use excerpts from their respective publications, to the following copyright owners:

The Bodley Head for the extracts from *Life and Letters of P. I. Tchaikovsky* by Modest Tchaikovsky, translated by Rosa Newmarch.

Mr Wladimir Lakond for excerpts from *The Diaries of Tchaikovsky*, translated from the Russian and annotated by Wladimir Lakond. Copyright 1945 by Wladimir Lakond; renewed 1973 by Wladimir Lakond.

James Brown Associates for excerpts from *Tchaikovsky: the Man behind the Music* by Lawrence and Elisabeth Hanson, published by Dodd, Mead and Company, copyright 1966 by Lawrence and Elisabeth Hanson.

Haskell House for excerpts from *Tchaikovsky, his Life and Works* by Rosa Newmarch.

W. W. Norton and Company and Kennikat Press for excerpts from *The Music of Tchaikovsky* by G. Abraham published by Kennikat Press.

Herbert Weinstock for excerpts from *Tchaikovsky* by Herbert Weinstock, published by Alfred A. Knopf, copyright 1943 by Herbert Weinstock.

V.V.

Illustrations

PART ONE

TCHAIKOVSKY AND HIS IMAGE

1 *What is so special about Tchaikovsky*

If a contest were arranged between historical characters to select the one whose image differs the most from what his personality really was, there is little doubt that Rasputin would win the race by several lengths, and it does not seem improbable that Joan of Arc and Tchaikovsky would tie for second place. Political reasons may account for Rasputin and Joan acquiring this doubtful privilege, but Tchaikovsky must have earned it somehow for himself. How? Why? What is so special about the man?

The first noticeable singularity is the emotional atmosphere which even now surrounds his name. Tchaikovsky can be defined as the man no one ever spoke an understatement about. A specific kind of electricity runs through crowds rushing to his concerts; a distinctive brand of slightly hysterical disapproval prevails among most of his critics. Statistics showing his popularity will not be necessary, since his popularity is what critics seem to reproach him with, but some samples of their peevishness might be useful.

Among sophisticated music-lovers it is now a common saying that everyone ought to outgrow his calf-love for Tchaikovsky. For some "his music is like the measles: you catch it once, probably in late adolescence, and then you are done with it."[1] A French critic called him a composer of spa-music. About the First Symphony, subtitled *Winter Dreams*, witty critics like to comment "Lots of daydreams, little winter."[2] About the Second, Cui, after wallowing in adjectives like 'very weak, poor, rough, commonplace, infantile, pompous, trivial,' suitably concluded by stating that 'the end was beneath all criticism.' Still the most significant stricture belongs to the gentleman who flatly declared that Tchaikovsky's music stank.[3]

Even when critics feel favourably inclined, there is something melodramatic in the way they express it. For them the scherzo of the *Pathétique* is nothing less but the "unshackling of evil forces leading up to the almost too naturalistic despair of the adagio lamentoso."[4] They find Tchaikovsky endowed with "a practically pathological sense of duty to audience and orchestra."[5] And of

B

course no two specialists can agree on what is sublime and what is ridiculous in the composer's work.

In that respect the adjective 'vulgar' has had a particularly rewarding career: not only cannot critics agree on what is and what is not 'vulgar' in Tchaikovsky, but, though reluctant to dismiss the word as inaccurate, they disagree on what it is supposed to mean. According to one of them the *Capriccio Italiano* is "in a literal sense a vulgar (i.e. popular)" work, "but one at which surely no musician ought to turn up his nose—least of all any of those who have no qualms over the slobbering vulgarities (in the other sense) of, say, the last two symphonies."[6] Another is willing to admit that the finale of the Third Quartet is 'vulgar,' provided this means that it is not "namby-pamby" stuff.[7] A third one objects to 'vulgarity' being used "in the opprobious sense of the word," wants to make sure that it is not understood in the sense of 'indecency' and sees in Tchaikovsky's 'vulgarity' "the musical equivalent of the 'vulgar tongue' which includes not only the language of the guttersnipe, but at the other end of its wide field the magnificent one of the English Bible."[8] A fourth one argues with some appearance of good sense that "these criticisms are . . . based on the myth that beauty and artistic worth are in some profound way connected with what is hidden and difficult, and that therefore all which is immediately pleasing and accessible must, of its very essence, be inferior." And he concludes: "There is no reason to expect vulgarity of triviality in the music of a man who, with all his faults, was neither vulgar nor trivial."[9]

In other terms not only emotionalism surrounds Tchaikovsky, but ambiguity as well. "He who of all composers presents for the not-so-very-musical layman no problems whatever, is for the connoisseur a very perplexing figure."[10] It is frankly comical to watch critics and especially biographers wriggling out of their introductions or prefaces and explaining how Tchaikovsky is popular without being great, or great in spite of being popular, and how they, the connoisseurs, cannot stand his major works, but enjoy some of the minor ones, which are oh! so much more refined.

Poets and novelists have been less reticent. Tolstoi wept shamelessly while listening to the First Quartet; Tchekhov "loved" Tchaikovky's music "very much"; Apuhtin advised him to let the weight of his fame crush the scum of his censors; and the great French American novelist, Julian Green, after spending all his life with the *Chanson Triste* ringing in his ear, flies into raptures over Tatiana's letter to Onegin, filled with "the frightening tenderness of love at twenty, the magic of night, the surging of a whole being toward another." True, he adds with characteristic coyness that sometimes he 'cannot help loving' the musician who expressed all that.

This problem of resisting Tchaikovsky's appeal for sophisticated reasons seems to have been shared by many, though not by composers and professional musicians. Hans von Bülow admired the 'loftiness, strength and originality' of his ideas; more than that, he considered that Tchaikovsky had "that best of styles in which intention and craftsmanship are everywhere concealed." Vincent d'Indy was an enthusiastic admirer of *Eugene Onegin*. Gounod put Tchaikovsky forward as a candidate to the Académie des Beaux-Arts; he was not elected that time, but a little later Ambroise Thomas nominated him again and this time he was elected by 32 votes out of 35.* Debussy seems to have admired his first symphonies. Saint-Saëns approved of Tchaikovsky's 'piquant charms and dazzling fireworks,' his talent, his 'astounding technique' and the subtlety of his art. Dvorak felt himself 'transported to another world' by *Eugene Onegin*. Mahler produced *Onegin* and *Iolanthe*. Fauré—surely one who cannot be suspected of partiality for the 'vulgar'—sent two of his compositions to "the master" and expressed his 'highest admiration.' Liszt, when listening to a piece by Tchaikovsky after other contemporary productions, contributed a concise but strong-felt remark: "At last here is music again!"† Stravinsky, by no means a sentimental composer himself, considered Tchaikovsky not only as the most Russian of all composers, but as one of the masters of all times. About *The Sleeping Beauty* he wrote: "It is a great satisfaction to see produced a work of so direct a character at a time when so many people who are neither simple, nor naïve, nor spontaneous, seek in their art simplicity, 'poverty' and spontaneity. Tchaikovsky in his very nature possessed these three gifts to the fullest extent. That is why he never feared to let himself go, whereas the prudes, whether *raffinés* or academic, were shocked by the frank speech, free from artifice, of his music. Tchaikovsky possessed the art of *melody*. . . . It is absolutely indifferent to me that the quality of his melody was sometimes unequal. The fact is that he was a creator of *melody*, which is an extremely rare and precious gift. . . . And how characteristic were his predilections in the music of the past and of his own day! He worshipped Mozart, Couperin, Glinka, Bizet; that leaves no doubt of the quality of his taste."

---

* To the Académie des Beaux-Arts and not, as Herbert Weinstock has it, to the Académie Française, which is concerned solely with literature and composed only of French citizens.

† He also transcribed for the piano the Polonaise from *Eugene Onegin*.

For my part, being no connoisseur, I feel no need to apologize to anybody for whatever admiration I may have for Tchaikovsky. It is true that through the accident of my own musical taste, I generally happen to receive more listening pleasure from more austere music than his (Monteverdi's madrigals, Beethoven's quartets, if the reader insists on knowing), but I certainly do consider Tchaikovsky as one of the major composers of the second part of the nineteenth century. Still—and this, I think, is the place to confess it—my interest in him is not mainly musical.

If Tchaikovsky had lived till he was 95, I should have sat on his knee and called him Uncle Peter. He would have thought me utterly delightful, not because I was, but because he thought nearly all children so. He would have dedicated one or two piano pieces to me and I could have written, as so many people did, my reminiscences of him, even though I had had very few, since I should have been but three at the time. As it is, I have little (though some) unpublished material to share with the public, and the fact that my great-grandmother was his first cousin, or that his grandfather was my great-great-great-grandfather, does not make me an authority on him. Nevertheless—let the envious brand me a snob if they like—I do enjoy a famous kinsman, and the not-so-very-distant relation definitely was the first motivation which kept me through the reading of his two or three first biographies. The biographies did the rest.

For a new interest had arisen. Probably a little warier and may be better equipped than the average Western reader, I found myself in the process of discovering fallacies heaped upon fallacies, and what with family pride, a sound hunting instinct and some respect for the public, I felt it would be a thrilling—even if sacred—duty to track, pinpoint and refute all the untruths with which my great-grand-uncle's life and character had been embellished.

That is in brief the story of this book and explains why I felt the need for a new biography.

2 What about other biographies?

At this point the reader is entitled to a sampling of what previous biographies have to offer. They constitute such a startling collection of delusions that a complete catalogue is out of the question; besides, some must be saved till later for better enjoyment. But at least some attempt at classification is in order. Tchaikovsky, by the way, seems to have foreseen what would happen to his memory in the West, since he noted himself that "foreigners deem it permissible to tell any fibs they like about whatever is Russian."

First category delusion caused by an excess of: *Innocence*. "Anyone who knows the Russians will be familiar with two outstanding characteristics common to the entire nation [*sic*]: they are a feeling people and they are subject to fits of sloth or what could be called paralysis of the will to action."[11] Moreover "the Russian tells the exact truth about himself, the Westerner does not."[12] As to our composer, "there is never anything concealed in the workings of Tchaikovsky's mind."[13]

Second category charitably entitled *Negligence*. Let us hope it is through negligence alone that a photograph of Tchaikovsky with his beloved nephew Vladimir Davydov, to whom he dedicated the *Pathétique*, was published with the caption "Tchaikovsky with his brother-in-law."[14] Let us hope it is through negligence alone that a photograph of the Tchaikovsky family, from which the commentator draws innumerable psychological conclusions, is described as showing the young composer standing "on the right of his mother with an arm crooked round her,"[15] when everybody can distinctly see he is standing with his arms crossed on his breast. Let us hope it is through negligence alone that a learned scholar informs us how in 1886 Tchaikovsky presented a laurel wreath to Glinka who, at that time, had been dead for twenty-nine years.[16]

Third category: *Ignorance*, with four sub-categories, as follows.

Ignorance of Russia as a whole. Tchaikovsky composes an opera, *The Oprichnik*, and we are warned that the *oprichniki* were a kind of secret police,[17] whereas they were about as secret as an American cop whistling his lungs out on Broadway. In fact, to make them as little secret as possible, they carried insignia composed of a broom and a dog's head. Tchaikovsky reviews the possibility of using Pushkin's *The Captain's Daughter* for an opera, and we are tipped that "the Pushkin work deals with the celebrated Pugachev rebellion against Peter the Great,"[18] which is hardly probable since Pugachev was born the year after Peter the Great died. Tchaikovsky composes *The Queen of Spades*, and we are called upon to admire in this opera the same misty atmosphere, typical of St Petersburg, which is to be found in Dostoievsky's *The Brothers Karamazov*;[19] unfortunately *The Brothers Karamazov* does not take place in St Petersburg, but in a provincial town with the ridiculous name Skotoprigonievsk. Tchaikovsky himself moves from St Petersburg to Moscow and we are led to believe that he changes his residence from the provinces to the capital, whereas at that time the capital had been St Petersburg for a century and a half and was to remain so for quite a number of years, while Tchaikovsky used to refer to Moscow not as to a big, 'fast' city,[20] but as to "that dirty old woman whom I love."

Ignorance of Russian language. It seems incredible that anyone would write the biography of a man whose language he does not thoroughly know, but most biographers naïvely confess their ignorance of Russian. The results are what should be expected. For instance we learn that Tchaikovsky received from Mrs von Meck a 10,000 francs *clock* and that, although he travelled all the time, he "hardly consented to be parted from this gift, even for the necessary cleaning and repair."[21] The reader must not visualize Tchaikovsky running around with a bronze or marble *clock* under his arm: the magnificent timepiece was a *watch* that fitted nicely into his pocket. In another instance, a well-intentioned translator implies that Tchaikovsky, while in church, smoked a cigarette on the sly;[22] a look at the original tells us that Tchaikovsky admired the effect of incense smouldering in the dusk.

Ignorance of Tchaikovsky's life. It all begins with the family name of his mother, which some transliterate as Assière, although it is a well-known French name spelt Assier. It goes on to the "large staff of serfs"[23] who were supposed to labour on the Tchaikovsky estate, although there was no Tchaikovsky estate and very few serfs: only one cook and his children. Further we are asked to believe that after his marriage the composer spent his honeymoon in Klin,[24] near Moscow, but, probably to spite his future biographer, it was to St Petersburg that he went. In Klin he did rent a house many years later, though he did not buy it, as he intended to and as we are told he did. Indeed his correspondence is at that period full of the plans of a future owner and, later, of his disappointment at having failed to become one.

Places and houses in general do not seem to agree with biographers, since one of them vainly tries to prove that Verbovka—about which Tchaikovsky is enthusiastic—and Kamenka —where he spent many months throughout his life, but which he despised—are one and the same place. Says the biographer: "The

Ukraine is famous for its beauty, the province of Kiev in the Ukraine contains the finest scenery and architecture, and Kamenka in Kiev province provided one of the best examples of both."[25] Says the composer: "A pity that Kamenka should be so paltry and poor in natural beauties" and elsewhere: "We sat on the terrace and as usual contemplated the wonderful (Kamenka) landscape consisting of barns, outhouses, pigsties, . . . shanties and the drugstore." When the biographer finally discovers Tchaikovsky's feelings towards Kamenka ("I never liked Kamenka"), he immediately makes up a sudden change in them: "It had *lost* all its charm and looked ugly and sordid."[26] Since Verbovka has still to be disposed of, our imaginative scholar writes it off as follows: "The house was named Verbovka, but the family always referred to it by the name of the village, Kamenka," although he mentions elsewhere that "This time Aleksandra was not at Kamenka (which was owned by the elder Davydov) but at nearby Verbovka." The truth of course is simpler. A look at the map will tell anybody that there are two villages, distant about eight miles from each other, one named Kamenka and the other Verbovka. Numerous allusions in Tchaikovsky's correspondence show that both villages included a country house, the first one belonging to Nikolai, the elder Davydov, and the second to Tchaikovsky's brother-in-law, Lev.

People do not fare much better than places. Tchaikovsky had a niece, Tatiana Davydov, of whom he was very fond. As she grew up, Tatiana became neurotic, hysterical, addicted to drugs. She drove her mother to distraction and altogether destroyed love and peace in the happy Davydov family. Moreover she got pregnant by a shabby music-teacher, was secretly delivered in Paris at Tchaikovsky's expense—he playing the part of the most attentive of nurses—never vouchsafed him a word of thanks and finally died in the middle of a brilliant ball, some think by suicide. All that is common knowledge. Still one learned biographer mysteriously writes: "For causes that cannot be determined, [he] developed a dislike for, almost an aversion to, his niece . . ." and adds a cute little footnote based on nothing at all: "It is possible that Tatiana was suffering from an illness from the exterior signs of which Tchaikovsky wanted to keep his attention."[27]

Ignorance of Tchaikovsky's music is the most ludicrous of all other ignorances. For instance, we find the most interesting psychological conclusions drawn from the fact that Tchaikovsky destroyed the score of his symphonic poem *The Voivode* ("The General," taken from a short humorous poem by Pushkin) composed in later years, and which the biographer[28] imagines to be inspired by an opera, also called *The Voivode* and written by the young Tchaikovsky on a romantic libretto by Ostrovsky, the two Voivodes being entirely different characters happening to have the same Army rank!

Fourth category: *Misrepresentation.*

When an absent-minded Tchaikovsky erroneously understands that the score of *Vakula the Smith* has to be delivered before 13th August 1874, instead of the same day in 1875, in order to take part in a contest, moreover indiscreetly inquires what other composers are competing and writes the address on the parcel containing the score in his own hand, we are advised that he acted 'unethically' and was ready to "embark on a series of almost Beethovian machinations."[29] Tchaikovsky himself seems to rebut his suspicious biographer when he writes: "Why couldn't you simply have asked (my friend) Kondratiev to tell me what an ass I had made of myself instead of imagining unworthy motives that never even entered my head?"

When Tchaikovsky expresses religious feelings which he was not supposed to have, the opinionated biographer tries his best to destroy the effect of his quotation by an unfounded but peremptory comment. Tchaikovsky: "I often pray to Him with tears in my eyes (where He is, what He is, I do not know; but I do know that He exists), and implore Him to grant me love and peace, to pardon and enlighten me; and it is sweet to say to Him: 'Lord, Thy will be done,' for I know His will is holy." The commentator, in a creative mood: "Line upon line the letter expresses faith (Tchaikovsky) could not feel. He was wrestling in the darkness of Rubinstein's death, and the result of his struggle is a brave flow of religious phrase, nothing more."[30]

Tchaikovsky was a staunch monarchist. That may be deemed an abominable vice, but cannot be denied. Consequently, it is entertaining to watch well-intentioned biographers disguise the disgraceful fact by not altogether faultless means. In one biography[31] we find this artless quotation: "I long to be in Russia, closer to the source of news, and to have a part in the demonstrations tendered to the new Tsar."* If we look it up in another biography, we may find a fuller version of it: a friend "came to tell me of the Emperor's death which was a great shock to me. At such moments it is very miserable to be abroad. I long to be in Russia, nearer to the source of information, and to take part

* Alexander III. Alexander II had just been assassinated.

in the demonstrations accorded to the new Tsar . . . in short to be living in touch with one's own people."[32] But only the original will tell us how Tchaikovsky really felt about the assassination of monarchs. "I received the visit of a Russian Navy officer who told me the awful news of the tragic death of our sovereign. This news so shocked me that I almost fell ill. At such dreadful times, when such calamities strike our whole people, when Russia is dishonoured by such events, it is painful to be far from home. I should have liked to fly to Russia, to learn the details, to find myself among my own people, to take part in the demonstrations of sympathy tendered to the new sovereign, and to join those who cry for revenge. Is it possible that once again the disgusting sore which plagues our political life will not be torn out and eradicated?"

In a less serious vein, but not without the same tampering with facts, we find one biographer telling us a charming little story about Tchaikovsky being invited to a wolf hunt. We learn that the composer 'could not endure the sight of blood or suffering;' we know all about the 'silent prayer he breathes for wolves to be scarce and shy;' we follow him all day long, 'blindly stumbling through the woods;' we are told that at noon he 'would give all his money and all his friends and all his talent for a warm bed,' but that, for an unexplained reason, he cannot go home, and that all the time he wonders 'why he is out here staggering round with this infernal gun.'[33] All that is very picturesque, but what we really know from the letter he wrote to a friend, is that Tchaikovsky, though he felt weak and sick, "remained with the hunt until five in the afternoon." As for enduring the sight of blood, though it is true that much later he stopped hunting, he was at that period a zestful if not a very lucky hunter, so that whenever he made a kill, his letters are full of his delight at bagging the game.

Fifth category: *Untruths*. Flat untruths can also be found in Tchaikovsky's biographies, and the trouble is they generally refer to a rather sensitive matter: Tchaikovsky's sexual life.

One scholar, for instance, affirms that "*As the years go by* references in his diaries to drunkenness become more and more frequent, and *there are many cryptic entries regarding a certain sensation Z.*"[34] That is untrue. There are all in all five mentions of sensation Z, spread over a period of about six weeks, the first being on 23rd April 1884, and the last on 4th June of the same year.

Another biography is even more misleading. The authors attempt to describe the new edition of Tchaikovsky's complete works, including his correspondence. This edition, published in the Soviet Union, contains a number of omissions, about which we understand, from the authors of the biography, "that the editors have deliberately excised passages which in their opinion reflect unfavourably on the subject personally or politically." That is fair enough. But on another page of the same work—and one much likelier to be perused by a superficial reader—the same authors, without any misgiving about contradicting themselves, make a completely different pronouncement: "We have satisfied ourselves that the editors have been justified in making these omissions which consist *without exception* of references to homosexuality."[35] That is absolutely inaccurate. The Director of the Tchaikovsky Archives himself wrote the present author to tell him so.[36] But even a casual glance thrown at the text by anyone acquainted with colloquial Russian would have told him as much: most omissions simply stand for what is known as 'unprintable language' to which Tchaikovsky was very partial when writing to close friends. Other omissions correspond to perfectly innocent passages, which had already been printed in previous editions and were omitted in this one only because they showed Tchaikovsky on the verge of hysterics. Only a few, to quote the Director of the Archives, refer to the composer's private life, about which more will be said later on. So it is quite unclear what the honourable biographers can have meant when they wrote that they 'had satisfied themselves' as to the nature of those omissions.

3 What about the Mad Russian?

It would have been a whimsical trick indeed if out of that mixture of stubbornness and naïveté any true image of Tchaikovsky had emerged. Well, it has not.

Of course there are several Tchaikovsky myths which do not coincide on all points, but they all revolve around "the Mad Russian" type, opinions varying only as to the extent and particular brand of his madness.

If, for the time being, we content ourselves with a brief survey of American and English myths—and mention only for curiosity's sake a fantastic and sordid novel by an otherwise unknown author and a childish though relatively pleasant movie in which Tchaikovsky appeared as the passionate lover of a grand-duchess—we have to face three main mythical orientations.

One can be found in Catherine Drinker Bowen's *Beloved Friend,* which presents a mad Russian on the weak and delicate side, a refined but sissyish character, more or less in love with Mrs von Meck, and otherwise a toy at the hands of Fate.

Herbert Weinstock's *Tchaikovsky* is on the contrary a dark psychopath, an 'unethical' personality, a typical homosexual suffering from a strong Oedipus complex. Mr Weinstock incidentally adopts a very high tone toward Miss Bowen's "fictionized and luridly coloured story" which "has now been rendered obsolete within its self-set limits by the publication in Russia of large amounts of further materials."

Lawrence and Elizabeth Hanson, definitely sweeter-tempered, are very tactfully appreciative of Mr Weinstock's book which "set a high standard in musical biography;" they try to "live up to" it, they "owe a great deal to this work" and they beg to "be allowed to pay this respectful and admiring tribute" to it. Nevertheless they very effectively (and appropriately) ridicule nearly all Mr Weinstock has to say and brilliantly dispose of the 'unethical character' and of the 'Oedipus complex' among other things. They try to present their *Man Behind the Music* as a jolly young man about town and a homosexual in spite of himself. This Mad Russian is a little more convincing than the others, though he is still wide away from the mark. Furthermore the constant carelessness—to say the least—of the authors, added to their irritating habit of misquoting French expressions, keeps their biography from being satisfactory in any way.

Although he does not actively participate in the Tchaikovsky mythology, John Warrack, in his beautifully if not always relevantly illustrated book, seldom attempts any serious psychological explanation of the composer's personality. His greatest fault is to take for granted much that other biographers have assumed to be true, no matter if their information happened to be sound, doubtful, twisted or flatly inaccurate. Historically he lacks objectivity, to say the least, and relies so candidly on gossip originating in the von Meck family that he should not be read without careful scrutiny of every detail which he imparts to the reader.

Finally, the most typical myth is Mr Ken Russell's one in his movie *The Music-Lovers.* Being a cocktail of all the other ones, it is maybe the least offensive because the most irrelevant. If only the spectator were warned that all the characters in the film are fictitious and have no relationship whatsoever to real people, *The Music-Lovers* could have been an interesting artist's interpretation of the Mad Russian myth. But the fact remains: there is not one particle of historic truth in it; and that fact is distressing, since the public has no way of checking fabrication against reality.

The real Tchaikovsky was not a Mad Russian or anything else as definite as that. He was mostly a living paradox (like nearly all of us) and one condemns oneself to twist reality if one sets out to prove that he was the incarnation of such and such an idea, vice or disease.

So, obviously, an exhaustive and authoritative new biography, founded on documents and verified facts, will be necessary one day, preferably when access to the Tchaikovsky Archives becomes easier, or when the professionals in charge of them are not bound any more by political suitabilities. But one thing can and must be done now: getting rid of the Mad Russian.

The need for a true portrait of the man is indeed much more urgent than for an accurate story of his life, and that for two reasons: on one hand, most biographers have erred less often in telling, listing, dating, than in interpreting; on the other hand, Tchaikovsky's life was somewhat monotonous and a chronological biography would amount to giving accounts of trips and concerts, which may be useful to the specialist but presents little interest for the layman. That is why the last pages of the present part contain a tightly condensed life story of the composer and the portrait approach has been selected for the rest of the book.

4 Sources

Sources are plentiful. If only biographers would consult those the titles of which they dutifully compile in their interminable bibliographies—up to 56 "primary" sources in one biography,[37] the intimation being that many others were also used—the results would probably be somewhat different from what they are. But most of these sources are in Russian; many are yet unprinted;

some contain little new information about the composer. That does not mean that it would be uninteresting or useless to peruse them all, to extract and distil whatever they may contribute to our knowledge, but at the present time this is impossible, especially for a Westerner and in all likelihood also for a Soviet, and nothing is to be gained by pretending it has been done. For our own purposes, we shall be content with far fewer sources, since what we are after is the most intimate portrait of Tchaikovsky we can find, in other words a self-portrait, mainly based on his own writings, of which most are now available (in Russian of course). Although occasionally other sources will be quoted, most of the information that will be found from now on in the present work will be borrowed from the seven publications listed and commented upon below. Some problems will also have been checked out personally with the Director of the Tchaikovsky Archives.

Tchaikovsky's first biography, consisting mainly of extracts from his correspondence, was published in 1900 by his brother Modest under the title *The Life and Letters of Peter Ilich Tchaikovsky*. The American public knows only a thoroughly condensed version of this work, published a little later by Rosa Newmarch. It is now the fashion to criticize Modest's contribution as misleading. Mr Weinstock, for instance, claims he has "found there is scarcely one page in Modest's *Life and Letters* without some misstatement of fact, accidental or deliberate, or some purposeful elision." This, although obviously based on Rosa Newmarch's version of the work, is still grossly exaggerated. It may be noted that Mr Weinstock gives no example of the misstatements he refers to, whereas his own book is full of them: we already have branded seven and more will follow. As to the elisions, it was scarcely to be expected that the composer's brother, writing seven years after his death, when practically all Tchaikovsky's contemporaries were still alive, would indulge in any sensational gossip. In fact, Modest's book, though obviously incomplete, is still one of the most reliable sources easily available in the West, especially for what regards Tchaikovsky's public life, as well as for family relations and basic events and dates. Incidentally the reader should realize that Russians have always felt somewhat differently from Westerners about biographies: they like to separate a man's life into public and private and have a strong reluctance to pry into the second one, considering it to be the man's most intimate property. That is still the fashion in Soviet Russia as will be seen later.

In the twenties, when most family archives had become the State's property, several volumes of Tchaikovsky's correspondence were published, and, for a time, the Russians forgot their customary discreetness. The correspondence with Mrs von Meck was published *in extenso** and many facts of Tchaikovsky's private life were revealed in footnotes, some of which appear now to have been somewhat hasty and ungrounded. This correspondence is not available in English, but many extracts from it can be found either in Modest's work or in Catherine Bowen's romanticized *Beloved Friend*.

Later came the publication of the Archives of S. I. Taneiev, including letters from Tchaikovsky to Taneiev himself, to N. G. Konradi and to three ladies: Désirée Artôt, Yu. P. Shpajinsky, A. P. Merkling.† None of those are available in English

Tchaikovsky's correspondence with his friend and publisher P. I. Jurgenson was also published, but with omissions, the nature of which is not always clear, although some of them deal as usual with 'bad' language. With typical Russian prudishness, the editor states that "less printable words are replaced by initials followed by periods; unprintable words are omitted, while a figure in brackets indicates the number of omitted words (in many cases of over-indulging, even so-called less printable words and expressions are omitted, and the same numbering system used). *This is an abridged edition*." The correspondence with Jurgenson is available only in Russian.

One of the main sources if not of information at least of coordination is *Days and Years of P. I. Tchaikovsky*, published in the Soviet Union in 1940 and containing a systematic chronicle of the composer's life, day by day. As could be expected, this chronicle is oriented more toward his musical achievements than toward his private problems, but it solves, once and for all, many problems of date and place, which, as we now know, is not to be disdained. *Days and Years* has not been translated.

Tchaikovsky's *Diaries* were published in English in 1945 and, in spite of some gross mistakes in translation and inadequate comments, can still be profitably used.

Finally the publication of Tchaikovsky's complete literary works, including correspondence, has begun in the Soviet Union. A total of thirteen volumes is expected; eight are in print but not translated. This very interesting and beautifully indexed edition has not been exploited in the West and contains much valuable information, although numerous omissions (87 in volume VI, 87 in volume

---

* Only some of her longest letters were given in extracts.
† The author's great-grand-aunt.

VII, 63 in volume VIII, etc.) make it somewhat difficult to use. These omissions have already been mentioned on page 26 and will again play a part in the fourth part of this book, *Tchaikovsky and His Secrets*.

5 *A man's life*

Before embarking on our main enterprise and trying to track Tchaikovsky in all the intricacies of his very complex self, it may be convenient to get a simplified idea of the principal occurrences of his life.

Peter Tchaikovsky was born on 10th May 1840, which—for those interested—makes him a Taurus. Since his family belonged to the hereditary *dvorianstvo*, he was not a nobleman in the British sense of the word, but rather 'a gentleman by birth,' a member of the gentry, though not of the landed kind, comparable (though definitely not similar) to the French *noblesse d'épée*.

A quaint little legend runs in the family concerning its origins which otherwise are uncertain. The reader must know that the Russian word *chaika* which means a sea-gull can also be applied to a kind of canoe used by Cossacks. During one of the plundering expeditions of the Zaporogues against Turkey, these professional soldiers were joined by a mysterious character, who proved to be not only a valiant fighter, but also a good sailor, and saved several of their canoes during a storm, thereby deserving the nickname Chaika. When the Zaporogues returned to the Sech, their permanent camp in Russia, Chaika went with them. At the Sech the rules were liberal as far as banqueting and carousing were concerned, but strictly forbade anyone to bring a woman to camp. One night the sentinels must have heard unmistakable noises coming from Chaika's tent; anyway they discovered him with a lady, whom he had brought disguised as a Cossack. Chaika was seized and subsequently tried by his peers, who could not help but condemn him to the only suitable penalty: death. Then the chief of the whole troop got up, twirled his huge moustache and said:

"Brother Cossacks, your decision is just, but everything must be done in the right order and according to tradition. When our good friend Chaika came back with us to the Sech, we forgot to change his nickname to a real family name, as is our custom."

"True," said the Cossacks.

"Therefore I propose that from now on he should be known as Chaikovsky* and no more as Chaika."

"Agreed," said the Cossacks.

"But if that is so," concluded the chief, "we have no reason to punish the man Chaikovsky: 'twas Chaika who brought the wench into the camp."

As the Cossacks were fond of their gallant comrade, they

ЧАЙКОВСКІЕ

The Tchaikovsky coat of arms

scratched their scalps, ruffled the funny tuft of hair that they left growing in the middle and decided that Chaikovsky was clearly innocent. If they had thought otherwise, the *Pathétique* would still be hovering in the limbo where works of art expect the summons of their authors.

The descendants of Chaika or whoever was the real founder of the family—the Tchaikovsky coat of arms is *azure seagulls white* with a play on the two meanings of *chaika*—served the Tsar for several generations, mostly as officers in his army. The composer's uncle and namesake Peter, my great-great-grandfather, fought against Napoleon and earned the privilege of sitting in presence of the

* Chaikovsky is the proper English transliteration. Elsewhere the French transliteration Tchaikovsky has been used as more familiar.

Chart 1. Tchaikovsky Genealogy

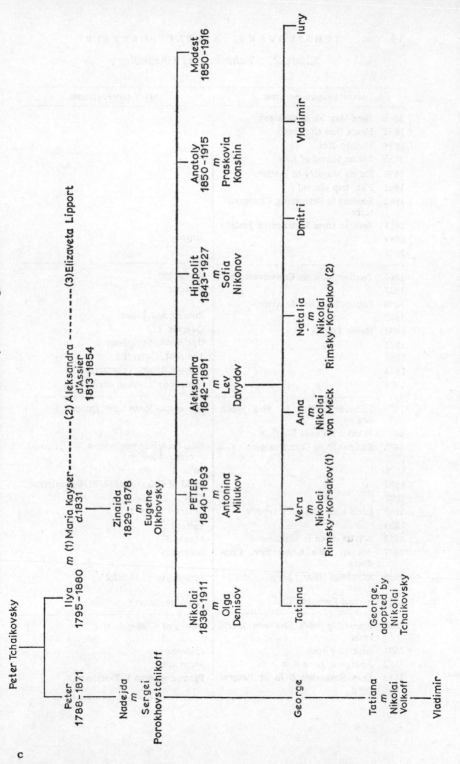

Chart 2. Tchaikovsky Chronology

MAIN EVENTS OF LIFE	MAIN COMPOSITIONS
1840 Born May 10, in Votkinsk	
1852 Hears *Don Giovanni*	
1854 Mother dies	
1855 Enters School of Law	
1859 Enters Ministry of Justice	
1861 First trip abroad	
1862 Student St Petersburg Conservatoire	
1863 Resigns from Ministry of Justice	
1864	*Storm*
1865	
1866 Teacher Moscow Conservatoire	Symphony 1
1867	*Voivode*
1868 Engaged to Désirée Artôt	
1869	*Romeo and Juliet*
1871 Meets Tolstoi	Quartet 1
1872	*Oprichnik*, Symphony 2
1873	*Tempest*, Quartet 2
1874	*Vakula* (later: *Tcherevichki*)
1875	Symphony 3. Piano concerto 1
1876 Friendship with N. von Meck begins	*Francesca. Swan Lake.* Quartet 3
1877 Marries Antonia Milukov	
1878 Resigns from Conservatoire	*Eug. Onegin.* Symphony 4. Violin concerto. Liturgy
1879	Suite 1
1880	*Maid of Orleans.* 1812. Piano concerto 2
1882	Trio
1883 Paris with Tatiana Davydov	*Mazepa.* Suite 2
1884	Suite 3
1885 Settles down in Maidanovo	*Manfred*
1887 Aachen with Kondratiev. Conducts	*Sorceress*
1888 European tour. Meets Désirée Artôt	Symphony 5. *Hamlet*
1889 Second European tour	*Sleeping Beauty*
1890 Friendship with Mrs von Meck ends	*Queen of Spades.* Sextet
1891 American tour	*Iolanthe*
1892 Settles down in Klin	*Nutcracker*
1893 Dies November 6 in St Petersburg	Piano concerto 3. Symphony 6

Tsar. The composer's father, Ilya, elected for a more peaceful avocation and became a mining engineer. At the time of Tchaikovsky's birth, his father held a prominent position in the mining town of Votkinsk, with many servants (not serfs) and a hundred Cossacks at his disposal. This was certainly not wealth but it looked and felt very much like it.

Ilya Tchaikovsky married three times. The chart on page 33 might help the reader to acquaint himself with a genealogy which will have its importance later on (Chart 1). His first wife, Maria, gave him one daughter, Zinaida, and died. His second wife, Aleksandra, granddaughter of the Marquis d'Assier, a French émigré, gave him six children: Nikolai, Piotr (or Peter, the composer), Aleksandra (who married Lev Davydov and had several children to whom the composer was deeply attached), Hippolit, Modest (the composer's biographer) and Anatoly, the last two being twins. All these boys made brilliant careers, respectively in the Army, the Navy, literature and government. The composer's mother died when he was fourteen; later his father married for a third time but had no more children.

Tchaikovsky's life can be conveniently separated into four periods, as can be seen from Chart 2.

First period: preparation. Age: birth to 25. Place: mainly St Petersburg. Tchaikovsky leads the life of most children of his class. Very early he shows a deep interest in music and begins to study the piano. His father having retired and moved to St Petersburg, the capital, Tchaikovsky enters the somewhat exclusive School of Law. He is an excellent student; on graduating from the School, he obtains a position at the Ministry of Justice and leads a brilliant social life on the fringe of high society. Music attracts him more and more. He becomes a student of the St Petersburg Conservatoire and soon resigns from the Ministry, in order to devote himself entirely to music. This means sacrificing most of his worldly pleasures, as he has to earn his living by giving lessons and accompanying singers on the piano. He composes his first pieces.

Second period: creation. Age: 26 to 35. Place: Moscow. Tchaikovsky becomes a professor of harmony at the Moscow Conservatoire, composes his three first symphonies, his First Piano Concerto, three operas, *Romeo and Juliet* and *The Swan Lake.* He writes music articles for newspapers, meets important people, is engaged to be married, but the marriage does not come off.

Third period: recognition. Age: 36 to 49. Travels. Tchaikovsky becomes acquainted by letters with the wealthy Mrs von Meck who becomes his patroness. He marries, falls ill and begins a long period of extensive travels. He resigns from the Conservatoire and from marriage practically at the same time. He composes three suites, two symphonies, his Second Piano Concerto, the Violin Concerto, *The Sleeping Beauty*, three symphonic poems including *Manfred*, four operas including *Eugene Onegin*. He begins to tour Europe as a director of his own works. Everywhere he meets growing enthusiasm. First Russia, then Europe, recognizes him as a leading composer of his day. He becomes the first Russian composer with a European reputation.

Fourth Period: fame and death. Age: 50 to 53. Settling down in Klin. Mrs von Meck breaks with the composer. He tours the United States with a tremendous success. After trying several country houses he finally settles down in the one which has now become the Tchaikovsky Museum. He composes two operas, *The Nutcracker*, the *Pathétique*, and dies, famous and independent, on 6th November 1893.

Such was the life. But who was the man who lived it?

NOTES TO PART I

1   Bowen.
2   Hanson.
3   The German critic Hanslick in his article "On the beautiful in Music."
4   Michel Hofmann.
5   Hanson.
6   R. W. Wood in G. Abraham.
7   Hanson.
8   E. Blom in G. Abraham.
9   M. Cooper in G. Abraham.
10 R. W. Wood in G. Abraham.
11 Hanson.
12 Hanson.
13 E. Lockspeiser in G. Abraham.
14 Hanson.
15 Hanson.
16 Lakond.
17 Michel Hofmann.
18 Weinstock.
19 Michel Hofmann.
20 Hanson.
21 Newmarch's translation of Modest. Same mistake in Weinstock.
22 Lakond.
23 Hanson.
24 Michel Hofmann.
25 Hanson.
26 This and the following quotations in this paragraph: Hanson.

27   Weinstock.
28   Hanson.
29   Weinstock.
30   Weinstock.
31   Weinstock.
32   Newmarch's translation of Modest.
33   Bowen.
34   E. Lockspeiser in G. Abraham.
35   Hanson. Italics mine. V.V.
36   Letter no 128, 22nd February 1971, from G. A. Shamkin, Director of
     the Tchaikovsky Archives and Museum, Klin, U.S.S.R.
37   Hanson.

PART TWO

TCHAIKOVSKY AND HIMSELF

1 *Happy to the point of self-oblivion*

Maybe there is something not altogether healthy in our curiosity for the personality of an artist. Maybe we ought to be thankful for the work of art, and let it stand alone, self-sufficient, anonymous, as the great cathedrals of the Middle Ages. Any artist is a demi-god and maybe we ought to be satisfied with the godly half of him, the one which is universal and holds no secrets. But that would be contrary to human nature. When we receive a gift—and what could be a more munificent gift than a work of art?—we like to know something about the donor. What child would refuse to learn a little more about Santa Claus if only he could? And is not our curiosity also a form of gratitude, maybe not the most discreet, but certainly the most guileless one? So we ask naïve questions about our demi-gods, and the first query that comes to our mind is humble, human, it has to do with what preoccupies us most when we ourselves are concerned: "Was the demi-god happy?"

It is of course a childlike question. He was and he was not, and then, what is happiness anyway? Happiness is like painting: you need the paint and the brush and the canvas and then the talent. So we should rephrase our question and before inquiring into the paint and brush situation ask a little more elaborately: "Was he gifted for happiness?"

Those gloomy belated post-romantics who profess that Tchaikovsky never composed anything but adagio-lamentosos would shrug their shoulder at such foolishness. 'Tchaikovsky, happy? The word sounds indecent applied to him!' But the composer himself felt differently. In fact few pleasure seekers seem to have extracted as much enjoyment from life as he did, and that not only while youth was there to help but even when he had aged prematurely and looked much older than he was.

At 30, we find him in a poetic mood. "You must know that nothing is divine as a dawn in May, and life is indeed beautiful, in spite of everything." By everything, he means that he is gaining

weight, his nerves bother him, he is bored with his teaching job,
he has less money than he would like, and he is not quite sure
about the fate of an opera.* "In short, there are quite a few
thorns, but thank God, there are roses too: the smell of spring,
the joy of friendship, a dewy dawn in May, an azure sky, sparrows
waking up and cats mysteriously mewing in the absence of any
human sound."

At 38, he still remembers a wonderful holiday he spent
at a friend's country house, five years before. He was 'in a
state of exaltation, extasis, beatitude.' He "cannot express the
felicity he felt," when, to crown a day of wandering, he would sit
by his window and "listen to the majestic silence of the wilderness,†
rarely troubled by the indistinct rumours of the night."

At 39, he exclaims enthusiastically: "O God, how happy I am
now! Did I ever dream that I should enjoy life so much?"

At 40, when most men are in need of more heavily seasoned
delights, a beautiful landscape and a full moon are enough to send
him into ecstasies: "Oh! oh! oh! What minutes life affords us!
Everything can be forgotten for their sake. . . . I float in an uninterrupted swelling of enchantment." Or else he finds happiness
'in a long walk under a cloudy, windless sky,' in the silence of
motionless trees, sweet fragrance of flowers, the sounds of
the countryside, dear, joyful, children's voices and a concert
which the birds have improvised for him! "Oh! what blissful
hours!"

At 46, with the help of a little vodka, it is true, and after having
directed the rehearsal of his dearest offspring, *Cherevichki*,
Tchaikovsky discovers that he is "happy to the point of self-
oblivion."

At 47, although he is "immensely delighted" with the "complete success" of a concert, he begins complaining somewhat
fastidiously about drops of gall in the honey; and what is the drop
of gall? "A formal, boring supper." That, we may say, is a little
ungrateful.

At 48, famous at home and in foreign lands, he sits in his box
in friendly Prague and watches his *Swan Lake* performed with a
"huge success." What more could an artist wish for? And Tchaikovsky is passionately appreciative of his fate. He enjoys "a moment of
absolute happiness. . . . But only one moment," he adds, in one

* *Undine*
† At this point, one translator has Tchaikovsky enjoying himself in an
'oasis' in the middle of a 'desert.'

of his more Faustian and insatiable veins. Truly it cannot be said that the man lacked a voracious appetite for the joys of life!

2 *Something unattainably beautiful*

And so we ask: that appetite, which carried him to such peaks of rapturous enjoyment, with what did he feed it?

Above all with work. Tchaikovsky was never so happy as when he composed. No qualms in front of a white page for him, as for Mallarmé; no torment in front of a messy canvas, as for Cézanne; he still participated in the blissful flow of romantic, unquestioned creation, and did not deem it his intellectual duty to whimper about the agonies of artistic travail. But that will be examined in detail in another chapter. What we are after now is the happiness of Tchaikovsky the man, and this was ensured most of all by the fervent contemplation of Nature.

There was nothing in Nature he did not love. He loved good weather, which he called "stunning, marvellous, divine;" he loved foul weather, although people laughed at him for it; he loved flowers and argued for hours with his brother Modest about the superiority of the lily-of-the-valley over the violet; in honour of the lily-of-the-valley he even wrote a charming little poem; and his love for flowers spoilt his visit to Niagara Falls. "The verdure (there) is quite fresh and in the grass the dandelions, my darlings, are showing off. Wished terribly to pick several of these yellow beauties with the fragrance of freshness and spring, but at every step there sticks out a board with a reminder that even wild flowers cannot be picked." Indeed he loved flowers and trees as one might love people, and an untimely frost inspired him with pity for 'the withered buds, the shrunken and blackened leaves:' "How will this end? How will we spend the summer if nothing is green?"

There was for him a deep relationship between Nature and life itself, the one being somehow the visible embodiment of the other. Alone in a millet-field, Tchaikovsky literally falls upon his knees and thanks God for the profound joy he is experiencing. A walk along a stream, 'in the deep delight of the forest at sundown' makes him in love with life. 'Such moments,' he says, 'are a promise of immortality and meanwhile one wishes to live, in order to experience them again. . . .' After having felt estranged from Nature for a time, he exclaims: "Thank God, I have again become fully receptive to Nature, seeing and comprehending in each leaf and flower something unattainably beautiful, reposeful, peaceful, giving me again an intense love of life." That feeling seems to have been at its most naïvely pathetic in his heart at the time when he was nursing a dying friend: "The poor old man is weeping all the time. Is not that a foreboding of the farewell he will soon have to bid to earthly destiny? God preserve us from dying in such a season: you cannot imagine *how ideally beautiful is the weather!* " We do not generally think of parting from nice weather as the most cruel of the ruptures wrought by death, but such was Tchaikovsky's deep relationship with Nature that for him it was indeed so.

Besides standing for life and love of life, Nature also was beauty and source of beauty to him. 'Conversing with Mother-Nature filled his whole spiritual being with an unconquerable aspiration for beauty.' In fact, the joy he found in Nature was somehow of the same kind as the joy he found in listening to music. He never ceased to compare them: sometimes he would find that "even art cannot give those moments of ecstasy afforded by Nature," sometimes he would give his preference to music, more demanding because more ideal: "Without music, it would be easier to tolerate everything that is petty, vulgar and commonplace. Nature has the same effect on me, but it lacks the charm of living sounds, it does not excite so much the imagination and the heart; but music, oh! music: I shall die listening to it or I shall go mad. . . . The more we are affected by meanness, jealousy, rivalry . . . the more we need those heavenly minutes that music dispenses us; the more also it drives us to despair."

It is worth noting that this great listener loved above all Nature's silence. "In the evening I often pace my verandah and enjoy the utter stillness. That strikes you as peculiar: how can anyone enjoy the absence of all sound, you will ask? If you were a musician, perhaps you, too, would have the gift of hearing, when all is still in the dead silence of night, the deep bass note which seems to come from the earth in its flight through space."

And so he lived, with the silence of nature and the sound of music in his ears, finding his purest happiness in the complementary harmony of both.

3 I hate chaotic hours

To enjoy it, he wanted first of all order. As should only be expected his biographers tell us that "he had no idea of time, orderliness, discipline"[1]—this goes with the Mad Russian legend—but facts hardly uphold their opinion. As his brother Modest remarked, a glance at his works (76 of them plus many arrangements), at his correspondence (Modest alone collected four thousand letters); at his literary production (61 articles, plus translations); all that turned out by a man who died at 53, will suffice to convince the most sceptical that his nature knew no moods of *dolce far niente*. But Tchaikovsky was more than a hard worker: he had, as we shall see, the strictest idea of precisely 'time, orderliness and discipline.' "My secret consists in working every day at regular hours. From this standpoint I possess an iron will over myself and when I do not particularly feel like working, I know how to force myself to conquer my reluctance and get in the mood."

Weeks were organized in consequence. "With your permission, I shall write you only once a week for a while. Until the opera is finished, I must plan all my days and my correspondence with the strictest regularity. I shall write you every Wednesday." Since Wednesdays were for his patroness, Mrs von Meck, other days were assigned to other correspondents; at such periods, even his beloved brothers, the twins, were meted out one day each.

Days were timed with so-called military precision. "At 6.30 I give Alexis his French lesson; exactly at 7 I sit down to play, not my music, but, for instance, the piano transcriptions of Beethoven's and Mozart's quartets, of Massenet's and Goldmark's operas; exactly at 7.20 we have a game of cards; exactly at 8 supper is served, etc, etc." Tchaikovsky did not even allow himself to go to sleep earlier if he felt like it: "In the evening I waited impatiently for 10 o'clock, in order to go to bed."

Thanks to such a regime, he was able to write up to eighteen letters a day, and to compose *The Queen of Spades* in two months and a half. Of course, after a period of hard toil, he would feel tired and grant himself a rest. What he called a rest was time devoted to the orchestration of the finished work, since "orchestration is but an intellectual job, like embroidering on canvas from a ready-made pattern."

Such a life was what Tchaikovsky liked and wanted. "Thanks to my work and the regular order of my life (from that standpoint I am no artist at all: I hate chaotic hours) the days slide by unnoticed. And the silence here is ideal; God only knows how I love this silence."

Silence, order, joy at recognizing the smell of an already visited house, delight at seeing his 'dear room' again, a fondness for the *Gemütlichkeit* of a boiling samovar served punctually at the same time every day, or of a clock tick-tocking into the night, a liking for old houses with thick walls, thick doors and few right angles, an appreciation of good cuisine, driven to the point of sulking the whole evening because chicken and sour milk were served instead of another dish, disgust at any pretentiousness (for instance 'icecream presented in form of a huge lifelike rose'), and a certain modest fastidiousness in the choice of his lodgings—"I am used to live if not always in luxurious surroundings, at least in clean and decent ones"—who could imagine a more bourgeois conception of happiness?

Only one trait of the bourgeois, but maybe the most important, is missing: the lust of ownership. True, at one period, Tchaikovsky strongly desired to acquire a house: "My room is still sweet and dear to me, only, I believe, because it is mine. So what would happen if I had a home of my own???" Yet, even then, what he desired was not so much an earthly possession, as a place where he could meet himself, be alone with himself: "I am already fortyfive and I feel that I cannot go on wandering through the world without having a nook of my own where would be all my things, books, scores, memories, in short everything which constitutes *un chez soi* [a home]." Anyway he never managed to buy such a place and instead played at furnishing the one he rented. He left no estate to speak of and practically no personal belongings, although he had earned a good deal of money and led the life of an independent man. But he felt no desire to own anything. The story of the handsomely-bound biography of Joan of Arc which Mrs von Meck gave him and which he returned, saying there was no place for a treasure like it in his wanderer's life, is very enlightening. He had a fine taste for comfort, and a supreme indifference to wealth. It seems that he knew exactly what material possessions are made for: to be used, enjoyed, given, squandered, left to be stolen,* never hoarded, never worshipped; goods in this world, rubbish in the next. He was independent in both meanings of the word.

4 Do not deny, dear friend, this excessively reasonable plea

His way of treating money is so enlightening as to the kind of man that he was that it deserves some attention.

He was, of course, an extraordinary spendthrift. His friends were shocked at the 'fabulous tips' he used to hand out. "You seem to be," wrote his sensible friend and publisher Jurgenson, "a meteor leaving a golden trail in the hands of waiters, doormen, coachmen etc." When somebody naïvely asked him where he invested the money he earned, he replied: "Why! In the Kokorev hotel where I stay in Moscow! Where my next investment will be, I cannot say until I know my itinerary." Losing money was also not an uncommon occurrence with him.

He knew his habits and was sincerely ashamed of his thriftlessness. To his sister he wrote: "You know I have a weakness; as soon as I have any money I squander it in pleasure. It is vulgar, wanting in good sense, I know. . . . Money vanishes like smoke." To his patroness: "Whenever I am in need of money, it means that I am spending lavishly and without sense. The funds you give me are enormous; I never before dreamed of such richness, and the fact that I, at my age, cannot keep within my budget speaks badly for me. I hope it will never happen again." To a friend: "At fifty years of age I put myself in situations in which only the most dissipate of young boys can find themselves." And he had little hope of reforming: "Although I have firmly resolved to correct the state of my finances during next winter, I do not really hope to do so, so many such firm resolutions have I already formed in the past."

* He forgave and did not prosecute the thief who had stolen the precious watch given to him by Mrs von Meck (above, page 22).

All that does not mean he did not know how to count. He knew the value of his work and billed his publisher accordingly. His accounts were always clear in his mind; he had a remarkable memory for numbers and dates; he always knew how far he was "in the red." But in the red he was, all the time.

And so his fate was to be a beggar all his life. He never made any difference between the money his publisher Jurgenson paid him and the money his friend Jurgenson, one and the same character, lent him in the hope of future receipts; he begged for both. "Please send me 300 roubles. I wanted to wait till I get to Moscow and then start to squeeze you dry, but I shall have to begin from here. I should like to wring out from you all I can, i.e. all you owe me, and I warn you that in Moscow I shall be pitiless. So, be prepared for a new blow of the evil fortune which put you on my way and doomed you to perpetual squeezing."

He begged money from his friends, sometimes in a "jocular style"—strung out through his letters were a few bars of melody set to the refrain of "Don't deny, dear friend, this excessively reasonable plea"—sometimes in a more tragic—though not necessarily serious—vein: "For God's sake send me four roubles or I shall starve!" He begged money from his brothers; he accepted money from his servant; finally he fell into the hands of money-lenders, both friendly and professional: at one point, for instance, he owed 1,000 roubles plus interest to his brother-in-law, 1,000 roubles plus interest to his publisher, 500 roubles to a money-lending Jew, 500 roubles to a money-lending general, 600 roubles to his servant Alexis from whom he had borrowed his life-long savings, plus a few small debts. Driven to despair, he finally "applied for assistance to the Tsar."* After the letter was written, he would gladly have destroyed it, but his servant had already taken it to the post. Some days later he received a donation of 3,000 roubles. He was glad to get the money, but always remembered this incident with shame. At the same time, he was deeply touched by the favour with which the Tsar had received "such a brazen appeal" and "resolved to take the first opportunity of giving some return for this gift: the Coronation March was the outcome of this mingled feeling of shame and gratitude."

Though always begging, Tchaikovsky never forgot his dignity. He could not forgive Jurgenson's brother for refusing him once, and was afraid the same thing would happen to his friend: with his customary frankness he told him so: "I am very upset at

* Alexander III.

always having to ask you to pay for me, now Alexis, now Modest, now somebody else, while maybe it is difficult for you to do so. Nevertheless, if at any time I ask for the impossible and you have to say no, I shall hate you with all my soul." He scarcely exaggerated. His last years were saddened by a financial misunderstanding with Jurgenson. Though he tried to treat him as a friend, their past intimacy was lost.

It is true that in exceptional circumstances, Tchaikovsky stopped begging and demanded his due. For the opera *Mazepa* Jurgenson had offered 1,000 roubles; the composer replied: "*Mazepa* contains hundreds of songs, a whole symphonic tableau, and another symphonic number which is not without merit. If consistency is to be respected, *Mazepa* should bring me at least ten times as much as ten songs or ten negligible piano pieces. On the other hand, as I know how difficult it is to sell big compositions as compared to short ones, I think it fair enough to put *Mazepa* at the following price: 2,400 roubles." To another publisher, Bessel, he wrote with commendable firmness: "I must warn you that this time I shall do all I can so that my labours do not remain unrequited: circumstances are forcing me to abandon the frivolous way in which I used to treat my own interests." And to an ex-friend, Vladimir Shilovsky Count Vasiliev, he addressed this masterpiece of distinguished insolence, meticulous precision and beneficent generosity, which can be appreciated only if reproduced *in extenso*:

Volodia!

I have learned from reliable sources that you are complaining to the whole world of my ingratitude, adding that you have given me 28,000 *roubles*!!! I would be lying were I to say that I am completely indifferent to *the rumours you are spreading*. I find them unpleasant—but accept them as just punishment for my indiscriminate methods of *obtaining* money and for my genuine interest in you. In rare instances similar money transactions between friends— one of whom is rich, the other poor—entail neither punishment for the recipient nor poisonous accusations and misunderstandings from the giver. Ours evidently is not one of those rare instances. I am guilty, therefore, not because I took the money (I see nothing *dishonourable* or *shameful* in that), but because I took that money from *you*; that is, from a man who I well knew would sooner or later tell of it *à qui voudra l'entendre.**

And so the fact that you are now revealing our money relations to all and sundry wounds me to some extent, but does not surprise me in the least—I have always expected it. I am, however, greatly astonished by the arbitrary figure with which you so generously

* To anybody.

D

endow your gifts to me. I have of course no legal means of preventing you from spreading about me whatever wild tales you choose, or of forcing you to make an accurate reckoning of the sums of money you have given me in the ten years we have known each other. But I do not consider it superfluous to point out that you have magnified the sum total of your generosity—and proportionately the degree of my black ingratitude—most unsparingly. I have an exceptionally fine memory in such matters, and I shall tell you to a kopeck exactly how much I got from you. You can later verify my reckoning from your ledgers. You will find I'm not even *an iota wrong*. However, I warn you that I do not consider as debts either the things you gave me when you left for Nice in 1869—the piano, bed, screen, etc.—costly though they were, nor the money you spent on our trips abroad in 1868 and 1870. In 1868 I accompanied you as your teacher working for a specified salary, and in 1870 in the capacity of something between companion, teacher, and uncle. The cost of my Dec[ember] 1871 trips to Nice, however, I am including in my reckoning. And so I begin, recalling to you after each figure where and how it was given to me. . . .

[Here the reckoning is detailed.]

That's all. I leave it to you to make the most thorough checkup, in complete confidence that if I have made some insignificant mistakes, they are in your favour. For inst[ance], I am not quite certain whether you gave me 1,300 or 1,500 roubles in 1875, while the two suits and coat that you bought at Zimmerman's for me cost, I believe, less than the 150 roubles I have allowed for this item.

I shall now make the final reckoning. 100, 100, 300, 900, 600, 150, 300, 200, 600, 1,500, 2,000, and 800—altogether *7,550 silver roubles*. This is both a great deal and very little. A great deal from the point of view of the absolute value of money. Very little if one takes into consideration the innumerable spiritual tortures this money cost me; very little when one remembers that you are a rich landowner and I a poor artist; very little indeed when one recalls your endless protestations of love and readiness to make sacrifices for my sake; and, finally, it amounts to but a zero when compared with your everlasting promises! Do you know, once (in May 1872) you definitely promised me an annual income of 20,000 roubles within a few years? You of course do not remember this—but it's a fact, an indubitable fact. Tell me, please, what is 7,500 roubles handed out during a ten-year period compared with such a sum? Nevertheless, I shall do you complete justice: when you gave me the money, you did so out of a sincere desire to help a friend; you rescued me from great difficulties, and God knows I was grateful to you then and still am grateful. At the same time, I submit, is it becoming a gentleman to brag of having been my "benefactor," and, while doing so, to sin so against truth by magnifying the sum fourfold!

However, the purpose of my letter is not to reproach you, but to ask a favour. Since I took from you a total of 7,550 roubles only, a sum which you arbitrarily increased to 28,000, I consider, not without basis, that 20,450 roubles are still coming to me. However, I shall be more modest in my demands. I need much less. The fact is that now (when I depend only on the sporadic earnings from my *morceaux malingres et rachitiques*,*) I am not in a position to be of as great and dependable assistance to Bochechkarev† as I was. And so it occurred to me to ask you to give him a life pension of 300 silver roubles a year (i.e. 25 roubles a month). Do please grant this request. Nik[olai] Lvov[ich] is today a poor, pitiful, and sick old man. And for you the sum is so insignificant! As for my gratitude to you, it will be so great, I promise not to be in the least offended should I hear that you continue to spread the rumours of having given me 28,000 roubles and of the blackness of my soul. Good-bye. I hope you have a pleasant summer.

But such demands—even though Tchaikovsky was not asking anything for himself—are exceptional. Most of the time we find him as busy refusing money as anxious to get some.

Sometimes it is a matter of pride with him. "Never was I in such need of money and never did I turn up my nose so high." Either he does not want to write bad music which would sell well; or though he accepts Mrs von Meck's regular allowance he returns two thousand francs she sent him as a supplement to have one of his works printed; or he finds Bessel too vile to 'honestly despoil him of a certain sum, devil take him;' or he ridicules the idea of accepting any money from the City of Moscow for arranging a Glinka chorus: "These things should be done gratuitously, or not at all." Sometimes he introduces nice differences between his patrons: "From you, [Jurgenson] as from my friend and publisher, I can accept five roubles for little pieces; but why should I execute Alekseiev's‡ fancies for money? I will not." Sometimes, it is a matter of figures: for the Coronation March, he probably would have accepted five thousand, but five hundred is out of the question: he will do the work for nothing. Sometimes, he makes fun of his own conceit: "Mrs von Meck asked if she should send my June allowance now, and instead of writing to her: 'Dearest friend, as soon as you can!' I decided to play the gentleman and replied that it did not matter, that I could wait, etc. This is June 1st, and I have not heard any more about the money!'

More often, he is just abnormally mindful of the interests of other people. He will not write music which he does not feel like

* My weak and washy pieces.
† Nikolai Lvovich Bochechkarev was an old friend of Tchaikovsky.
‡ The Mayor of Moscow.

writing and which Jurgenson would publish only to oblige him. If he submits many pieces at one time, although he thinks they are worth 915 roubles, he suggests taking only 800. He wants nothing for arranging the quartet *Night** 'because he has not put much of himself into it.' *Manfred* will be so difficult to sell that Tchaikovsky makes a gift of it to Jurgenson and his European correspondent Mackar. A German publisher offers the composer to take all his future works, at Tchaikovsky's own terms, but that would be unfair to Jurgenson who was publishing Tchaikovsky when he was completely unknown, and so all the German gets is a "polite but decisive refusal." The composer lives at Mrs von Meck's expense in Paris, but when he learns how much she pays for his room (35 francs a day), he is horrified and changes to a 20-franc room in order to save the difference for her.

Tchaikovsky's unreasonable spending and his reluctance to accept just any kind of money do not entirely account for the straits in which he perpetually found himself. The truth is he was "constitutionally unable to say no to a borrower"[2] and a borrower is just a modest name for anybody who would ask or—accept— money from Tchaikovsky. Many friends and their families lived at Tchaikovsky's expense, a few without knowing it. Jurgenson was instructed to help people not only out of Tchaikovsky's present, but even out of his future means. Young people of both sexes were granted unofficial Tchaikovsky scholarships. Some members of his family considered his purse as their own. When Anatoly asked his older brother for money, he received replies like the following: "Do excuse me, old chap, that I cannot send you more than twenty roubles for the moment; at the first possible opportunity I'll send more." When his cousin Anna Merkling did not ask for anything, she found money thrust on her with as much thoughtfulness as tact, and this happened more than once: "Will you really not take money from me if you need it for moving? Please, do not be too delicate; such ceremonies between us would be ridiculous. Just in case, I am sending you a check on Jurgenson for 100 roubles. If you need more, no ceremonies for God's sake. Some day we shall settle all that. . . . And you have not to go yourself: send your maid."

At one time, having had many expenses following the illness of his niece Tatiana and the secret birth of her illegitimate son, Tchaikovsky was desperate for money, when he learned that a certified letter had arrived for him. He felt sure it was from Mrs

* By Mozart.

von Meck, who had somehow guessed his situation and was sending him unexpected help. He felt at the same time ashamed and
delighted. Alas! When he opened the letter, he found that it was
from his cousin Henke who was in sore need of 150 roubles. And
another followed the same day, from a Mrs Levenson, who wanted
100 roubles, and not by mail if you please; by telegraph!

In fact Tchaikovsky was surrounded not only by people whom
he wanted to help but also by predators whom he just could not
refuse. Here is one of many samplings: "Never before was I so
pestered for money as today by everybody and from all sides. Gave
out a lot (a painter; a clerk; a man whose children were burned;
women; old men, etc., etc.,). And the main thing is that all accost
me from a tavern while I am passing by." Sometimes he reached
the point where, having not refused anybody, he finally "was sorry
for himself" as he humorously wrote to his brother.

Those are facts proved by innumerable witnesses. It is of course
impossible to figure out exactly how much Tchaikovsky's kindness
cost him. His income, from his music, Mrs von Meck's allowance,
and a pension granted by the Tsar, was considerable but not really
large enough for such munificence and it is doubtful if any sum
that he earned or got was not spent or given even before it was
received. Still, some biographers[3] insist that part of the money
went to paid lovers. In theory, there is nothing impossible about it,
but not the slightest indication of such a special budget has been
found, and one can only wonder that its existence should be presented as a fact to an unsuspecting public. The implied reasoning
of these biographers is often of the following kind: "There is no
proof that Tchaikovsky was a homosexual. But we know he spent
lots of money. Surely, since he was probably a homosexual, he
spent it on lovers. Since he spent it on lovers, his homosexuality
is now proved."

5 *I am going to fly a kite*

An artist is not exactly a person: he is more like two persons who
live in the same body, one a normal man, the other an inspired
lunatic. Curiously enough, in Tchaikovsky the lunatic required as we
have seen routine and order; the normal man was the one who

cared for less systematic pleasures. If we believe Modest, there was even a time, around the mature age of twenty, when the future composer was given to the 'feverish pursuit of pleasure,' feared to 'be overwhelmed in this slough of a petty, useless and vicious existence,' struggled through 'moments of agonizing despair' but finally 'stepped from the shadow into God's daylight.' It is doubtful that Modest would have thus darkly alluded to his brother's homosexuality, (it is even doubtful he would ever have written those passages if Peter Tchaikovsky had been a real homosexual and he, Modest, had tried to hide it); therefore it will be better to confess that we do not know of what precisely consisted the slough. Tchaikovsky did not become a heavy drinker until later, and in all probability Modest must have been referring—maybe not without some envy—to his older brother's brilliant and dissipated social life.*

One vice—if we care to call it a vice—Tchaikovsky decidedly had: an immoderate love not of gambling as such but of cards. He played whist with frenzy. When out of luck, he was 'awfully angry;' when in luck, he was 'embarrassed and tried to lose;' when there was no whist, he felt terribly disappointed. Whist had become, he confessed it himself, 'almost a necessity for him, even shamefully so.' Still, he could console himself with 'Fool' a simple game that he would play with his servant Aleksei, up to ten games in a row. Most of the time his luck would be bad and Aleksei, seeing his vexation, would beg him to stop playing, but he would insist on going on and on. Nothing of all that is very original, although it is interesting to notice, for further use, that Tchaikovsky felt embarrassed when in luck.

His other pleasures were—drinking and smoking maybe excepted —of a more innocent nature.

He was a handsome, well-groomed man, and he loved to dress well. Here is a good-natured self-portrait of the composer in Paris:

I walk in the streets wearing a new grey overcoat [demi-saison] and the most refined of top hats. My neck is decorated with a silk plastron and a coral pin, my hands are clad in purple gloves. Before

---

* There has been in the family a hitherto unpublished legend according to which Tchaikovsky would have been addicted to drugs, mainly straight morphine. This would explain some mysterious passages in his correspondence, which are generally credited to homosexuality, but some of them would still remain unclear. Besides we have discovered no facts supporting that theory. As to the Russian word 'vice', it was used very freely in the nineteenth century to mean any moral fault.

every mirror in the Rue de la Paix and on the boulevards I stop and admire myself. In show windows I also contemplate the reflection of my graceful person. In general I have become something of a dandy (which has happened before from time to time). I fondly caress the dream of buying myself a golden chain and pin. I had a new suit made and have ordered a dozen shirts. Money flies and in a few days I shall not have one franc left, but I do not care, since I expect some from N. F.*

Besides being fond of the theatre, the circus and even the music-hall, he had lots of hobbies, outdoor and indoor, some ordinary, some rather unexpected. Outdoors he mainly loved to walk, as he considered himself "an ardent lover of fresh air." "When he was not busy with music during his walks, he recited aloud or improvised dramatic scenes (almost always in French);" sometimes he collected bugs and made up little poems about them. At one period he was 'transformed into a kind of Diana' and went shooting 'nearly every day.' Thus he acquired the somewhat jocular "fame of an outstanding hunter." Shortly before his death he began riding a tricycle, which must have been a curious sight. He was not particularly fond of water sports although he would occasionally swim and let himself be rowed somewhere in a boat. He enjoyed fishing. Toward the end of his life he 'found more and more delight in the cultivation of flowers, and thought of devoting himself entirely to this occupation when his powers of composition began to decline.' As any Russian he taught tricks to dogs and had a passion for mushrooms. During the season, he would go mushrooming every day and bring back whole baskets of white and of red ones.† On the subject of mushrooms he became easily lyrical:

As I walked through the woods yesterday I found a quantity of mushrooms. Mushrooming is my greatest delight in summer. The moment in which one first sees a plump, white mushroom is simply fascinating! Passionate card-lovers may experience the same feeling when they see the ace of trumps in their hand. All night long I dreamed of large, fat, pink mushrooms. When I awoke I reflected that these *mushroomy dreams* were very childish. And, in truth, one would become a child again if one lived long all alone with Nature. One would become far more receptive to the simple, artless joys which she offers us.

Indoors, he would indulge in amateur theatricals, more often than not as stage manager, or 'sing bravura airs with a facility of

* N. F.: Mrs von Meck (Nadejda Filaretovna).

† One biographer contests the fact. I can think of no motive, unless perhaps envy . . .

vocalization any prima donna might have envied.'⁴ It seems typical that 'although he shrank from sharing his deeper musical emotions with anyone, he was quite willing to take part with those who regarded music as a mere recreation.'⁵ He liked parlour-games; he liked listening to somebody who would read aloud, as Russians often do: his friend the critic "Laroche was his favourite reader, not because he showed any particular talent that way, but because at every phrase his face expressed his enjoyment."⁶ He played chess and, if alone, games of patience. He also had more esoteric ways of spending his time: hemming and marking pocket-handkerchiefs, or burning various perfumes which he loved to mix and blend like an alchemist and which gave him frightful headaches.

His strangest hobby probably was dancing. Sometimes he dreamed that he was a dancer, and that as late as the age of 49. In his youth "he was passionately fond of imitating ballerinas and all their special mannerisms. . . . He used to give entire performances of this ballet-baiting in the evening."⁷ Later he used to treat the citizens of St Petersburg to the same kind of show: every time he went to see his beloved cousin Anna Merkling, he would, after leaving her, dance a few farewell steps under her balcony. It is well known that Saint-Saëns had the same interest for choreography, and that when the two composers met in Moscow, they improvised a ballet, entitled 'Pygmalion and Galatea, on the stage of the Conservatoire. "Saint-Saëns, aged forty, played the part of Galatea most conscientiously, while Tchaikovsky, aged thirty-five, appeared as Pygmalion. Nicholas Rubinstein formed the orchestra. Unfortunately, besides the three performers, no spectators witnessed this singular entertainment."⁸

A sense of merriment, of boisterous fun, from the most childish to the most whimsical, was in the man. This explains why he was so good with children. Modest says that he was incomparable as an inventor of games: "I have never met anything like them. He did not condescend to play with us, he became like one of us, improvised and created one game after another in the gayest of moods, all originating in his strange and magically charming nature." He was 39 when he amused himself by "rolling huge snow-balls and pushing them off the cliff." And still later we find him humorously wondering at himself: "I am going to fly a kite. This is my new rage. At forty-six!!! But what a wonderful kite!!! with rattles!!!" (The exclamation marks are his.) A few months afterward his rage had changed: he 'desired to amuse himself by swinging, with all his forty-six years and his head of grey hair.'

But his love for quaint frolics went further. The Tchaikovsky

Museum possesses a sixteenth-century Latin translation of three tragedies by Euripides, on which the composer wrote with his own hand: "Stolen from the Doge's Palace in Venice on December 3/15 1877* by Peter Tchaikovsky, Privy Counsellor and Professor at the Conservatoire."

Also he was not above playing a practical joke, although the results might sometimes be disconcerting with even a fantastic twist to them, as in the quaint story told by Modest. It happened at a post house:

We were in the best of spirits and partook of a luxurious lunch with wine and liqueurs. These stimulants had a considerable effect upon our empty stomachs, so that when we were informed of the fact that there were no fresh post-horses at our disposal, we lost our tempers and gave the overseer a good talking to. Peter Ilich quite lost his head, and could not avoid using the customary phrase: "Are you aware to whom you are talking?" The postmaster was not in the least impressed by this worn-out phraseology, and Peter Ilich, beside himself with wrath, demanded the report-book. It was brought, and thinking that the unknown name of Tchaikovsky would carry no weight, Peter Ilich signed his complaint: "Prince Volkonsky, Page-in-Waiting." The result was brilliant. In less than a quarter of an hour the horses were harnessed, and the head-ostler had been severely reprimanded for not having told the post-master that a pair had unexpectedly returned from a journey.

Arrived at Vorojba, Peter Ilich hurried to the ticket-office and discovered with horror that he had left his pocket-book, containing all his money and papers, at the post-station. What was to be done? He could not catch the train, and must therefore wait till the next day. This was tiresome; but far worse was the thought that the post-master had only to look inside the pocket-book to see Peter Ilich's real name on his passport and visiting-cards. While we sat there, feeling crushed, and debating what was to be done, my train came in. I was forced to steam off to Kiev, after bestowing the greater part of my available cash—some five or six roubles—upon the unhappy pseudo-Prince.

Poor Peter Ilich spent a terrible night at the inn. Mice and rats— of which he had a mortal terror—left him no peace. He waged war all night with these pests, which ran over his bed and made a hideous noise. The next morning came the news that the post-master would not entrust the pocket-book to the driver of the post-waggon; Peter Ilich must go back for it himself. This was a worse ordeal than even the rats and the sleepless night. . . . As soon as he arrived

* Double dates are given according to the Julian and Gregorian calendars. The Julian calendar was the official one in Russia. It is still used by the Russian Church.

he saw at once that the post-master had never opened the pocket-book, for his manner was as respectful and apologetic as before. Peter Ilich was so pleased with this man's strict sense of honour that before leaving he inquired his name. Great was his astonishment when the post-master replied, *"Tchaikovsky"*! At first he thought he was the victim of a joke, but afterwards he heard from his friend Kondratiev that the man's name was actually the same as his own.

Even in his sleep, Tchaikovsky's mind was working in pursuit of the droll and the fanciful, as testifies this strange political dream. "I attended a meeting at which Renan* pronounced a speech which he concluded by these strange deductions: "There exist four things which should be valued on earth: *France, rêve, tombeau, roi.*"† I turned to the man sitting next to me and asked him what it meant. He replied that Renan was a royalist and had already been shot for it; after his death he dared not speak openly but had to resort to puns. Those four words meant: "France, dream of your handsome king."‡ In my dream I was deeply impressed by the wit of the deceased but still silver-tongued Renan."

6 *My only way of doing without work*

Tchaikovsky was a great traveller, which, once again, is a paradox, since as soon as he had left Russian territory he became homesick, and still spent half his time in foreign lands. The truth is that his restless nature craved for these changes of place, landscape and climate and he enjoyed the fact of being elsewhere more than going to some special spot. He was clear-minded about that and wrote wistfully to a friend: "In autumn I shall have to travel again: this is my only way of doing without work." And so, whenever he needed a rest, he would travel.

He was not, it must be confessed, an exemplary tourist. Most of all he liked to stay in Florence which he had already exhaustively seen and where his "tourist's conscience" was at ease, whereas in Rome or Naples, for instance, he would have felt obliged to spend

* Ernest Renan, the French essayist.
† France, dream, tomb, king.
‡ *tombeau* (tomb) sounds like *ton beau* (your handsome).

his time in churches and museums. Venice he dutifully visited, and found it fascinating, but still, 'if he had to remain there for long, he would hang himself on the fifth day from sheer despair.' What he loved was pleasant, superficial impressions from new sights. He 'went into ecstasies' over the chimpanzee in the Berlin Zoo, who lived in intimate friendship with a dog; 'it was delightful to see the two play together, and the chimpanzee laughed in the drollest way when he took refuge in some place where the dog could not get at him.' The Dome of Milan, the Tower of Pisa and the Eiffel Tower also pleased Tchaikovsky very much; he adored the beautiful carriages in Hyde Park and the electric lights which were beginning to shine in some Paris streets.

His best trip was to the United States. Put at his ease by American friendliness, he enjoyed wholeheartedly New York, its inhabitants, whom he found kind and sympathetic, 'magnificent' Central Park, where some of his contemporaries still remembered seeing grazing cows, and even 'four-miles-long' Broadway: "The houses are simply colossal. I cannot understand how anyone can live on the thirteenth floor. . . . I went on the roof of one such house. The view was splendid, but I felt quite giddy when I looked down." This mixture of enthusiasm and awe he extended to his relationship with American railways, which he admired, but not without a hint of homesickness: "The cars are much more luxurious than ours, despite the absence of classes. The luxuries are entirely superfluous even, as, for example, the frescoes, the crystal ornamentations, etc. There are numerous dressing rooms, i.e. compartments in which are the washstands with hot and cold water, towels (regarding towels, there is an amazing supply here, in general), cakes of soap, brushes etc. You can roam about the train and wash as much as you like. There is a bath and a barber shop. All this is convenient and comfortable—but, for all that, our cars nevertheless are more attractive to me for some reason."

7 Quid licet Jovi

One American idiosyncrasy found no grace with Tchaikovsky and he spoke his mind about it without undue shilly-shallying: "These remnants of English Puritanism, shown by such absurd trifles as, for example, the impossibility of obtaining a drink of whisky or a glass of beer on Sunday except by deceit make me very indignant. It is said that the legislators who made this law in New York State are themselves awful drunkards."

This was indeed a sore spot with Tchaikovsky. The truth is he was something of a drunkard himself.

It is an enigma why, whereas they certainly cannot be suspected of covering up Tchaikovsky's weaknesses, most of his biographers have tried to minimize his indebtedness to what is modestly known in the United States as The Influence. Maybe after all the composer himself was right, and "these remnants of English Puritanism" have something to do with it. At any rate, when Tchaikovsky frankly confesses to his brother Anatoly: "I drink a considerable amount. I cannot do without it. . . . I have so accustomed myself to this secret tippling that I feel a kind of joy at the sight of the bottle I keep close by," a well-intentioned biographer hurries to add: "During the rest of his life [he] intermittently drank a little too much. He was never a sot or even a frequent drunkard."[9] And when Tchaikovsky says that he is drunk every night, another biographer rushes to the rescue with a tactful generalization: "Let no Western reader think this meant he was roaring drunk and carried to bed. No, Peter was Russian and his system was inured to alcohol."[10]

All these nice qualifications—'a little too much,' 'intermittent,' 'Russian and inured'—are very touching but they can hardly reduce the number of gallons of brandy, vodka, and wine that Tchaikovsky consumed throughout his life. Of course standards vary, and maybe the biographers whom we just quoted have higher ones than ours. We, for our part, tend to agree with Tchaikovsky himself and shall confess that he drank a lot. The following extracts from his diary will give the reader an idea of what some people mean by 'drinking *a little* too much,' and 'not being a drunkard.'

1886—19th April, Was unable to walk as far as home. Was drunk.
2nd May. Was a bit tipsy at lunch and dinner.
4th May. Went home. Hardly found it. Knocked at other doors in vain. Fright and horror. Found it, at last. . . . I was *a little* drunk.
21st May. Had an enormous quantity of grog. . . . Was drunk.
22nd May. Drunkenness.
29th November. Drunk as a sailor.

The most curious entry is to be found under 28th January 1887. On rereading his diary for the past days Tchaikovsky found this threatening metaphysical resolution: "Will find out who, how and what." With typical ingenuity, he added: "What does this mean? Must have been drunk when I wrote it."

Let us not forget that Rimsky-Korsakov said about him: "He could drink a great deal . . . and yet keep his full powers, both physical and mental. Few of us could keep up with him in this respect."[11] And Rimsky-Korsakov, being a former officer of the Imperial Navy, must have remembered a few things about drinking. In other words, when Tchaikovsky said he was drunk, he knew what he was talking about.

He drank for a purpose, to be able to write his letters, to be able to sleep, to fight home-sickness, he drank alcohol as other people drink medicine, he also drank for conviviality's sake and, at first, was unhappy about it all. At some periods Moscow herself was repulsive to him because of the drinking that went on in his set. He gave up drinking more than once. In April 1866, he had given up "vodka, wine and strong tea;" in January '78 he writes to his brother Anatoly: "It is true that lately I have often resorted to strong drinks, but only in moderate quantity, only to become merrier and sleep well. . . . All that will end soon." In October of the same year, he addresses Mrs von Meck as another Beatrice: "I give you my word to think about you whenever I have to struggle against temptation; from your friendship I shall draw the strength to resist."

Frankly there is something pathetic in the great man's affectionate relationship with his bottle, and something still more pitiful in his desperate efforts to renounce his addiction. In the later part of his life he overcame if not his taste for spirits at least his shame at having such a taste and indulged in it freely and manlily.

As early as 1879, he gives sound advice to his friend Jurgenson, who had had an accident after a drinking bout: "You are hereby allowed not to drink till my arrival. But as soon as I reach Moscow we shall have to revive old traditions, even if only once. As to the lesson that you got, keep it in mind, and learn, at the expense of a few bruises, that wine is not to be pounced upon but imbibed little by little." The day when his divorce would finally be granted he proposed to organize 'a capital spree.' Later, after Jurgenson had once again made a fool of himself, he consoled him quite sincerely: "I assure you, there is nothing to be ashamed about. First, you were very charming and amusing when you were drunk; second, I am convinced that from time to time, it is good for one's health to get really tight." In the meantime, he had become an advocate of drink as a matter of principle:

They say it is harmful to abuse alcohol, and I do not mind agreeing with that. But a man like me, who has sick nerves, simply cannot do without that alcoholic poison against which Micluha Maclaw protests. A man with that strange name declares himself very happy that he does not know the pleasures of vodka and other liquor. But how unjust it is to judge others by oneself and to forbid other people what one happens to dislike. Now I, for instance, I am drunk every night and cannot live otherwise. . . . In the first stage of drunkenness I am completely happy and, when in that state, I understand infinitely more than when I go without Micluha Maclaw's poison!!! Nor does my health especially suffer from it, as far as I know. As to the rest: *Quid licet Jovi non licet bovi.**

8 *Unfit for a woman to read*

Greater or smaller amounts of happiness may be offered to us, and we may have more or less talent to take advantage of them, but our style in so doing is at least as important as our efficiency: the 'how well' is as essential as the 'how much.' Speaking of drinks, you may prefer to grasp a mug of beer with both hands and empty it with head tilted backward, or to cup a sniffer of cognac in your warming palm, or to twirl the stem of a champagne glass between your fingers. Although as far as wine drinking was concerned, Tchaikovsky was no gourmet, and even preferred ordinary wines to so-called great bottles, in his relationship with life he was most fastidious and delicate.

His intelligence had something to do with it, of course. One has to think of Tchaikovsky as of a clearly superior man (although not extraordinarily intelligent) who could afford to care for noththing but quality. No complex of inferiority for him. In a very select school, from which he graduated thirteenth in a class of more than fifty, and where mathematics alone seem to offer any serious difficulty to him, he got the maximum grade (12 points out of 12) for eleven subjects out of eighteen (varying from Financial Law to French Philology); the lowest one he obtained was 10 out of 12 (something like an A — in the American system). In the Ministry of Justice, where we are told he was "a bad civil servant, constantly

* What is bad for some people can be good for their betters.

scolded by his superiors" and is supposed to have felt "like a kind of paria despised by everybody,"[12] he was nothing of the kind. On the contrary, in spite of an extreme absent-mindedness (he went so far as to tear off scraps of documents entrusted to him and chew them up, or at least he did it once) he worked very successfully, 'received regular promotions, in less than one year had become senior assistant to the chief clerk'[13] and left the service with the rank of Privy Councillor (equivalent to the rank of colonel in the Army: not so bad after just four years* of service, for a man who called himself 'a mediocre clerk'). This aura of success followed Tchaikovsky to the musical field. Not only did he attain at a very early age an international fame which to many composers comes only after their death, but from the start music repaid him generously for his efforts. He astounded his teachers by submitting two hundred variations on a theme when he was asked for twelve, and graduated from the Conservatoire with the following appreciations: "Theory of composition—excellent. Instrumentation— excellent. Orchestration—good. Piano—very good. Conducting— satisfactory." Although he deliberately 'cut' the oral examination, he received his diploma 'with a silver medal' (in other words *cum laude*). Later, when he sent his opera *Vakula the Smith* to a contest, the judges unanimously awarded him the prize. At 45, he became one of the directors of the Russian Musical Society and resigned five years later at his own wish. No wonder, as Modest put it, "he never once submitted blindly to any influence, nor swore by anyone *in verba magistri*." Once again, he was essentially independent.

But there was more than intelligence in this taste for quality, in this repugnance for whatever did not meet his standards. There was what may only be called naturally refined feelings, with a touch of elusiveness, a nervous recoil before the realities of life.

He hated surprises, even good ones, and once berated Jurgenson for not asking his advice before preparing him a surprise.† A ludicrous demand, but typical. It is equally typical that he considered suicide not so much immoral as "vulgar and in bad taste." Also that he hated being toasted and making speeches, and that he refused the offer of an anniversary concert in his honour ("I would rather shoot myself, writes this enemy of suicide, than to be the object of these anniversary ovations which have become so disgustingly cheap"). Other artists may flood their friends with newspaper cuttings, but Tchaikovsky felt 'embarrassment and aversion at

* 13th May 1859–1st May 1863.
† Jurgenson had secretly published the score of *Eugene Onegin*.

buying newspapers with articles about himself, grasping a pair of scissors, and mailing the cuttings.' Other artists may like exposing their private lives to the public—and the less appetizing the life, the more publicity they think it deserves—but Tchaikovsky "assailed by a sudden terror lest he might die with no friends at hand, and that someone should pry into these life secrets . . . ordered his fire to be lit, and burnt"[14] several volumes of his diaries.

To embarrass another person was a torment to him. He did not attend a Saint-Saëns concert, because he knew the house would be empty and did not want to witness the composer's discomfiture. He asked friends to send him telegrams summoning him to Moscow when he was bored with his family and did not want to offend them by departing without a reason. He chivalrously defended the purity of the relationship between Turgenev and Mme Viardot, although they were nothing to him.

On the other hand, he was easily horrified, and the very things which caused revulsion in him are characteristic. Serov "was not *kind* and this alone is sufficient to deter me from dedicating my leisure time to him." The play *Lysistrata* is "of boundless obscenity. Guitry* seemed to me a vulgarian." Zola's *La Bête humaine* "is so artificial that one never for a moment feels any sympathy with the actions or sufferings of the characters. It is simply a story of crime . . . larded with obscenities." Rousseau's book of Confessions "contains much cynical information which makes it almost unfit for a woman to read." (Yes, Tchaikovsky was something of a prig, but let us not forget that he lived in the heart of the Victorian age, and that of all the countries at that time, Russia was probably the most Victorian.) The French in general found little favour with him; he agreed with Mrs von Meck as to their 'awful coarseness' concealed under polished manners, and could not understand that Turgenev had made his second homeland in Paris, this capital of "insolent, self-assured bores, who deeply despise everything except Paris and France." His servant's dissipations—Aleksei was a pantry Casanova—outraged him. He was so disgusted with the sordidness of his publisher Bessel, that he refused to correspond directly with this "Quasimodo among music merchants." When an indiscreet impresario annoyed him too much, he paid him off not to see him any more. When his niece's fiancé, a prince and hitherto considered as a nice fellow, insulted her by coming to see her in a state of intoxi-

* Lucien Guitry, the French actor.

The Tchaikovsky family in 1848: (left to right) Peter Ilich, Aleksandra Andreyevna, Aleksandra Ilyinishna (seated, in front), Zinaida, Nikolai, Hippolit and Ilya Petrovich

Nadejda Petrovna Porokhovstchikoff née Tchaikovsky—the composer's first cousin and the author's great-grandmother

(left to right) Modest, Nikolai Kondratiev, **Anatoly** and the composer

cation, he approved of her breaking with him. He was sure that the editor of Bellini's correspondence would not have published it if only he had realized what an unpleasant image it gave of the Italian composer: "He is all absorbed in self-adoration, raves about every bar he wrote, tolerates no critique of his music, finds hostility, intrigue and envy everywhere." The most piquant example of Tchaikovsky's shuddering antipathies is doubtless the mixture of pity and disgust which he felt for the marvellous castrated soprano who sang in the Cathedral of Lateran. . . .

There may of course have been some exaggeration in such a squeamish attitude to the less savoury aspects of life, but it only reveals the genuineness of Tchaikovsky's feelings, which admitted of no pettiness, no meanness, no conceit and no dirt. With what simple loftiness and with what a sure instinct of what is generous and what is not, he brands Tolstoi's contemptuous attitude towards Beethoven, whom the great writer enjoyed depreciating, "frankly doubting his genius. That," notes Tchaikovsky, "is a trait unbecoming a great man. To abuse and deliberately refuse honour to a genius who has been recognized by all the world, is an indulgence practised, as a rule, only by small souls."

9 *The blooming fellow I used to be*

So far we have toyed with the idea of Tchaikovsky's happiness, but our main concern was to isolate the man, to find, so to speak, his identity, before delving into his relationship with other people, with society, with his work. Let us not deceive ourselves: there is something basically arbitrary and artificial about such a method; anatomy and physiology do not agree very well; but then every method is artificial, and physiology could not have been invented if it were not for anatomy. So let us go on with our dissecting and inquire into one of the most essential ingredients of Tchaikovsky's self: his health. And we will have once again to split the problem, and to investigate first his physical health, then his mental one.

Doctors have done that before us, but 36 years after the subject's death, so that their opinion can be but the interpretation of

E

the symptoms as described by the subject himself. And the subject was rather health-conscious. Listen to this pitiful declaration. "A cinder got into my eye. . . . Mlle Marie examined my eye and said she could see nothing. Nevertheless it is still there now." Or to this plaintive confession: "I believe no doctor ever heard of an illness such as mine. I caught a very severe cold accompanied by headaches. At first I completely lost the sense of smell; then it came back, but somehow distorted, making all odours inconceivably disgusting, so that from morning till night I was sick."

Against such mysterious diseases, the composer took strict precautions. Having been ill after working at night on his first symphony, he never did it again: "after that not one of his compositions was written during night hours." At one period of his life he visited a gymnasium thrice a week; at another he became addicted to cold baths and they had 'a wonderful effect' on his health. And his whole life, "wet or fine, [he] always went for a walk after dinner. He had read somewhere that, in order to keep in health, a man ought to walk for two hours daily. He observed this rule with as much conscientiousness and superstition as though some terrible catastrophe would follow should he return five minutes too soon."[15] When the weather was really too ugly, he would take his two hours' walk on the veranda, "being afraid of catching a cold." This health-consciousness must have played a few tricks on the composer, who was sensitive to surroundings, atmosphere, and all the ingredients of health of which doctors do not always account. When he was ordered to take waters at Essentuki in the Caucasus, he decided to stay at home and take them there, 'for in Essentuki (a very dull place) his depression would have come back and destroyed all benefit from the treatments!' When his doctor was absent and he had to see a new one, he had an adventure worth telling in full.

The famous doctor did not impress me favourably. I must tell you that doctors inspire me with some kind of superstitious awe. I like to deal only with those who know how to treat their patients as people and suffering people to boot, not as *something* that complains and is to pay a certain amount of money. This is why I wanted so much to see Saligoux who was affectionate and sympathetic, while taking care of me. Mr d'Archambault had me waiting for a long time in some magnificent sitting-room, then, appearing from under a portière, gestured me in. I had scarcely begun to tell him the history of my illness, when he said coldly and with some contempt, "Yes, I know all that by heart. You need not tell me all

that."* Then he indicated to me the different symptoms of my
illness, instead of questioning me. Finally he sat down to write his
prescription,* and then, standing up, he told me: "Sir, your disease
is incurable, but you can live with it till you are one hundred!"*
Having listened to his prescription which consisted of four points:
(1) Taking some kind of chalk before lunch and dinner; (2) drinking
a glass of Hauterive water a quarter of an hour before meals; (3)
bathing in Barèges water* and (4) avoiding a huge number of different foods, I put the fee on the table and went out without any re-
assurance, without any faith in his prescription, and with the feeling
of having been to see not a human doctor but some salesman of
medical advice. . . .
   The strangest thing of all is that Archambault did not even ask
me what was my profession, why I was so nervous. A doctor ought
to know all that! He simply asked my nationality, and when I
answered that I was Russian, remarked: "Hard climate there."*

So much for doctors, but what was really wrong with Tchaikovsky?
He suffered, so family tradition tells us, of nervous diarrhoea,
and that information is upheld by most of the symptoms he mentioned. Sometimes the pain in his intestines was 'unbearable.' He
developed a catarrh of the stomach and his liver was accused of not
staying in the right place. He was very young when he began complaining of "little apoplectic strokes" as he called them, which
seem to have consisted of insomnia, intestinal cramps, throbbing
in the head, trembling and sudden pains in the feet. Later he had
frightful headaches which he described at some length: 'a special
kind of headache which came when his nerves were completely
unsettled; a pain resembling toothache which nearly made him
lose his mind; a feeling as if a nail had been hammered into his
brain, which came when he had strained himself too much over
work.' Some crises lasted for fourteen days, and prevented him
from working. But how serious they really were we shall never
know.
Nevertheless, when he was not complaining about a specific
ailment and declaring that "he could not live through the night,"
Tchaikovsky was generally worth hearing on the subject of his
own health, about which he reasoned with astonishing clear-
sightedness. Whenever it was not too warm—he hated the heat
indoors and outdoors—he felt perfectly well and confessed as
much: "In fact, my constitution is extraordinarily strong and
healthy. I have two weak points: nerves and stomach. Concerning
the first, who in our time has healthy nerves? And as to my

* In French in the original.

stomach, its illness consists, to quote a certain doctor, of an excess of health. I suffer from an excess of digestive juices, which causes frequent heartburns etc. Of course that is an unpleasant pathological phenomenon, but there is an excellent remedy against it: abstinence. Unfortunately, in spite of all my readiness to be abstinent, it is possible only up to a certain point. For instance, wine is undoubtedly bad for my stomach; but, on the other hand, I cannot do entirely without wine, because it is sometimes required by my nervous condition." At another time: "My flesh feels all right. . . . I am still the same blooming fellow I used to be. As to my soul, it has received a wound from which I shall never recover. . . ."

And yet at another time he complained of 'a worm gnawing at his heart,' of 'some mysterious purely physical illness responsible for his changes of mood;' but having had his physical heart checked and pronounced in perfect condition, he had to conclude: "So the blame must rest with the nerves . . . but what are nerves? Why, on the same day, without visible reason, do they behave normally and then lose their elasticity and energy, do not respond any more to artistic impressions, are incapable of work? It is all a riddle."

Yes, a riddle, to which the key might well be the word Tchaikovsky used himself: nerves, this net of threads that sew body and soul together.

10 On the verge of insanity

There is little doubt that Tchaikovsky was actually neurotic. His constant fears are there to prove it, most of them irrational, as Tchaikovsky himself realized, since, though he considered himself 'an awful coward,' he still knew that he was not afraid of burglars and such dangers. Now ghosts he dreaded, although he admitted never having seen one, and bad dreams, and mysterious knocks, and the wind, and lightning 'on which he kept an anxious eye while reading Sappho by the mingled light of the moon and a lantern,' and being surrounded by high oppressive mountains, and being pursued by bats, and getting lost in the garden without his pince-nez, and—oh! horror!—encountering a mouse: "if a solitary one . . . strays into my room, I am condemned to a night of sleeplessness and torture. May Heaven protect me! "

It seems that real dangers could frighten him only if disguised as bugbears. Overflowing brooks 'courageously crossed in narrow but deep spots,' steep slopes from which he imagined himself rolling down, thirteen-storey buildings on Broadway which made him dizzy, a rough or tossing sea as much as a real storm, volcanoes exhaling 'a horrible pillar of smoke and fire,' an absent mad dog who might come back, wolves roaming in the forest and Italian bandits (though not Russian housebreakers), such were his most realistic terrors. It is interesting to know that he "descended in an elevator below the Niagara Falls, walked through a tunnel and finally stood right below the Falls' mostly 'so as not to be tortured by the thought that he was cowardly.' Moreover, he himself summarized his whole relation to fear very neatly by noting that he was afraid 'not of cholera but of quarantine.'

The truth is that he was prone to fall into extreme states of anxiety. Already as a child, "a trifle wounded him deeply. He was brittle as porcelain. With him there could be no question of punishment, the least criticism or reproof, that would pass lightly over other children, would upset him alarmingly." Such is the testimony of his governess, Fanny Durbach. When, nearly half a century later, he learned that she was still alive, and went to Montbéliard (France) to visit her, he had not become less sensitive or less brittle: "I have nothing to write about but fits of weeping. Really it is surprising that this phenomenal, deadly home-sickness does not drive me mad. . . . Tomorrow this feeling will give place to another, scarcely less painful emotion. I am going to Montbéliard, and must confess to a morbid fear and horror, as though I were entering the kingdom of the dead."

These fits of anxiety had of course their ridiculous side, of which Tchaikovsky was perfectly conscious and even made fun. When he failed to retrieve some letters from the general delivery, he worried so much that 'he was afraid the clerk would light his stove with them.' When he was photographed—which he was quite often—he 'did not know how to pose, had cramps in the muscles of his cheeks, and, as a result, looked fatter than he really was' unless it gave him 'a savage and almost blood-thirsty expression.' The Kondratiev-Pendennis episode gives a good idea of the tragi-comic emotionalism in which he constantly lived and which he describes with fetching frankness. The story began when, in the midst of the worst crisis of his life, his marriage, the composer sent a frantic S.O.S. to his old friend:

I wrote to Kondratiev a letter in which I described all the horror and hopelessness of my situation. The meaning of this letter, to be found naturally between lines, was "I perish—save me, help me, and hurry!" Kondratiev is very well off, absolutely free, and ready —according to himself—to all kinds of sacrifices for his friends. I was certain he would rush to my assistance. . . . It was already in Clarens that I received a letter which had arrived in Moscow a week after my flight. In this letter my friend expresses deep regrets concerning my plight and he concludes by saying: "Pray, my friend, pray. God will help you to get out of this situation." Cheap and effective. Last night I was reading the third volume of Thackeray's wonderful novel *Pendennis*. One of the characters who is very much alive often reminds me of Kondratiev: it is Major Pendennis. One episode happened to recall my friend's image to my mind with particular vividness. I jumped out of bed and immediately wrote him a letter in which, with quite unnecessary fury, I attacked him by means of an irony which scarcely veiled my resentment. After reading your letter, I was ashamed. I immediately wrote him another one, begging him to forgive me for a fury which was both excessive and uncalled for.

At 38, he still was clear-headed enough to joke about his own temper: "I am very superstitious," he wrote, "and as soon as my moral and physical happiness becomes more than ordinary, I begin to be afraid. Isn't that like Sobakevich in *Dead Souls*?* Having enjoyed bouncing health for forty years, he tells Chichikov that this must be a bad omen." But eighteen months later this attitude was already becoming a mania: "It may be a good thing that circumstances prevent me from staying here† too long. The constant ecstasy in which I live here must finally react detrimentally on my nerves. I have become extremely sensitive to all kinds of impressions; I weep all the time and without any cause: for a book, for a piece of music, or simply for Nature's beauty. I live with an abnormal, a fourfold intensity here. Sometimes my thoughts, my soul soar so high, that I nearly forget that I am on earth." And the drop of gall in the honey about which we already found him complaining tasted more and more bitter as the years went by. "Why should I be sad? The present is all right; in the future, I expect the presentation of my opera,‡ of which I am proud: everything is in order, and still I am displeased with something, I feel miserable, I surrender to a secret but sometimes painfull dejection. . . ." "After thirty-four years of wanderings, full of

* Gogol's novel.
† In Simaki, an estate belonging to Mrs von Meck.
‡ *The Queen of Spades*.

worries, anxiety, suffering and nostalgia, I have finally arrived home. This morbidly passionate dream has come true. So what? I do not know how and why, but instead of an untroubled joy and calm, I feel a vague sadness, an insatisfaction, even some nostalgia, and, most strange, I constantly catch myself thinking that it would be good to take a trip somewhere. What can be more curious than such a fact? I have work to do, the weather is wonderful, solitude I always loved and craved for, and with all that I feel if not unhappy at least sad and wistful. . . ." "What could be better than this trip* which is so profitable to my career as a composer? But God only knows how deeply unhappy I am and how often I cry from exhaustion, like a child."

So we have now the other side of the picture. The happiest of men was also the most unhappy, and this may not be inconsistent. Some rich temperaments jump from summits into abysses, and if pedestrian minds prefer trudging along on flat tablelands, the artist does not care.

It is true that Tchaikovsky's nervous tension brought about even physical consequences, like rash; it is true that his brother Modest was concerned, especially in later years, and hinted at 'new and unknown presences,' spoke about 'an inexplicable, restless, despondent condition of mind' and even declared: "It seemed as though he had become the victim of some blind force which drove him hither and thither at will." We do not know whether such a 'mysterious force' existed; and if it did, we do not know whence it came. Described by Modest it sounds like demoniac possession, and the idea might be worth investigating by specialists: unfortunately or rather fortunately the present author lacks the necessary knowledge and experience and will have to be content with some more common explanations.

As a child, Tchaikovsky was already subject to nervous tension that kept him from school. When he began working at the Conservatoire, he had a "terrible nervous breakdown" attributed by Modest to his brother's want of experience in composition and habit of working by night as well as by day. "The doctor who was called in to see him declared he had narrowly escaped madness. . . . The most alarming symptoms of the illness were his hallucinations and a constant feeling of dread. That he suffered intensely is evident from the fact that he never again attempted to work through the night." After his unlucky experience with marriage, he had "a dreadful nervous attack, the manifestations of

* First European tour as a conductor (1888).

which Anatoly never disclosed. Peter became unconscious and remained so for forty-eight hours. The doctor feared for his life."[16] Rumours of insanity were heard in both capitals, and the composer relates himself, with no lack of humour, how 'a former Director of the St Petersburg Conservatoire sent an emissary to find out whether Tchaikovsky were really as mad as the newspapers had said.'

Obviously, Tchaikovsky had no objection to having been mad. The word comes now and again in his correspondence, and he uses it without any kind of reluctance, even maybe with a certain pleasure. Describing the state in which he was a few weeks after his marriage, he writes unhesitatingly to Mrs von Meck:

> The rumour of my madness was not quite unfounded. When I remember all the crazy actions which I performed, I cannot escape the conclusion that I actually was overtaken by a temporary madness from which I am only emerging now. Many things of the recent past appear to me as a dream, as an awful nightmare in which a man with my name, appearance and character, behaved as one does behave in a dream, senselessly, wildly, without rime or reason. This was not I, conscious of my identity, healthy of will, guided by reason and logic. . . . During that bizarre and terrible period, during that nightmare that blinded my reason, I turned for salvation to those who are dear to me, and they came to rescue me from the precipice. To you and to my two dear brothers I owe the fact that I am not only alive but also healthy, physically and mentally.

And to Anatoly: "I have completely recovered from my madness. There is no doubt that during several months I have been a little mad, and only now, being completely well again, have I learned to consider objectively all I have done during this short period of madness. The man who in May decided to marry Antonina Ivanovna, in June, as if nothing was the matter with him, composed a whole opera,* in July got married, in September ran away from his wife, in November hated Rome, etc, was not I, but another Peter Ilich, of whom nothing remains now but a misanthropy which will probably never disappear."

So there is a case for madness. But what exactly did Tchaikovsky mean by the word? Does one recover from insanity by taking a trip to Switzerland and Italy, while writing a symphony† and a few other works? Or did Tchaikovsky never recover? Or was he never really mad? Are we perhaps the dupes of the Russian epistolary style which, at that period, was not particularly rich in un-

* *Eugene Onegin.*
† The Fourth.

derstatements? Should we read neurosis for madness, and imagine Tchaikovsky perfectly normal, just a little excited at times? In such an attitude too there might be some exaggeration. If Tchaikovsky's declarations of madness should not be taken too literally, his lucid analysis of the state in which he was and his allusions to a split personality ought not to be disregarded altogether. The composer was not a normal being: what artist is? But of course we should keep in mind that his vocabulary could never be accused of being flat, unimaginative, or colourless. Six years after his "little madness," at a time when he was a successful composer who had on his own initiative resigned from the Conservatoire and was beginning to settle down, he wrote to his brother Modest letters such as this one: "I found your letter when I came home an hour ago; but I have only just read it, because my mental condition was such that I had to collect myself first. What produces this terrible state?—I do not understand it myself. . . . Everything has tended to make to-day go pleasantly, and yet I am so depressed, and have suffered so intensely that I might envy any beggar in the street. It all lies in the fact that life is impossible for me, except in the country or abroad. Why this is so, God knows —but I am simply on the verge of insanity."

Yes. Maybe. On the verge. On the right side of the verge. Never much further.

11 My nerves had to have a paroxysm

There may have been a few examples of well-balanced artists, who painted their pictures or composed their cantatas as they would have ploughed their fields or milked their cows, but not among the Romantics. And the question which arises now is: what was the relationship between Tchaikovsky's nerves and his art? Did his art make him neurotic? Did his neurosis make him an artist? This, of course, is not a question but a trap: to ask it would be to show a total ignorance of the way artists function. How could we separate the sensitivity from the creation or the inspiration of the artist from the feelings of the man? The neurosis worked both ways: it was harmful and productive at the same time.

Being an artist is not the most restful profession. If Modest seemed to disapprove of a libretto, Tchaikovsky worried. If his music was performed to his satisfaction, he could hardly keep back his tears. If he dreaded to hear a work of his which he had outgrown, it was torture: "The circumstances in which I listened to *The Tempest* should have afforded me complete peace of mind. They did not. The evening before, I began having diarrhoea and being sick. From morning until the time when I heard the first chords, my perturbation went *crescendo* and, while they were playing, my heart ached so much that I thought I would die any minute." The feeling that he had something to give to the world was not soothing either: he was constantly afraid he would die leaving his work unfinished. We mentioned before that creation was joy to Tchaikovsky and so it was, but it still was not a peaceful joy, and certainly not assuaging for his nerves.

> I spent the last days in a very high creative fever. I have begun *The Maid of Orleans*, and you cannot imagine how difficult it is. The difficulty is not in the absence of inspiration, but on the contrary in an excess of it. (I hope that you will not accuse me of bragging.) I was possessed by a kind of fury: three whole days I was tortured and tormented by the abundance of material and the scarcity of time and human energies. I should have liked to do everything in one hour, as it happens in dreams. I was biting my nails, my stomach functioned poorly, in order to sleep I had to increase my portion of wine. Yesterday night, as I was reading the book about Joan of Arc which Mrs von Meck has presented to me[*] . . . and came to the trial, the abjuration and the execution (she never ceased crying while they were leading her to the stake, and begged to be beheaded, not burnt) I broke into awful sobs. I suddenly felt such pity, such pain for all mankind and was seized by such sadness!

And he adds, with the humour which seldom left him:

> Then I suddenly imagined that you were all ill, that you had died, that I was such a hapless fellow (as if I had been exiled here against my will) etc. Well, in a word, I was very excited, my nerves had to have a paroxysm. After that, I fell happily asleep and woke up with a feeling of great joy, for Aleksei, having entered my room, opened the windows, and I saw that the weather was divine. . . .

On the other hand, the tension in which Tchaikovsky found himself when he composed had its compensations. Sometimes he succeeded in terrifying himself with his own music, as in the

[*] Cf. above, p. 46.

scene where Hermann comes into the room of the old Countess, but also his terror was such that he felt that 'it would not be possible for an audience not to feel the same.'

His governess Fanny, a sentimental lady whose testimony ought to be treated with some circumspection, was the only witness to tell a pretty little story about the first musical party that Tchaikovsky attended as a child. He "was very happy, but before the end of the evening he grew so tired that he went to bed before the others. When Fanny visited his room she found him wide awake, sitting up in bed with bright, feverish eyes, and crying to himself. Asked what was the matter, he replied, although there was no music going on at the time: 'Oh, this music, this music! Save me from it! It is here, here,' pointing to his head, 'and will not give me any peace.'" The implication, of course, is that the poor child was already listening to some prefiguration of the *Pathétique*.

It does not really matter what percentage of the story is true. No such stories are told about Bach for instance, and other sedate composers. But they would, from one standpoint, be true even of them. An artist's life is not an average kind of life; there are times when, feeling that too much is demanded from him, that he too would like to be irresponsible like other people, he must exclaim: "Oh, this music! Save me from it!" But the other side of the picture should not be neglected. Tchaikovsky himself knew perfectly well how good music was for him, and frankly confessed: "I am saved by work, my work which is also my delight. Besides, having been successful several times, I feel quite encouraged, and the depression which was reaching the stage of hallucinations and insanity, visits me seldom now."

It is difficult of course to determine the exact proportion of madness and reason in Tchaikovsky's creative work. For our part we should be tempted to say that there was exactly enough madness to create the slight lack of balance necessary for any kind of movement, any kind of creation, and nothing more, but this may be an extreme view. It will be easier to evaluate Tchaikovsky's strength of will as opposed to his nerves in an occupation where there was nothing to expect from the nerves and everything from the will: namely, conducting.

Rosa Newmarch writes that "to those who understood Tchaikovsky's sensitive shrinking from publicity, the alacrity with which, during the last years of his life, he accepted engagements to conduct his own works, was a problem beyond solution." And she adds: "according to his own account, he took no pleasure in conducting." Obviously she relies mainly on Kashkin's testimony which is true enough, if applied to the right period: 1868, when the composer was 28 and tried to direct the dances of *The Voivode*.

When I went behind the scenes, writes Kashkin, to see how the *débutant* was feeling, he told me that to his great surprise he was not in the least nervous. Before it came to his turn I returned to my place. When Tchaikovsky actually appeared on the platform, I noticed that he was quite distracted; he came on timidly, as though he would have been glad to hide, or run away, and, on mounting to the conductor's desk, looked like a man who finds himself in some desperate situation. Apparently his composition was blotted out from his mind; he did not see the score before him, and gave all the leads at the wrong moment, or to the wrong instruments. Fortunately the band knew the music so well that they paid no attention whatever to Tchaikovsky's beat, but laughing in their sleeves, got through the dances very creditably in spite of him. Afterwards Peter Ilich told me that in his terror he had a feeling that his head would fall off his shoulders unless he held it tightly in position.

But as soon as 1877, Tchaikovsky, after having completely abandoned his conducting attempts, tried to resume them: "Although I did it very clumsily, timidly and diffidently, I had great success when I recently conducted my *Marche Slave* at the Bolshoi Theatre. In general, I shall now try to find opportunities to conduct my own works in public. I have to conquer my insane bashfulness, for, if my plan to go abroad materializes, I shall have to serve as conductor." His plan did not materialize at that time, and he did not look too hard for opportunities to conduct his works. After eleven years the problem arose again, and Tchaikovsky felt less than enthusiastic about it: "Imagine, my dear friend," he wrote to Mrs von Meck, who had just encouraged him not to conduct if he felt so bad about it, "that all my life I suffered and cringed because of my inaptitude to conduct. I thought that there was something shameful and dishonourable in lacking self-control to the point that only to think about appearing before an audience with the baton in hand sent me shivering from panic. I feel that this time too, although I have promised to conduct, I shall lack the courage and refuse, when the moment comes." But he did not. A month later he confided in his friend Jurgenson: "I shall not tell you all the torments through which I went when finally [the rehearsal was scheduled]. The closer the dreaded day, the more insufferable my torture. Many times I decided to give up conducting. But finally, having somehow conquered myself, I arrived, was enthusiastically greeted by the musicians, made a manly speech, and gallantly began to wave the stick. I know now that I can conduct and on the day of the production I probably shall not even be afraid."

Rosa Newmarch's 'problem beyond solution' is carefully explained by the composer himself. "By fatality, the circumstances were such that I could not avoid trying to test myself for the last time in the conductor's role. This was determined partly by the insistence of my friends, partly by the knowledge that if I were to triumph in that painful struggle against myself, innumerable consequences, all profitable to my music, would result from it, and finally by an invincible desire to prove to myself that I was wrong to believe in my complete incapacity to conduct. Who knows, maybe my health will not even suffer from it."

And he soon began to enjoy what had cost him such a tremendous effort. "Conducting is not very easy for me and requires a great tension of the whole nervous system. But I have to confess that it gives me also considerable joys. First, I am pleased by the thought that I have conquered my native morbid self-consciousness. Second, it is very pleasant for the author of a new opera to direct his own work without having to interrupt the conductor all the time to ask him to correct this and that mistake. Third, I see such sincere and ever-present expressions of sympathy for myself on the part of all participants, that my heart is deeply touched by it. . . . I am much less nervous now before a new opera than I used to be when I remained inactive during rehearsals. I think that if everything goes well the result will not be a weakening of my poor nerves, but, on the contrary, a good effect on them."

And a few months only had elapsed when this man who 'took no pleasure in conducting' wrote: "I did not imagine how deep, how strong, how indescribable is the happiness felt by a conductor standing at the head of an excellent orchestra. It is a feeling which cannot be compared to anything else. At times, it reaches a kind of quivering ecstasy. . . . At that concert I felt that I really had mastered the will of the hundred people who followed my baton."

Happy and in full control of himself, he arrived in the United States, and the *New York Herald* noted on 6th May 1891: "There is no sign of nervousness about him as he taps for silence. He conducts with the authoritative strength of a master and the band obeys his lead as one man." Pleased, but always full of his charming diffidence, Tchaikovsky jotted down in his diary: "The Third Suite is praised to the sky, but hardly more than my conducting. Is it possible that I really conduct so well? Or do the Americans exaggerate?!!!"

12 *Forgive me for loving myself better than you*

This book is supposed to be Tchaikovsky's self-portrait, and so far we have found the composer disposed to be candid and clear-sighted when speaking about himself. Nevertheless his sincerity has been doubted, and the point deserves investigation. Everything starts from an entry in his diary, which we will quote *in extenso*:

> It seems to me that letters are never entirely frank. I am judging, at any rate, by my own. No matter what or to whom I write, I always worry about the impression my letter will make, not only on my correspondent, but even on some accidental reader. It follows, therefore, that I am showing off. Sometimes I try to make my letters sound simple and sincere, so, that is, that they should give such an impression. But in no letters except those written under emotional stress am I ever myself. For that reason the latter sort of communication always remains a source of regret and repentance, at times even painful. When I read the letters of famous people, published after their death, I am always worried by an indefinable feeling of falseness and lies.

Carefully leaving out everything that has to do with Tchaikovsky's impression of other people's letters, one biographer takes a high moral tone to declare that Tchaikovsky "accused himself not only of egotism, but of insincerity and sham. . . . This admission is bad enough, and as if to show that he deserves not to be condemned but to be pitied for such duplicity he adds 'These letters are constant sources of remorse and regret, sometimes even very painful ones.' "[17] The trick is clever, but something less than honest. What Tchaikovsky wrote is: '*I am* just as *insincere* as everybody else *in my letters*;' what we are led to believe that he wrote is 'I am . . . insincere . . . in my letters.' For once, we will have to agree with another biographer who says: "The difference between Peter Ilich and most men is not that he had certain symptoms and the others do not; it is that he frankly confessed them as he confessed everything."[18]

Confession is a big word. The same biographer notes: "his letters to [his sister Aleksandra], which were to continue for the rest of her life, were filled with self-reproaches. They were so violent that the reader who examines his life at this time is perplexed to find his sins so white." There may be some naïveté in this remark. Tchaikovsky's style is always violent, whether in self-reproach or expression of any other feeling, and we should be conscious of it. For instance, he always uses two adjectives when one would do, and the stronger the better (agonizing for painful, blissful for pleasant, etc.) We certainly do not agree with the critic who wrote, in a style worthy of Tchaikovsky himself: "It may be unorthodox in modern musical criticism to point, in a symphony, to a sense of guilt or of sin; but they are there, in his letters as in his music, expressed with the same horrifying terror as in the poetry of Baudelaire."[19] We should very much like to know which key is the best to express 'horrifying terror,' and what is the aptest orchestration of 'guilt and sin.' More than that: we suspect that if the learned critic had never heard about Tchaikovsky's alleged homosexuality, he would not have found a sense of sin or guilt, neither in the ascending scales nor in the descending ones. Still it is true that Tchaikovsky was sensitive to his own faults, and that he confessed them with a childlike honesty, and without a hint of 'duplicity' or 'sham.'

He accused himself of 'vulgarity, foolishness and weakness' in his relationship with his publisher Bessel; of laziness (he of all men); of envy for Rimsky-Korsakov's 'mastery' in *The Snow-Maiden*; of being negligent towards the children of Maidanovo, whom he had treated affectionately in former times; of lacking willpower; of reading too fast and not remembering what he read; of a funny mixture of anger and pleasure when he was faced by very bad music:

> Played *Nero** after supper. I am still astonished at the impudent liberties taken by its composer. Oh, you ridiculous clown! By God, I am seized with anger looking at this score. But then I play this abomination because I am conscious of my superiority—at least as to sincerity—and that gives support to my energy. You think that you write vilely, but seeing such trash which nevertheless was performed seriously—your soul feels better. I am ashamed that I feel so much anger over this work—but why should I make pretences in my diary?

More seriously, he accused himself, and very often of selfishness.

> I explain my melancholy, not only by my weakness and the sensitivity of my nerves, but also by my bachelor's surroundings, by the

---

* An opera by Anton Rubinstein.

total absence of any element of self-sacrifice in my life. Indeed I fulfil as well as I can the duties of my vocation, but with no benefit to individuals. Were I to vanish from the face of the earth today, Russian music would maybe lose a little by it, but it certainly would cause unhappiness to no one. In a word I live a selfish bachelor's life. I work for myself alone and care only for myself. This is certainly very peaceful, but sterile, lifeless and narrow.*

Maybe Tchaikovsky was over-critical of himself. From Venice he wrote to his brother Modest: "Instead of going abroad and spending money, I ought really to have paid your debts and Anatoly's—and yet I am hurrying off to enjoy the beautiful South. . . . So forgive me, dear Modia, for loving myself better than you and the rest of mankind. . . . My egotism, is limitless, or I should not have gone off on my trip while you had to remain at home. . . ." But when he expressed passionate wishes for the happiness of these two brothers, he also wondered if it was not for a selfish reason, since his brothers' happiness was necessary to his own.

Six years before his own death he went to Germany, which he disliked, to spend a few weeks with his dying friend Kondratiev. This friend was not so close that Tchaikovsky could have derived any satisfaction from bidding him farewell: he did it only so that Kondratiev, who had refused to help him in a former occasion,† would not remain alone. Nevertheless, he was full of remorse. "The idea of this remorse is: life passes, is going towards its end, while I have reached no conclusions; I banish vital problems or run away from them when they arise. Do I live as I should? Am I acting right? For instance, now: I am here and everybody is admiring my sacrifice. But there is no sacrifice at all. I am complacent, am a glutton at the *table d'hôte*, do nothing and spend money on nonsense, when others are in need of necessities. Am I not a real egoist? Even towards close ones, I am not what I ought to be."‡

---

* In Rosa Newmarch's version of Modest's biography of his brother, this passage has undergone strange modifications. Although the extract quoted is much larger than the one we have retained, two sentences are skipped (from "I explain my melancholy" through "no benefit to individuals"), and replaced by "Indeed, my life is of little worth to anyone," which changes the whole colour of the text. As to the phrase "Russian music would maybe lose a little by it," it becomes "it would be no great loss to Russian music." So Tchaikovsky is made to whimper again when in fact he was in a sober mood of self-analysis.

† Cf. above, page 70.

‡ In V. Lakond's translation of Tchaikovsky's diaries. "Do I live as I should?" becomes "Is that how I live?" In Rosa Newmarch's translation of the same passage: the 'close ones' become neighbours!

The Davydov family:
(from left to right) Vera,
Vladimir (Bob), Iury,
Aleksandra (Sasha, the
composer's sister),
Tatiana, Lev, Dmitri,
Natalia, Anna

The composer in 1863

(*left*) Désirée Artôt

There is one instance* when Tchaikovsky's mood for confession allowed him to rise to a height from which he could see his whole past, and judge it and himself with a startling objectivity: such level-headedness is seldom given to men, much less to creative artists. This letter is addressed to his brother Anatoly:

I wanted to be the first composer not only of Russia but of the whole world; I wanted to be not only a composer but a first-class conductor; I wanted to be a man of extraordinary intelligence and enormous knowledge; I also wanted to be elegant and fashionable and brilliant in drawing-rooms. What did I not want? Only little by little, at the price of a whole series of insufferable torments have I learned my real value. I should like to spare you the same torments. I laugh for instance when I remember how I suffered from not being able to become a member of high society and a fashionable man.† Nobody knows what torture this nonsense cost me, and how I struggled to conquer my unbelievable self-consciousness, which, at one time, had brought me to the point where I lost sleep and appetite for two days if I was to dine at the Davydovs!!!‡ And through what secret anguish did I go before I acknowledged that I just could not be a conductor.§ How much time I spent realizing that I belonged to the category of indifferently intelligent people and not to extraordinary ones? How many years did it take me to understand that, even as a composer, I am just a gifted man and not an inconceivable phenomenon. Only now [. . .]‖ do I begin to understand that nothing is more futile than desiring to be what my nature is not.

No wonder that Tchaikovsky was fascinated by Rousseau's *Confessions*, although he felt 'hatred and contempt' for certain aspects of the author's personality. But Rousseau had described with 'an unbelievable precision' some traits of his own nature, which belonged also to Tchaikovsky: for instance 'the intolerable necessity of small talk,' which, to the composer, appeared as the most painful of society's bonds, because of its basic insincerity. Tolstoi's *Confession* also deeply impressed the composer: he felt he had

* This crucial passage is, as many others, published in any Western language for the first time.
† The corresponding terms in Russian do not lend themselves very easily to translation. Tchaikovsky was a gentleman living among gentlemen. Many of his friends were noblemen. Later, one was Grand-duke Konstantin. Tchaikovsky was received in the highest society, but still like an outsider: he did not belong to it.
‡ The family of the composer's brother-in-law. They belonged to Russian aristocracy.
§ Written in 1878.
‖ Passage omitted by publisher of Tchaikovsky's correspondence.

F

suffered the same 'torturing doubts and tragic misgivings' as the writer.

Tchaikovsky's flagellations of himself, his perpetual doubts about the quality of his life, which have systematically been attributed to the alleged particularities of his sexual life, seem in fact to be a typical Russian trait. What compatriot and contemporary of Tchaikovsky did not suffer because he was not leading a life of self-sacrifice? This characteristic Tchaikovsky had in common with most of Tolstoi's, Dostoievsky's, Turgenev's heroes. His salvation was his work, as he expressed it in a very pathetic, and a perfectly outspoken letter to Mrs von Meck: "How I shall work, how I shall try to prove to myself that I really deserve all you do for me! Very, very often, I feel embarrassed because you give me too much happiness. Then if I do not compose, if I do not work, I begin to despise myself and fall into great despair because of my nothingness and unworthiness, and because of the difference between what you think of me and what I really am. When I work, when what I do satisfies me, then the abyss fills and I reach the measure of all the kindness and affection you have shown to me."

13 Torrents of tears

Tchaikovsky did not always word his confessions in such dramatic terms. In fact he was very good at making fun of himself. He laughed at his absent-mindedness; he laughed at his fondness for nice clothes; he laughed at his excess of imagination and at his perpetual need of money. Here he tells with good-natured self-deprecation the story of one of his visits to Mrs von Meck's estate:

> On the way to Brailov I suffered from the heat and also from nervousness: would the horses come for me? had not N.F. given orders for me to be thrown out as soon as I should appear? and other nonsense. Lately I have been growing insane over the idea that either N.F. had become indifferent to me, or that, on the contrary, she had increased her solicitude, so that, in the secret of my heart, I was hoping for a little sealed box which she would have left for

me and which would contain . . . a few thousands, which I devil-
ishly need. I arrive in state, I walk in, I ask for letters, I am told
that some are waiting for me. I go to my study and I find two letters
and the little sealed box! . . . In much agitation I open everything . . .
but instead of the thousands I find a watch and a note requesting
that I accept it as a present. It had been ordered during the winter,
in Paris, and had just arrived. The watch must cost several thousand
francs; on one side is Joan of Arc on horseback, on the other Apollo
with two muses, both pictures on a background of black enamel
with golden stars. Most delicate and elegant work. Goodness! what a
darling is N.F.! But, between you and me, I should have preferred
not the watch but the money it cost.

He even laughed at his vanity as a composer, declaring that he
felt quite at home in a foreign city as soon as he saw his name 'on
all the boardings and posters,' that no music had ever been written
to compare with the Third Suite, that history was made up of two
eras: before and after *The Queen of Spades*, and that, having
played *Eugene Onegin* in front of an audience composed exclusively
of the author, he received 'a heap of compliments.' A comparable
event took place during the composition of *The Maid of Orleans*:

A very interesting event has just taken place. There exist, as you
well know, three remarkable characters with whom you are
acquainted: (1) Mr N.N., a rather poor poet who has never written
anything but a few verses for Russian songs published by you; (2)
Mr B.L., former musical critic for *The Russian News*, and (3) Mr
Tchaikovsky, composer and ex-professor.*

An hour ago, Mr Tchaikovsky invited these two co-citizens of his,
who happen to share his lodgings, to the piano and played for them
the second act of *The Maid of Orleans*, an opera on which he is now
working. Mr Tchaikovsky, who is on the most intimate terms with
N.N. and B.L. having easily conquered his natural timidity, performed his new creation before them with extreme competence,
enthusiasm and inspiration. You should have seen the raptures of
the two gentlemen! You could have believed that they had taken
a personal part in the composition of the opera (it is true that Mr
N.N. wrote the libretto, but that does not make him the author of
the opera), so proudly they strutted around the room, putting on
airs and deeply moved by the beauty of the music! Finally the composer, who tried for a long time to keep a modest appearance, became equally frantic, and the three characters ended by running to
and fro on the balcony, hoping that fresh air would calm down their
shattered nerves and appease their impatience to hear the following acts as soon as possible (the first one had already been com-

* Tchaikovsky signed N.N. some of his translations and B.L. some of his
articles.

pleted and performed). In vain did Messrs N.N. and B.L. represent to Mr Tchaikovsky that operas cannot be tossed off as pancakes: he went into despair over the weakness of human nature, which cannot get onto paper in one week all that has accumulated in the head.

Tchaikovsky went further than that. He even made fun of that tendency to exaggerate his emotions (both in the living and the describing) which, as we have seen, nonplussed his historians, and authorized so many doubtful interpretations of his motives.

Tchaikovsky is to see his publisher Bessel: "I was already imagining . . . how he would blow on me all the mephitic miasmata of his breath." Tchaikovsky expects his brother Modest and young Nikolai Konradi, Modest's pupil; they are late: "With my capacity to exaggerate every mishap, I immediately imagined the awful picture of a sick child whom my brother could not leave for a minute, his panic, helplessness and difficulties." Telegrams, early trains follow and when the composer finally reaches his brother, he finds the boy sleeping off a slight cold. Tchaikovsky wants to go on with the First Suite and the first part of the manuscript seems to have been lost in the mail: "I am terribly angry. If it does not come to-morrow morning, I shall give it up and tear the rest. By the way, that is a lie. I shall not tear it." Tchaikovsky says good-bye to his brother: "As soon as I was in the carriage and had taken leave from you, I began to shed tears with great application. I remembered our meeting in Milan! How joyful it was! How charming was the trip to Genoa. . . . Here: torrents of tears. All that had been, and precisely because it had been and could not come again, it seemed so wonderful to me. Nearly six months had elapsed since that time . . . tears again. Etc. etc., till I finally and unexpectedly fell asleep. After all, there is really nothing much to grieve about." Tchaikovsky has a happy meeting with his brother: "Since I cannot live without torturing myself, I suffer from the idea that . . ." utter nonsense follows* and Tchaikovsky knew it himself, but the quotation is interesting: it shows that the composer was conscious of his need to suffer for nothing at all.

* Mr Konradi, the father of Modest's pupil Nikolai, had allowed his son to spend a vacation in Italy, so that Modest could live with his brother, and Tchaikovsky was afraid that such a favour had made Modest and him "the slaves" of Konradi.

14 Insolent enough to beg

Self-deprecation does not mean lack of pride. It can even mean the contrary. Tchaikovsky said as much: "I am supposed to be a modest man, but I must confess that my modesty is truly a secret but very, very great pride. Among all living musicians there is not one before whom I should freely bow. But nature, who put so much pride into my soul, did not give me the aptitude and talent to sell my goods with a profit . . . I am abnormally timid, maybe from too much pride."

We have already mentioned it and shall do so again: if anything, Tchaikovsky was a living paradox. This modesty and this pride of which he himself was conscious did not go unnoticed by other people. Rubinstein, who would have liked Tchaikovsky to succeed him as Director of the Conservatoire, felt that the composer was too yielding to occupy such a post; Vsevolzhskiy, Director of the Imperial Theatres, wrote to the composer: "You are a truly Russian talent, a real, not a counterfeit one; therefore there is no complacency in you." But The Powerful Handful* of St Petersburg must have felt differently, since, though he was ready to defend them when the need arose, he knew very well how to preserve his independence toward them. Few of his contemporaries would have thanked the important Balakirev for proposing a subject for a cantata, and added that they would attend to it at some other time; fewer still would have written to the famous and formidable critic Stasov to decline the privilege of using an opera scenario drafted by the great man himself;† but Tchaikovsky did so, and with a perfect blend of suavity and independence: "Therefore, I shall beg you to accept my warmest and most sincere gratitude for your work, for the condescending readiness with which you come to my assistance. At the same time, accept my apologies for not taking advantage of a scenario so cleverly, so effectively conceived. I am guilty for the second time. In the midst of your various occupations, you were so kind as to write two whole scenarios for me, and I made use of none!‡ Still you must believe how deeply I

* Otherwise known as The Five (Balakirev, Cui, Borodin, Musorgsky, Rimsky-Korsakov) protected by the critic Stasov.
† From the novel Cinq-Mars by Alfred de Vigny.
‡ The first one was an adaptation of Othello.

value your patronage; if I do not express enough gratitude, it is only because I do not know how. And nevertheless I shall be insolent enough to beg that, if you should happen to think of a subject that would suit me, you kindly mention it to me."

It seems that Modest did not lack psychological insight the day when he wrote: Tchaikovsky "was yielding and submissive in matters of daily existence, although inwardly he protested against all attempts to influence and coerce him, and generally reserved his freedom of opinion, at least as regards music. This self-assertion did not, however, come naturally to him, and for that reason he loved solitude."

Some people mistake vanity or arrogance for pride; and those might think that Tchaikovsky was a self-effacing man. But he was nothing of the kind. From the day when, at 22, he told his brother Nikolai, with gleaming eyes, "you will be proud some day to own me as a brother," he never doubted that his fate would not be a common one. "I am only afraid of a want of purpose: perhaps idleness may take possession of me and I may not persevere," he wrote to his sister Aleksandra at the early dawn of his career; but even then he did not doubt his talent, for he added: "You know I have power and capacity." He was 37, and most of his great works were yet to come, when he wrote to Jurgenson: "I am an artist who can and must bring honour to his country. I feel in myself a great artistic strength. I have not yet done the tenth of what I can do. And with all the strength of my soul I want to do it." This was a brave declaration, and if it meant pride, Tchaikovsky was not one to be afraid of the word: "Pride is expressed differently in different people: for my part, it makes me avoid meeting men who do not recognize my merits or have no knowledge of them. I cannot stand modestly before some Saint-Saëns or other and feel his patronizing glance on me, when, in my own mind, I consider myself Alps higher than he is."

The pride did not belong exclusively to the musician. Tchaikovsky the man was not to be slighted. He had been invited to spend some time in the estate of his friend Kondratiev, and could not sleep because "the flunky Aleksei* had flunky Bacchanals every night. . . . Once, not able to contain myself any more, I came out of the pavilion in which I lodged, and created an inexpressible scandal. I woke my host up and declared that if Aleksei was not thrown out the next day, I should leave. Aleksei was not thrown out and consequently here I am." In the same mood the

* *Not* Tchaikovsky's personal servant Aleksei Sofronov.

very young Tchaikovsky refused to send the *Voivode* dances to be performed unless he received a written request, signed by all the Directors of the Russian Musical Society. In the same mood, a much older Tchaikovsky refused a position in the same Society: "The role which you magnanimously assign to me, i.e. the role of a man whose voice in purely musical questions can be neglected and disobeyed, I dislike. If I am important to them, if they want me to participate actively in what they do, then let them submit to my decisions."

Sometimes his pride would be calculated. Since he wanted a very special cast for *Eugene Onegin*, and was afraid of a conventional performance if the opera was presented in a state theatre, he decided he would never ask for such a presentation but would wait to be 'humbly begged' to allow the opera to be performed: "Then I shall say: 'all right, but you have to do everything as I say; if not, you may go to hell.' " When the German conductor Bilse made openings which Jurgenson would have had Tchaikovsky disregard, the composer answered: "With my hand on my heart I can say that not only did I not make one step, but I never moved my little finger in order to deserve the attention of some Bilse or other. That passive pride I have. But it is quite another matter when he is making the advances: then I melt, I soften, I am ready to grovel (by letter, of course)."

But he did not grovel often. More frequently we find him haughtily refusing some benefit—for instance the prestigious position of Russian representative at the International Exhibition in Paris—because to get acquainted with the musical Paris world would be "most awful for me. To compliment, to flatter, to ingratiate myself with all that riff-raff, is loathsome to my nature." If a German publisher orders Russian dances from him, Tchaikovsky snorts: "See what a wonderful composer I must be: German publishers are ordering Russian reels from me!" and replies that he is used to write what he pleases and not what will please Mr So and So. If, invited to conduct in Vienna a concert related to a large theatrical-musical exhibition, he discovers that the orchestra is not good enough, he refuses to fulfil his engagement. He accepts musical orders, not literary ones: "Send the text or order instrumental things, but clearly and precisely."

When Tchaikovsky was a beginner, the critic Stasov had no rival in Russia, and ruled its musical world with a very high hand. But the young composer, for whom the mature critic who favoured self-taught artists could do much, did not hesitate to upbraid him for an article about Mozart: "I find your commentary on Mozart offensive for me, since I am a musician and spoiled by schooling not less than my idol."

After Tchaikovsky had enthusiastically toured the United States once, he was invited to go back for a much larger tour. But the terms, although commercially they could be justified, he found slighting, because the fee offered per concert was lower than the first time. And so, in perpetual need of money as he was, he cabled with an almost royal conciseness: "No. Tchaikovsky." And that was all.

The story of his relationship with the makers of the Knabe pianos is not very important in itself but significant. At his arrival in New York, he was greeted and entertained by a Mr Mayer, whose kindness he could not praise enough. American disinterested hospitality was so pleasant after French greed! After several days of dinners, drinks, presents, etc., which Tchaikovsky innocently accepted, Mr Mayer finally got down to business: the composer was to write a testimonial in favour of the Knabe pianos. Slightly disgusted, Tchaikovsky did not refuse but suggested that Mr Mayer write the testimonial himself: the composer would sign it. Mr Mayer, who knew his publicity, did not mince matters: his text was short and to the point. It read as follows: "I consider the Knabe pianofortes without doubt the best in America."—'Notwithstanding his deep gratitude to Mayer,' Tchaikovsky replied that he could not tell a lie, and that he did value some other makers' far more highly. He did write a testimonial, but never consented to sign 'the phrase which ranks these pianos as the first.'*

Telling a lie was naturally out of the question, but also Tchaikovsky did not wish to be compromised by or with anything which was not first class. Not only did he object to productions of his works which did not do them justice, but once in his life, after composing *Navy Volunteers*, a march much too patriotic to be good, he even refused to own it as a child of his, and asked Jurgenson to find a pseudonym to sign it with.† He was aiming high, much higher than patriotic marches and publicity for piano makers. He was aiming for fame in the highest meaning of the word.

If fame is destined for me, it will come with slow but sure steps. History convinces us that the success which is long delayed is often more lasting than when it comes easily and at a bound. Many a

---

* Rosa Newmarch's version modestly disguises the names Knabe and Mayer under code names: Three asterisks and Z, respectively.
† It was signed P. I. Sinopov.

name which resounded through its own generation is now engulfed in the ocean of oblivion. An artist should not be troubled by the indifference of his contemporaries. He should go on working and say all he has been predestined to say. He should know that posterity alone can deliver a true and just verdict. I will tell you something more. Perhaps I accept my modest share with so little complaint because my faith in the judgment of the future is immovable. I have a foretaste during my lifetime of the fame which will be meted out to me when the history of Russian music comes to be written. For the present I am satisfied with what I have already acquired. I have no right to complain. I have met people on my way through life whose warm sympathy for my music more than compensates me for the indifference, misunderstanding, and ill-will of others.

Tchaikovsky did not desire fame like a child. He knew that some aspects of it would be harrowing for him, and still he strove for it, because he knew that such was his fate, that being a great artist he was condemned to fame, that it was part, so to speak, of his identity itself:

Fame! What contradictory sentiments the word awakes in me! On the one hand I desire and strive for it; on the other I detest it. If the chief thought of my life is concentrated upon my creative work, I cannot do otherwise than wish for fame. If I feel a continual impulse to express myself in the language of music, it follows that I need to be heard; and the larger my circle of sympathetic hearers, the better. I desire with all my soul that my music should become more widely known, and that the number of those people who derive comfort and support from their love of it should increase. In this sense not only do I love fame, but it becomes the aim of all that is most earnest in my work. But, alas! when I begin to reflect that with an increasing audience will come also an increase of interest in my personality, in the more intimate sense; that there will be inquisitive people among the public who will tear aside the curtain behind which I have striven to conceal my private life; then I am filled with pain and disgust, so that I half wish to keep silence for ever, in order to be left in peace. I am not afraid of the world, for I can say that my conscience is clear, and I have nothing to be ashamed of; but the thought that someone may try to force the inner world of my thoughts and feelings, which all my life I have guarded so carefully from outsiders—this is sad and terrible. There is a tragic element, dear friend, in this conflict between the desire for fame and the fear of its consequences. I am attracted to it like the moth to the candle, and I, too, burn my wings. Sometimes I am possessed by a mad desire to disappear for ever, to be buried alive, to ignore all that is going on, and be forgotten by everybody. Then, alas! the creative inspiration returns. . . . I fly to the flame and burn my wings once more.

So what was fame for Tchaikovsky? 'An increase in the number of people who derive comfort and support from their love of his music.' How close it sounds to Prince Andrei's dream of military glory in *War and Peace*: to desire fame is to desire to be loved, and to desire to be loved is to love.

Not in every case. There is a petty appetite for journalistic notoriety. To have one's picture in the papers, one's name in the news *at any price*, is not one of man's higher ambitions. Tchekhov tells us the hilarious story of the man who was in raptures at finding himself named in the newspaper, because the police had found him drunk on the street. How many of our contemporary celebrities are even worse than Tchekhov's hero: they provide the scandal, in order to get the publicity that goes with it! Not so Tchaikovsky: he makes that clear enough. Even when he had achieved what he considered the foretaste of fame to which he was entitled during his lifetime, his modesty made of pride or his pride made of modesty did not abandon him.

His cousin Anna Merkling gave a letter of his to a collector of autographs and was afraid he would mind. But why should he? "My writings are not so precious that you should never let hold of them! And if there are cranks who find something valuable in them, so much the better for my vanity and for their collection." Somehow all Tchaikovsky's personality is clearly shown in that incident, or at least all its lighter side: this mixture of good-naturedness, good taste, and good sense, this gentle humour directed at himself, there is something there that is specifically Tchaikovskian, although we are not used to associate it with his name.

At no time did the man show himself beneath the artist in the use of the fame which surrounded his last years. We shall see later how he helped other composers, younger than he, how often he was ready to sacrifice his own advantage to theirs, but sometimes he would renounce his rights only because he felt that he owed it to himself. He wrote to the conductor Napravnik: "You have not forgotten your promise to conduct one of the concerts of the Moscow Musical Society? . . . We beg you to lay aside your modesty and to include at least two important works of your own. I implore you most emphatically not to do any of my compositions. As I am arranging this concert, it would be most unseemly were the conductor I engaged to perform any work of mine." And then, of course, there is the extraordinary example of the symphonic poem, *The Voivode*. Many a young composer must have destroyed a score which displeased his audience, and although there is always something pathetic in an artist's burning his own cherished work, such a reaction is not necessarily to be admired. But Tchaikovsky was 51; he was famous throughout Russia, Europe and America; nothing he wrote displeased his audiences any more; he directed himself the performance of his latest composition; the audience was prodigal of ovations and applause; the critics shared the enthusiasm; and still, on hearing *The Voivode*, he disliked it; he found that it was not good music, and he tore it up.

15 *The snub-nosed monster*

Such was the man in his relationship to his own self, to his intelligence, to his body, to his image. We could end the first part of our investigation here. But the most personal, the most intimate remains yet to be told. Who can boast of knowing what kind of man he is before he has seen himself in the mirror which death so obligingly holds up to us? What is more intimate than death anyway? When somebody asked the French writer Jean Paulhan how he wished to die, he replied: "Not unconsciously. I was already cheated out of my birth: I do not want to miss my death." We have now to see how "the disgusting snub-nosed monster" treated Tchaikovsky and how Tchaikovsky treated him— or her, since death is feminine in Russian.

It is not of necessity true that those who love life most dread death more than others: it is more a question of how you love it. In Tchaikovsky's love for life there was a gentleness, one could almost say a detachment, which gave it a melancholy touch without decreasing its passionate quality. He summarized all that rather aptly himself when he wrote: "To regret the past and to hope for the future, never to be satisfied with the present, this is my life." His attachment to the past was very strong: "Nothing delights me more than to plunge into my past. Memory is like a moonray: it lights up the past so that what was bad remains unnoticed while what was good seems even better." But he was satisfied to let youth go: if he had been offered a chance to relieve it, he would have refused. And his impatience with the present was decidedly of a Faustian type: "My nature constantly expects I know not what incredible enchantments, and is constantly unsatisfied. Yesterday I could not wait for dinner. After dinner I could not wait for my walk. During my walk I could not wait for tea. After tea I could not wait for the moon to rise. After that I hoped for supper, and then for the time to go to bed." Only in sleep did Tchaikovsky find any appeasement to this perpetual unrest: "I slept well. Sleep may be the best thing in life: on the next morning it gives us the strength to resume our eternal expectation of things unknown."

And so, as the most effective kind of sleep, death sometimes seemed welcome to him: "I reached such disgust of life that I even called for death. . . ." "Death is really the greatest happiness and I call for it with all my soul." At the time of his unfortunate marriage he even, according to Kashkin, made a clumsy attempt at suicide: not finding the courage to drown himself, he decided he would catch pneumonia and so he walked into a body of water, at night. He stayed there, with water up to his waist, as long as he could stand the cold. It could not have been very cold, by the way, since the ludicrous nocturnal scene took place in Moscow, in the middle of September. "I came out with the firm conviction that death would be sure to come now, through pneumonia or some other illness having to do with cold. . . . But my health was so good that this icy bath had no consequences whatsoever." The joking reference to the 'icy bath' sounds authentic. And it does not seem that this attempt should be taken too seriously: Tchaikovsky wanted to escape from his wife and he did not even catch a cold: the incident is ridiculous from both standpoints; he himself knew it, and it would be stretching evidence to make him look like a suicidal type.

On the contrary, he frequently referred to his horror of death: "That snub-nosed monster is always abominable and repulsive, but I particularly hate it when it destroys a man in his prime. . . ." Kondratiev "is awfully despondent . . . tears. I understand him: he abhors the death that approaches him—and I too abhor it deeply." "As a man who passionately loves life (in spite of all its calamities) and who hates death just as passionately, I always feel deeply shaken when dies a creature whom I know and cherish. But never does death appear so abominably dreadful and absurd as when dies a dear, nice and healthy child."

Tchaikovsky died at 53, so prematurely that rumours of suicide were circulated, avidly seized upon by journalists, and are still to be heard from time to time. There is not the slightest bit of evidence to support such a version of his death, and even his more sensational biographers seem to have abandoned it.

The truth is that during his last years he had aged very much. In 1884, he was already keenly conscious of passing time: "Soon I shall be forty-four years old. How long I have lived and—truthfully, without false modesty—how little accomplished! Even in my own present occupation, why there is nothing—I swear—that is perfect and exemplary. I am still searching, doubting, wavering. And in other things? I read nothing, know nothing. Only on whist do I spend endless, precious time." And two years later: "How much there is yet to be done! How much to be read! How much to learn! I am terribly reluctant to die as yet, even though at times I imagine that I have lived, oh, so long." But, maybe more than fleeting time, the death of his friend Kondratiev wounded him to the quick. "The six weeks which I spent in Aachen, in the company of a man in great pain, condemned to die, but not managing to do so, were inexpressibly agonizing for me. It is one of the darkest periods of my life. I aged very much and grew thin. I am tired of life, and filled with a mournful apathy; I feel as though it will be soon time for me to die too, and this proximity of death makes whatever was important and essential in my private life seem petty, insignificant and completely aimless." That was written in 1887. He lived six years more, during which he composed two symphonies, two operas and two ballets including the joyful *Nutcracker*, but that does not mean he was not already wounded to death. When he came back from Aachen, he was so thin and pale and had aged so much in six weeks that 'all his relatives and friends were dismayed. A week spent in the country and in solitude put him right,' but to what extent? Rosa Newmarch notes that "at fifty he began to show some signs of the troubles he had suffered and the hard mental work he had accomplished. He could no longer give himself up so entirely to composition; he needed more rest and distraction, and unfortunately his sight began to be affected. He could no longer read with comfort and thus he was deprived of one of his chief sources of occupation during the long evenings which he spent alone in his country house." He was very much annoyed with some of the more humiliating results of age: his growing absent-mindedness and especially the loss of a front tooth which gave a "special hissing sound" to his sibilants and made them indistinct.* In America he was unpleasantly surprised at being taken "for a veritable patriarch."† In 1888, he had already

---

* Russian is particularly rich with sibilants.

† "Tchaikovsky is a man of ample proportions with rather grey hair, well built, of pleasing appearance, and about sixty years of age." The *New York Herald*, 6th May 1891. Tchaikovsky was fifty.

written: "Old age is knocking at the door; death also may not be far away." And in 1891: "I am aging fast, I am tired of life, I thirst for quietness and a rest from all these vanities, emotions, disappointments, etc. etc. It is natural for an old man to think of a prospective dirty hole called a grave."

It is only in his last months that he forgot to expect death: on the contrary, he seemed to be embarking for a long and healthy old age. Such are the whims of fate. On 9th (21st) October 1893, he attended a meeting of old friends, in Moscow, among whom was Kashkin, who remembers what happened that evening: "Unconsciously the talk turned to our recent losses: to the death of Albrecht and Zverev. We thought of the gaps time had made in our circle of old friends and how few now remained. Involuntarily the question arose: Who will be the next to take the road from which there is no return? With complete assurance of its truth, I declared that Tchaikovsky would outlive us all. He disputed the probability, but ended by saying he had never felt better or happier in his life."

After that meeting—which seems memorable only because two weeks later the composer was dead—he travelled by train to St Petersburg, where the *Pathétique* was to be created.

During these last days he was neither very cheerful, nor yet depressed. In the circle of his intimate friends he was contented and jovial; among strangers he was, as usual, nervous and excited and, as time went on, tired out and dull. But nothing gave the smallest hint of his approaching end. . . .

On Tuesday, 19th (31st) October, he went to a private performance of Rubinstein's *The Maccabees*. On the 20th (1st November) he was still in good health and dined with his old friend Vera Butakov (*née* Davydov). Afterwards he went to see Ostrovsky's play, *A Warm Heart*, at the Alexander Theatre. During the interval he went with Modest to see the actor Varlamov in his dressing-room. The conversation turned upon spiritualism. Varlamov described in his own humorous style—which cannot be transferred to paper—his loathing for "all those abominations" which reminded one of death. Peter Ilich laughed at Varlamov's quaint way of expressing himself.

"There is plenty of time," said Tchaikovsky, "before we need reckon with this snub-nosed horror; it will not come to snatch us off just yet! I feel I shall live a long time." From the theatre, Tchaikovsky went with his cousins, Count Litke and Baron Buxhövden, to the Restaurant Leiner. Modest joined them an hour later, and found one or two other visitors—of whom Glazunov was one. They had already had their supper, and Modest was afterwards told his brother had eaten macaroni and drunk, as usual, white wine and soda water. They went home about two a.m. Peter Ilich was perfectly well and serene.

On the morning of Thursday, 21st October (2nd November), Tchaikovsky did not appear as usual at the early breakfast-table. His brother went to his room and found him slightly indisposed. He complained of his digestion being upset and of a bad night. About eleven a.m. he dressed and went out to see Napravnik. Half an hour later he returned, still feeling unwell. He absolutely declined to send for a doctor. His condition gave no anxiety to Modest, who had often seen him suffer from similar derangements.

He joined his brother and nephew at lunch, although he ate nothing. But this was probably the fatal moment in his indisposition for, while talking, he poured out a glass of water and drank a long draught. The water had not been boiled, and they were dismayed at his imprudence. But he was not in the least alarmed, and tried to calm their fears. He dreaded cholera less than any other illness. After this his condition grew worse; but he attributed all his discomfort to a copious dose of Hunyadi which he had taken earlier in the day, and still declined to send for his favourite doctor, Bertenson. Towards evening Modest grew so anxious that he sent for the doctor on his own account. Meanwhile Tchaikovsky was tended by his brother's servant Nazar, who had once travelled with him to Italy.

About eight p.m. Bertenson arrived. He saw at once that the illness was serious, and sent for his brother in consultation. The sufferer had grown very weak, and complained of terrible oppression on his chest. More than once he said, "I believe this is death."

After a short consultation the brothers Bertenson, the two leading physicians in St Petersburg, pronounced it to be a case of cholera.

All night long those who nursed him in turn fought against the cramps; towards morning with some hope of success. His courage was wonderful, and in the intervals between the paroxysms of pain he made little jokes with those around him. He constantly begged his nurses to take some rest, and was grateful for the smallest service.

On Friday his condition seemed more hopeful, and he himself believed he had been "snatched from the jaws of death." But on the following day his mental depression returned. "Leave me," he said to his doctors, "you can do no good. I shall never recover."

Gradually he passed into the second stage of the cholera, with its most dangerous symptom—complete inactivity of the kidneys. He slept more, but his sleep was restless, and sometimes he wandered in his mind. At these times he continually repeated the name of Nadejda Filaretovna von Meck in an indignant, or reproachful, tone. Consciousness returned at longer intervals, and when his servant Aleksei arrived from Klin he was no longer able to recognize him.

A warm bath was tried as a last resource, but without avail, and soon afterwards his pulse grew so weak that the end seemed imminent. At the desire of his brother Nikolai, a priest was sent for from the Isaac Cathedral. He did not administer the sacrament, as Tchaikovsky was now quite unconscious, but prayed in clear and distinct tones, which, however, did not seem to reach the ears of the dying man.

At three o'clock on the morning of 25th October (6th November) Tchaikovsky passed away in the presence of his brothers Nikolai and Modest, his cousins Litke, Buxhövden, and Vladimir Davydov, the three doctors, and his faithful servant Aleksei Sofronov. At the last moment an indescribable look of clear recognition lit up his face— a gleam which only died away with his last breath.[20]

There is no reason to doubt any part of Modest's sober narrative. And very little can be added to it, except that such an utter lack of rebellion, such a willingness to go with good grace seem somehow characteristic. That Tchaikovsky died of cholera, as his mother had died 39 years before, has been abundantly exploited but, twist the facts as you like, it can only be a coincidence. What we should not disregard is that "look of clear recognition" which lit up his face at the last moment as it surely lit up Ivan Ilitch's, in Tolstoi's tale. Modest's words aptly describe the expression which we find on the composer's death mask: spiritual, all-intelligent and all-kind. One can imagine no fitter expression in death for the little boy who, at the age of eight, wrote in approximate French the following quaint little poem:

> *Ah! l'homme qui est bon n'a pas peur de mourir!*
> *Oh! il sai bien que son ame entrera chez Bon Dieu*
> *Aussi les enfants pur, bon, pieux et sage.*
> *Oh! ils seront des anges aux cieux!*
> *Moi je voudrai être comme cela un*

> Ah! a good man is not afraid to die!
> Oh! he knows full well that his soul will go to good God!
> So will children pure, good, pious and nice.
> Oh! they will be angels in heaven!
> I should like to be one like them

NOTES TO PART II

1 Hanson.
2 Hanson.
3 Hanson, Weinstock and Michel Hofmann.
4 Modest.
5 Modest.

(*above left*) Nikolai (left) and Anton Rubinstein; (*above right*) P. I. Jurgenson

(*right*) The composer's manservant Aleksei Sofronov and his wife

Tchaikovsky and his wife, Antonina Milukov

6 Modest.
7 Modest quoted by Hanson.
8 Modest.
9 Weinstock.
10 Bowen.
11 Quoted in Bowen.
12 Michel Hofmann.
13 Hanson.
14 Quoted by Newmarch from N. D. Kashkin's reminiscences.
15 Modest.
16 Bowen.
17 E. Lockspeiser in G. Abraham.
18 Hanson.
19 E. Lockspeiser in G. Abraham.
20 Newmarch's translation of Modest.

G

PART THREE

TCHAIKOVSKY AND OTHERS

1 Puppies are the pearls of creation

Adam did not last very long alone. Man is a social animal. A view of a man isolated from the world is a very partial view indeed. We need others in order to become our real selves. And Tchaikovsky not less than most.

Although on this point he was, as on many others, a paradox of a man, we still feel justified in stating that he was a live fountain of sympathy, that his need for love was in direct proportion to the amount of love he poured out upon the world, that his heart was a permanent spring bubbling with slightly indiscriminate affections. It is certainly not a coincidence if the most laudatory adjective of his vocabulary was, for things, ideas, persons, places, styles, etc, 'simpatichny': inspiring sympathy.

Except a very few pet detestations including his publisher Bessel (but who loves a publisher?—and still Tchaikovsky managed to love Jurgenson), it really seems that the composer's capacity for love was limitless. And of course he began with animals. To him belongs the honour of having described Venice, the most prestigious of all cities, as 'a dead and gloomy place where no horses and even no dogs were to be found.' His fondness for animals started when he was a child, and tender souls have had a tendency to exaggerate its precocious effects. Modest says that young Peter wrote a whole group of poems about his love of animals, but only one, on 'The Death of a Bird', has been preserved; and Fanny Dürbach, the governess, tells us a touching tale[5] about the boy snatching a kitten which was to be drowned and touring the neighbourhood to find a home for it, which sounds a little contrived; nevertheless the essence of those stories is true: animals, all kind of animals except mice, appealed to Tchaikovsky and he was faithful to them throughout his life.

He liked rabbits; he liked cats; during his stay at Mrs von Meck's estate, Brailov, he even had a love-affair with a parrot; he nearly took him to Simaki, another von Meck estate where he was to go after Brailov, and refrained from doing so only out of consideration for the feelings of a parlour maid who also loved the parrot. And when the musician and the bird met again, much later, Tchaikovsky was 'very happy to see his old friend from Brailov' and expressed concern over his health: the bird was losing its feathers—what could be done about it? He even decided to acquire such a parrot[8]—he found the species 'simpatichny'—but finally never realized his wish.

Still his deepest tenderness was for dogs. "Children are enchanting, he wrote. Only puppies are better: they are the pearls of creation. Here [in Florence] there is a race of dogs completely unknown in Russia, called Lupetto, and Lupetto dogs are often to be sold on the Lugarno. How delightful they are! If my Aleksei did not hate dogs (when servants do not like them, their life is very miserable), I could not help buying one."[9] To Mrs von Meck he gave longer explanations about his feelings for canine friends. "I sympathize wholeheartedly with your passion for dogs. I love them dearly myself, but I think that I must be the only dog lover of my kind. First, I prefer mongrels; second I cannot keep a dog in my house and in all my life have had only one house-dog. . . . This is because I worry continuously about them; all the time I think that they are hungry, that they want something and cannot say so, that they are sick, etc etc. Moreover my Aleksei does not like them, and when servants are not attentive and patient enough to animals, they cannot be happy."*

There are different ways of loving animals, and Tchaikovsky loved them most because of their helplessness, because of their dependence on man. He noted in his diary "the sight of a poor horse, mercilessly beaten" and, although he never missed the opportunity of going to a Zoo,† he broke into sobs when he saw a rabbit fed to a snake. About hunting, he had mixed feelings, and finally abandoned it for two contradictory reasons: (a) he did not shoot well enough, (b) he could not get used to spilling blood, although how he managed to spill blood if he was a bad shot remains unclear.

---

* All that daringly condensed by Bowen into: "Alexis hated dogs, so his master dared not have more than one."
† Cf. above page 59.

2 A father's rights

Though they did not quite reach the exalted level of puppies, children also were entitled to Tchaikovsky's admiration and fondness. Testimonies abound to the effect that he was extremely successful with them. "He treated them particularly nicely and kindly," writes Kashkin's daughter Sofia. ". . . He seemed to know that grown-ups must not talk to children in a special way, talking down to them, but simply, as if they were grown-up too. He always did this, that is why I and other children were so happy to be with him; he felt one of us and conveyed this to us so that we all understood without a word said." Who these children were was of no importance to him. He had served his apprenticeship as nurse by taking care of his brothers, the twins, and was always ready to baby-sit for his sister Aleksandra, but he also 'got on friendly terms with his grand-niece Kira* and was treated with benevolence by his grand-nephew Mark,* a wonderful, superb child, with a big shock of blond hair.' Sometimes he travelled with "his beloved Dinochka, the nine-year-old daughter of [his friend] Kondratiev, who was so devoted to him that he had not the heart to leave her." Sometimes he would join the children of the village, for a chat: "Saw Egorka Tabach flying a kite. Talked with him and some other boys and girls. These children, though ugly, are so charmingly engaging in their display of the pure Great Russian spirit, that I could not help being moved. (One of the girls asked for twenty kopeks; then one hundred roubles and later a five-kopek piece! !)." His godson, the son of his servant Aleksei, seemed to him "a wonderfully attractive child" and was a source of "great amusement" for him. As to the three-year-old daughter of Legoshin (a servant of Kondratiev), Tchaikovsky was positively "fascinated by her prettiness, her clear, bell-like voice, her charming ways, and clever little head. He would spend hours romping with the child, listening to her chatter, and even acting as nurse-maid."

The story of the song *Pimpinella* is well known. Tchaikovsky

* Children of Nikolai von Meck, son of Nadejda Filaretovna von Meck, Tchaikovsky's patroness, and Anna Davydov, daughter of Aleksandra, Tchaikovsky's sister, and Lev Davydov.

learned it from a young street-singer in Florence. "How I pity the boy! His father, uncle and other relatives exploit him so! In Carnival time he sings from morning till night and will go on singing until his voice is ruined forever. Even now it is already a little cracked, as compared to the first time I heard him. It adds a new grace to its marvellously *simpatichny* quality, but this will not be for long."

The death of a child was always particularly offensive to him.* Without unnecessary pathos but with a deep feeling he writes to Mrs von Meck about the forester's daughter: "Yesterday I received sad news from Kamenka. In the neighbourhood lies a little wood, the goal of my daily walk. In the heart of the wood lives a forester with a large and *simpatichny* family. I never saw more beautiful children. I was particularly devoted to a little girl of four, who was very shy at first, but afterwards grew so friendly that she would caress me prettily, and chatter delightful nonsense, which was a great pleasure to me. Now my brother-in-law writes that this child and one of the others have died of diphtheria. The remaining children were removed to the village by his orders, but, he adds, 'I fear it is too late.' "

Tchaikovsky had no children of his own, at least none of which we know. The only one of whom he elected to be responsible was Georgi, the illegitimate son of Tatiana Davydov and her music teacher, Stanislav Mihailovich Blumenfeld. The composer spent more than five thousand roubles and played nurse to his niece at the time of the delivery. Later the child was entrusted to a French couple for three years and once again the composer paid the expenses. When the boy was three, he was adopted by Tchaikovsky's older brother Nikolai, but it was the composer who had to go to Paris to fetch the child and to arrange all necessary official papers, which cost him no little money and more worry. Between 1883 (birth) and 1886 (adoption) little Georgi was somehow Tchaikovsky's responsibility, since no one in the family but he and his younger brother Modest, not even Tatiana's parents, knew what had happened. When the composer saw the three-year-old child, he was at first appalled at his resemblance with his mother: would not the Davydovs guess that their adopted nephew was in fact their grandson? Apparently the child was not particularly appealing: at least Tchaikovsky found him such an 'awful nuisance' that he was terrified 'to think about the journey.' But the frightening journey was enough to melt the composer's heart.

* Cf. above page 92.

Back at home, he wrote to Jurgenson: "I have safely brought the child to St Petersburg, and now he has already settled down at my brother Nikolai's. Yesterday he was baptized, I being his godfather. I am very sad to lose a father's rights over this charming boy, but one has to rejoice at knowing that he is in good hands."*

Another boy, also marked by ill fortune, played an important part in Tchaikovsky's childless life: Nikolai Konradi, Modest's deaf and dumb pupil. And again it was the sorrowful fate, the utter defencelessness of the child, which impressed Tchaikovsky in his favour. "The child is very weak, and it is healthy for him to be outdoors. You cannot imagine what a wonderful boy he is! I feel for him a sort of tremulous tenderness. It is impossible to refrain from tears when one sees how he treats my brother. It is not affection, it is some kind of passionate adoration. When he has been naughty and my brother punishes him, it is a torment to look at his face, so touchingly does it express repentance, love, a prayer for forgiveness. He is extraordinarily intelligent. The first day, when I saw him, I had only pity for him; his infirmity, I mean his deafness and dumbness, the unnatural sounds which he utters instead of words, all that inspired me with an unconquerable aversion. But this lasted only a day. After that, everything became dear to me in this wonderful, intelligent, affectionate and unfortunate child."

Tchaikovsky's enthusiasm grew during the next days. When the wind blew, the composer dared not leave the child, for fear something would happen to him. And when the time of the separation came, he grieved: "I cannot imagine how I shall live without him. I have become so attached to him, I love him so much that neither his father nor his mother can love him so. The more you know him, the more you value him. I have never seen or met a child with a purer soul, with more kindness and love in him. I cannot live without listening to his chattering."†

In later years, the friendship between Tchaikovsky and young Konradi became less intimate mainly because Modest wanted to go on managing his pupil's fortune, even when Nikolai was an adult and quite able to do it himself. This of course did not go without some bitterness on all sides; nevertheless Nikolai carefully preserved the composer's letters and let most of them be published. These letters would deserve a special study, so much do

* Under the name Georgi Nikolaevich Tchaikovsky, the boy is mentioned in the composer's will.
† Nikolai Konradi was learning to speak; Modest was teaching him.

they have to tell us about Tchaikovsky's attitude towards children. The first notes are written to a retarded boy; the next ones to a very dear though very young friend who is progressing intellectually at a fast pace; the last, to an adult. The gradual sophistication of Tchaikovsky's style, the continuously rising level of the subjects he treats, are a marvel by themselves, but the most characteristic aspect of it all is still to be found in this 'one-of-us-ness' that Sofia Kashkin so aptly pinpointed: to the wealthy adult, to the brilliant adolescent, to the Wunderkind, to the slightly repugnant deaf and dumb child, Tchaikovsky always wrote as to an equal. And here we reach one of the deepest insights we will ever have into Tchaikovsky the man: he knew of course that he was more gifted in many ways than many people, and less gifted in some ways than some, but he never felt either superior or inferior to any; he had an instinct which has always been rather rare and seems to grow rarer and rarer as society becomes more and more mixed: an absolute faith in the equal dignity of all men.

3 Not like a servant but like a pal

This instinctive faith he expressed very clearly when speaking about Kondratiev's manservant Legoshin: "What pleasure there is in Legoshin's frequent presence; he is such a wonderful personality! Good God! And there are people who turn up their noses at a valet because he is a valet. Why, I do not know anyone whose soul is purer and nobler than Legoshin's. And he is a valet! That people are equal regardless of their position in society was never so absolutely apparent as in the present instance."

Tchaikovsky treated servants accordingly, and nearly everybody responded to the warmth he radiated. Not only was his departure from the Swiss pension in which he used to stay "highly dramatic: the landlady wept; the landlord shook me warmly by the hand; the maid (a very nice creature) also wept, so that I, too was reduced to tears;" but even in New York he managed to thaw the hotel's personnel: "in general I observe a curious difference in the behaviour toward me of all the employees in the hotel at the beginning of my stay and now. At first, they treated me with that coolness and rather offensive indifference that bordered on enmity. Now they all smile, are all ready to go to the four corners of the earth at my first word, and even the young people serving on the elevator begin to talk about the weather every time I go up or down. But I am far from the thought that all this is the result of tips which I hand out rather liberally." And with this last remark we tend to agree, although the tips helped, of course. But there was more in Tchaikovsky's tips than just money: when he left the hotel he probably tipped the servants, but it is not the way he mentions the episode in his diary: there he writes that he "said good-bye" to the servants. They knew the difference.

The amount of attention he spent on those servants who approached him personally is truly remarkable. Nazar's* illness is doubly characteristic from this point of view, since Tchaikovsky's kindness did not stop at the sick man but was extended even to his doctor: "Nazar still cannot walk without two sticks, but he feels much better. A funny doctor takes care of him; for a long time already it has been obvious that there is nothing seriously wrong with Nazar, but for a week the doctor has been coming every day, and has never left without assuring me that he would come again. The old fellow is so *simpatichny* and apparently so badly off that I do not find the courage to ask him to stop his visits." A letter Jurgenson received one day from his bachelor friend is still more typical, although Jurgenson must have been slightly startled on reading it: "My dear fellow, will you please ask Anna Vasilievna† to buy me immediately a perambulator for a sick two-year-old child, and let the store ship it here at once." The next day came the explanation: "The wife of Kondratiev's manservant is visiting with me, or, I should say, with Aleksei. She is very weakly and sickly, the child is paralysed, cannot walk, and the poor mother has worn herself out carrying it all the time in her arms. I could not look at her tortured face any more and I decided to acquire a perambulator so that it would be possible to drive the poor little mite instead of carrying it."

The fact is that Tchaikovsky was terribly dependent on the sympathy of all people in general and of underlings in particular. His servants' moods affected him so much that he described them in his diary: "The quarrelling, crying and cursing of Arisha whose disposition, it turns out, is getting worse and worse. And that spoiled my enjoyment during supper." On the other hand how

---

* Nazar temporarily replaced Aleksei who stayed at home to take care of his sick wife.

† Jurgenson's secretary.

happy he was when he had met with friendliness! At a hotel: "The head clerk was especially likeable, as also the chambermaids who were Poles judging by their language." At a bank: "Money. Courteous clerks." On a ship: "The steward in my cabin, Schroeder, is a very kind young German; two other *gracious* Germans serve at table; this is *very important* to me." On the train from New York to Niagara: "The employees, i.e. the conductors, the waiters in the dining car and in the buffet in the smoking car, are Negroes who are very obliging and polite." Tchaikovsky knew himself pretty well on that point as on most others, and, after having been a little annoyed by the number of servants at Mrs von Meck's when he stayed there in her absence, he soon made friends with them because he saw that they were ready to love him. "In order to feel at ease I need the people around me to serve me not only out of duty but also with friendliness, and I always try to earn a *simpatichny* attitude on the servants' part. Here I have completely succeeded. I see that they serve me not only out of duty but also out of affection, and that is highly pleasant for me. They are all so kind, so attentive!" And on leaving: "Nadejda Filaretovna! How ungrateful of me! I nearly forgot to tell you that I am unbelievably satisfied with the service of (1) kindly, distinctive, original Leon, (2) intelligent, *simpatichny* Efim, (3) gallant Mihailo, the Russian, whose cuisine . . . was excellent, and (4) the doorman and the housemaids." And on being invited back: "[I felt] the inexpressibly strong desire to find nothing changed. Were Marcel, Efim, Leon still there? That question was extremely important for me since, by nature I am a peculiar person: I get used very fast to certain surroundings and suffer from any change. I was met by Marcel Karlovich and Efim, and I cannot tell you how happy I was to see them both. If another than Efim had been sitting on the coachman's seat, a great part of my joy would have been lost."

Aleksei Sofronov, Tchaikovsky's gentleman's gentleman, who was a 14-year-old lad when Tchaikovsky took him into his service and stayed with him from 1875 till the composer's death, naturally deserves our special attention.

Tchaikovsky loved him dearly. At first he even found that Aleksei had only one fault: when travelling—for instance the whole way from Vienna to Florence—he slept, slept and slept. This of course was annoying, but, on the other hand, he was so affectionate, that you had to forgive him. One could spoil Aleksei all one wanted, he remained attentive and willing to please: if anything, his feelings grew finer from good treatment. And he was so sensitive, as his master discovered from perusing—rather indiscreetly, it must be confessed—the young man's secret diary! Then, the spoiling having finally succeeded, matters became a little more complicated. In 1879, Tchaikovsky was still satisfied with Aleksei but not without a few reservations: "It is remarkable how nice he is when you keep him in his flunky position . . . and how he gets immediately spoiled . . . if you treat him not like a servant but like a pal. In Paris, he reminded me a little of last year Aleksei, i.e. he argued all day, acted in a conceited manner, and altogether lost the tender and affectionate attitude which he assumes when he finds himself in the position of a servant." In 1886 Tchaikovsky still grumbled a little at his man: Aleksei was having a birthday party in his master's house and was glad to have the master leave; he accompanied his master to the Caucasus 'for the sake of adventure and not out of affection;' he was bickering about everything and becoming unbearable 'in the sense of being pleasant company.' "In general," wrote Tchaikovsky, "I value and like Alesha* fully only when living in the country, where all is normal and there is nothing to argue about."

These problems did not prevent Tchaikovsky from pouring on Aleksei all the affection of which he was capable and from 'spoiling' him. The master took the servant to see shows for which he had no interest himself. He took care of him when he was ill.† He shared all his problems, and though at one point he states that 'he is horrified at his servant's dissipations,' he does not seem to have done much to limit them. In fact, we find him 'very happy' when Aleksei travels with somebody's chambermaid and ready to help 'up to a certain point' when Aleksei starts a love affair with a charming Swiss girl, Marie. This affair ended rather unfortunately, since the certain point was soon left behind, Marie became pregnant, and her lover showed no intention of marrying her: once again Tchaikovsky's open purse settled at least the material

* Diminutive for Aleksei. Cf. also Lona.
† Here arises a mysterious point in the history of the sources (Cf. Part I, Section 4). Tchaikovsky's letter to Mrs von Meck written on the 9th (21st) January 1878 contains the story of an illness of Aleksei's and of the care Tchaikovsky took of him. As Tchaikovsky was at first reluctant to tell Mrs von Meck about it, and as he does not name the disease which caused sores to appear on Aleksei's body, we can surmise that its origin was of a venereal nature. But since no details are given and Tchaikovsky's care in that case does not exceed what would only be expected from a good master worrying about the health of a good servant, it is unclear why the whole passage has been omitted in Tchaikovsky's *Complete Works*.

aspect of the case. When Aleksei got married to a Russian modiste, Tchaikovsky hired his 'fetching little wife' to do his laundry and found her very *simpatichny*. When she fell ill, he was deeply sorry for the young couple, "the more so that he saw no way of saving her life. The knowledge that he was of no use, but rather a hindrance to the care of the invalid—for Aleksei was the poor soul's only nurse—made Tchaikovsky anxious to save his man all the personal services with which he could possibly dispense. For this reason he cut short his stay in Moscow and returned to St Petersburg. . . ." And he wept when he learned of her death.

He used to worry about what would happen to Aleksei when he would not be there any more: "Having served me many years, and in spite of the fact that I never gave him a position higher than the one which Fate had intended for him, he has become used to being treated not only as a servant but also as a friend. If I die, it would be hard for him to work in a house where servants are treated harshly. He is an excellent servant and I can guarantee that he would make himself useful." In consequence, Tchaikovsky asked Mrs von Meck to hire Aleksei if she were to live longer than the composer. Such a course of action however did not become necessary, since when Tchaikovsky died he was able to take care of Aleksei in his will: one seventh of his monetary holdings, all his furniture and personal effects and six hundred roubles a year from his royalties went to the faithful Aleksei, who was even able to buy Tchaikovsky's house in Klin and to start, with the help of Modest Tchaikovsky and Vladimir Davydov, one of the composer's nephews, what has now become the Tchaikovsky Museum and Archives.

One episode of the master-servant relationship gave cause to somewhat distasteful insinuations. A cautious biographer remarks that "the wildly emotional tone in which Peter Ilitch wrote about and to Aleksei forcibly suggests that, whatever the private relations between master and servant were, his personal feeling was not far from love."[1] A less cautious one states flatly that "his servant Aleksei Sofronov . . . is mentioned in the most amorous terms." Tchaikovsky himself would have been horrified at the phrase "not far from love": why "not far"? Of course he loved his man, and loved him tenderly; but did he love him "amorously"? That is the question.

Obviously it will never be possible to prove that Tchaikovsky was innocent of the kind of feelings suggested here: no such proof can exist. On the other hand, if a relationship of this kind existed, although proofs might not be available, still it is imaginable that they would turn up. In other terms, it would have been preferable to wait for some evidence before raising a doubt which, once raised, can never be put out of mind.

The incriminating episode is Aleksei's absence, when he was drafted for four years in the Army. Tchaikovsky went to see him in his barracks, had nervous breakdowns on account of him, visited him when he was ill, and finally found even a way of protecting him against the sergeant who, for some reason, had taken an unjust dislike to him. The colonel of Aleksei's regiment admired Tchaikovsky's music and soon it became possible to arrange for supplementary leaves and various favours. In return the composer had to suffer: "I have made the acquaintance of the colonel, and, in accordance with his wife's wishes, I go to their place and have to spend whole evenings accompanying her singing and talking small talk. This is a heavy sacrifice on my part."

Tchaikovsky missed his servant very much and refused to travel without him, especially to Mrs von Meck's estate of Simaki, where he had been so happy previously when Aleksei was with him. He finally accepted the invitation, when the soldier got leave of absence for two months. In some instances, the composer's feelings of bereavement were expressed in such a style that we can scarcely be surprised at seeing our virtuous biographers shake their heads. To Modest he wrote: "Regularly every evening, at nightfall, I think about Aleksei, about times gone by which will never come back, and I cry. This has become a habit with me. I sleep very well though. . . ." "During the whole month of September Aleksei will be free and we will go to spend some time in Brailov. I cannot think about such happiness without crying. . . . At the present time, Aleksei is my sore spot. I should not exaggerate at all if I told you that there is not one second during the whole day in which I do not think about him and suffer for him. Even at night I dream about him all the time; recently I saw him dead." To Aleksei himself Tchaikovsky wrote with an affection which must have been very gratifying to the poor fellow in his barracks: "My dear Lona! This morning I got your letter. I felt glad and sad at reading it. Glad because I want to have frequent news of you, and sad because your letter makes my pain worse. If you could know and see how listless and despondent I am because you are not here! Yesterday, we went to the wood and were drenched by the storm. When I came back and went into your room to change my clothes, I suddenly and vividly remembered what joy I used to feel when I came home and saw your dear face. I remembered how you used to scold me for having soiled my clothes, and I felt so sad, so sad, that I cried like a child! Ah! dear good Lona! You must know that even if you had to stay one hundred years in the Army, I should never forget you and should always wait impatiently for the happy day when you would come back. . . . The weather is warm. But I feel gloomy and bored. Would you believe it, I cannot even write anything. I have lost interest in everything because, you, my dear, are not with me." Of course the composer hired another valet: "He is clean, orderly and attentive. With my reason I have to be fair to him, but I cannot conquer a kind of instinctive antipathy towards him because he has taken Aleksei's place."

There is little doubt that our eyebrow-raising biographers, if they had personal valets, would not write to them and about them in such a style. They are shocked at the idea that Tchaikovsky's feelings for his servant could be "not far from love." But we need not be such snobs, and the least we can say, knowing Tchaikovsky, his loving nature and his impetuous style, is that an amorous interpretation of this affection appears to be somewhat less than obvious.

True, Tchaikovsky loved the lad and missed him and wanted him to know that he missed him. He even wondered himself at the excess of his feelings: "I can imagine how somebody who did not know me would burst out laughing on reading this, how he would be surprised to discover that one can be listless and despondent for a valet. But what can I do if that valet was at the same time my friend, and a devoted and loving friend at that." To Mrs von Meck, his patroness, from whom he certainly would have tried to hide any excessive attachment which he might have felt for his man, he told the same tale of listlessness and despondency, and explained very clearly, without any apparent reticence, why he missed the fellow: "More than ever I feel how much I need him just now, when there is so much bitterness in my soul and when faithful attachments and an environment to which I am used would be so soothing for me. I know that his very presence, the knowledge that a being absolutely devoted to me and who has been my constant companion for many years is at hand, would give me much moral strength to conquer the secret despondency which is gnawing at me, and my aversion to work. . . ." "As I am very used to him and love him very much, I still cannot imagine myself somewhere abroad, without his service and his presence around me." *Service* and *presence*: the stress has been heavily laid on the presence, but Tchaikovsky thought at least as much of the service: "With Aleksei I knew that every paper which I need,

Nadejda von Meck

Москва. 15 Іюля 1877 г.

№ 20

Вчера пріѣхалъ я въ Москву и отправившись въ Консерваторію получилъ письмо Ваше, дорогая Надежда Филаретовна. Въ томъ состояніи нервной возбужденности, въ которомъ я теперь нахожусь, Ваши дружескія рѣчи, Ваше тёплое участіе ко мнѣ, — подѣйствовали на меня самымъ благотворнымъ образомъ.

Надежда Филаретовна! Какъ это ни странно, какъ это ни смѣло, но я долженъ, я принужденъ опять обратиться къ Вамъ за матеріальной помощью. Вотъ въ чемъ дѣло. Предоставленной Вами суммы у меня оставалось совершенно достаточное количество денегъ для путешествія на Кавказъ и вообще для того, чтобы не стѣсняясь въ расходахъ провести лѣто совершенно по воля. На судьбу явилась женитьба. Всѣ эти деньги ушли на свадьбу и на сопряженные съ нею расходы. Между тѣмъ я былъ совер

Tchaikovsky's letter of 15th July 1877 to Mrs von Meck

every object which I might want while working, would be systematically arranged each in its own place. Being terribly absent-
minded and constantly absorbed by my musical combinations, I
need to have somebody around me to take care of me and of my
belongings. At present I am completely lost."

It can also be added that Aleksei's military service had a very
bad influence on him, that he became much coarser than he had
been and even positively unclean, which hardly could please his
master. And at the time of Aleksei's illness, although Tchaikovsky
did for him all he could, he still "prepared himself to endure his
loss with good courage." Mrs von Meck, who 'was very fond' of
Aleksei and sent him gifts like, for instance, a silver purse, found
nothing strange in the composer's affection for his man: "How I
pity you, my dear Peter Ilitch, that you have so many worries and
are deprived of your Aleksei: I know how painful such a depriva-
tion can be."

So, although there is no possibility of proving that Tchaikovsky's
relations with his servant were pure, there is little reason to
suspect that they were not. In our time we naturally tend to disregard the familiarity, indeed the intimacy which necessarily arose
between two men who lived together as only families live now, and
who, each in his own way, were entirely dependent on each
other. It is maybe a sign of the evolution of the world that while
we always think now in bisexual terms—what we might call the
Executive and Secretary Complex—our fathers had a different idea
of the couple: Don Quixote and Sancho Panza were much more
inseparable, if not more useful to each other, than man and wife.

4 How strange, how obscure is man's heart

If there was one thing Tchaikovsky hated, it was social constraint,
which so often forces us to behave insincerely; and if there was
something he was good at, it was being himself (which, by the
way, is a rare talent). "What happiness to live again as you want
and not as others order you to! What delight to be able to work,
read, play, walk, without any hindrance, instead of playing a
thousand parts a day. How false, how absurd is life in society!

H

Speak, when you want to be quiet, be courteous and feign emotion at the courtesy of others when you want to run away from them; sit when you want to walk; walk when you feel like resting; starve when you are hungry; eat and drink when you want to sleep; in short, from the first minute of wakefulness till the last one before you close your eyes, do every possible violence to yourself for the sake of your duty to society!" Not feeling like doing violence to himself, Tchaikovsky always behaved with the utmost naturalness, and this aptitude—some would say this fault—which endeared him to underlings—also opened before him the doors of higher circles. No one was less affected than he: whether you were a beggar or a prince, you knew that you had to deal with someone who, except for a joke, would never stoop to pretend that he was what he was not. And so, in spite of all his love for solitude, he enjoyed, from his youth on, society at its best. At eleven he is already dancing in the Club of the Nobility; at 46 he mentions in his diary his 'social successes'; at 52 he does not hide his pleasure at finding 'the Polish countesses fascinatingly amiable to him.'

The truth is that he liked people in general. When he was young and poor, he would have loved to belong to the superficial English Club which he found 'delightful,' but 'it cost too much.' Older and longing for solitude, he used to cry for companionship as soon as he was alone. His friend the critic Laroche said of him: "The number of people who made a good impression on him, who pleased him, and of whom he spoke in their absence as 'good' and 'simpatichny' sometimes astounded me." He was confident in his capacity to read people's personalities: "I have the aptitude of evaluating the merit of a person at one glance. From the first time," he told his friend Mrs Shpajinsky, "you seemed very simpatichny to me and from the first time I knew that you were a good person in the whole meaning of that word." We believe that one of the biographers is right in remarking that he "was much more than a sympathetic man, he was that rare creature, a noble-minded one. He was incapable of spite or meanness, and in fifty-three years not one nasty action and very few unfair words were recorded against him."[2]

Although eye-witnesses are generally supposed to disagree, practically all testimonies concerning Tchaikovsky's manners, his attitude towards people, concord. Sofia Kashkin remembers "a general impression of a friendly man, a man with whom you feel you can be simple and at ease." The actor-director Stanislavsky was impressed by the composer's 'unusual modesty.' Mrs Eichenwald, the singer, states that "everybody fell in love with him, women, men, children, grand-mothers. A procession followed him all the time through Moscow. . . . He had no mannerisms, not the slightest affectation." The composer Glazunov tells of a visit which Tchaikovsky payed to Balakirev's musical circle: "How should we treat this outsider who was not a member of our group? We decided to be very reserved with him. The result was a certain stiffness in the amosphere when Tchaikovsky arrived. It did not last long. We were all staggered by his dignity, his refinement and well-bred self-command that we thought of as exclusively European. We began to breathe freely and when he spoke, the atmosphere of reserve—you could call it dis-approval—melted away *because he obviously felt no constraint whatever.*"* And Tchaikovsky himself describes the impression he produced on the famous Carnegie, whose Hall he inaugurated:

> This singular man, Carnegie, who rapidly rose from a telegraph apprentice to be one of the richest men in America, while still re-maining quite simple, inspires me with unusual confidence, perhaps because he shows me so much sympathy. During the evening he expressed his liking for me in a very marked manner. He took both my hands in his, and declared that, though not crowned, I was a genuine king of music. He embraced me (without kissing me: men do not kiss over here), got on tiptoe and stretched his hand up to indicate my greatness, and finally made the whole company laugh by imitating my conducting. This he did so solemnly, so well, and so like me, that I myself was quite delighted. His wife is also an-extremely simple and charming young lady, and showed her interest in me in every possible way.

Such a warm personality attracted many acquaintances—Tchai-kovsky himself said he knew no man who spent so much as he on postage stamps—and a few real friends. Modest counts six of them: Nikolai Rubinstein, Albrecht, Jurgenson, Kashkin, Laroche and Hubert. "This little circle," says he, "was destined to give un-failing support to the growing reputation of the composer, and to remain in the closest personal relations with him to the end of his life. Amid these friends he found encouragement and sympa-thy all the time when he stood most in need of them." We can hardly accept this statement as correct since in 1878, Tchaikovsky already referred to Laroche and Kashkin as to "men . . . whose society had once been pleasant" to him; Albrecht he patronized all his life; to Hubert it seems that he was much less attached than to Hubert's wife "Batashka;"† Jurgenson and Rubinstein stand apart, and it would be unfair not to add young Taneiev,

* Author's italics.
† Cf. p. 183.

Tchaikovsky's pupil, disciple and admirer, who did not win for himself the fame of a composer, but whose infatuation for Countess Leo Tolstoi, the writer's wife, has at least earned him a place in the history of literature.

Soviet historians tend to criticize Jurgenson for exploiting Tchaikovsky's talent for his own capitalistic aims, but this seems far-fetched. Of course Jurgenson the publisher profited from Tchaikovsky's music, but there is no reason to doubt the sincere friendship of Jurgenson the man. His letters to the composer are full of affection; he calls him tender—and hardly translatable —names, like "*Petia milia*," tells him about his own family problems and confesses with ingenuity how he wanted 'to fool' Tchaikovsky by hiding the orchestra scores of *The Voivode* so as to prevent the composer from destroying his work. Tchaikovsky on the other hand worries about his publisher's interests: "You are poisoning my life. When I get carried away with composing, I suddenly remember that you will have to take care of all that and this thought chills me." With the exception of the shadow which came over their relationship at the end* it can almost be said that their friendship was a perfect one.

Not so with Nikolai Rubinstein. The first of the two Rubinstein brothers whom Tchaikovsky met was Anton, the Director of the St Petersburg Conservatoire and Tchaikovsky's teacher: a few words about him are necessary here. He never approved of his famous student and his student's feelings towards him seem to have vacillated between passionate respect and deep antipathy. Modest, who is supposed to have done everything he could to hide his brother's homosexual tendencies, appears to have done a very poor job of it when he wrote: "I still remember the excitement, rapture and reverence with which the future pupil gazed on his future teacher. . . . His eyes followed his 'divinity' with the rapt gaze of a lover for the unattainable beauty of his fancy. . . . He stood as near to him as possible, strove to catch the sound of his voice, and envied the fortunate mortals who ventured to shake hands with him. . . . This feeling . . . practically lasted to the end of Tchaikovsky's life. . . . Externally he was always 'in love' with Rubinstein, although—as is always the case in love affairs—there were periods of coolness, jealousy, and irritation, which invariably gave place in turn to a fresh access of . . . sentiment. . . . In Rubinstein's presence Tchaikovsky became quite diffident, lost his head and seemed to regard him a superior being. When at a supper

* Cf. p. 49.

given during the pianist's jubilee, someone, in an indelicate and
unseemly way, requested Rubinstein and Tchaikovsky to drink to
each other 'as brothers,' the latter was not only confused and indignant, but in his reply to the toast, protested warmly, saying
that his tongue would never consent to address the great artist
in the second person singular—it would be entirely against the
spirit of their relations. He would be happy if Rubinstein addressed
him by the familiar 'thou,'* but for his own part, the more cere-
monious form better expressed a sense of reverence from the pupil
to his teacher, from the man to the embodiment of his ideal." But
on this point, Modest's testimony is frankly misleading. We have
found very few expressions of enthusiasm on Tchaikovsky's part
concerning his master, whom he admired as a musical interpreter,
but to whom he granted few other qualities. As a composer, Anton
Rubinstein was nothing but a 'ridiculous clown' producing 'trash.'
As a man, he was "intolerable with his mania for organizing
celebrations for himself. Admit that he is an ace and is deserving
of ovations, but how he can still enjoy them—I do not understand."
True, Tchaikovsky recognized that Anton Rubinstein stood higher
than the mire of intrigues which surrounded him, but he never
forgave the great man's late interest for his work: "What a curious man, this Anton Rubinstein! He could pay no attention to my
piano compositions ten years ago. Would he perform a single note
of mine then? What a service that would have been! I am nevertheless grateful to him even now, but the difference is great."
More than that, Tchaikovsky was deeply shocked by Anton's
attitude at the time of Nikolai's death: he decided he himself would not attend the funeral service in Moscow because he
did not want to be a witness to "the strange, incomprehensible and
offensive behaviour of Anton Rubinstein. . . . I do not want to
accuse him; I shall just tell you that here (at the funeral service
held in Paris) he behaved as if not only he was not pained by
his brother's death but glad of it." As to the "Second person
singular incident," Tchaikovsky himself remembered a completely
different version of it: he refused to "say thou" to Rubinstein not
out of bashfulness but on the contrary, because he did not want
the man for a friend, and spoke of reverence and ceremony only
out of good-breeding, in order not to create a public incident.

* Russian, like most languages, has two second persons: one is more
familiar, the other more courteous. Compare French *tu* and *vous*. Two men
who have been using the courteous *vy* form can decide to drink each other's
health 'as brothers' and then switch to the familiar *ty*. Germans have a
similar custom.

All that of course is of secondary importance, since Tchaikovsky's friend was Nikolai, the Director of the Moscow Conservatoire, with whom the composer had a long and stormy relationship.

It all began in 1866, when Tchaikovsky was hired by the Moscow Conservatoire as a teacher, and was persuaded by Rubinstein to share his lodgings with him. One biography presents a somewhat personal version of the meeting. Tchaikovsky (a gentleman by birth, a graduate of one of the best schools in St Petersburg, the capital, an honoured guest in Prince Golitsin's estate) is described as a provincial, whom Rubinstein (a Jewish musician, with high protections but no real position in society) would have initiated to elegant life after dining him at the "Var" (the learned biographer probably means the *Yar* restaurant). It would have been thanks to Nikolai Rubinstein that Tchaikovsky became "a man of the world in the best sense."[3] Little of that seems to have been true, although it is a fact that Rubinstein lent the young composer a coat and even insisted on giving him half a dozen shirts. The initiation did not go much further.

The lodging arrangement was not very satisfactory, not only because of the noise without which Rubinstein could not live, but mainly because Tchaikovsky was too considerate ("I have a little room next to Rubinstein's bedroom and truly I am afraid of disturbing him at night with the scratching of my pen, for only a small partition divides our rooms") and Rubinstein was not considerate enough ("Rubinstein and Tarnovsky have discovered that I am easily startled and amuse themselves by giving me all manners of shocks all day long"). However, due to Rubinstein's need for companionship, the arrangement lasted for nearly six years,* before Tchaikovsky could find a delicate way of escaping and settling down on his own.

After that comes the incident of the First Piano Concerto, which Tchaikovsky submitted to the judgement of his friend:

> "Well?" I asked and rose from the piano. Then a torrent broke from Rubinstein's lips. Gentle at first, gathering volume as it proceeded, and finally bursting into the fury of a Jupiter-Tonans. My concerto was worthless, absolutely unplayable; the passages so broken, so disconnected, so unskilfully written, that they could not even be improved; the work itself was bad, trivial, common; here and there I had stolen from other people; only one or two pages were worth anything; all the rest had better be destroyed, or entirely rewritten.

*1866–71.

Tchaikovsky was deeply offended, but the friendship continued, although the dedication of the Concerto to Rubinstein was erased and replaced by a dedication to Hans von Bülow.

Tchaikovsky's marriage, nervous illness, and flight abroad come next. At that time (1877) "Rubinstein acted promptly and generously; he granted Tchaikovsky unlimited leave of absence and persuaded the board of the Musical Society to vote a special sum of money as a token of appreciation for his eleven years of work in the Conservatoire."[4] This sum was modest and Tchaikovsky felt the need to tell his friend what other income he enjoyed:

> You will wonder of course where I get the money to travel like I do, and this is where I ought to tell you some kind of fib. But since you would not believe my lies, I shall tell you the truth but ask you to leave it between us, because the person who has provided me with quite a sufficient amount of money asked me to tell it to no one. She even wrote me that you had been to see her, and that she hopes that you did not conclude from her interest in me that she wanted to help me materially. This person is no other than Mrs Meck. I can even tell you the figure: she sends me fifteen hundred francs a month. I beg you, not one word of it to anyone, except maybe Karlusha.* She is extremely desirous that no one should know of it.

Two months later, Tchaikovsky wrote to Mrs von Meck herself to tell her what he thought of Rubinstein, who, at that time, was severely criticized in Moscow and even ridiculed under the nickname of Jupiter.

> Concerning Nikolai Rubinstein you are almost right: he is not quite the hero he is sometimes thought to be. He is an exceptionally gifted and an intelligent man, although he has little education; he is energetic and astute. But he is marred by his passion for adulation, by his utterly childish weakness for all kinds of obeisant and obsequious manifestations. His aptitude as an administrator, his cleverness in dealing with men in power, are astounding. His nature is not petty, but has grown petty because of the absurdly obsequious idolatry which surrounds him. It must be said that he is honest in the highest meaning of the word, and disinterested, i.e. he has been plotting and manoeuvring not for narrowly material objectives, not for gain. He has to have the first place, and so he protects his own infallibility by various means. He tolerates no contradiction and immediately suspects a hidden foe in any man who dares disagree with him. He will not hesitate to use intrigue and injustice to destroy such a foe. All that originates in the fear of losing be it only one inch of his exalted position. His despotism is often revolting.

* Diminutive for Karl (Albrecht).

He is not above showing his strength and power in front of miserable, defenceless people. If he meets with opposition, he retreats immediately and shows some inclination for intrigue. His heart is not particularly kind, although he likes to brag about his fatherly kindness and, in order to be popular, plays the part of a genial fellow. All his faults come from his passionate lust for power and shameless despotism. But, Nadejda Filaretovna, what services he has rendered to music! For their sake we must forgive him everything. Good or bad, the Conservatoire which he has rather artificially implanted in the Moscow soil, propagates healthy musical ideas and tastes. Twenty years ago, Moscow was a barbarous land from the point of view of music. I often get angry at Rubinstein, but when I remember how much his energetic activity has done, I am disarmed. True, he acted mainly for the gratification of his own ambition, but his ambition is a noble one. We should not forget also that he is an excellent pianist (the best in Europe, I think) and a very good conductor.

Our relationship is a very curious one. When he has drunk a little wine, he becomes sickeningly affectionate and reproaches me with being insensitive, and not loving him enough. In his normal state, he is very cold with me. He is very fond of making me feel that I owe him everything. In fact he is a little afraid of my waywardness.

Soon after that, a storm broke out. Rubinstein offered to Tchaikovsky the post of Russian Delegate to the Paris Exhibition. Tchaikovsky, after many qualms and misgivings, refused, on account of his nerves. Rubinstein, in a letter which has been lost, reproached him with laziness and with 'putting on.'* Tchaikovsky was 'mad with rage,' and wrote to his brother Anatoly: "How right I was not to love that man! How heartless, dried up, and crazy about playing the benefactor he is!" To Mrs von Meck, he poured out his heart: Nikolai Rubinstein's "letter breathes savage wrath. This would not matter so much, but that the whole tone of the communication is so dry, so lacking in cordial feeling, so exaggerated! He says my illness is a mere fraud, that I am only putting it on . . . and that he deeply regrets having shown me so much sympathy because it has only encouraged my indolence!!!" To Rubinstein himself he replied with dignity and firmness:

All you have written to me, and also your manner of saying it, only proves how little you know me, as I have frequently observed on former occasions. Possibly you may be right, and I am only *putting it on*; but that is precisely the nature of my illness. . . . From your letter I can only gather the impression that in you I possess a

* The Russian '*blajit*' is untranslatable. *Putting on* and *indulging* at the same time.

great benefactor, and that I have proved an ungrateful recipient of your favours. It is useless to try this tone! I know how much I am indebted to you; but, in the first place, your reproaches cool my gratitude, and, secondly, it annoys me when you pose as a benefactor in a matter in which you have proved yourself quite the reverse.

No rupture followed. Indeed, in the same letter, Tchaikovsky entrusted his Fourth Symphony and *Eugene Onegin* to the care of 'the one man who had rightly understood his works' (and was playing everywhere the Piano Concerto which had displeased him so much).

A little later, Mrs von Meck advised Tchaikovsky to ask Rubinstein to use his influence with the composer's wife, to keep her quiet, and it is not the least mysterious feature of Tchaikovsky's marriage that Rubinstein indeed seems to have had some influence with her.* Approximately at that time, the composer confided in his brother Modest: he had always hated Rubinstein, he said, even when he shared his lodgings, and had gone on living with him to avoid a distasteful quarrel. But only half a year had elapsed when Tchaikovsky wrote to Anatoly: "How strange, how obscure is man's heart! I have always—or at least for a very long time—thought that I disliked Rubinstein. Recently I dreamed that he was dead and that this was a great sorrow for me. Now I cannot think about him without compassion in my heart and a most positive feeling of love." Also it was to Rubinstein, the wonderful pianist who performed Tchaikovsky's sonata with all his skill, that the composer owed what he called "one of the most marvellous minutes" of his life.

In 1881, Rubinstein died. Tchaikovsky, who, at one point, had had the intention of telling Mrs von Meck 'the whole story of his relationship to Rubinstein' but finally had decided that it would be too 'disgusting to acquaint her with all these empty, petty and repugnant intrigues,' was immediately reconciled to the memory of his difficult friend, and composed his first and only Trio, dedicated to the dead man. For two years he refused to have it performed publicly, letting only Rubinstein's friends play it in private. It was finally created at an anniversary concert held in honour of Rubinstein. Not only did Tchaikovsky pay this homage to his friend; he visited his tomb, expressed indignation at the publication of a novel in which Rubinstein was ridiculed, and, although he still confessed he had never particularly loved the man, declared

* Cf. p. 209.

that 'now everything was naturally forgotten, except his good qualities which outnumbered his weaknesses.'

All that raises one question: what kind of a friend was Tchaikovsky? What did he expect from friendship? How did he treat his friends? In several biographies we find that much has been made of a tragic episode which happened when he was ten: he lived at the house of a friend, and brought back from school scarlatine infection: "the eldest son, the pride of the home, developed the complaint and died of it."[5] There is really no reason to suppose that this tragedy marked Tchaikovsky for life, and that he took himself for "an instrument of Fate, of the Fatum which he was to cite so often," but it is true that, Fatum or not, he never committed himself entirely to any of his friendships.

At times he was—and he recognized it himself—incapable of forgetting the smallest slight. When the violinist Kotek refused to play his concerto under the pretext that he was not prepared, Tchaikovsky wrote him in as many words: "I shall never forgive you," and when Kotek died, Tchaikovsky was decidedly sad, but not so sad that he could not be diverted from his sadness by correcting proofs. At times, on the contrary, he would quarrel and make up with apparent levity: in 1866, he became friendly with young Vladimir Shilovsky; in 1879, he wrote him the insulting letter quoted on page 49, in 1882, he had made friends with him again and they were carousing together at the Saratov Restaurant; in 1883, he told Modest: "Never has his stinginess been so insolently displayed. All his faults have become worse and stick out as disgusting carbuncles."

Such incoherent conduct seems to indicate a kind of detachment, maybe not indifference, but a strangely elusive quality: it is significant that to his brother Anatoly Tchaikovsky wrote: "If you have any powers of observation, you will have noticed that my friendship with Rubinstein and the other gentlemen of the Conservatoire is simply based on the circumstance of our being colleagues and that none of them gives me the tenderness and affection of which I constantly stand in need."* This is important particularly as most of Tchaikovsky's so-called friends were precisely members of the Conservatoire. In other words, we are coming to the conclusion that this loving soul had practically no real, intimate, male friends, with maybe one exception: Jurgenson. Was it his fault? Was he incapable of the generosity which any kind of friendship requires of us? Let us investigate deeper.

* Cf. Modest's optimistic statement on p. 115.

5 How could I not try to save a man?

"I cannot be at peace, I cannot use and enjoy material and moral advantages, when I know that a man who is close to me, or whom I have met by chance, is in need," wrote Tchaikovsky, and we know that he lived up to this Dostoievskian creed.

His generosity with money has already been mentioned and of course it had its small, ridiculous sides, like the time when he decided he would withstand the incessant begging of his little neighbours, which he was only too prone to encourage: the resolution did not last, since the urchins waylaid him on a bridge which he had to cross and he surrendered. To the two friends who accompanied him he told that he had given the children "scarcely anything" but they knew him too well to believe him.[6]

Tchaikovsky's habit of giving did not stop there. Modest quotes the following examples not only of generosity but also of tact:

"Dear Friend,—I want to help X. in some way. You are selling the tickets for his concert. Should they go badly, take fifteen or twenty places on my behalf and give them to whomsoever you please. Of course, X. must know nothing about it."

"If you are in pecuniary difficulties," he wrote to Y., "come to your sincere friend (myself), who now earns so much from his operas and will be delighted to help you. I promise not a soul shall hear of it; but it will be a great pleasure to me."

"Please write at once to K., that he is to send Y. twenty-five roubles a month. He may pay him three months in advance."

Instances when Tchaikovsky did not spare his purse are indeed innumerable. Jurgenson was to help Albrecht's family not only out of the composer's present but even out of his future funds. His first piano teacher was to get the help she asked for. The twins' governess was to receive a pension her life long. Mrs Shpajinsky could make Tchaikovsky 'extremely happy by accepting some material service from him.' Maybe N. A. Plessky, a lady-friend of the Davydovs, wanted to have a small house built? The composer's funds were at her disposal. And when Kotek, the unforgivable Kotek, fell ill, Tchaikovsky quite naturally left "instructions that all expenses in connection with the illness were to be charged to him."

It can of course be said that monetary generosity is just thriftlessness and not generosity at all. But Tchaikovsky went much further than spending currency on his friends and acquaintances: he gave them his time and attention, which, for an artist, is even more remarkable than for an ordinary man. For one thing, he, the nervous, the anxious, the fastidious, was always ready to nurse a sick friend.

Vladimir Shilovsky is sick. Tchaikovsky rushes from St Petersburg to Paris where he fears to find him on his death-bed. "The young man was extremely weak, but able to travel to Soden at the end of three days. The atmosphere of ill-health in which Tchaikovsky found himself—Soden is a resort for consumptive patients—was very depressing, but he determined to endure it for his friend's sake.

'The care of Volodia,'* he wrote, 'is a matter of conscience with me, for his life hangs by a thread . . . his affection for me, and his delight on my arrival, touched me so deeply that I am glad to take upon myself the rôle of an Argus, and be the saviour of his life.' "[7]

Later it is Kotek's turn to be dying and Tchaikovsky hurries to Davos, having at once forgotten his friend's unforgettable† sins: how could he live quietly anywhere without knowing how Kotek really feels? Besides the violinist has expressed the desire to see him.

As to Laroche—who was not dying, just slouching his life away—Tchaikovsky takes care of him not only in hotels but even in his own house, spending his very precious time to pen articles which Laroche, too lazy to write himself, condescends to dictate. 'He needs a nurse," says the composer, "and I have undertaken the part, having no work on hand just now."

But his most tender care seems to have been spent on Kondratiev, the same Kondratiev who did nothing for him but advise him to pray when he was in trouble.‡ On learning that Kondratiev is dying in Aachen, Tchaikovsky begs an advance from Mrs von Meck and hastens off to Germany. "There are minutes when I think I should give anything to tear myself from this awful boredom, but, on the other hand, the sick man values my presence so much, is so happy that I am with him, that I do not say a word about leaving." And the health of the dying Kondratiev becomes a matter of deep, of personal concern to Tchaikovsky who notes every detail in his diary: "During my visit there was no perspiration. Went away upstairs and was waiting nervously. The per-

* Volodia: diminutive of Vladimir.
† Cf. p. 122.
‡ Cf. p. 69.

spiration came after an hour had passed. Thank God. . . .! [The servant] made me happy in the morning with the news that [Kondratiev] slept well and that he is better in general. However, in the course of the day, the improvement was extremely relative. He was quiet and submissive. In such a condition, he especially arouses my pity. Wanted to cry at times. His only joy now is food, but even for that, the spark, i.e. the appetite, was lacking today. As a matter of fact, I wept a little, while working on the orchestration of the piece (cello), when he tried to relish his food and could not."

Nursing is not enough. Tchaikovsky is continuously interceding with somebody for somebody else: with Alexander III for the Tiflis opera, with the newspaper *Voice* for Kiev artists who were offended at not hearing anything about themselves from the capital, with the landlady of the hotel where Aleksei had seduced a maid, so that she would hire the maid back (which the landlady virtuously declined to do), with Mrs von Meck for a number of characters, including Catholic peasants who wanted a Roman Catholic chapel, and a young workman who had used a boat reserved for the composer's exclusive use and been fired for the misdeed: 'it does not matter too much if the fellow was not in real need of work, but what if this was his way of earning his daily bread?' All Tchaikovsky's friends were supposed to be as generous as he, and he never hesitated to ask favours for other people:

I venture to approach you, dear friend, with the following request. An employee in a counting-house, here in Kamenka, has a son who is remarkably gifted for painting. It seemed to me cruel not to give him the means of studying, so I sent him to Moscow and asked Anatoly to take him to the School of Painting and Sculpture. All this was arranged, and then it turned out that the boy's maintenance would cost far more than I expected. And so I thought I would ask you whether in your house there was any corner in which this lad might live? Not, of course, without some kind of supervision. He would only need a tiny room with a bed, a cupboard, and a table where he could sleep and work. Perhaps your servants would look after him, and give him a little advice? The boy is of irreproachable character: industrious, good, obedient, clean in his person—in short, exemplary. I would undertake his meals. . . .

I have also unearthed a musical talent here, in the daughter of the local priest, and have been successful in placing her at the Conservatoire.

The composer himself was not blind to the risk of being exploited and even made ridiculous by undeserving wards, but what of that? Anything was better than not helping somebody who needed help.

Yesterday I received a letter from Mr Tkachenko, the same unknown young man in whose life Fate made me interfere so strangely and unexpectedly.* I did not like this letter and it made me fear for the future. I expected him, I confess, to thank me for my help. Not at all. He hastens to assure me that I vainly assure him of the existence of virtue (although I said nothing about such matters), that I shall not succeed to prove to him that it is worth while to live, that he does not want the money which I sent him and will do without it, but that he will come to Moscow on the tenth, and he promises to give me a hearing. Strange and unclear! It seemed that the young man was perishing from lack of help and sympathy. Here comes a man who offers him both and is welcomed by vulgar declarations about the drying up of virtue in men. . . ! If Mr Tkachenko is revealed to be nothing but a humbug, I shall be very much vexed with myself. But what could I do? How could I not try to save a man from destruction?

The school which Tchaikovsky organized at his own expense in the village of Maidanovo may have been a venture more worthy of his interest than the salvation of Mr Tkachenko. On arriving in Maidanovo, the composer was impressed by the poverty of the people, but also by their apparent happiness and content. The less they complained, the more he wished to do something for them, especially for the children, who had such *simpatichny* faces. At first he was depressed by his own powerlessness to help, but then, having consulted with the local priest, he discovered that it would be possible to found a school, if he were to donate an annual sum for it. This he of course consented to do and in two months' time action followed:

The school . . . was opened . . . with a religious service, a speech by the priest, and the distribution of books to every pupil, as an encouragement. So far there are twenty-eight of them. Today I spent all the morning at school and attended the classes of the deacon and of the priest. Their method of teaching leaves much to be desired. In particular I was astonished by the earsplitting yelling which takes place during the lessons, because the deacon forces the pupils to shout whatever they are assigned to learn. If I were a pupil of this deacon's in this school, I should run away from the intolerable din. But, since I am utterly ignorant of pedagogy, I abstain from criticizing this strange method and feel glad that, good or bad, still some studying is going on. Both the deacon and the

* Tchaikovsky had saved Tkachenko from a more or less real suicide.

priest treat the children very kindly, with patriarchal simplicity and benignity.

The remarkable thing is that Tchaikovsky helped not only friends, servants, children, but even—most strange for a musician —musicians.

They could be professional conductors hired through the composer's recommendation and whose concerts he would subsequently feel obliged to attend, like Laube; they could be young law students who dreamed of a musical career, and whom he would encourage by telling them that 'he too had left the Law for music,' like Khessin; they could be poor French artists, to whom he would abandon the royalties of a specially written piece; they could be famous men, his rivals, in defence of whom he would write articles, like Balakirev,* or on the publishing of whose works by his own friend and publisher Jurgenson he would insist, like Rimsky-Korsakov.

They could also be the whole rising generation of young Russian composers. Tchaikovsky interceded with the Director of Imperial Theatres on behalf of Taneiev, whose opera should be produced, and of Arensky, from whom an opera should be ordered. He wrote to newspapers about Konus, obtained an annual pension for him, worried about his works, recommended them to his publisher and conducted them himself. Rachmaninov frankly confessed that his opera "Aleko succeeded more because of the great kindness of Tchaikovsky than because of the actual music." Indeed the tact displayed by the great man when dealing with the beginner was no less striking than the kindness: instead of offering to split the programme as a favour, he "had said to the youthful composer in his easy way: 'You know I've just finished Iolanthe? It doesn't fill an entire evening. Would you object if it were performed with Aleko?' "[8]

That Tchaikovsky felt that it was his duty to help beginners cannot be doubted. In 1892, he was asked what he proposed to write next. He replied that he thought it was time he stopped writing and gave way to young blood. To the reporter's question

---

* A particularly gaudy version of this incident is to be found in one biography (Hanson). Balakirev was in danger of his life for ignoring Grand-Duchess Elena Pavlovan! Tchaikovsky rushed to his rescue, risking his own future! Finally, thanks to the assassination of the liberal Alexander II and the crowning of the 'reactionary' Alexander III, Balakirev was appointed Director of the Imperial Chapel! All this is of course pure balderdash, of the kind which seems for some reason inseparable from Russian histories written by well-meaning Westerners.

'is there any worthy new blood in Russia?' Tchaikovsky named Glazunov, Arensky and Rachmaninov, who, by the way, had just finished bungling rather dishonestly a four-hand arrangement of *The Sleeping Beauty* which Tchaikovsky had ordered from him. To Ippolitov-Ivanov, whose opera he was trying to have produced, Tchaikovsky, always critical of himself, wrote: "I am commissioned to write a one-act opera and a ballet. . . . In this way I am involuntarily a hindrance to the younger composers, who would be glad to see their works performed at the Imperial Opera. This troubles me, but the tempation is too great, and I am not yet convinced that the time has come for me to make room for the younger generation." He meant: to cease composing. A few months later, he wrote to his friend Grand-Duke Konstantin: "I often think it is time to shut up shop. A composer who has won success and recognition stands in the way of younger men who want to be heard. Time was when no one wanted to listen to my music, and if the Grand Duke, your father, had not been my patron, not one of my operas would ever have been performed. Now I am spoilt and encouraged in every way. It is very pleasant, but I am often tormented by the thought that I ought to make room for others." These were not empty declarations. In 1883 Tchaikovsky already offered to have some of his own works published under the name of Nikolai Aleksandrovitch Alekseiev, so that this good administrator could become a Director of the Conservatoire. In 1886 he asked that his *Romeo and Juliet* overture should be stricken from the programme of a concert organized by Rimsky-Korsakov and that a piece by Arensky be performed instead. In 1887—and he was not yet the famous man he was going to be, his first European tour had not even taken place—he asked the same favour for Ippolitov-Ivanov: "let one of my works be excluded from the programme, so that Ivanov's can be performed."

6 How could you manage to turn your back?

And yet . . . and yet. Just as Tchaikovsky appeared to us first as the happiest of men and then as the unhappiest, he was undoubtedly that strange animal: a misanthropic philanthropist.

Of misanthropy he accused himself with his usual willingness to see himself as he was, or a little worse. He was 27 when he wrote to his sister Aleksandra: "I have the opportunity . . . of constantly convincing myself of the fact that a disease called misanthropy has made its nest in my heart; I am subject . . . to frightening fits of hatred of men." When Mrs von Meck expressed the desire to patronize his art without making his acquaintance, he was not in the least surprised: "The very fact that we both suffer from one and the same malady draws us together. This malady is— misanthropy, but misanthropy of a peculiar kind, at the base of which there is certainly no hatred and contempt for people. People who suffer from this complaint fear not the harm that may be caused by intrigues but the disillusionment, the craving for the ideal, which are the consequence of every intimacy. There was a time when I was so possessed by this fear of people that I nearly went out of my mind. The circumstances of my life were such that I couldn't escape and hide myself. I had to fight it out with myself, and God alone knows what this struggle cost me. . . . From what I have said above, you will easily understand that I'm not at all surprised that, loving my music, you do not strive to make the acquaintance of its composer." When he had earned European fame, his old trick of escaping from Russia to Europe in order to live incognito did not work any more: "Because of the Russian concerts in Paris just now, the newspapers are full of my name and the more publicity pursues me, the more I dread it. I cannot meet even strangers without real distress, and as my acquaintance in St Petersburg is wide, I have to hide all day to avoid chance meetings. In the evening I dare not go to public places. My life is like that of a fugitive from the law! I have become quite a misanthrope, my friend, and seem to have lost the ability to live with other people."

The composer's misanthropy took sometimes comical forms, as when he pretended he was travelling with a woman, in order to get rid of Weniavsky on a train (Weniavsky winked at him "You sly dog, you!" and left him in peace), or when he demanded to be introduced as a Mr Petrovsky so as to escape recognition. But at other times Tchaikovsky became seriously angry, and then his misanthropy took up a more dramatic character. His dear cousin Mitrofan Tchaikovsky, of whom everybody in the family was very fond, came to spend a few days in the country with the composer and insisted on going for a walk with him: the daily walk was completely spoilt, and it is only because Tchaikovsky managed to take a second walk the same day, all by himself, that he forgave his

I

unsuspecting relative. The reporter Flerov irritated him twice: first by staying with him from five in the afternoon till midnight and asking him 'what pictures, what images, floated in his mind when he composed such and such a piece;' second by describing in a newspaper how the composer won prizes at a lottery, which was untrue and anyway unimportant, but Tchaikovsky 'loathed nothing so much as being exposed to the public.' He 'could have killed' the man. American journalists displeased him by noticing his "brusque and jerky bows": "It angers me that they write not only about the music but also about my personality." The Germans did worse: "I have just read in the *Fremdenblatt* that the famous Russian composer P. Tschaikowsky *weilt in Berlin** and that, according to my wishes, tomorrow, the thirtieth, there will be a solemn Fruhschopp, to which all my numerous (! ! !) friends and admirers (! ! !) are invited. . . . They may send the police after me but I shall die before I go to this ridiculous Fruhschopp." The Russians, when they appointed him Musical Delegate at the Paris Exhibition and hinted that this position would be profitable for his career, outdid everybody else: "I shall do nothing whatsoever to advertise my wares. If they want to play and sing my music, so be it; if they do not, very well, I spit, spit, spit upon it all! ! ! Must I tell you once again that if I were rich I should live in a desert and visit rarely even Moscow, which I love deeply? In August I shall resume teaching, which occupation I hate with all my heart. I shall live . . . in quiet and seclusion, with a few intimate friends . . . and until my last breath I shall spit upon the world, its opinion, its fame and the honours it has to give."

But where did such misanthropy come from? Tchaikovsky himself admitted that he was shy, and this was probably true at least in part. Shy with servants: "Marcel . . . was very attentive and amiable. His coat and hat were infinitely superior to mine, so that I felt quite embarrassed"—and happy when they did not press their services upon him: "I observed that Marcel had received his instructions; he did not attempt to converse, nor to stand behind my chair, but just served what was necessary and went away." Shy with people he knew, especially when he had been the subject of their gossip: "I shall die here† like a dog rather than show myself on the streets of Moscow, at the Conservatoire, in theatres, at concerts, etc. Here also there are people, of course, but they do not care about me." Shy with persons he had never met like the French publisher Mackar: "Decided to go to Mackar.

* Is staying in Berlin.
† In Switzerland, after the scandal which followed his marriage.

What suffering I went through and how excited I was—it is impossible to describe. Ten times I approached the place and each time went away—even a large glass of absinth did not help. Finally I walked in. He was expecting me. I imagined him to be otherwise; less tall. His gaze is amazingly similar to Bessel's. We had a talk (while there, someone came to buy my works) and I left. It goes without saying that it was as though a load was taken off my shoulders."

For years Tchaikovsky struggled against this shyness, but around the age of 37, after emerging out of the breakdown caused by his marriage, he resigned himself to his own self-consciousness, and began to run away shamelessly from people he did not want to see: "Musicians for me are worse than anybody else. Previously . . . I should probably have made an effort . . . I considered it my duty to fight my pathological shyness. Now I cannot fight any more and I am not ashamed of it. Experience has taught me that there was no point at all in such useless tormenting of oneself." His appointment as Delegate plunged him into sheer panic, but at least he found the courage to refuse it: "I cannot go to Paris. It is not cowardice, it is not laziness: I just cannot. These past three days, after receiving the news of my appointment, I have been ill, I have been going mad. Death would be better than that. I wanted to force myself into it, but I did not succeed. I know now, by experience, what it means for me to force myself into things and to go against my nature, whatever it is. I cannot see people, I have to be isolated from all noise and bustle. In a word, if you want me to come back whole to be hugged by you, do not demand that I go to Paris: nothing good would result from it either for Russian music or for me personally. If you saw in what state I am, you would yourself advise me against going. Quiet, quiet, quiet and work: that is what I need." This of course was the letter of a sick man, but Tchaikovsky had practically recovered when he declared: "I have made up my mind to disregard all proprieties, all civilities, all the unavoidable observances of social forms when they are burdensome to me. I have tortured myself long enough. It is time for me to begin living the remainder of my life as I want to live, freely, without submitting to the tyranny of social relations." And he was perfectly sane when he wrote a long letter to Mrs von Meck in order to explain to her why, contrary to her wish, he did not go to visit Turgenev in Paris.

All my life I have been tormented by obligatory relations with people. By nature I am a retiring person. Every acquaintance, every new meeting with a person unknown to me has always caused me the greatest moral tortures. I can hardly even explain of what these tortures consist. Maybe it is timidity which has become a mania, maybe a total lack of need of social intercourse, maybe a false fear of seeming to be what I am not, maybe an inaptitude to say effortlessly things which I do not think (and without this no first acquaintance is possible)—in short I do not know what it is; but, as long as my position did not allow me to avoid meetings, I met people, I pretended to find pleasure in it, I was forced into playing different parts (for, when one lives in society, this cannot be avoided) and suffered abominably. Again, to tell that story would be to tell an awfully long and an awfully funny tale. God only knows how much I suffered through that, and if now I feel so quiet and happy, it is because I can live, at least here and in the country, without seeing anybody, except those in front of whom I can be myself. *Not once in my life* did I take one step to become acquainted with this or that interesting personality, and if it happened of itself, by sheer necessity, I finally felt only disappointment, sadness and fatigue. To give you a simple example: two years ago, Count L. N. Tolstoi, the writer, expressed a wish to make my acquaintance. He is very much interested in music. Of course I weakly tried to hide from him, but did not succeed. He came to the Conservatoire and declared to Rubinstein that he would not leave before I had come down to meet him. Tolstoi is enormously talented and his talent is very *simpatichny* to me. There was no way of refusing an acquaintance which would normally be thought flattering and agreeable. We met, and of course I played the part of a man who would have been both flattered and pleased, telling him that I was very happy, grateful and so on: a whole series of inevitable lies. 'I want to know you more intimately,' he said; 'I should like to talk with you about music.' Then and there, we had barely shaken hands, he expounded to me his musical views. According to him, *Beethoven is inept.* That was the beginning. In other words, a great writer, a genius in the knowledge of hearts, had begun by uttering, in a self-assured tone, a piece of nonsense which could only be insulting to a musician. What should one do in such a case? Argue? I argued. But how could such an argument be serious? To tell the truth, I should have admonished him. Perhaps another man would have done so, but I only suppressed my torments and went on playing a comedy, pretending I was serious and delighted. Later he called on me several times, and, although the impression I formed during our acquaintance is that Tolstoi is a somewhat paradoxical but also a direct and kind person, even sensitive to music in his own way (he cried and sobbed in front of me when I played to him the Andante of my first quartet, at his request), still his acquaintance afforded me nothing but trouble and pain, like any other one. . . . As far as I am concerned, *it is possible to enjoy a person's society only when, due to several years of contacts and to mutual interests (especially family ones), one can be oneself* in front of him. Failing that, any society is *painful*, and I am mentally organized in such a way that this pain I cannot tolerate. This is why, my dear friend, I do not call on Turgenev.

But was all this really shyness? Was it *only* shyness? Did not Tchaikovsky come closer to the mark when he expressed anguish at the idea of wasting time on socializing, time which a composer could easily find means to put to better use? True, he avoided Russian ladies because he was afraid of their invitations and was dismayed by Grand-Duke Konstantin's invitation to go around the world with him on his battleship. But was it because he was too shy or because he felt that his fate was to write music and not to lounge in pleasant company? And, as he was a paradox of a man, would it not be true, at least *partly* true, to say that he had mixed feelings about society, and that there were times when he found it not only difficult but even unpleasant to shun it altogether? Oh! he hated bores, there is no doubt about that: "I often go to the opera, but I do not enjoy it much. The impossibility of escaping from innumerable acquaintances bores me dreadfully. No matter where I hide myself, there are always idle people who poison my pleasure in the music by their kind attentions. They will worry me with the usual commonplace questions: 'How are you?' 'What are you composing now?' etc. But the invitations are the most intolerable. It requires so much courage to refuse them."

So he found it difficult to refuse invitations. Was that out of shyness?

"On arriving home I found Count Stroganov's card. I cannot get rid of these aristocrats whose understanding is unable to grasp the thought that a man might not consider their acquaintance as the greatest happiness in the world. This Count Stroganov had already invited me . . . and I had replied that I was too busy to visit anybody. Now he will not take no for an answer and calls on me. What shall I do? Not to call on him would be rude; to call would mean that I wish to be acquainted. Impossible to run away from these gents!" There is little trace of shyness here, and still less in Tchaikovsky's qualms after receiving invitations to a formal dinner at Count Bobrinsky's and to a reception at Countess Sollogub's: "I am afraid I shall have to leave soon, since I know for a fact that other invitations are awaiting me and since a foolish reluctance to offend by refusing makes me accept them: I cannot find enough strength of will to refuse offhand." Is there not even a trace of complacency in the following avowal: "Imagine, my dear friend, for the last few days I have hardly ever been out of a tail coat and white tie and associating with the most august personages. It is all very flattering, sometimes touching; but fatiguing to the last degree. I feel so happy and comfortable in my room in the hotel, not being obliged to go anywhere, or do anything."

As to being or not being flattered by Tolstoi's interest and attention, we should not forget that Tchaikovsky wrote in as many words: "Recently Count L. N. Tolstoi spent a few days here. He came to see me several times, and even spent two whole evenings. I am awfully flattered and pleased by the interest which I inspire in him, and am myself completely charmed by his ideal personality."

Tchaikovsky was conscious of this social paradox which affected him differently at different periods of his life. To Taneiev who had suspected the sincerity of his misanthropy he wrote:

> I wish, I want, I love interest, praise, love for my music; but I never sought interest for my personality, my appearance, my conversation. Not to sign my name under my compositions out of misanthropy would be ridiculous and inane, since I have to differentiate myself from others who speak at the same time as I. I want my name, real or borrowed, it does not matter, to be the label which distinguishes my wares, and I want this label to be appreciated, to be sought and known on the market.

And to Mrs Shpajinsky:

> What happiness it is to be at home, to be oneself, to shed the intolerable mask which one has to put on in society, when one forces oneself to be a man of fashion, to talk instead of keeping quiet, to smile amiably when the soul finds no reason to smile, to talk endlessly when one has to work, etc, etc. But on the other hand how to avoid plunging from time to time into the abyss of society? When you are an artist and pour out your musical thoughts to the crowd . . . how could you manage to turn your back . . . on that same crowd if, by various expressions of sympathy, they try to tell you that they feel for you? You must be grateful, and I eagerly try to show my gratefulness by avoiding to decline any invitation, appointment, etc, for I see in them the expression of real sympathy. But how much does it cost me!

Such was the evolution of Tchaikovsky's misanthropy, and when fame came, he accepted it with its servitudes. But this did not solve the paradox. In 1878 he had already expressed his love of solitude: "I have come to the conclusion that I can find full satisfaction from life only if I live in the country and most of the time alone." And he was always glad when, during his daily walk, he had not met a single soul. People strolling under his windows annoyed him. For long spells of time, he was happy alone. At other moments, companionship was indispensable to him. With characteristic clear-mindedness about himself, he noted in his diary: "Curious fact. I seek solitude and suffer when I have found it."

7 An uninterrupted paean of praise

Paradoxes are not made to be solved but observed. It is not the least vice of historians that they always try to rub paradoxes out: they like their histories flat. This is one sin which we do not want to commit. Tchaikovsky loved mankind, hated mankind; loved solitude, hated solitude: all this is true, at least in part, and if a majority of facts point one way, we still do not want to wipe out the minority: on the contrary, we want to preserve it with care, because we believe that life is made of paradoxes and contradictions, and we want to have our Tchaikovsky as much alive as we can.

Still there is one conception, which has been systematically neglected for reasons that will soon be apparent, and which may —certainly not flatten and deaden the information we have gathered—but present it as more complementary than contradictory: not that opposites can ever be reconciled—that indeed is not even to be desired—but they can be shown as the different sides of the same block of truth.

Peter Tchaikovsky was, by essence, a family man. When he wrotes to his brother Anatoly "A quiet life with someone I love, and work to do is what I need," we believe that he was sincere and that he was right: this was what he needed. His bourgeois tastes have already been pointed out* and we ought not to be surprised that his ideal of life was of the same character. This, by the way, opens an interesting avenue of thought: we have been taught by post-romantic folklorists to expect a Bohemian in every artist; but as a matter of fact no true artist can be a true Bohemian, because an art is first of all a craft, which necessitates training, time, atten-

* Cf. p. 45ff

tion, industry, hard work, and some sense of order. It would be worth while to debunk the myth of Bohemian artists by showing how much toil and method goes into the shortest poem, the smallest canvas, the simplest song. And although a family life may not be the easiest one for an artist, it is true that the intimate, simple companionship of a beloved family can seem to him— especially from outside—the least exacting, the most reassuring form of human fellowship. Tchaikovsky had no children, as little of a wife as he could, but he had parents, brothers, sisters, nieces, nephews, and all the fellowship he could get from them he drank in with happiness and avidity. No wonder if his other friends never became indispensable to him: he was old-fashioned enough to find friends among his own kin.

He was seven when he wrote a pitiful poem entitled 'Prière d'une petite fille tout à fait orpheline' (Prayer of a little-girl-who-is-quite-an-orphan); he was 50 when he told Anna Merkling: "The joy of life does not consist at all, as you say, in spending the whole year on touring foreign countries, but in having at home somebody to love, whose interests to share, for whom to suffer and to rejoice."

When, after his marriage and nervous breakdown, he was invited to spend some time at his sister Aleksandra's home in Kamenka, he wrote to her and to his brother-in-law that the hope to see them shone for him like the hope of dawn: "One moment will suffice, I think, for my complete recovery: to see all of you is enough to get reconciled to the most dreadful, to the most bitter feelings." And he was not only anxious to receive care and love; he was genuinely interested in the family, for instance in Aleksandra's children, for each of whom he had a special epithet: "How I wish to see soon Tatiana, so proud and graceful; Vera, the fragrant violet; Tassia, who is like an appetizing cucumber just plucked from its garden bed; Mitia, the warlike, the chivalrous; Bobik, the poetical and finally the incomparable Uka."

Not only did Tchaikovsky feel a need for family companionship, but he was always welcome among his nephews and nieces; not only was he highly successful with them, but he was perfectly conscious of his success: "You cannot imagine with what impatience I was expected and how I was needed here. My nieces want to produce a play. They did not want to choose one without me, or to undertake anything about producing it; moreover I have become somehow indispensable to their summer life. Without me they do not drive to the woods, they do not play music, in a word they get bored. And so how they expected me! How they urged me to come back sooner!" This relationship with the younger generation of the family he kept up during his whole life, acting as cicerone at the Franco-Russian Exhibition to his Davydov and Litke, cousins and nephews, or being a constant visitor at his niece Anna's house, of whose children he was very fond. At times this misanthropist 'dreaded solitude' so much that he nearly joined Anna on her wedding trip!

His love of anniversaries is also typical of a real family man for whom the smallest incidents became memories to be cherished, if only they happened to his kith and kin. "The day after to-morrow will be the anniversary of our famous trip to Monte-Carlo, and, on the fifth, of our departure from here and our arrival in Pisa. . . ." "Yesterday was the anniversary of my dinner and today is the anniversary of Lova's illness. . . ."* "I am opening this letter to tell you that I am awfully sad at the idea that I shall not see you. Do you know what happened exactly a year ago? We met at the station and went to the Russian bath with Nikolai Lvovitch, who danced, was merry and full of life."† His animosity toward his non-musical cousins, and his deep conviction that he did not like relatives (he even felt a little remorseful for being so heartless) emphasizes the seriousness with which he took all blood relations: "How I enjoy a life free from the obligation to meet strangers! Among strangers I count my relatives. Have you many relatives, my friend? I think not. Mine are numberless and they all live in St Petersburg. This is a great hardship. In spite of blood ties, most of these people are completely foreign to me and their company brings me nothing but the necessity to seem glad when I am not. They pester me with solicitations and invitations. And since it is very unpleasant to offend people without a reason, I have to pay a daily tribute to boredom. The most intolerable is that they all feel it their duty to talk to me about music and to ask me 'to play something new.'" A homeless man, fleeing from cousins into the arms of brothers and nephews, Tchaikovsky cuts a somewhat pathetic figure, especially when misinformed ladies make matters worse by inconsiderate remarks: "I sat on the platform in full view of the audience, having Grieg and his wife as neighbours. Afterwards a friendly critic—Fritsch—told me that he saw a lady point out the Griegs and myself to her daughter, saying 'Look dear, there sits Tchaikovsky, and by his side his children.' This was said quite seriously, and is not so very surprising, because

* Lova, diminutive of Lev: Lev Davydov.
† Bochechkarev.

I am quite grey and elderly, while Grieg, who is forty-five, and his wife, look extraordinarily young and small at a distance."*

Various interpretations have been given of Tchaikovsky's relations with different members of his family. Seriously, if any conclusion may be drawn from his own letters, it is that all these relations, although they varied in tenderness and depth, were of a perfectly ordinary nature. A little too ordinary to be very interesting in a biography.

His father, Ilya Petrovich Tchaikovsky the mining engineer, is usually presented as a downright fool, but in a recent biography he becomes the brilliant man of the family.[9] This is not very important and will not be discussed here. Much more serious is the imputation that Tchaikovsky suffered from an Oedipus complex. The reasoning behind it is of the type we have already encountered: 'Maybe Tchaikovsky was a homosexual; most homosexuals suffer from an Oedipus complex; therefore Tchaikovsky had an Oedipus complex; since he had an Oedipus complex, he was obviously a homosexual.'

There is no evidence at all pointing in that direction. Clever or foolish, Ilya Petrovich seems to have deserved love and respect from his son. As a child, Peter Tchaikovsky was once reproached by his governess for not studying well enough, while his father was spending money on his education: "When he was undressing for bed," tells Fanny Dürbach, "and I had forgotten all about the incident he suddenly burst into tears, began to insist that he loved his father deeply, that he was filled with gratitude towards both parents, and reproached me for injustice." It is true that, according to Modest, there was one period when "Tchaikovsky's attitude to his father and aunts was slightly egotistical and contemptuous. This was only a passing phase. He was not actually wanting in affection for his own people, but was simply bored in their society." Some biographers are under the impression that the composer's father showed hostility toward his son's musical career. The source is a manuscript by A. I. Brullov, mother of Nikolai Konradi, who describes in the following terms Tchaikovsky's emotion at reading César Cui's review of his Ode to Joy: "When I read this terrible judgment, I hardly know what happened to me. . . . And the thought of going home, where Father would begin to prove how right he was in opposing my musical career, oppressed and tortured me." But Mrs Brullov's memory or imagination must have been playing tricks on her. Modest tells us that, on the contrary,

---

* The incident took place in 1888: Tchaikovsky was 48.

Tchaikovsky's "father, on his own initiative, had actually proposed that he should devote himself entirely to music," and the composer wrote as much to his sister: "Papa affirms that it is not yet too late for me to become a musician." And there was obviously no bitterness in the charming incident which took place during the first night of Tchaikovsky's first opera to be performed in St Petersburg, *The Oprichnik.* 'In a box on the second tier sat the composer's old father with his family. He beamed with happiness. But when Modest asked him which he thought best for Peter, this artistic success or the Empress Anne's Order, which he might have gained as an official, the incorrigible old civil servant replied: "The decoration would certainly have been better." '

Tchaikovsky never reproached his father for marrying a third time after the death of his mother, and was on the best terms with his "tasty little cream puff" of a stepmother, whom he found "half-educated but very intelligent and extremely kind." When he wrote letters home, he added tender kisses for "Papa, the dear little old man, and for Lizaveta Mihailovna."* Whenever he spoke about his father, it was always in the most affectionate terms, even when old Ilya Petrovich began his second childhood: "He is still very alert and healthy in body, but feeble in mind. Only his old love for his children is left, and the angelic kindness that always distinguished him but which is now especially touching. It can truly be said that he cannot hurt a fly. . . ." "I have a little time to see those whom I should most like to see. My father, who is wonderful in his angelic kindness, I see only by snatches. The dear little old man weeps from joy every time I visit him. It is very encouraging for us that his health is good: yesterday night he went to the theatre and was not even tired."

In 1878 when Tchaikovsky was 38, he wrote: "For the first time in my life I felt uncomfortable with Papa: this comes because I have kept from him the catastrophe of last year† and remember how he admired" the bride. A man who has an Oedipus complex and waits till he is 38 to feel uncomfortable in the presence of his father is a very special case. But this does not deter stubborn Oedipists who insist on their point with an obstinacy worthy of a better cause: "In his outward manner, Tchaikovsky in later years, *was far too conventional* ever to express any hostility towards his father or even to allow himself to think of such a feeling. Nor is

---

* Elizaveta Mihailovna née Lipport, Ilia Tchaikovsky's third and last wife. At first the composer did not approve of her, but he soon changed his mind. Cf. p. 144.

† Arising from Tchaikovsky's marriage.

there ever any suggestion of antagonism in his correspondence; the letters he wrote to his father, though few and far between, are consistently affectionate. *But one cannot avoid the suspicion that he was merely paying lipservice* to a sentiment which was *probably* less profound than he would care to believe. On receiving the news of his father's death he wept, but he *seems* to have been far more concerned by the fact that he had received no word of praise after the performance of a recent work."*[10] To quote from a biographer who showed good sense in several circumstances "those who pursue the well-known spectre of the Oedipus complex have lost no time in pointing out that the death of Ilya Petrovitch did not cause Tchaikovsky the grief he had felt when he lost his mother.† This is a typical example of wishful thinking. No one knows what [he] felt —grief is not measurable—and those who say they do are talking nonsense. Moreover Aleksandra Andreievna‡ was forty-one when she died, her husband eighty-five! Forty-one was young even in those days, eighty-five a great age."[11] If we go back to the sources, here is what we find.

To Anatoly, who wrote him to describe their father's death, Tchaikovsky replied: "Your letter is infinitely sad and at the same time some inexpressible light radiates from it. . . . I think that the soul of our dear deceased lit up your thoughts when you wrote it." To Mrs von Meck: "I have finally received a letter from Anatoly who tells me the detailed history of my father's illness and death. The tale is deeply touching. I wept a lot when reading it, and I think that these tears, shed for the departure from this world of a man who was pure and possessed the soul of an angel, have had a beneficial influence on me. In my soul I find serenity and resignation. My brother says that he was conscious of death, but calmly and serenely conscious of it." And to Jurgenson, several days later: "My family grief did not shock me. Life hardens people and accustoms them to losses. But I am awfully sad to think that never again shall I see my dear, beloved, old father."

The composer went to see his stepmother: "It was inexpressibly sad to see the familiar little apartment without its main inhabitant. What wonderful women there are on earth! My stepmother, whose life with an old man of eighty-four was exhausting, cannot recover from her grief! Only women know how to love so."

Tchaikovsky's mother did not fare better than his father at his

---

* The italics are mine. V.V.

† Tchaikovsky was 14 when his mother died; nearly 40 when he lost his father.

‡ Tchaikovsky's mother.

biographers' hands. Her real image is completely blurred now, and we probably shall never know whether she was the heroine that her French blood makes her in the eyes of French biographers or the cold and lazy 'fine lady'[12] in which believe those who believe all Fanny Dürbach's (the dismissed governess's) recriminations. This again does not matter very much. Whoever she was her son loved her, and we are told that his attachment to her "was not the ordinary love of a boy for his mother. It had the intensity of a lover's passion. One school of psychoanalysts might call it an Oedipus complex, another say that psychically the boy found the world too difficult and had a subconscious desire to leave it by re-entering the womb from which he had issued. Whether [Peter Ilich's] frantic and undiminishing love for his mother was the result of congenital abnormality or whether abnormality developed out of that love, it is impossible to read his childish letters to her, feel his crushed and despairing reaction to her death, or even look at his remarks about that death decades later, without becoming certain that there was a causal connection* between his emotional relationship to [Aleksandra Andreievna] and his homosexuality."[13] Much also has been made and in the most gaudy terms of a scene in which Tchaikovsky indulged, at the mature age of ten, when his mother was leaving him, for the first time of his life, as boarder in a school, and going back home, about fifteen hundred miles away. "As the moment of her departure drew near, Peter Ilich excited himself into a state close to hysterics. Nothing the frantic woman could say quieted him. Promises to return soon unloosed more tears. Embrace after embrace only made his forehead hotter, his eyes redder, his sobs less controllable. When Aleksandra Andreievna at last stepped into the waiting carriage, the boy had to be forcibly restrained from going with her. And as it began to get under way, he broke from those holding him, ran to the carriage and clung desperately to one of the turning wheels."†[14] This, we are told, was "the first symptom of that fierce identification with his mother from which he was never able to free himself." That he felt crushed when she died is also considered as a misdemeanour on his part. He is *accused* of having written: "I shall never reconcile myself to the thought that my dear mother, whom I loved so much, actually is not, or that I shall never be able to tell her how, after twenty-three years of separation, she is as dear to me as ever." And to crown his demonstration the prosecuting biographer[15] exclaims:

* How anybody can be certain of a causal relation between A and B without knowing if A causes B or B causes A remains a secret.
† Practically, this seems a little difficult to do and remain unscathed.

"In another letter *he admits** that 'her death had a great influence
on the fate of myself and our entire family.' " Those two little
words 'he admits' are quite a programme: Tchaikovsky could not
have said, declared, proclaimed, remarked, that his mother's death
had an influence on him (and his entire family): he had to *admit*
it.

Rather sensible objections have been opposed to this interpretation of the facts: "If every boy who sincerely believed himself
heartbroken when his mother dies were written off as a neurotic,
the masculine half of the world would consist almost exclusively of
them. . . . Had he been a victim of the Oedipus complex as so many
have alleged, [Peter Ilich] could never have accepted another woman
in the place of his mother. . . . To say that [he] did not resign
himself without a fight after his mother's death is to say the
obvious. Certainly he never forgot her—why should he? But if we
go by his actions . . . it becomes clear that he overcame this shat-
tering loss courageously. . . . It is 1891 and his sister has just died
suddenly. He is worried about her son Vladimir, one of his great
favourites. Then he recalls his own mother's death and feels less
worried. 'I know from my own experience,' he says, 'that one gets
over such shocks with fair ease at his age.' "[16]

So much for Oedipus. But the 'fair ease' should not be interpreted as a lack of heart: once again Tchaikovsky appears as clear-
minded, not a cynic but a realist; he knows that shocks are shocks,
but that life goes on. Still there is no reason to disguise the fact
that he was deeply attached to his mother and to his mother's
memory. With his love for anniversaries, he kept piously mentioning the one of her death: "Twenty years ago today my mother
died. . . . Every minute of that awful day remains in my memory
as if it were yesterday. . . ." Thirty-second "anniversary of
mother's death. . . ." When he found the letters he had written
to his parents as a child, he was deeply moved because he was
reminded of his 'feverishly passionate love' for his absent mother,
and he never forgot her hands, which were very beautiful: "Such
hands do not exist nowadays," he used to say, "and never will
again."

Tchaikovsky was also deeply attached to his older sister Aleksandra, or Sasha. Her family was his family; he spent many
summers with them at Kamenka or Verbovka; he wrote her the
most affectionate letters, and, at least during the two first periods
of his life (Cf. Chart II, page 34), was very sensitive to her

* The Italics are mine. V.V.

opinion of him. "I have already told you what an important part
you play in my life—although you do not live near me. In dark
hours my thoughts fly to you. 'If things go very badly with me, I
shall go to Sasha,' I say to myself; or 'I think I will do this, I am
sure Sasha would advise it;' or 'Shall I write to her? What would
she think of this. . . . ?' What a joy to think that if I could get
away from these surroundings into another atmosphere I should
sun myself in your kindly heart! "

When Mrs von Meck, on learning that Aleksandra wanted to
travel and could not do so because of her children, suggested that
the children should come and visit her, Tchaikovsky was offended:
she could help him but she was not to meddle in family affairs.
He replied rather stiffly: "I am very grateful to you for inviting
my nephews, but they do not prevent at all my sister from taking
a trip. She is just reluctant to leave them for a time." All that had
to seem suspicious to somebody, and we find it seriously maintained that Tchaikovsky discovered in Aleksandra a second mother
on whom he transferred his unnatural passion for his real mother.
The extracts quoted above are followed by a nasty comment from
the prosecution: "Tchaikovsky had little reticence in describing
his feelings."[17] That is of course true; he had none, and we should
not try to read our own prejudices into what he wrote.

In fact Tchaikovsky, especially in the two latter periods of his
life, was often critical of Sasha, though still fond of her. She was
something of a tyrant, he said: "she has trained all the members
of the household not even to drive in a nail without her supervision." She "is a very good but a very strange person." She
"worries me very much. Her present fits, according to the Kamenka
doctor, are of a very malignant nature. They are somehow akin to
epilepsy, and, as he presumes, are the consequence of morphine
and all the other narcotics without which she cannot do. I shall
tell you (and I beg you to leave it between us)* that to morphine
she now adds alcohol. My sister resorts to this poison, which is
new for her, in constantly growing quantities."

He learned of her death when he was in Paris, through reading
a Russian newspaper in a library. He 'ran out of the room as if
he had been stung' and, naturally enough, was depressed for some
time. But when, two years later, his brother-in-law remarried,
he gently chid his cousin Anna Merkling for objecting:

> You reacted like a real woman, I mean with too much passion and
> too little thought, to Lova's marriage. You say that, for you, he

* Addressed to Mrs von Meck.

has slipped into the mud: this is exaggerated and cruel, just as it was definitely exaggerated to take him for an ideal man, to use your expression. There was never anything ideal about him: he has always been a kind and very weak fellow, which he still is. Like you I fear that Katia's* sickliness will spoil his life, but, in general, I rather approve his choice: first, she is of the family; second, she has always been very *simpatichny* to me and I never thought her foolish—on the contrary, she is full of tact, and I am sure she is not silly. At our age, we cannot be so absolute in our positive and negative judgments. Remember how angry we all were when my father married Lizaveta Mihailovna. So what? Nothing but undoubtedly good things followed this late and, as we thought, inappropriate marriage. I too, during the first minute, found it unpleasant that Lova was marrying again, but, having thought about his position, I bear him no grudge.

Another member of Tchaikovsky's family to have been the subject of not very well founded surmises is Aleksandra and Lev's son, Vladimir Davydov, known as Bob, whom the composer adored as a child, who became his favourite nephew in later years, and spent his last moments with him. It has been very loudly whispered that Bob was much more than a nephew for him, and, once again, this is the kind of imputation which cannot be disproved. The main evidence is that Bob shot himself thirteen years after the composer's death, and since homosexuals do happen to shoot themselves, Bob may very well have been a homosexual, and then it is fairly obvious that he was his uncle's lover. Other evidence is taken from Tchaikovsky's diaries and correspondence: he never fails to call Bob an angel or some other affectionate name, and exclaims about him with even more enthusiasm than he does about other children. But the most compromising elements are to be found, once again, in Modest's biography, which is supposed to have been written in order to hide the composer's singularities. Here are the suspicious passages.

Bob, I idolize you! Do you remember how I once told you that the happiness your presence gave me was nothing compared to all I suffered in your absence? Away from home, with the prospect of long weeks and months apart, I feel the full meaning of my affection for you. . . ."

I am counting—just as last year—the days, hours, and minutes till my journey is over. You are constantly in my thoughts, for at every access of agitation and homesickness, whenever my spiritual horizon grows dark, the thought that you are there, that I shall see you sooner or later, flashes like a ray of sunlight across my mind.

* Lev Davydov's second wife, a cousin of the composer.

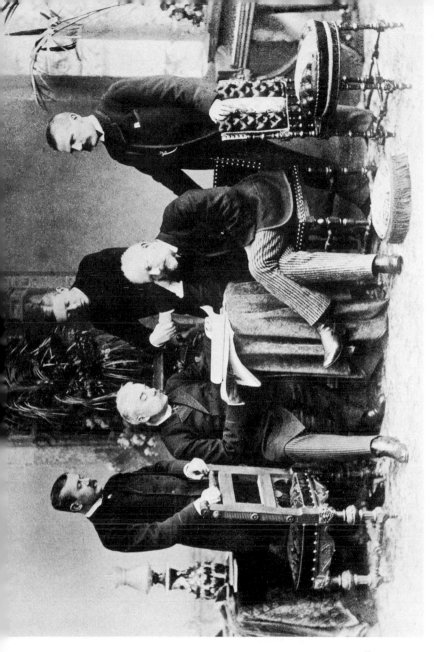

The Tchaikovsky brothers *circa* 1890: (from left to right) Anatoly, Nikolai, Hippolit, Peter, Modest

The composer in 1888;
Tchaikovsky as a Cambridge
Doctor, 1893

I am not exaggerating, upon my honour! Every moment this sun-ray keeps breaking forth in these or similar words: "Yes, it is bad, but never mind, Bob lives in the world;" "Far away in St Petersburg sits Bob, drudging at his work;" "In a month's time I shall see Bob again."

Either Modest was an extraordinary fool, or his real purpose was to make public what he is supposed to have tried to hide, or he considered his brother's relationship with their nephew perfectly innocent and did not dream that anybody could imagine it to be otherwise. Rosa Newmarch summarizes in the following terms Modest's own comments:

Up to the age of eighteen, these pleasant relations between uncle and nephew had not assumed any deep significance. But as Vladimir Davydov grew up, Tchaikovsky gradually felt for him a sentiment which can only be compared to his love for the twins. Tola and Modia, in their youth. The difference of age was no hindrance to their relations. Tchaikovsky preferred the companionship of his nephew; was always grieved to part with him; confided to him his inmost thoughts, and finally made him his heir, commending to this young man all those whom he still desired to assist and cherish, even after his death.

Before studying Tchaikovsky's attachment to the twins, which endured all his life and took the place of many other natural affections, it will be appropriate to mention here his half-sister Zinaida, who, in most biographies,[18] plays the part of the villain, for no reason that we could identify; his older brother Nikolai, who had been his playmate but was never very close to him; and his younger brother Ippolit, whom he suspected of amplifying his ailments in order to get more attention. None of these played an important part in Tchaikovsky's life; nevertheless he did not separate them from his favourites when he wrote to Mrs von Meck that 'the description of his family would be an uninterrupted paean of praise, but that nothing would be exaggerated in the eulogies he would squander on his relatives.' It is true that he squandered most on the beloved twins, so much so even, that one cannot help wondering why no one ever thought of suggesting incestuous homosexuality, which, after all, would have simplified matters for all parties concerned.

When they were born, "he could scarcely believe, he said, that they were not angels come down to earth," a rather remarkable declaration from a ten-year-old boy about two wrinkled babes. And after the mother's death, although how soon after is not entirely clear (immediately, according to the composer; six years later

K

according to Modest), he took them under his direct protection.
Modest tells the story:

After the marriage of our sister Aleksandra, the twins, Anatoly
and myself, then about ten years old, were often very lonely. From
three o'clock in the afternoon—when we returned from school—until
bedtime, we were left to our own resources. One long and wearisome
evening, as we sat on the drawing-room window-sill kicking our
heels, Peter came in and found us. From our earliest infancy he inspired us, not so much with love as with respect and adoration. A
word from him was like a sacred treasure. He, on the contrary,
took no notice of us; we had no existence for him.

The mere fact that he was in the house, and that we could see
him, sufficed to distract our dullness and cheer us up; but great
indeed was our astonishment when, instead of passing us by un-
observed as usual, he stopped to say: "Are you dull, boys? Would
you like to spend the evening with me?" To this day I cannot forget that memorable evening; memorable indeed for us, since it was
the beginning of a new existence.

The wisest and most experienced of teachers, the dearest and
tenderest of mothers, could not have replaced Peter Ilich in our life
from that hour; for he was all this, and our friend and comrade
besides. All we thought and felt we could tell him without any fear
lest it would fail to interest him. His influence upon us was un-
bounded. We, on our side, became the first care and aim of his life.
We three formed, as it were, a family within the family. A year later
Peter wrote to his sister:

"My attachment to these little folk grows from day to day. I am
very proud of this feeling, perhaps the best which my heart has
known. When I am unhappy I have only to think of them, and my
life seems better worth living. I try as far as possible to give them
a mother's love and care. . . ."

This care never ceased. Tchaikovsky had scarcely arrived in
Moscow to take up his position at the Conservatoire when he began writing them letters full of tenderness and advice: "Yesterday
at bedtime I thought a great deal about you both. I pictured to
myself all the horrors of the first night after the holidays, and
fancied how Modia would hide his nose under the bedclothes and
cry bitterly. How I wish I could have comforted him! It's not a
meaningless phrase, Modia, when I tell you to grind and grind and
grind, and to make friends with your respectable companions, but
not with that crazy fellow X. . . . I am afraid you will be left
behind in your class and be one of those who get into the master's
black books. I have no fears for Tola, so I send him no advice.
Tola, my dear, conquer your indolence as a correspondent and

write to me. Hearty kisses!" He was as anxious for them to have a good time as to work, and wrote to Aleksandra. "I am going to act as advocate for two mortals who are just crazy about Kamenka. You write that Tola and Modia might be left in St Petersburg, but I am determined not to tell them your point of view. They would utterly lose heart—especially Tola. One of my chief reasons for caring to spend the summer at Kamenka is to be with them, and your house is the only place where we can be together for a time. If you only knew how these little fellows cling to me (and I return their love a hundredfold), you would not find it in your heart to separate us. Arrange, my dear, for this visit to come off. Very likely I shall be able to take part of the expense off your hands." In a word, as a kindly biographer puts it, 'he was smothering them with effusive, well-meant attention.'

Told by the composer himself, the story is not substantially different.

Without exaggeration one can say that these two young men are, thanks to their moral and intellectual qualities, very pleasant to observe. I am attached to them by one of those mutual affections which even between brothers are not often to be found. They are much younger than I am; there is a ten year difference between us. When our mother died, they were four. Our sister was a boarding student. Our elder brother, a good person, but not particularly affectionate, could not take the place of a tender and loving mother. Of course I too have not been a mother for them, but from the first minute that they became orphans, I wanted to give them what a mother gives, because I knew by experience what indelible imprint is left in the soul of a child by a mother's tenderness and caresses. And from that time between them and me a special relationship was created: just as I love them more than myself and am ready to sacrifice anything for them, they are boundlessly attached to me. Both went to the School of Law. *Anatoly* is doing well in civil service: he is now assistant-prosecutor in St Petersburg. *Modest* is extraordinarily gifted by nature, but has no particular inclination towards any definite activity: he did not do too well in the civil service, being more interested in books, paintings, music than in his reports. We were all worrying about his future when a mutual friend . . . had the idea to recommend him to a certain Mr Konradi who was looking for a tutor for his only son who is deaf and dumb. The matter was arranged, and Modest revealed himself an excellent pedagogue. He spent a year abroad to learn the methods of educating deaf and dumb children, and is now wholeheartedly devoted to his work.

The twins did not look alike; they had different personalities and Tchaikovsky's feelings towards them were somewhat different too. Modest, the playwright, annoyed him by the scrapes into which he got, and he told him so without beating about the bush: "I am told you have done something very dishonourable and nasty. I don't yet know what it is but I know your character well, you are so spineless that you will do absolutely anything to be able to go on the spree and have a good time. . . . Ah! Modka! I am seriously worried about you. Have you forgotten already how I spoke to you about your utter lack of purpose, the way you never think of doing something with your life." On the other hand Modest was closer to him intellectually, and they used to joke about the future biography of the composer by the writer, not knowing that such a biography would actually be written. And their love was deep and sincere: "I never realize all my affection for you so much as when away from home, and oppressed with loneliness and nostalgia" wrote Tchaikovsky to Modest, and also: "As a matter of fact nothing can really matter so long as there are people whom one loves as I love you and as you love me (pardon my conceit)."

Anatoly, the lawyer, was more reliable, but fitful, restless, a complacent victim to his own nerves. "I could now be perfectly happy if only my Tola did not mope" is a recurring sentence under the composer's pen. His love affairs were also a matter of concern for his older brother since, most of the time, Anatoly did not know his own mind; it was the same with the problems he created for himself in his work, but finally, 'having the talent to be liked by important people without servility or flattery,' he climbed very close to the top in his chosen career.

The relationship between Tchaikovsky and Anatoly was naturally passionate: what was not passionate in the composer's life? On entering Anatoly's empty room, Tchaikovsky 'felt his heart contract and this contraction went crescendo till night.' Rooms of absent people in general did not agree with him. We have already seen him crying in Aleksei's, and here he is again crying in Anatoly's: "All day I had struggled against tears and wished very much to conquer them, but, when I saw the empty rooms, when I realized what a loss for me was your departure, I lost control over myself. . . . I should like to express with words how much I love you but such words do not exist. It is a bottomless abyss of love. . . ." "You cannot imagine how I languish without you, how disgusting Venice, the Hotel Beau Rivage and everything, everything seems to me, because it all reminds me of you and you are far away. . . . And how infinite is my love for you! Only now that you are not with me do I realize the strength of my love for you, and I am tormented by the idea that when you were with me I did not know how to express this love. It is always like that with me." Anatoly's feelings seem to have been scarcely less passionate than his brother's: "his morbidity influences his relationship to me," wrote the composer. "Imagine! He is jealous of all the people whom I love, and this jealousy is sometimes expressed rather brutally and strangely. Moreover he constantly fears for me. He has incessant visions of dangers threatening me. He can be perfectly calm and happy only when I am with him." It is even probable that Anatoly was in the habit of covering Peter's photograph with kisses, as Peter covered Anatoly's. And if we find all this somewhat far-fetched, we should re-read one of Dostoievsky's earlier novels, and we shall discover there enough crying, weeping, kissing, fretting and loving to equip a whole family of Tchaikovskys for several generations. It is not to be denied that the composer's nervous system was somewhat unstrung; still, when judging our ancestors we should never forget that we live in a very cold century, when natural affections are reduced to a minimum—and that we are not the happier for it.

8 Do not forget the particle

We know enough now about Tchaikovsky and his feelings towards those who were closest to him to extend our range and try to place him or rather to see how he placed himself in the society of his time. It will scarcely come as a surprise that he was essentially faithful to the most traditional values on all levels.

Here again contradictions abound, but he is not responsible for them. Modest was the first to introduce confusion by declaring: "One of the most characteristic traits of Peter Ilich Tchaikovsky was his ironical attitude towards his family's traditions of noble descent. He never lost an opportunity of making fun of their armorial bearings, which he regarded as 'imaginary,' and clung obstinately to the plebeian origin of the Tchaikovskys. . . . He would not consider himself a scion of the aristocracy, because his [direct] ancestors could not boast of one *boyar*. . . . But if he was unconcerned as to family descent, he was far from indifferent as to nationality. The aristocratic pretensions of his relatives aroused his mockery, but the mere suggestion of their Polish origin stirred him to instant wrath." H. Weinstock followed suit by declaring on one hand that Peter Ilich "was always angered by any suggestion that some of his forebears might have been Poles. He wanted to insist on the Tchaikovskys' entire Russianness," and on the other hand that "It is sometimes stated, without the advancing of any proof, that Ilya Petrovich's father . . . was a nobleman. His father, in turn, is described as . . . [an] officer in a regiment of Cossacks." Catherine Bowen was not to be left behind: "The Tchaikovskys were indeed gentility, but gentility by virtue of talent, education and bearing rather than birth. . . . As for Peter himself, he cared not a pin for the social ladder, past or present; let one of his brothers discover a Tchaikovsky coat-of-arms or raise the family artificially to gentility, and ridicule descended swiftly upon them. . . . He wasted no time over the bourgeois stamp of his ancestry."

Unfortunately there is scarcely any truth in any of these statements.

First there is no written evidence to show that Tchaikovsky was irritated at the idea of having Polish ancestors. On the contrary, when Mrs von Meck asked him for details about his family, he answered: "There are a number of Poles bearing my name. I myself am probably of Polish descent, though I do not know positively who my ancestors were." So on the first point at least Modest was wrong.

As to the social rank of the Tchaikovskys, though it is true that they were not noblemen in the British sense—they had no title of nobility—it is established by documents that they belonged to the *dvorianstvo*, which was a class in the strictest sense of the term, with its distinctive duties and privileges.* Tchaikovsky was not only conscious of it, but he obviously had no intentions of renouncing his quality, since he signed his German letters 'Peter von Tchaikovsky' and, fondly believing, as many foreigners do, that the French particle *de* is a sign of noble birth, had his passport established in the name of 'Pierre *de* Tchaikovsky,' and insisted on being so addressed when he lived abroad: 'Do not forget the

* H. Weinstock should have guessed it, since he knew that the composer's great-grandfather was an officer. Russia would have been a very democratic country indeed if, at the beginning of the eighteenth century, she had recruited her officers among commoners.

particle, he wrote to his friends: it is there to uphold my aristocratic dignity.'

True, the tone is humorous. It is not less humorous in the following passage quoted by Catherine Bowen, though she obviously
took it literally and seriously: "I know only that my grandfather was a physician* and lived in the province of Viatka, and
then my genealogical tree becomes lost in darkness. Perhaps Mr
Victor Tchaikovsky and the other fellow bearing the same name
as I, who every day advertises in the *Moscow News* a corn plaster
he has invented—are distant relatives of mine." This druggist was,
we believe, a sore spot with the composer who used to say that if
he received a commission he was ready to set to music the adver-
tisement 'Come to Tchaikovsky for your corn plasters.' But what
did this harping on corn plasters mean, and are we to assume that
Modest invented Tchaikovsky's democratic attitude to please his
liberal readers?

The imbroglio is easily clarified. Tchaikovsky, poor, genteel,
bearing a name which was very common indeed, lived among the
nobility. Compared to theirs, his origin was obscure and the
musical jobs he did for them, accompanying singers and giving
lessons, did nothing to relieve his obscurity.† What was a proud
man to do? Boast of his *dvorianstvo* to descendants of the
oldest families of the Empire? He adopted the opposite attitude:
he systematically diminished his ancestry, declaring himself content with his talents and his 'wares'‡ as he used to say, not without a touch of irony. His natural simplicity and liking for simple
people must have helped him to develop this distinguished modesty, but it would be a mistake to read into it any excessively democratic feelings. He was still horrified when actors who were
supposed to play French gentlemen held themselves 'like flunkies,'
and still quite capable to share with Apuhtin a joke about a count
who had somewhat demeaned himself by becoming an indus-
trialist and manufacturing dyes. The count asked Apuhtin if he
thought that blue blood existed among merchants. "Certainly,
Count," replied Apuhtin. "With aniline."

---

* In fact it seems that he was a police official with the rather unexpected
talent of healing the sick.

† According to Modest, Tchaikovsky's indigence in 1866 was so dramatic
that he was seriously offered the position of inspector of meat. This was
obviously no time for snobbishness.

‡ Cf. p. 134.

9 Is there no strength or loyalty left?

"There is a republic here," wrote Tchaikovsky left to baby-sit at his sister's home. "Master and mistress of the house are away and chaos reigns." This jocular remark leaves little doubt as to what he thought about republics and further investigation confirms the impression. The composer reads "a marvellous work *although* written in a republican spirit," declares that peace and mutual understanding are impossible without someone in charge, and rages at the way the French treat their princes.

This does not mean that Tchaikovsky was a reactionary. Not only does his diary express "joy due to the news about *suffrage universel*" but he even had his own troubles with officialdom. Having published his *Liturgy* in spite of existing regulations (they forbade the publication of religious music without approval from the Court Chapel, which possessed a privilege in such matters) he—or rather Jurgenson—won the lawsuit which followed and so was instrumental in opening the realm of religious music to other Russian composers. Russian law, out of respect for the Church, did not allow impersonation of members of the clergy on the stage, and here again Tchaikovsky got into trouble, because of the Archbishop who was supposed to appear in his *Maid of Orleans*. The censor suggested that he be replaced by a pilgrim, and the composer did not restrain his rage: "How angry this revolting censure makes me! In all the world you would not find such arbitrary measures, such idiocy! Transform the archbishop into a pilgrim? They would have done better to make a pilgrim of Joan of Arc herself: it would have been more suitable."

Tchaikovsky lived through a very troubled period of Russian history. Anarchists, socialists, communists, nihilists, believed in political assassination as a permissible method of gaining power, and the police practised repression whenever liberal influences, which were then in fashion, did not prevent it. Tchaikovsky himself said a few pretty harsh things about the repressions. He was indignant at 'Count Tolstoi's works being persecuted as if they were revolutionary proclamations,' at Aksakov being exiled for speaking the truth, at the 'thousands of insane young people banished without trial to the limits of the earth;' he found the government 'dazed' and masses 'engulfed in their selfish interests.' His hair 'rose on end at the pitiless, cruel, inhuman way youths were sometimes treated for their mistakes,' and at one point he even expressed distrust of Alexander III and was favourable to the meeting of a *Zemsky sobor*, an assembly of Russian people. Here is the passage:

> For our dear and sorrowful country a very dark period has begun. All feel a vague restlessness and dissatisfaction; all walk there as on a volcano about to erupt; all feel that the situation is not firm and that unpredictable changes are bound to come. Oh! if only the Russian throne were occupied now by an intelligent and strong-willed Tsar, with definite aims, with clearly drawn plans! Alas! We are governed by a good, *simpatichny* man, poorly endowed with intelligence, badly educated, in one word incapable of taking in his weak hands the shaky mechanism of the State. As a matter of fact there is no real government over us at the present time.
>
> ... In my opinion since we have no exceptional men, this is the time or never, to look for indications and assistance in the people. Holding a meeting with all of us and asking for our help would be the only way to rejuvenate and reinforce authority. A *Zemsky sobor*, I think, is what the Russian land needs now. The Tsar may learn the truth from us; we can help him to eradicate rebellion and decide together what is necessary for Russia to be strong and happy.
>
> It is quite probable that I am a very poor politician. Maybe what I say is very naïve and unfounded, but only, when I happen to think about everything which is taking place in our country, I cannot find any other solutions and it is inconceivable for me how such a thought does not occur to those on whom our fate depends. Katkov* who calls all parliaments 'prattlements' and hates so much words like *popular representation* and *constitution* is wrong, I believe, to confuse the idea of a *Zemsky sobor*, which used to meet even in old times when the Tsar needed advice, with European chambers, parliaments etc. It may happen that precisely the *Zemsky sobor* would reject a constitution in the European sense; it is not a question of our immediately getting responsible ministers and all the procedure of British institutions, but of uncovering truth, of bestowing the people's confidence on the government and on showing it in what direction it ought to lead us.

It would seem that these outbursts of liberalism could have sufficed. But the specialists did not think so. If we read Tchaikovsky's biographies,[19] we cannot escape the usual melodramatic rubbish about poor nineteenth-century Russia, who finally begins to resemble the dead lion of the fable: no passing donkey can refrain from kicking it in the ribs. This is not only annoying, it

* A journalist.

verges on the dishonest, and often verges on it from the wrong side. At best we are told that "the composer took no very strong political views"[20] and that 'he did not care very much one way or the other'[21] whereas we have already seen that he did care and shall soon see that his views were very strong indeed. He was probably opposed to serfdom and even 'went to church on purpose to see what impression the reading of the Emancipation Manifesto would make on the peasants,' but it is already a little unfair to describe him as feeling that 'the manifesto promised a new era' and especially as the son of a serf-owner knowing 'the evils of serfdom as an institution'[22] when all we know about it is that he found the Emancipator's* personality 'decidedly unpleasant' although he recognized in him 'a good Tsar.' It is worse to truncate quotations in order to change their meaning and to comment upon them to rub it in. After an attempt on the Tsar's life, Tchaikovsky wrote: "I think the Tsar would do well to assemble representatives throughout all Russia, and take counsel with them *how to prevent the recurrence of such terrible actions on the part of mad revolutionaries.*† So long as all of us—the Russian citizens—are not called to take part in the government of the country, there is no hope of a better future." Only the second sentence is reproduced by two biographers, and one of them[23] adds that Tchaikovsky 'did not lack courage' which suggests that there was rebellious meaning in what he said. But the worst is yet to come. We present here, for curiosity's sake, an incident as told by the composer and then as retold by one of his faithful Boswells.

Tchaikovsky: "Brothers! Forgive me for not having written before. The journey was safely accomplished. The news of the attempt upon the Emperor's life‡ reached us at the station where we stopped for tea, but only in a very vague form. We pictured to ourselves that he was actually dead and one lady wept bitterly, while another began to extol all the virtues of the new sovereign. Only at Moscow I learnt the true account. The rejoicings here were beyond belief; yesterday at the Opera, where I went to hear A Life for the Tsar, when the Poles appeared on the stage the entire public began to shout, 'Down with the Poles!' In the last scene of the fourth act, in which the Poles put Susanin to death, the singer who was taking this part resisted with such realistic violence that he knocked down several of the 'Polish'

* Alexander II.
† The italics are mine.
‡ Karakozov's unsuccessful attempt upon Alexander II, 4th (16th) April 1866.

chorus-singers. When the rest of the 'Poles' saw that this outrage to art and to the truth delighted the public, they promptly fell down of their own accord, and the triumphant Susanin walked away, shaking his fists at them, amid the vociferous applause of the Muscovites. At the end of the opera the Emperor's portrait was brought on the stage, and an indescribable tumult followed."

The biographer: "The following day Peter Ilich went to the Bolshoi Theatre to hear a performance of *A Life for the Tsar*, in which Poles play a villainous role. He immersed himself in a copy of the score as the opera unrolled and utterly failed to hear or see the audience's unrest, which was turning the performance into an anti-Polish demonstration. Even when his neighbours began to mutter against him, disliking this silent man interested in the music and not in shouting against Poland, he kept his mind and eyes on the score. Finally his ejection from the theatre was angrily and vociferously demanded. He looked up, found himself the centre of unfriendly attention, did not know why, and rushed from the theatre as the Tsar's portrait was being brought onto the stage."[24]

The truth is that Tchaikovsky was a man of good sense and humane feelings, and that he firmly believed that a strong traditional method of government was the best for Russia. Not only did he declare that 'the spirit of Pobedonostsev is better than the spirit of Suvorov;'* not only did he criticize contemporary judges for seeking popularity through excessive liberalism; not only did he rejoice at an explosion of monarchist feelings among the common people, express sympathy "for our poor good Emperor, so sincerely concerned for the country's welfare, yet meeting such mortal disappointments and anxieties," look for treason in the Tsar's entourage—"Whose fault is it? Is there no strength or loyalty left among those whose duty it is to guard our Emperor"?, but, more than that, he took the care of expressing his opinions very clearly, and even, having between 1882 and 1885 changed his mind, of stating very firmly his trust in Alexander III's qualities as a statesman. He wrote to Mrs von Meck:

It seems to me you think too gloomily, too despairingly, of Russia. Undoubtedly there is much to be wished for here, and all kinds of deceit and disorder do still exist. But where will you find perfection? Can you point out any country in Europe where everyone is perfectly contented? There was a time when I was convinced that for the abolishment of autocracy and the introduction of law and

* Two administrators, the first a conservative, the second an extreme liberal, not to be confused with the eighteenth-century general.

order, political institutions, such as parliaments, chambers of deputies, etc., were indispensable, and that it was only necessary to introduce these reforms with great caution, then all would turn out well, and everyone would be quite happy. But now, although I have not yet gone over to the camp of the ultra-conservatives, I am very doubtful as to the actual utility of these reforms. When I observe what goes on in other countries, I see everywhere discontent, party conflict and hatred; everywhere—in a greater or less degree—the same disorder and tyranny prevails. Therefore I am driven to the conclusion that there is no ideal government, and, until the end of the world, men will have to endure in patience many disappointments with regard to these things. From time to time great men—benefactors of mankind—appear, who rule justly and care more for the common welfare than for their own. But these are very exceptional. Therefore I am firmly convinced that the welfare of the great majority is not dependent upon *principles* and *theories*, but upon those individuals who, by the accident of their birth, or for some other reason, stand at the head of affairs. In a word, mankind serves man, not a personified principle. Now arises the question: Have we a *man* upon whom we can stake our hopes? I answer, Yes, and this man is the Emperor. His personality fascinates me; but, apart from personal impressions, I am inclined to think that the Emperor is a good man. I am pleased with the caution with which he introduces the new and does away with the old order. It pleases me, too, that he does not seek popularity; and I take pleasure also in his blameless life, and in the fact that he is an honourable and good man.

Tchaikovsky made no mystery either of his opinion about revolutionaries of all kinds. About terrorists: "I nearly went mad from anger and rage at the news of yet another attempt against our sovereign's life. One wonders as much at the insolence and strength of this loathsome gang of bandits as at the resourcelessness shown by the police whose duty it is to protect and defend the Tsar." About nihilists:

I have just read the pamphlet you sent me (*La Vérité aux nihilistes*)* with great satisfaction, because it is written with warmth, and is full of sympathy for Russia and the Russians. I must observe that it is of no avail as an argument against Nihilism. The author speaks a language which the Nihilists cannot understand, since no moral persuasion could change a tiger into a lamb, or induce a New Zealand cannibal to love his neighbour in a true Christian spirit. A Nihilist, after reading the pamphlet, would probably say: 'Dear sir, we know already from innumerable newspapers, pamphlets, and books, all you tell us as to the uselessness of our murders and

* Telling the truth to Nihilists.

dynamite explosions. We are also aware that Louis XVI was a good king, and Alexander II a good Tsar, who emancipated the serfs. Nevertheless we shall remain assassins and dynamiters, because it is our vocation to murder and blow up, with the object of destroying the present order of things.'

Have you read the last volume of Taine's work upon the Revolution? No one has so admirably characterized the unreasoning crowd of anarchists and extreme revolutionists as he has done. Much of what he says respecting the French in 1793, of the degraded band of anarchists who perpetrated the most unheard-of crimes before the eyes of the nation, which was paralysed with astonishment. applies equally to the Nihilists. . . . The attempt to convince the Nihilists is useless. They must be exterminated; there is no other remedy against this evil.

About socialists: "I have read the proclamation which you mention. Nothing more revolting and cynical could be imagined. And how such revolutionary manifestations must delay those reforms with which sooner or later the sovereign would doubtless have crowned his career! What a strong reaction they motivate! That the socialists should speak for all Russia is foolish and insolent, but not less disgusting are their lies: they seem to extend their hands to moderate liberals of all shades by saying that they will leave the Tsar in peace if he organizes a Parliament. But they do not really want that: they go much further, they would like a socialist republic and even anarchy. But nobody will swallow their bait, and if, in some remote future, a representative form of government is installed in Russia, the first job of the *Zemskaia Duma** will be to eradicate the repugnant handful of killers who imagine that Russia is following them. These gentlemen do not understand that we all hate them as much (and maybe more) as does the sovereign, in whose person they insult all the Russian people. . . . One has to rejoice when the government is forced to take hard measures." About communism: "It is impossible to find any utopia more absurd, anything more in contradiction with the natural tendencies of man. And how boring and intolerably colourless life will probably become when and if equality of property is established. Life is a struggle, and if there were no struggle there would be no life, just a senseless vegetation."

Concerning Tchaikovsky's personal relationship to the Imperial Family, all or nearly all we generally gather from his biographies is that once, after having seen the dress rehearsal of *The Sleeping Beauty*, Alexander III commented "Very charming!", and that

* National Parliament.

Tchaikovsky noted in his diary "His Majesty treated me in a most offhand manner. God be with him." This of course is perfectly true, but, to say the least, incomplete.

The first personal service Tchaikovsky rendered to Alexander III was when he was not yet Alexander III, but the Tsarevitch, and about to marry a Danish Princess. In honour of this occasion Tchaikovsky composed his Festival Overture on the Danish National Anthem, which he dedicated to the Tsarevitch; he received in return a pair of jewelled cuff-links, which he immediately sold, being as usual in dire straits. This was in 1866. In 1881 he secretly asked from the new Tsar a grant of 3,000 roubles which he received a few days later. In 1883, Tchaikovsky composed a Coronation March and a Coronation Cantata. "I confess," he said "that I was both flattered and pleased to participate in these solemnities. . . . I feel much sympathy and love for the sovereign, especially as I know from good sources that he likes my music." For this Cantata Tchaikovsky must have had a particular affection since he chose to conduct it for his first American concert. To thank him for the music, the Tsar granted him 1,500 roubles. When Tchaikovsky discovered that the imperial gift was in form of a diamond ring and not in cash, he was cruelly disappointed. At the same time, he did not really wish to lose such a sign of the sovereign's favour. Finally, after pawning and redeeming it, he sold it to Mrs von Meck. In 1884, on learning that Alexander III had ordered *Eugene Onegin* to be produced as it was his favourite opera, Tchaikovsky decided to travel to St Petersburg, in order not to seem ungrateful. After receiving the Cross of St Vladimir, Tchaikovsky was finally presented to the reigning couple. "I will give you a brief account of what took place. Last Saturday I was taken with a severe chill. By morning I felt better, but I was terribly nervous at the idea of being presented to the Emperor and Empress. On Monday, at ten o'clock I went to Gatchina. I had only permission to appear before His Majesty, but Prince Vladimir Obolensky had also arranged an audience with the Empress, who had frequently expressed a wish to see me. I was first presented to the Emperor and then to the Empress. Both were most friendly and kind. I think it is only necessary to look once into the Emperor's eyes, in order to remain for ever his most loyal adherent, for it is difficult to express in words all the charm and sympathy of his manner. She is also bewitching. Afterwards I had to visit the Grand Duke Konstantin Nikolaevich, and yesterday I sat with him in the Imperial box during the whole of the rehearsal at the Conservatoire." And Modest comments: "He came home tired but happy."

In 1885 Tchaikovsky was invited to the Tsar's box during a production of *Eugene Onegin*, and received permission to write an opera on Pushkin's *Captain's Daughter*, which was also a sign of favour, since the subject was somewhat touchy from a political point of view.* "We had a long and friendly conversation, in the course of which he asked all about my life and musical work, and then took me to the Empress, who paid me the most touching attention." In 1886, Tchaikovsky dedicated twelve songs to the Empress.† The same year he became very friendly with Grand Duke Konstantin Konstantinovich: "In the higher spheres, besides the Emperor and the Empress who treat me with favour, I have a special, particular patron in the person of Grand Duke Konstantin Konstantinovich. During my stay in St Petersburg, I saw him and went to his house rather often. He has extraordinary charm. He is a good poet and recently, he has published a book of verse, signed K.R., which had great success and which all newspapers and magazines praised very highly. He is also interested in music and has written several quite charming songs. His wife is a very *simpatichny* young woman, remarkable, among other things, for having learned to speak and read Russian quite fluently in two years. In spite of all my timidity, particularly with people from higher spheres, I felt perfectly at ease among these *simpatichny* princes, and found real pleasure in their conversation." In 1887, Tchaikovsky dedicated six songs to his patron and received an autographed picture of the Empress "in a beautiful frame. This attention has touched me deeply, especially at a time when she and the Emperor have so many other things to think about." In 1888, Tchaikovsky was granted a pension of 3,000 roubles a year: "I am not so much pleased as deeply touched. It is indeed impossible not to feel gratitude for the Tsar, who takes into consideration not only military and administrative activities, but art as well." The same year Tchaikovsky saw the Tsar again and was disappointed because the sovereign was in a hurry and did not listen to the composer's account of pro-Russian manifestations in Prague, of which he had been the witness and the object. In 1889, four years before his death, Tchaikovsky envisaged blending his musical and loyal feelings in one great work. To Grand Duke Konstantinovich he wrote: "The news that the Emperor has deigned to inquire after

* The project did not materialize.
† It is of course a pure coincidence that in the catalogue of Tchaikovsky's works published by Lawrence and Elisabeth Hanson, all dedications of song albums are clearly indicated with only two exceptions: the Empress and the Grand Duke (Hanson, p. 368).

me gives me great pleasure. How am I to understand the Emperor's question about little pieces? If it is an indirect incitement to compose something in this style, I will take the first opportunity of doing so. I should immensely like to compose a great symphony, which should be, as it were, the crown of my creative work, and dedicate it to the Tsar. I have long since had a vague plan of such a work in my mind, but many favourable circumstances must combine before I can realize my idea. I hope I shall not die before I have carried out this project." But his hope did not come true. He died before leaving a dedication which might have proved embarrassing in our times.

10 I am Russian, Russian, Russian

Tchaikovsky's loyalty toward the Romanovs was second only to his deeper and even more passionate loyalty toward his native land.

> *Terre! apresent tu est loin de moi*
> *Je ne te voi plus, o patrie chérie!*
> *Je t'embrasse. O! pays adorée*
> *Toi, oh Russie aimé*
> *Vien! vien! aupre de moi*
> *Toi, place où je suis né*
> *Je te salut! oh, terre chérie*
> *Longtemps quand je suis né*
> *Je n'avais ni memoire, ni raison*
> *Ni de dons pour parler*
> *Oh, je ne savais pas que ma Patrie est Russie*

Country! Now you are far from me
I do not see you any more, dear fatherland!
I kiss you. O! adored land
You, oh beloved Russia
Come! Come near me
You, place where I was born
I greet you! oh, dear country
A long time ago, when I was born
I had neither memory nor reason
Nor gift of speech
Oh, I did not know that my Fatherland was Russia.

Manuscript of the Fifth Symphony

The composer's drawing-room at Klin—his father's portrait dominates the wall; (*below*) Tchaikovsky's death mask

So he wrote when he was a boy, and it is not the least strange aspect of Russian civilization that such poems to Russia were written in French by seven-year-old Russian children. His feelings never weakened, and he was certainly right when, defending himself against the Mighty Handful who accused him of being a Westerner, he exclaimed: "I am Russian, Russian, Russian!" His music is full of Russian themes; and if he did not feel the need to emphasize them by adopting folklore mannerisms, it proves only that he was Russian on the deepest level. He was passionately attached to everything Russian, and, apart from many charming descriptions of landscapes, which show a truly sensual love of his country, he often expressed his total endorsement of whatever his country stood for:

I am, and shall ever be, faithful to my Russia. Do you know, I have never yet come across anyone so much in love with Mother Russia—especially Great Russia—as myself? The verses by Lermontov which you sent me only depict one side of our native land: that indefinable charm which lies in our modest, plain, poor, but wide and open landscape. I go further. I am passionately devoted to the Russian people, to the language, to the Russian spirit, to the fine Russian type of countenance and to Russian customs. Lermontov says frankly: 'the sacred traditions of our past' do not move his soul. I love these traditions. I believe my sympathy for the Orthodox faith, the tenets of which have long been undermined in me by destructive criticism, has its source in my innate affection for its national element. I could not say what particular virtue or quality it is which endears Russia and the Russians to me. No doubt such qualities exist. A lover, however, does not love for such reasons, but because he cannot help himself.

This is why I feel so angry with those among us who are ready to perish of hunger in a garret in Paris and who seem to enjoy running down everything Russian; who can spend their whole lives abroad without regret, on the grounds that there are fewer comforts to be had in Russia. I hate these people; they trample in the mud all that to me is inexpressibly precious and sacred.

Although he often lived abroad himself in order to be less bothered by acquaintances, he could never get over his homesickness. Either he was "weeping every day," or he was 'looking forward with fearful excitement and impatience to the blessed day when he would return to his adored Mother Russia,' or he declared that he 'could not do without Russia for any length of time;' on the road to America he nearly 'turned round and ran back home.' True, he was rewarded for his courage, since in the United States he met a few Russians; the first one was a lady and Tchaikovsky made a scene: "This was the first time I had had the pleasure of talking to a Russian lady; consequently I made a fool of myself. Suddenly the tears came into my eyes, my voice broke, and I could not suppress my sobs. I fled into the next room, and could not show myself again for a long time. I blush with shame to think of this unexpected episode. . . ."

The composer was very sensitive to Russia's reputation abroad, which was not especially good, and he insisted on upholding his country's dignity on all occasions. "No doubt I should do much towards making my works known abroad if I went the round of the influential people, paying visits and compliments. But, Lord, how I hate that kind of thing! If you could only hear the offensively patronizing tone in which they speak of Russian music! One reads in their faces: 'Although you are a Russian, my condescension is such that I honour you with my attention.' God be with them! Last year I met Liszt. He was sickeningly polite, but all the while there was a smile on his lips which expressed the above words pretty plainly."

When Mrs von Meck suggested a French title-page for *The Maid of Orleans*, Tchaikovsky took exception to the idea: "Such advances to foreign nations are repugnant to me. Do not let us go to them, let them come to us. If they want our operas—then not the title-page only but the full text can be translated. . . . So long as an opera has not crossed the Russian frontier, it is not necessary—to my mind—that it should be translated into the language of those who take no interest in it."

Interest for Russia, if it existed, had to be of good quality: if not, Tchaikovsky was annoyed. "Yesterday I was at the 'Folies Bergère,' and it bored me terribly. The Russian clown Durov brings on 250 dressed-up rats. It is most curious in what forms the Parisians display their Russophile propensities. Neither at the Opera, nor at any of the more serious theatres, is anything Russian performed, and while *we* are giving *Esclarmonde*,* *they* show their goodwill towards Russian art by the medium of Durov and his rats! Truly, it enrages me—I say it frankly—partly on account of my own interests."

On the other hand, any sign of true sympathy for Russia moved him deeply. On reading Sarcey's† article about Tolstoi, he "could hardly keep from sobbing . . . out of happiness that our Tolstoi is understood so well by the French," and the triumphant reception

---

* An opera by Massenet.
† A French critic.

which he got in Prague in 1888 he attributed more to Russia's popularity than to his own. "This day is one of the most significant of my life. I have begun to dearly love these kind Czekhs. They deserve it! ! ! Lord! How much enthusiasm there was, and all that not for me at all but for my darling Russia. . . ." "I did not suspect how devoted the Czekhs are to Russia and how they hate the Germans."

The war against Turkey exacerbated the composer's nationalism. The prospective declaration he had found 'frightening,' but at the same time he was glad to see that 'our beloved fatherland is finally reaching the decision to sustain its dignity.' He himself had many troubles at the time, but "do you know what gave me heart and encouraged me to master my evil fate? It is the thought that at this time, when the future of the whole counry is at stake, when every day numerous families lose their fathers and fall into destitution, it is unseemly to get immersed into one's own private little affairs. It is unseemly to shed tears about oneself when the country sheds torrents of blood for the common cause." And later: "It seems to me that now I am no longer absorbed in my personal troubles, I feel far more keenly all the wounds inflicted upon our Fatherland, although I have no doubt that in the end Russia — indeed, the whole Slavonic world—will triumph, if only because we have truth and honour on our side." True, Tchaikovsky never thought of joining the Army, but at least he wrote a military march and refused payment for it: "I too am a patriot," he said.

As usual, the composer's feelings had their humorous side: here is how he won a victory for the Russian troops.

Do you know what enrages me in Venice?—The vendors of the evening papers. If I go for a walk across the Piazza di San Marco I hear on every side, 'Il Tempo! La Gazzetta di Venezia! Vittoria dei Turchi!' This 'Vittoria dei Turchi!' is shouted every evening. Why do they never cry one of our actual victories? Why do they try to attract customers by fictitious Turkish successes? Can it be that peaceful, beautiful Venice, who once lost her strength in fighting these same Turks, is as full of hatred for Russia as all the rest of Western Europe?

Beside myself with indignation, I asked one of them, 'Ma dovè la vittoria?' It turned out that a Turkish victory was really a reconnonaissance, in which the Russians had had about one hundred casualties. 'Is that a victory?' I asked him angrily. I could not understand his reply, but he cried no more 'victories.' One must acknowledge the amiability, politeness, and obligingness of the Italians. These qualities of theirs strike one very forcibly when one comes direct from Switzerland, where the people are gloomy, unfriendly, and disinclined for a joke. Today, when I met the same vendor of papers, he greeted me civilly, and instead of calling out, 'Grande vittoria dei Turchi'—with which words the others were recommending their wares—he began to cry, 'Gran combattimento a Plevna, vittoria dei Russi!' I knew he lied, but it pleased me all the same, since it expressed the innate courtesy of a poor man.*

Pure patriotism, without any element of xenophobia in it, is a very rare thing, and Tchaikovsky did not rise quite so high. His love for Russia was exclusive, and other nations found no grace with him. This was already true of him as a child, according to Fanny Dürbach. "Once, during the recreation hour, he was turning over the pages of his atlas. Coming to the map of Europe, he smothered Russia with kisses and spat on all the rest of the world. When I told him he ought to be ashamed of such behaviour, that it was wicked to hate his fellow-men who said the same 'Our Father' as himself, only because they were not Russians, and reminded him that he was spitting upon his own Fanny, who was a Frenchwoman, he replied at once: 'There is no need to scold me; didn't you see me cover France with my hand first?'"

Later his manners improved but his feelings did not. "I dislike Germans very much, and everything German is distasteful to me, although it is impossible to deny that life here is very cosy and comfortable. . . ." "At heart I am an echter Russe† and this is probably why the German as such is obnoxious, foreign, offensive, repulsive to me. Intellectually I am fair; I am surprised at the order and cleanliness of Berlin, I like the cheapness of things, the accessibility of all pleasures, I admire the cuisine of the St Petersburg Hotel, I find the Museum and the Aquarium excellent, and nevertheless I cannot stand more than two days of German air." The French were not treated better: in Paris "at every approach, in every stranger's kindness one feels an attempt at exploitation." England fared worse. On political grounds, Tchaikovsky felt very strongly about "that shameless nation that has passed the limits of decency." He even exclaimed: "How I hate that awful race!" He was the more surprised to be made welcome in England when he went there to get his honorary degree from Cambridge University: "At Cambridge I stayed with Professor Maitland. This would have been dreadfully embarrassing for me, if he and his wife had not proved to be some of the most charming people I ever

* As a matter of fact, Tchaikovsky overestimated his man: Plevna was indeed one of the main Russian victories.
† A real Russian.

met; and Russophiles into the bargain, which is the greatest rarity
in England." For the Jewish community Tchaikovsky had little
sympathy and even disliked Kamenka partly because of its numerous Jewish population. Hiding the fact, as has been* the fashion
so far, amounts to taking him for a racist, which he was not: his
intimacy with Rubinstein is there to prove it. The only nation
which Tchaikovsky liked, although he strongly objected to its
cuisine, was the United States of America. "Amazing people,
these Americans. . . ! The frankness, sincerity and generosity of
this city, its hospitality without hidden motives and its eagerness
to oblige and win approval are simply astonishing and, at the same
time, touching. This, and indeed American customs, American
manners and habits generally are very attractive to me." In his
praise the composer went even one step further and bestowed
on Americans the highest possible compliment: he compared them
to Russians. "One must give credit to American hospitality," he
wrote "only in our own country would one encounter anything
like it."

Among capitals, he liked New York,† he loved Paris, he adored
Vienna, but he disliked London where 'he could not find anything.'

All that, of course, is not very serious. His loathings and his
hatings were only the expression of homesickness. One might say
though that anything not Russian was somehow not entirely real
for him. Italy is characteristic: he lived there for months in a row,
but we find few impressions of Italian life in his letters although
he spoke the language, and still less traces of Italian influences in
his music, although he frequently went to the opera and to concerts. The *Capriccio Italiano* and *Pimpinella* are there to show his
curiosity for Italian themes, but that is all. The most foreign characters in his operas as Joan of Arc or Iolanthe, sing melodies which
could not have been born anywhere West of the Niemen. It is interesting to note, especially in our time of world-citizenship, that
Tchaikovsky's national heritage and his musical genius were inseparable in his mind as indeed they are for us who listen to his
works. Besides weaving all his music from typically Russian
material, he was constantly concerned‡ with 'the honour he could
and should bring to his native land:' "Let me prove my patriotism
as I prove my soul," he exclaimed, "by the music I write."

* Cf. p. 23.
† Cf. pp. 59–60.
‡ Cf. p. 86

11 *I am learning to love God*

There is yet one Other who remains and whose friendship with Tchaikovsky has to be told. The story unfolded itself during the composer's whole life, and since evolution in these matters is finally what counts, it has to be told in chronological sequence. Other methods necessarily result in incomplete, although not always dishonest, quotations like "I long to believe in a future life—When I can say the longing has become belief, then I shall be happy,"[25] or in sheer nonsense, like blasphemous interpretations of the *Pathétique*,[26] or in oversimplified summaries, like the following: "his general attitude to Christianity—characteristic of a great many educated Russians of his day—may be summed up in three phrases: acceptance of Christian ethics, regretful rejection of the doctrines of the Orthodox Church, artistic (or sentimental) pleasure in the ritual of that Church."[27]

We have seen that Tchaikovsky's childish poems expressed accurately enough the deepest trends of his nature. Here is one more, written when the 'poet' was seven years old:

> *L'ENFANT PARLE À SON ANGE GARDIEN*
> Tez *ailes dorees ont vole chez moi* (?)
> *Ta* voi *m'a* parler
> *O! que j'etais heureuse**
> Quant *tu* venait *chez moi*
> *Tes ailes* son blanc *et* pur *aussi*
> *Viens encore une* foix
> *Pour parler de Dieu puissant!*

> THE CHILD SPEAKS TO HER GUARDIAN ANGEL
> Your golden wings flew to me
> Your voice spoke to me
> Oh! how happy I was
> When you came to me
> Your wings are white and pure also
> Come once again
> To speak of mighty God!

---

* The feminine *heureuse* may indicate that this is another of little Peter's poems about Joan of Arc.

Years went by, and the young boy, who had a beautiful voice, was encouraged to sing in church. He never forgot singing the soprano part in sacred trios in front of the Metropolitan, and thus actively participating in the divine liturgy. "How proud I was then to take part in the service by my singing! How happy I was when the Metropolitan thanked and blessed us for this singing."

More years went by and Tchaikovsky detached himself from the Church, as young people will. He was 30 when he wrote to Anatoly that the guardian of Vladimir Shilovsky 'wanted to convert him at any price.' "He has given me a number of religious books, and I have promised to read them all. In any case I now walk in ways of godliness. In Passion week I fasted with Rubinstein." Obviously the word *convert* indicates some estrangement from Christianity.

The same regretful estrangement seems to have prompted the composer to write, six years later, to Modest:

I have thought a lot about you last night and today. I am very glad that you are religious. In theory I do not agree with you on any point, but if my theories were to shake your faith, I should be angry with you. I am as passionate in my readiness to argue with you concerning questions of faith as in my desire that you should keep your religious beliefs. Religiousness in the form in which I see it in you testifies to the excellent quality of the metal of which you are wrought.

After that comes the marriage, the pseudo attempted suicide, the breakdown, and a more thoughtful attitude towards life and death. In 1877, Tchaikovsky writes:

Thinking over all that has happened to me, I have several times wondered about a Providence taking care of me among others. Not only did I not perish when it seemed that there was no other way out, but I am all right now, and in the future success and happiness seem to dawn. I must tell you that concerning religion my nature has become double and I still have found no conciliation. On one hand, my reason obstinately refuses to recognize as true the dogmatic aspect of Orthodoxy as well as of all other Christian confessions. For instance, much as I have thought about the dogma of punishment and reward, I never could find any sense in it. How can one separate so sharply the sheep from the goats? Reward for what, and even punish for what? A firm faith in an eternal life is just as difficult to grasp for me. From that standpoint, I am completely captivated by the pantheistic view of life and immortality.

On the other hand, my education, the habits of childhood, the accepted poetic representations concerning Christ and His teaching,—all this causes me to turn to Him with prayers in sorrow and with gratefulness in happiness.

The same year the composer and Mrs von Meck begin to exchange ideas on ethical and metaphysical subjects and Tchaikovsky develops his opinions in two letters which have often been quoted but nearly always incompletely. It seems fairer to present *in extenso* all the passages concerning philosophy and religion.

. . . Now it is evident that theoretically you have separated yourself from the Church and from dogmatic belief. I perceive that after years of thought you have framed for yourself a kind of religio-philosophic catechism. But it strikes me you are mistaken in supposing that parallel with the bulwarks of the old, strong faith which you have overthrown, you have raised new ones, so sure and reliable that you can afford to do away entirely with the old lines of defence. Herein lies precisely the sceptic's tragedy: once he has broken the ties which bind him to traditional belief, he passes from one set of philosophical speculations to another, always imagining he will discover that inexhaustible source of strength, so needful for the battle of life, with which the believer is fully equipped. You may say what you please, but a faith—not that which proceeds from mere deficiency of reasoning power and is simply a matter of routine—but a faith founded on reason and able to reconcile all misconceptions and contradictions arising from intellectual criticism—such a belief is the supreme happiness. A man who has both intellect and faith (and there are many such) is clad, as it were, in a panoply of armour which can resist all the blows of fate. You say you have fallen away from the accepted forms of religion and have made a creed for yourself. But religion is an element of reconciliation. Have you this sense of being reconciled? I think not. For if you had, you would never have written that letter from Como. Do you remember? That yearning, that discontent, that aspiration towards some vague ideal, that isolation from humanity, the confession that only in music—the most ideal of all the arts—could you find any solution of these agitating questions, all proved to me that your self-made religion did not give that absolute peace of mind which is peculiar to those who have found in their faith a ready-made answer to all those doubts which torment a reflective and sensitive nature. And, do you know—it seems to me you only care so much for my music because I am as full of the ideal longing as yourself. Our sufferings are the same. Your doubts are as strong as mine. We are both adrift in that limitless sea of scepticism, seeking a haven and finding none.

Are not these the reasons why my music touches you so closely? I also think you are mistaken in calling yourself a realist. If we define 'realism' as contempt for all that is false and insincere—in life as in art—you are undoubtedly a 'realist.' But when we consider that a true realist would never dream of seeking consolation in music, as you do, it is evident you are far more of an idealist. You are only a realist in the sense that you do not care to waste time over sentimental, trivial, and aimless dreams, like so many women. You do not care for phrases and empty words, but that does not mean you are a realist. Impossible! Realism argues a certain limited outlook, a thirst for truth which is too quickly and easily satisfied. A realist does not actually feel eager to comprehend the essential problems of existence; he even denies the need of seeking truth, and does not believe in those who are searching for reconciliation and religion, philosophy, or art. Art—especially music—counts for nothing with the realist, because it is the answer to a question which his narrow intellect is incapable of posing. For these reasons I think you are wrong in declaring you have enrolled under the banner of realism. You say music only produces in you a pleasant, purely physical, sensation. Against this I distinctly protest. You are deceiving yourself. Do you really only care for music in the same way that I enjoy a bottle of wine or a pickled gherkin? Nay, you love music as it should be loved: that is to say, you give yourself up to it with all your soul and let it exercise its magic spell all unconsciously upon your spirit.

Perhaps it may seem strange that I should doubt your self-knowledge. But, to my mind, you are, first of all, a very good woman, and have been so from your birth up. You honour what is good because the aspiration towards the right, as well as the hatred of lies and evil, is innate in you. You are clever, and consequently sceptical. An intelligent man cannot help being a sceptic; at least he must at some period of his life experience the most agonizing scepticism. When your innate scepticism led you to the negation of tradition and dogma you naturally began to seek some way of escape from your doubts. You found it *partly* in the pantheistic point of view, and *partly* in music; but you discovered no perfect reconciliation with faith. Hating all evil and falsehood, you enclose yourself in your narrow family circle in order to shut out the consciousness of human wickedness. You have done much good, because, like your innate love of nature and art, this doing good is an invincible craving of your soul. You help others, not in order to purchase that eternal happiness which you neither quite believe in nor quite deny, but because you are so made that you cannot help doing good.

. . . My feeling about the Church is quite different to yours. For me it still possesses much poetical charm. I very often attend the services. I consider the liturgy of St John Chrysostom one of the greatest productions of art. If we follow the service very carefully, and enter into the meaning of every ceremony, it is impossible not to be profoundly moved by the liturgy of our own Orthodox Church. I also love vespers. To stand on a Saturday evening in the twilight in some little old country church, filled with the smoke of incense; to lose oneself in the eternal questions, *whence*, *why*, and *whither*; to be startled from one's trance by a burst from the choir; to be carried away by the poetry of this music; to be thrilled with quiet rapture when the Royal Gates of the Iconostasis are flung open and the words ring out, 'Praise the name of the Lord!'—all this is infinitely precious to me! One of my deepest joys!

Thus, from one point of view, I am firmly united to our Church. From other standpoints I have—like yourself—long since lost faith in dogma. The doctrine of retribution, for instance, seems to me monstrous in its injustice and unreason. Like you, I am convinced that if there is a future life at all, it is only conceivable in the sense of the indestructibility of matter, in the pantheistic view of the eternity of nature, of which I am only a microscopic atom. I cannot believe in a personal, individual immortality.

How shall we picture to ourselves eternal life after death? As endless bliss? But such endless joy is inconceivable apart from its opposite—eternal pain. I entirely refuse to believe in the latter. Finally, I am not sure that life beyond death is desirable, for it would lose its charm but for its alternations of joy and sorrow, its struggle between good and evil, darkness and light. How can we contemplate immortality as a state of eternal bliss? According to our earthly conceptions, even bliss itself becomes wearisome if it is never broken or interrupted. So I have come to the conclusion, as the result of much thinking, that there is no future life. But conviction is one thing and feeling and instinct another. This denial of immortality brings me face to face with the terrible thought that I shall never, never, again set eyes upon some of my dear dead. In spite of the strength of my *convictions*, I shall never reconcile myself to the thought that my dear mother, whom I loved so much, actually *is not*; that I shall never have any chance of telling her how, after twenty-three years of separation, she is as dear to me as ever.

You see, my dear friend, I am made up of contradictions, and I have reached a very mature age without resting upon anything positive, without having calmed my restless spirit either by religion or philosophy. Undoubtedly I should have gone mad but for *music*. Music is indeed the most beautiful of all Heaven's gifts to humanity wandering in the darkness. Alone it calms, enlightens, and stills our souls. It is not the straw to which the drowning man clings; but a true friend, refuge, and comforter, for whose sake life is worth living. Perhaps there will be no music in heaven. Well, let us give our mortal life to it as long as it lasts.

These passages can be summarized in an expression of melancholic scepticism. But they are only the starting point of Tchaikovsky's drifting towards a more orthodox form of faith.

In 1878 he composes a liturgy.

In 1879, he thinks about God and expresses dismay at the idea that 'our Russian Lord God' could be the same as the one invoked by 'sordid Roman padres and other foreign preachers.' The Madeleine church in Paris appears to him as the summum of idolatry.

The same year he is impressed by the reading of *The Brothers Karamazov*. "I was deeply shaken, moved into sobbing and hysterics, by the scene where Father Zosima receives suffering people who come to him to be healed. Among them appears a woman who has walked five hundred *versts* to get consolation from him. She has lost all her children. Having buried the last one, she has lost the strength to struggle against her sorrow, she has abandoned her house, her husband, and has become a vagabond pilgrim. The simplicity with which she describes her utter hopelessness, the striking force of the natural phrases by which she expresses her infinite woe at knowing that she will never, never, never see and hear him again, and especially her words 'I would not even come near him, I would not say anything, I would hide in a corner if I only could see him for one minute,' all that rends my heart apart. Yes, my friend. It would be better to die oneself twenty-four times a day for one thousand years than lose those whom we love and look for consolation in the doubtful thought that 'we shall meet in the other world'! Shall we? Happy are those who do not doubt it."

In 1880, Tchaikovsky goes to the Comédie Française and is impressed by a production of Corneille's *Polyeucte*: "The last act . . . in which Felix, conscience-striken and illumined by Christ, suddenly becomes a Christian, touched me profoundly."

In 1881 begins for him this last part of life which comes to every man, when friends of his own generation, those whose death seems intolerable and inexplicable, begin to die. Rubinstein is the first to go, and Tchaikovsky's mood turns toward serious and humble meditations. To Mrs von Meck, a declared atheist, he writes:

It is possible to be a Christian in life and deed without clinging closely to dogma, and I am sure that un-Christian feelings could only dwell in you for a brief moment, as an involuntary protest against human wickedness. Such really good people as you do not know what *hate* means in the true sense of the word. What can be more aimless and unprofitable than hate? According to Christ's words, our enemies only injure us from *ignorance*. O, if only men could be Christians in truth as well as in form! If only everyone was penetrated by the simple truths of Christian morality! That can never be, for then eternal and *perfect* happiness would reign on earth; and we are imperfect creations, who only understand goodness and happiness as the opposites of evil. We are, as it were, specially created to be eternally reverting to evil, to perpetually seek the ideal of aspire to everlasting truth—and never to reach the goal. At least we should be indulgent to those who, in their blindness, are attracted to evil by some inborn instinct. Are they to be blamed because they exist only to bring the chosen people into stronger relief? No, we can only say with Christ, 'Lord, forgive them, they know not what they do.' I feel I am expressing *vague* thoughts *vaguely*—thoughts which are wandering through my mind, because a man who was good and dear to me has just vanished from this earth. But if I think and speak vaguely, I *feel* it all clearly enough. My brain is obscured today. How could it be otherwise in face of those enigmas—*Death, the aim and meaning of life, its finality or immortality?* Therefore, the light of *faith* penetrates my soul more and more. Yes, dear friend, I feel myself increasingly drawn towards this, the one and only shield against every calamity. I am learning to love God, as formerly I did not know how to do. Now and then doubts come back to me; I still strive at times to conceive the inconceivable with my feeble intellect; but the voice of divine truth speaks louder within me. I sometimes find an indiscribable joy in bowing before the Inscrutable, Omniscient God. I often pray to Him with tears in my eyes (where He is, what He is, I know not; but I know He exists), and implore Him to grant me love and peace, to pardon and enlighten me; and it is sweet to say to Him, 'Lord, Thy will be done,' because I know His will is *holy*. Let me also tell you that I see clearly the finger of God in my own life, showing me the way and upholding me in all danger. Why it has been God's will to shield me I cannot say. I wish to be *humble*, and not to regard myself as one of the elect, for God loves all His creatures equally. I only know He really cares for me, and I shed tears of gratitude for His eternal goodness. That is not enough. I want to accustom myself to the thought that all trials are good in the end. I want to love God always, not only when He sends me good, but when He proves me; for somewhere there must exist that kingdom of eternal happiness, which we seek so vainly upon earth. The time will come when all the questionings of our intellects will be answered, and we shall know why God sends us these trials. I want to believe that there is another life. When this desire becomes a fact, I shall be happy, in so far as happiness is possible in this world.

Today I attended the funeral service in the church, and afterwards I accompanied the remains to the Gare du Nord, and saw that the leaden coffin was packed in a wooden case and placed in a luggage van. It was painful and horrible to think that our poor Nikolai Grigorievich should return thus to Moscow. Yes, it was intensely painful. But there are germs of faith in me, and I took comfort from the thought that it was God's *inscrutable* and holy will.

And he concludes this act of humility by the following words: "As to praying God, I shall tell you, my dear, incomparable friend, that it is my greatest happiness and delight to pray God for you and to call his blessings upon you."

The same year he writes an Evening Church Service* and expresses admiration at the fortitude which an old lady derives from her Christian faith. "It was very sad for me to see old A. I. Davydov, the mother of my brother-in-law, the last of the Decembrists' wives who followed their husbands to Siberia.† Last year she already lost one eye; now, having shed too many tears due to the Tsar's death‡ and different family troubles, she has lost the second one. But the strength of her religious feeling is such that she endures this calamity with perfect calm and resignation to God's will."

In 1882 Tchaikovsky's love of nature takes a religious colouring: "All Naples, Vesuvius, Castellammare, Sorrento, lie before us. At sunset yesterday it was so divinely beautiful that I shed tears of gratitude to God." In 1883 he expresses his willingness to submit to God:

In my youth I often felt indignant at the apparent injustice with which Providence dealt out happiness and misfortune to mankind. Gradually I have come to the conviction that from our limited, earthly point of view we cannot possibly comprehend the aims and ends towards which God guides us on our way through life. Our sufferings and deprivations are not sent blindly and fortuitously; they are needful for our good, and although the good may seem very far away, some day we shall realize this. Experience has taught me that suffering and bitterness are frequently for our good, even in this life. But after this life *perhaps* there is another, and—although my intellect cannot conceive what form it may take—my heart and my instinct, which revolt from death in the sense of complete annihilation, compel me to believe in it. Perhaps we may then understand the things which now appear to us harsh and unjust. Meanwhile, we can only pray, and thank God when He sends us happiness, and submit when misfortune overtakes us, or those who are near and dear to us. I thank God who has given me this conviction. Without it life would be a grievous burden. Did I not know that you, the best of human beings, and above all deserving of happiness, were suffering so much, not through an insensate blow aimed by a

* Known in the West as Vesper Mass, although Vigils would be more correct.

† In December 1825 a few aristocrats rebelled against Nicholas I. They were defeated and some of them sentenced to exile in Siberia. Their wives chose to follow them.

‡ Alexander II.

blind destiny, but for some divine end which my limited reason cannot discern—then, indeed, there would remain for me in life nothing but despair and loathing. I have learnt not to murmur against God, but to pray to Him for all who are dear to me.

In 1884 he already considers himself as a believer, and comments upon Tolstoi's *Confessions* from a believer's point of view: "They made a profound impression upon me, because I, too, know the torments of doubt and the tragic perplexity which Tolstoi has experienced and described so wonderfully in the *Confessions*. But *enlightenment* came to me earlier than Tolstoi; perhaps because my brain is more simply organized than his; and perhaps it has been due to the continual necessity of work that I have suffered less than Tolstoi. Every day, every hour, I thank God for having given me this faith in Him. What would have become of me, with my cowardice, my capacity for depression, and—at the least failure of courage—my desire for *non-existence*, unless I had been able to believe in God and submit to His will?"
The same year he expresses persisting doubts.

I do not wish to die and even should like to reach deep old age, but I should refuse to become young once again and live my whole life from the beginning. Once is enough. Of course . . . one regrets the past, and nobody likes to immerse himself in memories more than I do; nobody feels the vanity and flight of life more than I, and nevertheless I do not want to be young. To each age its charm and pleasant sides. The question is not to be eternally young, but to suffer as little as possible physically and morally. I do not know what kind of an old man I shall be, but, for the time being, I cannot be blind to the fact that the amount of good things of which I take advantage now is much superior to the one which was at my disposal when I was young. Therefore I see no point in fretting because I am forty-four; it could even be seventy or eighty: what does it matter so long as body and mind are sound. Also one should not be afraid of death. From that standpoint I cannot brag. I am not so impregnated with religion as to consider death as the certain beginning of a new life and I am not enough of a philosopher to resign myself to the abyss of non-being in which I might have to dive. There is no one whom I envy so much as perfectly religious people.

Religion preoccupies him more and more. He attends the liturgy and feels "very perceptive to religious impressions; nearly all the time I stood with tears in my eyes." He discusses religious themes with Balakirev and is "deeply moved." In 1886 he re-reads the Bible and is shocked, as many Orthodox believers, by the contrast between the two Testaments: "What an unfathomable gulf lies between the Old and the New Testament! Read the psalms of David, and at first it is impossible to understand why they have taken such a high place from an artistic point of view; and, secondly, why they should stand beside the Gospels. David is altogether *of this* world. He divides the whole of humanity into two unequal portions: sinners (to which belong the greatest number) and the righteous, at whose head he places himself. In every psalm he calls down God's wrath upon the sinner and His praise upon the righteous; yet the reward and the punishment are both worldly. The sinners shall be undone, and the righteous shall enjoy all the good things of this earthly life. How little that agrees with Christ's teaching, who prayed for His enemies, and promised the good no earthly wealth, but rather the kingdom of heaven! What touching love and compassion for mankind lies in these words: 'Come unto Me, all ye that labour and are heavy laden'! In comparison with these simple words all the psalms of David are as nothing."

Philosophic questioning becomes a habit with him. His friend Kondratiev makes him angry and he exclaims: "What a riddle that man is! Good and evil alike give him pleasure." He goes to Moscow and, on entering the Uspensky Cathedral, he hears his own liturgy performed: he is overjoyed. To Mrs Shpajinsky, a friend in trouble, he writes: "You are in a situation where religion could greatly relieve your sorrows. I do not know if you are religious. I hope you are." He finishes the rough sketches of his opera *The Sorceress* and 'thanks God for this kindness.'

In 1887 he is impressed by the spiritual help which Kondratiev has received from Father John of Kronstadt.* He goes to a Catholic church and dislikes the service: "Ours is so much better." And finally he is amazed at his own evolution during the past year: "How short is life! How much I have still to do, to think, and to say! We keep putting things off, and meanwhile death lurks round the corner. It is just a year since I touched this book, and so much has changed since then. How strange! Just 365 days ago I was afraid to confess that, in spite of the glow of sympathetic feeling which Christ awoke in me, I dared to doubt His divinity. Since then my *religion* has become more clearly defined, for during this time I have thought a great deal about God, life, and death. In Aachen especially I meditated on the fatal questions: why, how, for what end? I should like to define my religion in detail, if only I might be quite clear, once for all, as to my faith,

* Now canonized by the Russian Orthodox Church.

and as to the boundary which divides it from speculation. But life and its vanities are passing, and I do not know whether I shall succeed in expressing the *symbol* of that faith which has arisen in me of late. It has very definite forms, but I do not use them when I pray. I pray just as before; as I was taught. Moreover, God can hardly require to know how and why we pray. God has no need of prayers. *But we have.*"

These words would have been suitable to conclude a spiritual ripening which had taken nearly half a century to reach this point. But Tchaikovsky found better. The last mention of God that we were able to find in his diary or correspondence comes after the completion of *The Queen of Spades*. It has a slightly prophetic ring: "*Finished everything* . . . I thank God that He has given me the strength."

NOTES TO PART III

1   Weinstock.
2   Hanson.
3   Hanson.
4   Hanson.
5   Modest. Cf. also Michel Hofmann.
6   Bowen.
7   Modest.
8   Hanson.
9   Hanson.
10 E. Lockspeiser in G. Abraham.
11 Hanson.
12 Hanson.
13 Weinstock. Cf. also Michel Hofmann.
14 Weinstock.
15 E. Lockspeiser in G. Abraham.
16 Hanson.
17 E. Lockspeiser in G. Abraham.
18 Cf. in particular Hanson, Michel Hofmann.
19 Especially Weinstock and Hanson.
20 Modest.
21 Hanson.
22 Weinstock.
23 Weinstock and Hanson: Hanson.
24 Weinstock.
25 Quoted by Bowen.
26 Michel Hofmann.
27 G. Abraham.

PART FOUR

TCHAIKOVSKY AND HIS SECRETS

M

1 Driving the fair sex into hysterics

It is idle but not uninteresting to wonder what Tchaikovsky would have thought of his biographers in general and of us in particular. He would probably have hated the lot, since any prying into his private life, any discussion of his personality, was loathsome to him. But history has to be written, and truth is better than untruth. So we shall proceed.

Tchaikovsky's secrets were and still are well-guarded. He himself destroyed most of his diaries. Modest may have tampered with a few others. Many letters addressed to brothers, friends, etc., never reached a publisher. And now the Tchaikovsky Archives, under strict orders from whoever is in charge, have deliberately adopted a secretive course. The thick layer of publicity, pseudo-history, pseudo-psychology, misunderstandings, misleading prejudices and interpretations which covers whatever information is available does not help matters. It is impossible to go back to the original sources since, in many cases, there are no sources; and yet it is necessary to reconstruct an image of Tchaikovsky which would have at least some resemblance to the real man.

It is now common knowledge—we should say: common surmise —that Tchaikovsky was a homosexual. One could be content with that. After all, his private life was his own business. But the fact is that nothing that we know about the man corresponds to the usual representation of a homosexual. There may be some naïveté in imagining that all homosexuals are alike. Of course they are not. But they have certain common denominators which are generally easy to recognize and we fail to find any of those in Tchaikovsky. What that means we do not know. Anyway conjectures and even deductions are out of our scope: we are trying to present a self-portrait and prefer to leave it unfinished rather than brush in any part ourself.

We know nothing or next to nothing about Tchaikovsky's alleged men lovers. We know nothing about any mistresses that he may have had. It is better to confess it now than to hint at some obscure knowledge hidden in the magician's hat, but which, for some reason, will never out. It is better also to state at the outset that we are not going to prove that Tchaikovsky was homosexual or heterosexual or both or neither. We shall try and present facts. So much the better if they are contradictory. Where unproved suppositions have been assumed to be true, where downright fallacies have been developed, we shall expose them. But we shall reach no conclusion and are conceited enough to see cause for pride in such deliberate restraint.

The question that is now hovering in the reader's mind was once asked from Tchaikovsky himself in as many words. He was 38 and Mrs von Meck wrote to inquire if he had ever known non-platonic love. This question coming from a mother of twelve, who was herself 47 at the time and addressed to a man who had just bungled his marriage, must have seemed unexpected to the composer; to us it seems absurd. But if we insist on judging nineteenth-century Russia by twentieth-century Western standards we are condemning ourselves to numberless misapprehensions. We would do better to keep an open mind. Did Mrs von Meck really mean what she wrote? Could she have been so naïve as that? Probably not. She was just phrasing her question modestly. What she must have meant is: "Tell me something about your love life." But the phrasing itself is indicative: that the woman she was could have expressed herself in such terms tells us a lot about the style in which it was customary to refer to such matters. And Tchaikovsky was not taken aback by the question. He answered it primly, truthfully and vaguely: "Yes and no," he wrote. "If you had phrased your question differently, if you had asked me whether I had ever discovered complete happiness in love, I should have answered no, and no again. Besides, it seems to me that the reply to that question is to be heard in my music. If, however, you ask me whether I have ever experienced the entire power and inexpressible tension of love, I must answer yes, yes, yes. For time and again I have laboured to render in music all the anguish and ecstasy of love." Which means, transposed into our crude modern vocabulary: "I am no virgin, but I do not intend to discuss my love affairs with you. Whatever I want to say I say in my music. Will you please listen to it.' Mrs von Meck, by the way, must have anticipated such an answer, since her question was followed by a comment which we cannot help finding far-fetched, but which may very well be a penetrating summary of the truth: "Peter Ilitch, have you ever loved? I think not. *You love music too much to love a woman.*" (Or a man, she could have added if she had suspected Tchaikovsky of a singularity of this kind.)

References to love affairs are not very frequent in what remains of Tchaikovsky's diaries or in what is available of his correspondence. In 1861, he writes to Sasha: "In love no luck." We think that it would have taken a greater cynic than he was to mention homosexual affairs, even unlucky, to his sister. In 1866 he is "very much taken" with a young lady whom he would like to call by her diminutive, Mufka, but cannot find the courage to do so. In 1878 he has a date, 'of which he gets rid not without trouble' in order to go and listen to a street singer. In 1879 he explains to Modest that "being in love consists of the fact that nothing beautiful exists in all the world except She": hesitating between three girls means that you do not love any of them: "to me it happened scores of times." On 4th June 1884, Tchaikovsky "dreamt about M. and as a result of it was in love a little, even more than a little, all day. . . . It's nothing, nothing. . . . Silence. . . . ! ! !" What sex was M. we do not know. In 1886, the composer was 'completely in love' with a princess Mania. As far as fleeting mentions of love are concerned, that is nearly all. But that love was an important preoccupation of his is clear, although it is typical that he did not reserve the term, as we tend to do now, for the sexual variety of that passion. He wrote to Stasov, the critic, who was supplying him with subjects for operas: "I need a subject where a single dramatic motive predominates, for example love (maternal or sexual makes no difference)."

The fact that there were no women at Tchaikovsky's deathbed has been abundantly exploited: "*Keine Frau im Tode, wie es keine Frau im Leben gab*," no woman in death as in life, remarks for instance the German biographer Kurt Pahlen. This is true in the flesh, not in the spirit: a woman's name, not a man's, was on the composer's lips when he died.* Still there is no disputing that he lived surrounded mainly by men. On the other hand nothing could be unfairer than to declare, as has been done, that 'although he had no special partiality for men, he felt frank disgust towards women.' That is an absolutely gratuitous affirmation, upheld by no evidence, contradicted by much. Without trying to deduce anything from our findings, it is necessary here to show what were Tchaikovsky's real feelings towards women.

Some of his dearest friends, Julia Shpajinsky, Anna Merkling, Nadejda von Meck, were women. Three women, as we shall see later, played an essential part in his life. His diaries are full of women, most of them mentioned in a tone of commendation: they

* Cf. p. 95.

are 'charming, sweet, pretty,' etc. It is obvious that when Tchaikovsky saw a pretty woman he looked at her at least twice. Of some he speaks with serious admiration, of many with the superficial pleasurable tickling which a normal man feels when he mentions a pretty woman. If the composer holds preliminary examinations at the Conservatoire, he is not without noticing that "many pretty girls presented themselves." If he goes to a dress ball, he spends the whole evening dancing and flirting with a masked lady whom he finds "exceedingly attractive." If he travels by ship and is a little bored, the arrival of three "new women passengers (Greeks: a blond, a brunette and an old lady)" is enough to restore his good humour. If, in a hotel, he has to push his way through 'a crowd of ladies who are standing in the corridor to stare at him, he reads in their eyes 'with involuntary pleasure, signs of enthusiastic sympathy.' If he is invited to a grand evening with many Polish aristocrats, he finds the ladies 'amiable, cultivated, interesting, and *simpatichny*." If a pretty maid serves his dinner, he is not above flirting with her. "*A propos* of the carrots which had been served to me I asked her what she preferred: carrots or men's kisses? She answered resolutely: kisses."

Curiously, and maybe a little pathetically, one of the recurring notations in diaries and letters is admiration for somebody else's wife: with Mrs Rimsky-Korsakov Tchaikovsky was on excellent terms; Krotkov, the composer, he wrote off as "absolutely insane, but his wife is pretty;" he was "quite in love with both the wife and the sister-in-law" of the violinist Brodsky, and had a complicated relationship with his own sister-in-law Pania, Anatoly's wife, whose behaviour he sometimes found "unbecoming," but whose "magnetic eyes" disturbed him and who touched him as he had "never been touched in his life" by weeping when he started to speak about leaving. Many other examples are available.

Vera Davydov, later Butakov, was more than a friend, obviously a flame of his. They contemplated farming together: "as regards myself it is no joke" wrote the composer. But apparently marriage frightened him more than farming attracted him: "I quite see how all this ought to end. But what can I do if I sense that my feeling for her would turn to hatred if the question of marriage between us ever became serious?" Their relationship began in 1863 and lasted for years. What they were for each other is unknown. In 1884, she had not forgotten the past, but, for some reason, these memories were obnoxious to Tchaikovsky and he stated in his diary that he would not wish for "all that to begin again."

Moscow gossip linked Tchaikovsky's name with the name of Aleksandra Batalina, who married his friend Hubert a little after his own marriage. She made piano arrangements of his works, presented him with embroideries, and in general behaved as a very close friend indeed. He generally referred to her as Batasha, or Batashka, an extremely familiar diminutive built on her family name. What their relationship was is unknown, but it remained intimate till the composer's death.

With Emma Genton, Kondratiev's governess, Tchaikovsky had a complicated connection. He reproached himself with being "cruel" to her. What he meant we do not know. We do not know either why his own maid Arisha gave him so much trouble. One day she was leaving and somebody was crying, one day she was back in heavenly weather and 'everything was the same,' then she left once again and Tchaikovsky made a note of his sadness in his diary. There is no point in adorning Tchaikovsky's life with ancilliary conquests, and we are perfectly content to concede that there was nothing at all between him and the chambermaid to whom he let his friend Laroche "make love," but it begins to be obvious that Tchaikovsky felt no kind of estrangement from any kind of women. We might add that the laconic "Girls" without explanation or comment is not an exceptional notation in the diaries.

Among literary and historical characters many women appealed to the composer. He read with intense delight the correspondence of Catherine the Great: "What an intelligent, what a captivating woman!" He "experienced something like falling in love" with a heroine of Daudet.* And of course, as any self-respecting Russian, he was completely infatuated with Pushkin's Tatiana from *Eugene Onegin.* He is said to have thought of setting Tatiana's famous letter as a solo song long before he decided to make an opera of the whole poem, and he began composing the music for it even before he prepared his libretto. "I had so familiarized myself with the figure of Tatiana," he told Kashkin, "that she had become for me a living person in living surroundings. I loved Tatiana and was terribly indignant with Onegin."

His other works show the same partiality for women. In the second act of *The Voivode* he felt the need to introduce a female character which did not belong there. He composed but one scene of a *Boris Godunov* which he had in mind, and it was the scene between the Pretender and Marina by the fountain. He wanted to write an opera on a play called *Vanka the Steward,* the

---

* Alphonse Daudet, the French novelist.

subject of which he found *simpatichny* "mainly it appears because it centred on a love scene in a garden at night." The little music which he wrote for it he used later in "a love scene in a room with doors open on a garden at night": it was the scene between Maria and Mazepa. He nearly wrote an opera on the theme of *Romeo and Juliet*; he even considered at one time that 'fate had to some extent ordained him for this task,' and what attracted him most was the possibility of writing two love duets completely different one from the other: "in the first, brightness and serenity; in the second, a tragic element," and—most important—in the whole work there would be "nothing but love, love, love." It is of course ironic that nothing came out of such enthusiasm, but, on the other hand, it must not be forgotten that Tchaikovsky had already composed one of his most beautiful symphonic poems on the same subject. It may also be worth mentioning that of the ten operas which Tchaikovsky composed, five have women's names or designations for titles, and that in at least two of the other five, women are in fact the main characters: Tatiana in *Eugene Onegin* and Oksana in *Vakula the Smith*. Tatiana is more than that: she is probably the most attractive female character of Russian opera as a whole.

These facts are so manifest, so indisputable, that we see no reason to go beyond and to identify *The Swan Lake* as "a hymn dedicated to the Russian woman,"[1] or to deduce the composer's sexual preferences from his music, as has been quite seriously done: "When the music of *Francesca da Rimini* is not martially vigorous it is sultry, sensual, exotic and at the risk of undue harping on argument it must be said that Tchaikovsky was to offer few better proofs than this symphonic poem that he was not a natural homosexual; otherwise, such a theme and such treatment of it would have been quite beyond him!"[2]

We really need not gamble so extravagantly on conjecture and personal interpretation. Determining from our seat in the concert-hall whether the composer *naturally* or *unnaturally* preferred boys or girls is quite out of our range of possibilities. But we may ask Tchaikovsky himself what he thought of women, and his answer, although it will certainly not be complete, is at least bound to be a little more to the point.

"Only women know how to love so," said Tchaikovsky about his stepmother. "If you want attention, conscientiousness and punctuality, always entrust your work to a woman," he advised

* The exclamation mark is mine. V.V.

Jurgenson. "In family life, one of the main joys comes from the presence of young girls," he observed to Mrs von Meck. "By their virginal charm and purity they embellish the daily family atmosphere, and without them, whatever comfort one has, one lacks the warmest element of a happy family life." And to Mrs Shpajinsky he wrote with his usual fervour. "What can be higher, better, more divine, than kind, Russian, especially feminine souls! ! !"

Once he confessed to Anatoly "I am in a period of complete indifference to the fair sex," which implies that this was not ordinary with him. One month earlier, after having performed the First Suite in the presence of a few friends, he had written, with humorous bombast: "I am beginning to be proud of my works, now that I see what an extraordinary effect some of them make. Everyone here is crazy over the Andante, and when I played it with my brother as a pianoforte duet, one girl had a fit of hysterics (*faktisch*! ! !). Driving the fair sex into hysterics, isn't that the highest triumph for an artist?"

Jokes apart, there are two instances when Tchaikovsky lifted the veil on his innermost relationship to women. In the first one, he reacts to the news of Anatoly's future marriage, and gives us an interesting element of meditation by quoting Tolstoi's *Anna Karenina* and one of its heroes, Levin. What Tchaikovsky clearly means in that passage is this: 'If I had had a comparable opportunity, I should have felt like you or Levin.' The reader no doubt remembers that Levin entertains for his bride a mixture of respect and tenderness bordering on idolatry. Here is the very revealing text:

Tola, my dearest, I have just received your letter with the details of your engagement. I am heartily glad you are happy, and I think I understand all you are feeling, although I never experienced it myself. There is a certain kind of yearning for tenderness and consolation that only a wife can satisfy. Sometimes I am overcome by an insane craving for the caress of a woman's touch. Sometimes I see *simpatichny* women's faces (not young women's by the way), and I should like to lay my head in their lap and kiss their hands. Difficult to express all that. When you are quite calm again—after your marriage—read *Anna Karenina*, which I have read lately for the first time with an enthusiasm bordering on fanaticism. What you are now feeling is there wonderfully expressed with reference to Levin's marriage.

This passage should not be made to prove anything. It probably could have been written by a homosexual or a heterosexual, both natural and unnatural. Modest published it. It clearly speaks of anything but physical desire. All that is beside the point. The only thing which it shows is that Tchaikovsky's attitude towards women was, to say the least, positive.

This is even more distinctly expressed in the following letter, which Tchaikovsky wrote to the singer E. K. Pavlovsky, to persuade her to undertake the main part of his opera *The Sorceress*. This letter, besides showing the composer as extremely receptive to feminine charm, contains one of his most striking declarations about his music and himself. This statement again should not be used to prove this or that. It is interesting and perplexing enough in itself. Here is a composer who has already written to a friend 'If you want to know the story of my love life, listen to my music' and who tells another: 'the fundamental requirement of my soul is to illustrate in music Goethe's words *Das Ewig Weibliche zieht uns hinan.** The fundamental requirement of his soul, nothing less. A text containing such a confession deserves to be quoted at length.

My conception of Nastasia's type is quite different from yours.

Of course she is a *loose woman*, but her charm does not lie merely in her ability to talk well. That would be enough to attract the people to her inn. But it wouldn't be enough to turn the young Prince from a . . . bitter enemy, who has come to kill her, into a lover. In the depths of this loose woman's soul lie a certain *moral power and beauty* which up to now have had no opportunity to unfold themselves. *This power is love.* She is a strong womanly nature who can love only once and can sacrifice *everything* for her love. While her love is still unborn Nastasia squanders her power so to speak in small change, i.e., she makes a joke of compelling everyone who comes in her way to fall in love with her. She remains a *simpatichny*, charming, though spoiled woman; she knows she is charming, is content to be, and—since she is neither guided by religious faith nor, being an orphan, has received a proper upbringing—pursues the single aim of having a good time. Then appears the man who has power to touch the slumbering better chords of her inward being and—she is transformed. Life loses for her its value so long as her goal is not reached; her charms, which hitherto have possessed an elementary, instinctive power of attraction, now become a powerful weapon which in a moment overcomes the hostile power, i.e., the hatred of the young Prince. Then both surrender themselves to the mad torrent of love which leads to the inevitable catastrophe —her death—and this death leaves the spectator with a sense of peace and reconciliation. At any rate, it will be so in my libretto, though it's different in the drama. Shpajinsky understands perfectly well what I want and will work out the characterization in accord-

* The eternal feminine draws us onward.

ance with my intentions. He will soften some of the rough
edges of Nastasia's *manières d'être* and bring the hidden power of
her *moral* beauty more into the foreground. He and I, later *you*
too (if you come to terms with this rôle), will so arrange it that
in the last act everyone will have to weep. As regards costume and
make-up, there's no need for headaches about that. We'll arrange
it so that there's nothing repellent. If Savina [the actress whom
E. K. Pavlovsky had seen play the part in its original, non-prettified
form] was badly dressed there's no need for you to be. . . . My
enthusiasm for *The Sorceress* has not made me untrue to the fundamental requirements of my soul: to illustrate in music Goethe's
words, *Das Ewig-Weibliche zieht uns hinan.* The circumstance that
the power and beauty of Nastasia's womanliness long remain covered
under a cloak of sin only heightens the theatrical interest. Why do
you love the rôle of la Traviata? Why are you so fond of Carmen?
Because power and beauty peep out from these characters, though
in coarse form. I assure you that you will also grow fond of
the Sorceress.

2 *This woman has done me much harm, and yet . . .*

"I know of one love in your life," wrote Mrs von Meck to Tchaikovsky, "but I think such love platonic." Tchaikovsky did not comment on the surmise, and it is generally believed that Mrs von
Meck was alluding to his love for the French singer Désirée Artôt.
    She arrived in Moscow in 1868 with a mediocre Italian com-
pany among which she was, according to Laroche, the one exception:

  A woman of thirty,* not good-looking, but with a passionate and
  expressive face. . . . Her voice was powerful and adapted to express
  intense dramatic pathos, but unfortunately it had no reserve force,
  and began to deteriorate early, so that six or seven years after the
  time of which I am speaking it had completely lost its charm. . . .†
It is not too much to say that in the whole world of music, in the

---

* She was 33.
† Such, as we shall see, was not Tchaikovsky's opinion.

entire range of lyrical emotion, there was not a single idea, or a single form, of which this admirable artist could not give a poetical interpretation. The timbre of her voice . . . was penetrated by such indescribable beauty, warmth and passion, that everyone who heard it was fascinated and carried away. I have said that Désirée Artôt was not good-looking. At the same time, without recourse to artificial aids, her charm was so great that she had won all hearts and turned all heads, as though she had been the loveliest of women. The delicate texture and pallor of her skin, the plastic grace of her movements, the beauty of her neck and arms, were not her only weapons; under the irregularity of her features lay some wonderful charm of attraction, and of all the many 'Gretchens' I have seen in my day, Artôt was by far the most ideal, the most fascinating. This was chiefly due to her talent as an actress. I have never seen anyone so perfectly at home on the stage as she was. From the first entrance to the last cry of triumph or despair, the illusion was perfect. Not a single movement betrayed intention or pre-consideration. She was equally herself in a tragic . . . or comic part.

Such was Laroche's impression of her. The style of that gentleman never suffered from an excess of simplicity and the portrait is not necessarily very accurate. But one thing is sure: Désirée Artôt was charming.

The young professor of the Conservatoire Peter Tchaikovsky, who had so far written one opera and had one symphony performed, did not resist. He began by declaring "Artôt is a splendid creature. She and I are good friends," and by spending hours with her, so that Prince Odoevsky noted in his diary: "Tchaikovsky seems to court Désirée Artôt a great deal." At that time, the composer was working on a symphonic poem to be called *Fatum*, "but his letters spoke more of Artôt than of it."[3] In fact they spoke of her in less and less doubtful terms. To Anatoly: "I have become very friendly with Artôt, and am glad to know something of her remarkable character. I have never met a kinder, a better, or a cleverer woman." To Modest: "Oh! Modia, I long to pour my impressions into your artistic soul. If only you knew what a singer and actress Artôt is! ! I have never experienced such powerful artistic impressions as just recently. How delighted you would be with the grace of her movements and poses. . . !" "I have not written to you for a long while, but many things make it impossible for me to write letters, for all my leisure is given to one—of whom you have already heard—whom I love dearly." Yes, anyone who was preventing Tchaikovsky from writing to the twins had to be loved, and probably not dearly but passionately. To Modest again: "Recently a concert was given here for the benefit of poor

students, in which 'the one being' sang for the last time before her
departure, and Nikolai Rubinstein played my pianoforte piece
dedicated to Artôt."

To his father Tchaikovsky wrote with fewer exclamation marks,
but even more seriously: "As rumours of my engagement will
doubtless have reached you, and you may feel hurt at my silence
upon the subject, I will tell you the whole story." He proceeds to
tell how their acquaintance started a few months before and how

> we began to experience a mutual glow of tenderness, and an under-
> standing followed immediately. Naturally the question of marriage
> arose at once, and, if nothing hinders it, our wedding is to take
> place in the summer. But the worst is that there are several
> obstacles. First, there is her mother, who always lives with her, and
> has considerable influence upon her daughter. She is not in favour
> of the match, because she considers me too young, and probably
> fears lest I should expect her daughter to live permanently in Russia.
> Secondly, my friends, especially N. Rubinstein, are trying might and
> main to prevent my marriage. They declare that, married to a
> famous singer, I should play the pitiable part of 'husband of my
> wife' . . . The risk of such a catastrophe might perhaps be avoided,
> if she would consent to leave the stage and live entirely in Russia.
> But she declares that in spite of all her love for me, she cannot make
> up her mind to give up the profession which brings her in so much
> money, and to which she has grown accustomed. . . . If she will not
> consent to give up the stage, I, on my part, hesitate to sacrifice
> my future; for it is clear that I shall lose all opportunity of making
> my own way, if I blindly follow in her train. You see, Papa, my
> situation is a very difficult one. On the one hand, I love her heart
> and soul, and feel I cannot live any longer without her; on the other
> hand, calm reason bids me to consider more closely all the mis-
> fortunes with which my friends threaten me. I shall wait, my dear,
> for your views on the subject.

It has been argued that "the mere fact that he thought it necessary to ask his father's advice . . . showed how undecided he was."[4]
This is only partly true: it was customary for a Russian of that
period to ask for his parents' blessing before getting married. The
reader remembers that in *War and Peace*, Prince Andrei, although
he is nearly middle-aged and a widower, needs his father's permission to marry. Nevertheless it is true that Tchaikovsky shows
indecision, which is perfectly natural since the situation is indeed
complex. Here are a professor and a singer, she older than he, she
endowed with an unquestionable talent, he with huge ambitions;
she used to a sizeable income, he having only a meagre salary;
they love each other, but if they marry, they will have to live in

a conventional society in which their differences will hurt more and more as time goes by and passion cools off; she will not stay in Russia; he will not "live at her expense and accompany her all over Europe." What can they do? It is not unreasonable to ask one's father's advice.

The advice came, and it was very typical of Ilya Petrovich as we imagine him. He begins by adopting the tone of a Polonius to state that "marriage is not a step to take heedlessly; it is a gambler's risk; it is the hazard of the brave." But his kind innocent heart saves him from the commonplace and he goes on with artless benevolence and simplicity: "As a father I rejoice; Désirée is surely worthy because my son Peter loves her, and my son Peter is a man of taste and talent who would naturally select a wife with like qualities." The two years' difference does not mean a thing. No more does a mother's wish in love affairs although it should be given some consideration. Money does not count so long as both work. Travelling will only bring opportunities of getting Peter's works performed throughout the world. "Artists have no country; they belong to the world." As to the risk of spoiling the composer's avocation, it does not exist: "Having sacrificed to your talent your service to the Crown, you will obviously not cease being an artist even if in the beginning you find little success, as it generally happens to musicians. . . . With such a companion as your chosen one, your talent is more likely to progress than to deteriorate." The mere idea that passion could cool off is ridiculous: "I lived twenty-one years with your mother, and during all that time I loved her just the same, with the ardour of a young man, and respected and worshipped her as a saint." With the superior good sense that some unintelligent people attain through their good heart, Ilya Petrovich asks the only important question: "Have you proved each other? Do you love each other truly and for all time?" He suggests waiting a little, because Time is the only verifier and old people know it well, but he ends his letter on a very affectionate note, as of he was already sure of a happy ending: "Tell me openly, my dear, what is your desired's character—be sure to translate to her that tender word Désirée."

It did not take much time to verify Miss Artôt's feelings. Tchaikovsky had scarcely written to his father when she married a Spanish baritone, Don Mariano Padilla y Ramos.

Tchaikovsky must already have felt that his engagement was about to be broken, since he had written to Anatoly "With regard to the love affair I had early in the winter, I may tell you that it is very doubtful whether I shall enter Hymen's bonds or not. Things are beginning to go rather awry." Nevertheless his reaction when he learned that he had been jilted was such as to cause comment and create a biographical problem.

The singer de Lazari was present when Nikolai Rubinstein, who had been opposed to his friend's marriage, announced the news to him. "Tchaikovsky did not say a word. He went pale and left." The same Lazari says that "several days later one could not have recognized him. He was again content, calm and devoted himself entirely to work." Modest, to whom Tchaikovsky had neglected to write when he was spending all his time with his fiancée, remarks that this disappointment "affected him less painfully than might have been expected." We may be mistaken in thinking that we detect some smugness in Modest's tone, but it is obvious that the impartial testimony of Lazari lends itself to various interpretations. "A man of thirty wholly in love for the first time and particularly a man of Peter Ilich's stormily emotional temperament, would hardly recover in a day or two from such brutal treatment by his beloved," declares one commentator.[5] The implication is to be sung to the well-known tune: Tchaikovsky cannot have loved Désirée Artôt because he was a homosexual, and since he did not love her, his homosexuality is proved. In order to create that impression, Lazari's text is even misquoted and the word which means 'content' becomes sometimes 'obviously happy.'[6] For our part, we should like to make a note of the *several days* mentioned by Lazari. It took Tchaikovsky several days to conquer himself. What was he supposed to do? Not come to the rehearsals of his first opera? Or cry for weeks on Mr de Lazari's shoulder? Tchaikovsky did the only thing which a heart-broken but well-bred lover could have done: he tried to absorb himself in his work, and took care "not to worry others with his private sorrows." "It was a notable victory for the last virtue with which Tchaikovsky is ever credited, self-restraint."[7]

The following events confirm our point of view, but before we get to them, we must not skip an interesting though cryptic remark of the composer's in a letter to Modest: "One must know the details of our relation to understand fully how comic is this dénouement." A false impression is given by adapting this remark into "it was necessary to know all the details of his relations with Artôt in order to realize fully how absurd her marriage was"[8] or into "after their intimacy a marriage to another man was farcical."[9] We know nothing about their intimacy and it is useless to pretend that we do.

About a year after the rupture, Désirée Artôt de Padilla y Ramos was to come back to Moscow. "I shall have very shortly to meet Artôt," wrote Tchaikovsky to Anatoly. "I cannot avoid a meeting, because immediately after her arrival we begin the rehearsals for *Le Domino Noir** (for which I have written recitatives and choruses), which I shall be compelled to attend. This woman has done me much harm, and yet I am drawn to her by such an inexplicable sympathy that I begin to look forward to her coming with feverish impatience."

Modest says that "they met as friends. All intimate relations were at an end." Do we hear a triumphant note in this declaration which may or may not be true? Anyway the statement is partly contradicted by Kashkin, who tells us two stories. The first is quoted by Modest himself and does not contradict him: "When, in 1869, Artôt reappeared at the Moscow Opera,† I sat in the stalls next to Tchaikovsky who was greatly moved. When the singer came on, he held his opera glasses to his eyes and never lowered them during the entire performance; but he must have seen very little, for tear after tear rolled down his cheeks." The second seems to show that there was no personal meeting in 1869, or else unfriendly ones. "Seven or eight years later I was present at an unexpected meeting between Tchaikovsky and the singer. We had gone to call upon N. Rubinstein at the Conservatoire, but, on being told that he was engaged with a lady in his private room, we sat down in the ante-room to wait until the visitor should take her departure. Presently the door opened and the lady appeared. Tchaikovsky recognized her at a glance and sprang from his seat, turning very pale. The lady gave a little cry of alarm, and in her confusion began to fumble for the door of the half-lighted anteroom. Having found it, she fled without a word. N. Rubinstein who had followed her out stood a silent and astonished spectator of this little scene. A year or two later Tchaikovsky met the lady once more, while travelling abroad, and resumed his friendly relations with her."

Kashkin is obviously confused as to his dates. Tchaikovsky met Artôt again in 1888, twenty years after their rupture and not ten. And 'seven or eight years later' is not a very precise indication. Probably the strange little scene took place in 1875, when we know that the singer appeared in Moscow in Meyerbeer's *Huguenots*. Anyway if Kashkin tells the truth it is evident that Tchaikovsky and Mrs Padilla had not met as friends in 1869.

---

* An opera by Auber.
† As Gretchen in Gounod's *Faust*.

Anyway in 1872, three years after the rupture, Tchaikovsky, after listening to Christine Nillson, declared: "with all her good qualities she does not please me nearly so well as Artôt. If the latter would only return to Moscow I should jump for joy." And he nearly did. When, in 1875, he saw her in *The Huguenots*, "she had grown disgracefully fat and had nearly lost her voice, but nevertheless she triumphed thanks to her talent." It may be worth noting that Modest does not mention this tribute of the composer to the artist.

No real meeting took place between the former fiancés for sixteen years more. And then, apparently by chance, they met at a dinner party, in Berlin. "I was inexpressibly glad to see her again," wrote Tchaikovsky to Jurgenson. "We made friends at once, without a word as to the past. Her husband, Padilla, smothered me in his embraces. The day after tomorrow she gives a big dinner. As a little old woman she is just as charming as she was twenty years ago." Obviously no bitterness had remained between them. Tchaikovsky corresponded with her in sometimes rather strained French, with a quaint mixture of tremulous adoration and careful aloofness. He dedicated several songs to her in the following terms:

I have just delivered to my publisher, P. Jurgenson, six songs which I have composed for You and of which I beg that You would accept the dedication. I have endeavoured to please You, Madam, and I believe that all six can be sung by You, I mean that they are suitable to the present range of Your voice. I wish that these songs might be so fortunate as to please You,—but alas I am far from sure of it, since I must confess to You that I have worked too much lately and it is more than probable that my new compositions are the product of a desire to do well rather than of real inspiration. Moreover one feels self-conscious when one composes for a singer whom one considers as the greatest of all the great.

She asked him for different favours, and he was happy to oblige whenever she did not want him to compose anything special: then he put her off. In 1889 he met her again in Berlin where she was "a great comfort" to him. In 1890 she recommended to him a libretto for an opera, by Capoul. He was not interested and said so with an exquisite courtesy bordering on insolence: "Since you recommend me Capoul's poem, it is more than probable that I am mistaken and that it would suit me perfectly. Only be kind enough to understand that at the present time it is impossible for me to ask him to send it to me so that I might read it. For I have neither the desire nor even the time."

Such was the end of a relationship to which we probably owe

N

Romeo and Juliet, since that hymn to unfulfilled love was composed in 1869, immediately after Désirée Artôt decided, as far as Tchaikovsky was concerned, to remain *désirée* and nothing more.

3 *I hate that beautiful, unknown being*

Miss Vera Davydov would maybe have agreed to become Mrs Tchaikovsky if she had been asked, but she was not. Miss Désirée Artôt was, but she accepted somebody else. Nevertheless the idea of marriage, having once entered Tchaikovsky's head, stayed there.

In 1870, he confided in his sister: "I have a deep yearning for the sound of children's voices and for some share in all the small matters of a home—in a word for family life." In 1872, he shared his problems with his father: "As regards marriage, I must confess that I have often thought of finding myself a suitable wife, but I am afraid I might afterwards regret doing so. I earn almost enough (3,000 roubles a year), but I know so little about the management of money that I am always in debt and dilemma. So long as a man is alone, this does not mean much. But how would it be if I had to keep a wife and family?"

So far he appears as the reasonable, clear-sighted man in whose part we have so often seen him. He wants a wife, a family, children; he is concerned about money: the bourgeois tastes once again. The only indication which he gives about the kind of wife he wants, 'a good plump little woman like a tasty cream puff,' resembling his father's third wife, confirms this impression of jovial common sense. Nothing could be less romantic and this again was to be expected after the very romantic disappointment which had come before. Even biographers' ravings about what it could have meant that he wanted a wife like his stepmother do not succeed entirely in obscuring the situation which is perfectly normal.[10] There is no reason to suppose, as it has been done, that he wanted to marry "to free himself from the oppressive domination of Nikolai Rubinstein":[11] he wanted to marry as it is normal at his age, to found a family.

Then something must have happened, and we do not know what. Around September 1876 he wrote to Modest a series of letters presenting his prospective marriage in a completely different light. The trouble is that the originals of these frantic letters are in the Tchaikovsky Archives, that no independent party has seen them, and that they have been carved into extracts by those who had access to them and wanted to prove a point. Modest cut out everything that smacked of homosexuality; on the contrary the Soviet editors of the correspondence with Mrs von Meck, who, for some reason, were determined to prove that the composer had been a homosexual, cut to measure other extracts, and bound them together into fasces which they placed in pointed footnotes. Then translators came and played havoc with it all. Conclusions will have to be postponed till the time when the 'September' letters are published *in extenso*; but for the time being we shall have to do with what we can get, and try to piece everything together.

On 19th August Tchaikovsky wrote to Modest from Verbovka: "I have now to pass through a critical moment in my life. By-and-by I shall write to you about it more fully; meanwhile I must just tell you that I have decided to get married. This is irrevocable." On 10th September: "I have thought much about myself and my future.* The result of all these reflections is that beginning today I shall seriously try to contract a legitimate marriage with anybody.† I am of the opinion that my tendencies are the greatest and the most unconquerable obstacle to happiness and I must struggle with all my strength against my nature. . . ." Here comes an unfortunate omission. The preceding passage seems to be a reference to homosexuality, but we must exercise caution with quotations taken out of context. For instance, how would we interpret the following passage: "Oh! if you only knew how I struggled against this fault and how much I suffered from this struggle against my unusual nature, how it tormented me, how I laboured to redress myself"? Does it not suggest some awful vice? But in fact Tchaikovsky used those terms to tell Mrs von Meck about his natural timidity. After the mysterious omission, of which even the length cannot be determined, the letter resumes: "I shall do all I can to marry this year, and if I do not have enough courage, in any case I discard my habits once and for all." On 17th September, quoted by Modest and so presumably innocent (Rosa

* Rosa Newmarch's translation (which, for all we know, may be more accurate than the Soviet quotation): "I have thought much *about you* and also about myself and my future." Italics mine. V.V.

† H. Weinstock's translation: "I shall seriously *prepare myself* to marry someone or other." Italics mine. V.V. The implications of "prepare myself" are obvious, but Tchaikovsky never wrote "prepare myself."

Newmarch's translation): "Time passes uneventfully. In this colourless existence, however, lies a certain charm. I can hardly express in words how sweet is this feeling of quiet. What comfort —I might almost say happiness—it is to return to my pleasant rooms and sit down with a book in my hand! At this moment I hate, probably not less than you do,* that beautiful, unknown being who will force me to change my way of living. Do not be afraid, I shall not hurry in this matter; you may be sure I will approach it with great caution, and only after much deliberation." The Soviet quotation starts only at "I shall not hurry" and gives a different version from Rosa Newmarch's: "you may be sure that, if I really tie myself to a woman, I shall do it with great deliberation."

On 28th September was written the main letter of this group. Modest did not quote it at all for obvious reasons. The Soviet edition quotes only parts of it.

There are people who cannot despise me for my vices only because they began to love me before suspecting that I was in fact a man with a lost reputation. Among them Sasha. I know that she guesses everything and forgives everything. Many people I love or respect treat me the same way. Do you think that it is not painful for me to know that I am being pitied and forgiven when, in reality, I am not guilty of anything! And is it not a torturing thought that people who love me can sometimes be ashamed of me! And that happened a hundred times and will happen again a hundred times. In a word I should like, by a marriage or in general by a public liaison with a woman, to shut the mouths of different contemptible creatures whose opinion I value not, but who can cause sorrow to people who are close to me. [Omission] The realization of my plans is not nearly so imminent as you think. I have sunk so deeply in my habits and tastes that it is impossible to discard them at once, like an old glove. Moreover I am far from possessing an iron character and since my letters to you I have already succumbed two or three times to the force of natural tendencies.

As far as one can judge from quotations out of context, the meaning of all this seems pretty clear at first sight. It is only on re-reading it that a few questions arise. How can Tchaikovsky declare that he is not guilty of anything when he admits later that he has already succumbed several times to natural tendencies? Does he mean that those tendencies are not really evil, just condemned by common opinion? But then why does he call them vices? Why does he think that it is his lost reputation and not his

* Is this an allusion to jealousy on Modest's part?

vices as such which could have prevented some people from loving him? Does he refer to the same fault when he speaks about his habits, his tastes and his tendencies, or are there two or three different objects? And if so, about which one of the two or three is he most unhappy? One would tend to deduce from the whole *first part* that Tchaikovsky is concerned about his reputation and not at all about his guilt. In fact he recognizes no guilt, and it would have taken a more modern man than he was to feel no guilt about homosexuality in the middle of the Victorian age. At no point have we found Tchaikovsky so free from prejudice, so uninterested in traditional morals, as to credit him with such liberty of thought. In other words, and the quotation remaining incomplete, only the following meaning can be safely extracted from the passage: "I want to marry to put an end to gossip." And the reference to a liaison with a woman suggests that this gossip concerned affairs with men. But at the same time the composer is careful to state "in reality I am not guilty of anything!"

The *second part* of the quotation, after the omission, contains the only real confession: "since my letters to you I have already succumbed two or three times to the force of natural tendencies." Nothing is there to indicate which letters and what tendencies are in question.

This of course does not prove anything besides the fact that it is impossible to work on quotations chosen to suit an editor's purpose. But as, in the present state of sources, a history of Tchaikovsky is necessarily also a history of his biographies, it will be worth mentioning here that H. Weinstock's treatment of such a crucial and difficult passage contains seven inaccuracies some of which can be ascribed to negligence, while others, to put it mildly, cannot.

(1) Where Tchaikovsky writes "about three times," which we tried to render by "two or three times," H. Weinstock translates "three times," which indicates a much more definite way of succumbing.

(2) Tchaikovsky succumbs to 'natural tendencies' or 'inclinations' in the original; to '*his* natural inclinations' in the translation. The possessive is there to indicate that these inclinations were natural to Tchaikovsky but not natural in general. In other words, the translation clearly indicates abnormality, whereas the original text suggests nothing of the kind. For all we know the composer may have patronized a brothel or got drunk.

(3) In the original, Tchaikovsky states quite clearly "I am not guilty of anything." In the translation he mentions "actions for

which I cannot be held responsible." The word 'action' has been introduced in the text out of nowhere, and the idea of responsibility has replaced the idea of guilt. In other words a denial has been, hey presto, transformed into a confession.

(4) Tchaikovsky speaks about his *vices* in the plural. The word having the very broad meaning which it had in Russia at the time, it cannot be made to signify anything in particular. So we find it replaced by the singular *vice* in the beginning of the quotation.

(5) All this is child's play compared to the next point. Where Tchaikovsky has: "There are people who cannot despise me," Mr Weinstock calmly writes "There are people who cannot help despising me."

(6) For no reason that we could find this letter written on the 28th (Soviet quotation) is ascribed to the 10th.

(7) Tchaikovsky says that "Sasha *guesses* everything." Mr Weinstock, although he translates the passage accurately, declares: "There is reason to believe that he always told her everything with complete honesty and assurance of sympathy." If he had told her everything, she would have had nothing left to guess.

To resume with Tchaikovsky's preparation for the ordeal of marriage. On 6th October, he wrote to Sasha a letter which seems to conclude the September group: "Please, my angel, do not worry about my marriage. First, I do not intend at all to decide to take such a step in the near future, and at any rate during this year (I mean this school year) it will certainly not happen. But during these several months, I want to get used to the idea of and to prepare myself for matrimony, which, for various reasons, I think very good for me. Be sure that I shall not throw myself thoughtlessly in the slough of an unhappy marriage. Sonia Peresleni (who, as a matter of fact, would probably have refused me) is definitively stricken from the list of candidates. I have had the opportunity to verify the extraordinary heartlessness of this young lady. If you add this heartlessness to her fancifulness, the result is not in the least suitable for me."

Obviously the mood had changed and, for unknown reasons, his decision to marry 'anyone' was dissolving. The winter, according to Modest, passed quietly: "Never was he more contented with his lot, or calmer in mind, than a few months before he entered the Conservatoire. It was the same at the present juncture. Shortly before that rash act, which cut him off for ever from Moscow,* which changed all his habits and social relations, and

* In fact: only temporarily.

was destined to be the beginning of a new life; just at the moment,
in fact, when we might look for some dissatisfaction with fate as a
reason for this desperate resolve, Tchaikovsky was by no means
out of spirits. On the contrary, in January and February 1877, he
gave the impression of a man whose mind was at rest, who had no
desires, and displayed more purpose and cheerfulness than before."

We have to wait till 8th May—and at that time contact had
already been established with the future Mrs Tchaikovsky—to
find again the word 'marriage' under the composer's pen. He wrote
to his friend the architect Klimenko: "I have changed much
(during the past five years) physically and mainly morally. I have
lost all desire to be merry and play the fool. Not a farthing of
youth is left in me. Life is awfully empty, boring and vulgar. I
seriously think of a marriage or some other stable liaison." Once
again translators have changed the character of this confession,
which in Modest's biography translated by Rosa Newmarch, is made
to end with the virtuous and nonsensical words "considering
matrimony as a lasting tie" and in Catherine Bowen's *Beloved
Friend* with the more ambiguous "matrimony or indeed any other
steady bond." This, although rather whimsical, would have been
unimportant if the phrase, addressed to a man who was never
an intimate friend, did not echo, nearly to perfection the one
written eight months earlier to Modest.

4 *Poor woman*

Chivalry is always a temptation and we can only sympathize with
Kurt Pahlen's attempt to rehabilitate Antonina Milukov. But the
result, to say the least, is not convincing, and in spite of the irony
of the situation—is it not ironical that a nymphomaniac should
have thrown herself at the head of the kind of man we know
Tchaikovsky to have been, even without mentioning his possible
singularities—there is no reason to disguise what is known of the
facts. Antonina was a nymphomaniac, she was a lunatic, she died
in a lunatic asylum, she was into the bargain very foolish and
rather vulgar. The irony is only apparent, especially if Tchaikovsky
really was more or less a homosexual; being also an honest and

not a foolhardy man he would probably never have found the courage to marry anybody: 'anybody' had to marry him.

We do not really know when and where the story begins. Probably in the early seventies at the Moscow Conservatoire, where Antonina was a student. But at that time she had no personal relations with Tchaikovsky, at least none that we know of. She had already left the Conservatoire when, according to Kashkin in the beginning of April 1877, she wrote a love letter to Tchaikovsky. In the beginning of May, still according to Kashkin, Tchaikovsky asked the pianist Langer for information about the girl and received 'a harshly negative description.' On the 8th of that month, the composer got from Antonina a crazy letter begun on the 4th and finished on the 7th. Obviously he had answered the first one and others had followed, since the lady wrote, in her usual whining tone:

For a whole week I was in agony, Peter Ilich, not knowing whether or not to write you. I see that my letters begin to annoy you. But is it possible that you may drop the correspondence before meeting me even once? No, I am sure that you will not be so cruel! God knows, perhaps you think me a fickle, infatuated girl, and because of that have no faith in my letters? But how can I prove to you the truth of what I say, and finally it is impossible to lie so. After your last letter I loved you twice as much and your faults mean absolutely nothing to me. . . . There is no such fault which would make me cease loving you. . . . I spend all day at home, I wander from place to place like an idiot, I think only about the minute when I shall see you. I shall be ready to throw myself on your neck, to kiss you, but what right have I to do that? You might think it insolent on my part. I have to repay your frankness with equal frankness and so I shall tell you that, although I did express my feelings I should be deeply pained if you interpreted it in a wicked way. I can assure you that I am an honourable and honest girl in the full meaning of that word and that there is nothing that I should want to hide from you. My first kiss will be for you and for no other. Good-bye, my dear. Do not try to disillusion me about yourself any more because you will only waste your time. I cannot live without you and so perhaps I shall soon make an end of myself. Let me look at you and kiss you so I may remember that kiss in the other world. . . . Once again, I beg that you should come to see me. If you knew how I suffer you would probably grant my prayer out of sheer compassion. Forgive me if I cannot entertain you with as much respectability as I should like, since I have only one room at my disposal, but I hope that I shall not degrade myself in your eyes by doing so. . . .

Miss Milukov was 29 at the time, and it is to be wondered how a delicate, possibly over-delicate, and clearly intelligent man of 37, like Tchaikovsky, could have been deceived by such vulgar nonsense coming from a girl who, in that period, was already something of an old maid. We shall see later how he tried to explain it himself after the catastrophe, but no explanation is really satisfactory. His lack of experience with women, his trustful nature, some charm that the girl must have had, his desire to settle down, his weariness with life, a certain fatalism, a certain weakness of character, all played their part. We must not forget that marrying for love was not exactly the thing to do in the nineteenth century, and Tchaikovsky's compassion for anyone poorer, weaker, simpler than he, probably hid from him the monstrous unsuitability of the marriage. *Eugene Onegin* too, which Tchaikovsky was composing at the time, played an important part in the intrigue.

Onegin, as the reader remembers, is a city dandy with whom a country girl, Tatiana, falls in love. She writes him a letter to tell him so. He declares himself honoured, but advises her not to squander her affections on men who have expressed no intention of entering the holy state of matrimony. "You have to learn some self-control," he concludes, and leaves. We, of the twentieth century, are crude enough to think that Onegin's behaviour was beyond reproach, that he acted like 'the perfect gentleman,' maybe even that he was foolish to miss an opportunity which must have been tempting. Not so Tchaikovsky and his contemporaries: for them since Tatiana had been so unconventional as to declare her love, the only decent thing to do was to be overwhelmed by such sincerity and immediately fall at her feet. The Chevalier de Charette, when he went to ask for his pretty neigbour's hand, began to express himself a little clumsily; the mother, who was a widow, thought that he was proposing to her and immediately said "yes!" A gentleman could not shame a lady by refusing her: Charette married the mother. And Onegin could have hesitated??! Tchaikovsky's feelings about the situation are not a matter of surmise. He told Kashkin that 'he loved Tatiana and was terribly indignant with Onegin, who seemed to him a cold, heartless coxcomb.' Now Peter Ilich was not a cold, heartless coxcomb, and the only way to prove it was become Miss Milukov's husband.

On 20th May, Tchaikovsky went to see her. On the 23rd or thereabouts he went to see her again. Some time between the 23rd and the 27th he proposed to her. June was occupied mainly with *Eugene Onegin*. On the 23rd, one month after proposing to Antonina, the composer wrote to Anatoly:

You guessed rightly that I was hiding something from you but you did not guess what. Here is what it is all about. At the end of May took place an event which I wanted to keep secret for some time from you and all the people who are dear and close to me, to prevent you from anxiously wondering how, what, whom, why, am I right, etc. I wanted to finish everything and then to make my confession to you. I am going to be married. When we meet, I shall tell you how it happened. I made my proposal at the end of May and wanted to arrange the marriage at the beginning of July and announce it to you all afterward. But your letter made me change my mind. First, I am not going to avoid meeting you, and it would be difficult to play a comedy, to invent reasons why I am not going to Kamenka with you. Second, I decided that to get married without Father's blessing would not be the thing to do. Give to Father the enclosed letter. Please, do not worry about me: I have carefully thought over what I am doing and I take this important step in my life quite calmly. This calmness must be made obvious to you by the fact that, with my wedding being so close, I was able to write two thirds of my opera.* The girl I am marrying is not very young, but quite respectable, and endowed with one main quality; *she is in love with me as a cat.* She has no fortune whatsoever. Her name is Antonina Ivanovna Milukov. . . . So I am not only announcing to you my future marriage but inviting you to it. You and Kotek will be the only witnesses. . . . Ask Father to be sure not to tell *anyone*; the same applies to you. I shall write to Sasha and to our brothers myself.

To his father he wrote:

My dear, beloved Father, your son Peter has made up his mind to marry. Not wishing to be wed without your blessing, he begs you to bless him for his new life. I am marrying Miss *Antonina Ivanovna Milukov. She is a poor but honest and decent young lady, who loves me very much.* My dearest Father, you know that at my age one does not decide to get married without calm consideration, and so do not worry about me. I am sure that my wife will do everything to make me peaceful and happy.

Probably on the 28th he received his father's answer, very endearing in the same old Polonius style:

Tola gave me the letter in which you ask for my blessing upon your marriage. I was so happy and enthusiastic that I crossed myself and even jumped for joy. God be praised! May the Lord bless you!

---

* *Eugene Onegin.*

I do not doubt that the person whom you have chosen is worthy of the same eulogies that you deserve from your father, an 83-year-old patriarch, from the whole family, and, to tell the truth, from all human beings who know you.

Is that not so, my darling Antonina Ivanovna? Beginning yesterday, I beg to be allowed to call you my God-sent daughter, and you to love the betrothed and husband whom you have chosen. In truth he deserves it. As to you, O bridegroom, inform me as to the day and time of the wedding: I shall come in person (if this meets with your approval) so as to bless you, and I shall bring the icon with which you were blessed by your godmother, Aunt Nadejda Timofeevna, an intelligent and kind woman.

All this makes it fairly obvious that Tchaikovsky was marrying without enthusiasm, but there is no evidence at all of the panic of September 1876. No reference to gossip or bad habits. The only indiscreet indication which dates from this period is Miss Milukov's reference to his attempts to disillusion her in him, which may mean something or nothing at all. Issues have been somewhat confused by biographers trying to divine what Tchaikovsky told her about himself,[12] but fascinating as such guesswork may be as a parlour-game we are not going to indulge in it. The only detailed, although, of course, incomplete, account of this period we owe to the composer himself who, on 3rd July confided in Mrs von Meck:

For God's sake forgive me for not writing to you earlier. Here is in short the history of what happened to me lately.

First of all let me tell you that in the most unexpected way I *became engaged* at the end of May. Here is how it happened. Some time before that I had received a letter from a young lady whom I knew and had met before. From this letter I learned that she had honoured me with her love for a long time. The letter was written so sincerely, so warmly, that I made up my mind to answer it, which I had always refrained from doing in similar cases. Although my reply did not encourage my correspondent in the least, the correspondence began. I shall not tell you all the details but the result was that I accepted to visit her in her home. Why did I do that? Now it seems to me that some fate was drawing me towards this young lady. When we met, I again explained to her that I did not feel anything for her, except sympathy and gratefulness for her love. But having left her I began to think over all the giddiness of my behaviour. If I did not love her, if I did not want to encourage her feelings, why did I visit her and how would all this end? The letter that followed showed that if, having gone so far, I should turn my back on the young lady, I should make her deeply unhappy and bring her to a tragic end. Thus a difficult dilemma was offered me:

either to save my freedom at the price of the young lady's ruin (*ruin* is not here an empty word: she does boundlessly love me) or *to marry* her. I could but choose the latter. The fact that my eighty-two-year-old father and all my family live in the hope of having me marry sustained me in that decision. And so, one fine evening, I went to see my future wife, and told her openly that I did not love her but that I should be for her, at any rate, a devoted and thankful friend. I described to her, in full detail, my character, my irritability, my nervous temperament, my shyness and finally my circumstances. Then I asked her if she wanted to be my wife. The reply was of course positive. I cannot describe to you in words the dreadful feelings which were mine during the days that followed. Nothing strange about it. Having reached the age of thirty-seven with an inborn antipathy towards marriage, to be drawn by the force of circumstance into the situation of a fiancé, and one who is not in the least fascinated by his betrothed, that is very painful. To change the whole organization of one's life, to take care of the welfare and peace of another person whom fate has bound to one, all that is not very easy for a confirmed and selfish bachelor. In order to take the time to think, to get used to considering my future with calm, I decided not to alter my previous plans and to spend a month in the country in spite of everything. So I did. The quiet country life among very friendly people and in the midst of an *admirable* nature was very good for me. I decided that it was impossible to avoid one's fate and that there had been something fateful in my meeting with that young lady. Besides I know from experience that very often in life that which frightens and scares proves to be beneficial, and that, on the contrary, one is disappointed by that which excited one's hopes for happiness and bliss. Let what must be, be.

I shall now tell you a little about my future wife. Her name is *Antonina Ivanovna Milukov*. She is twenty-eight. She is rather handsome. Her reputation is spotless. She worked for her living because she likes to be independent, but she has a very loving mother. She has no fortune whatsoever, has received no higher education (she was educated at the Elisabeth Institution), she seems to be very kind and capable of an unswerving attachment. We shall be married in a few days. What will happen later, I do not know. . . .

Wish me not to fail in courage in front of the future changes in my life. God knows that I am full of the best intention towards the companion of my life and that if we are to be unhappy, it will not be my fault. My conscience is at rest. If I marry without love, it is because the circumstances became such that I could not do otherwise. I behaved frivolously in reacting to the first expression of her love; I should not have replied at all. But having once encouraged her love by replying and visiting her, I had to act as I did. At any rate, I repeat that my conscience is clear: I did not lie to her, I did not deceive her. I have told her what she can expect from me and on what she must not count.

We are naturally free to think that this insistence on a clear conscience means "I have told her that I was a homosexual" or "I have told her that I did not love her."

On 5th July Tchaikovsky announced his forthcoming marriage to Modest and to Sasha. On 6th July the ceremony took place and the newly-married couple departed for St Petersburg, so that the bride could be introduced to her father-in-law.

Here again we have to ward off biographers' speculations. It may very well be that Tchaikovsky had told Miss Milukov that he would not be a real husband for her. It may also be that he had not. Commentators have always assumed that he never became his wife's lover, but we have reason to believe otherwise, although how good is the reason we do not know.* If he did not intend to consummate marriage, why did he consider as 'an attraction' the fact that she was in love with him 'as a cat'? In Russian, the expression is definitely not an ambiguous one; it is even rather crude and Modest left it out when he quoted the letter, but Tchaikovsky used it, and considered it 'an attraction.' Herbert Weinstock is indignant because it seems that the marriage was not consummated on the wedding-night, but since the wedding-night was spent in a train, we do not think that it ought to be held against such a conventional man as we know Tchaikovsky to have been.

On the 7th, Mr and Mrs Tchaikovsky arrived in St Petersburg and stayed at the Europe Hotel. What happened there we do not know since, once again, the sources have been tampered with and we have to be satisfied with the extracts which are available. On the 8th, Tchaikovsky wrote to the twins.

To Anatoly:

I should be an awful liar if I assured you that I am already completely happy, completely accustomed to my new position etc. After a dreadful day like 6th July, after this interminable spiritual torture, it is impossible to recover fast. But all calamities have their sunny side: I suffered intolerably to see how afflicted you were for me, but at the same time you were responsible for the fact that I fought so valiantly against my agony. . . . When the train started I was ready

* He "was a real husband to his wife, and only her personality estranged him from her." Letter No. 128, 22nd February 1971, signed by G. A. Shamkin, Director of the Tchaikovsky Archives and Museum, Klin, U.S.S.R. In the same letter, Mr Shamkin grants that Tchaikovsky had sexual singularities in his youth, but insists that he discarded them later. No evidence is furnished either way.

to scream, so choked was I with sobs. But I had to entertain my wife with conversation as far as Klin in order to earn the right to lie in the dark in my own seat and to remain alone with myself. . . . My main consolation was that my wife did not understand and realize my ill-concealed distress. Now and all the time she seems perfectly happy and satisfied. *Elle n'est pas difficile.** She agrees to everything and is content with everything. . . . We have had conversations which have made our mutual relationship still clearer. She consents absolutely to everything and will never raise any objections. She needs only to fondle and take care of me. I have kept a full freedom of action. . . . I have kept such freedom of action that as soon as my wife and I become used to each other, she will not bother me at all. One ought not to deceive oneself. She is very limited, but this is even good. I should be afraid of an intelligent woman. With this one I stand so high and dominate her so much that at least I have no fear of her.

To Modest the composer wrote with more common sense:

That day was, I must confess, rather painful, be it only because I had to suffer through the ceremony of marriage, the long wedding lunch, the departure with farewells etc. On the way I slept very well. Yesterday we spent a rather pleasant day, in the evening we went for a ride, and to an entertainment on Krestovsky boulevard. . . . My wife has one enormous quality: she blindly obeys me in everything, she agrees to everything, she is satisfied with everything and wishes for nothing besides the happiness of being a help and a consolation to me. I cannot yet say that I love her, but I already feel that I shall love her as soon as we are used to each other.

Once again, to draw conclusions from quotations arbitrarily clipped is not a satisfactory sport. Quite naturally we tend to be impressed by the sobs, the distress, the calamities. But we should not forget that the victim of it all slept soundly in the train and that, in the 8th, his nymphomaniacal wife seemed perfectly content to him. He was even ready to love her.

On the 9th, the lookout was a little gloomier. Tchaikovsky wrote to Anatoly: "In the morning, walking arm in arm with my wife on the Nevsky, I ran into Niks Litke and spoke to him but for some reason could not bring myself to tell him that the lady was my wife. On the way to the theatre in the evening I met Konstantinov. I said nothing to him and managed to escape for once in a while with no more than a loan of five roubles." And, having arranged with his wife that he would leave her at the end of the month to go to Kamenka for a rest, he adds: "I feel that the happiest day of my life will be the first of August."

* She is not difficult to please.

On the 11th things were still worse. "I am really living through a painful period of my life," wrote the composer to Anatoly. "Nevertheless I feel that I am getting used, little by little, to the new position. It would be completely dishonest and intolerable if I had deceived my wife on any point, but I have warned her that she could only expect brotherly love from me. Physically my wife has become clearly repulsive to me. I am sure that some time later the attacks will be renewed but for the time being attempts would be useless."

This passage is generally quoted to show that Tchaikovsky was not his wife's husband, but it could very well show the opposite. It is far from certain that the expression 'brotherly love' should be interpreted as 'platonic love.' Tchaikovsky may have meant that he was not in love with his wife but that he would give her brotherly affection besides the undisputed rights of a wife. How could she have become physically repulsive to him if they had had no physical contact? And he was the one to get used 'little by little to the new position.' That he did not desire her is clear; that he did not do as if he did is not. Anyway he afforded one generous biographer the chance of making a brilliant remark, which would make the composer not only a hardened homosexual but an ambidextrous one: "With one hand [Peter Ilich] wrote Modest his belief that in time he would learn to love Antonina. With the other, three days later, he told Anatoly that she had become physically loathsome to him."[13]

One year later, Mrs von Meck all but asked Tchaikovsky the fateful question: were you her lover or not? "You are the one who knows the temperament of the lady and the character of your relation to her when you lived together. For me one aspect of it remains obscure." The composer did not answer.

On 18th, 19th and 20th July, Mr and Mrs Tchaikovsky visited the bride's mother, who owned some estates not far from Moscow. "Here my torments increased tenfold. The mother and the whole family which I have entered excite antipathy in me. Their ideas are narrow, their opinions barbarous, they are all at swords drawn with one another; Besides my wife was becoming more abhorrent to me by the hour (unjustly perhaps)."

On 26th July Tchaikovsky left alone for Kamenka. On the 28th, he brought Mrs von Meck up to date concerning what 'he had lived through since the day of his marriage.'

I have already written you that I married through no urge of my heart, but because of a chain of circumstances inexplicable to me . . . I imagined first that I could not help loving a girl sincerely attached to me; second, I knew that my marriage was fulfilling the dearest dreams of my father and of other people close and dear to me.

But as soon as the wedding was over, as soon as I remained alone with my wife, knowing that from now on our fate would be to live our life together, inseparably, I began to realize not only that she did not inspire me with the most ordinary friendship but that I *loathed* her in the full meaning of that word. It seemed to me that I, or at least the best, or even the only good part of *me*, my music, was ruined forever. My future appeared to me as a dreary existence, as the most intolerable, agonizing comedy. My wife is in no way guilty towards me: she did not importune me to marry her. Therefore, to let her feel that I do not love her, that I consider her an insupportable nuisance, would be cruel and mean. All that is left is to pretend. But to pretend for a whole life, what could be worse?

Nevertheless he added: "If I am not mistaken in the knowledge of my own nature, it is very probable that, having rested and restored my nerves, once I am back in Moscow and at my ordinary activities, my attitude towards my wife will change completely. In fact she has many potentialities which could, later on, make me happy. She loves me sincerely and wishes only that I might be at peace and happy. I pity her very much." Two weeks went by and, on 11th August, he was in the same disposition, even better: "I am ashamed that I let myself go to such an extent. . . . I am sure I shall triumph in the end. I must fight this alienation that I feel towards my wife, and learn to appreciate her good qualities. There is no doubt that she has some."

Nevertheless, a little before leaving Kamenka, Tchaikovsky seemed somewhat despondent. Not without humour he wrote to Anatoly: "Oh! how little I love Antonina Ivanovna Tchaikovsky! What deep indifference that lady inspires in me! What little pleasure I derive from the prospect of meeting her again! On the other hand she does not terrify me: she bores me, that is all."

On 11th September Tchaikovsky travelled back to Moscow, to the apartment which his wife had furnished during his absence. We have no evidence as to how the meeting worked out, (although some biographers know all about Antonina's 'voracious lips' and her 'too brilliant eyes'), but on the next day the composer wrote to Mrs von Meck and to Anatoly to tell them that he was satisfied with his home: "The arrangements of our home leave nothing to be desired. My wife has done all she possibly could to please me. . . ." "Poor woman, she has gone through some miserable experiences in getting our home ready. . . . Our home pleases me; it is pretty, comfortable, and not altogether wanting in luxury."

Still "his only thought was to find a way of escaping somewhere" and he "called upon death with all the might of his soul."

We have little direct evidence concerning the next ten days. Through Kashkin we know that Tchaikovsky seemed tense in the Conservatoire, nervous about his wife's behaviour in company, and that he attempted to commit suicide as has already been described.* He even accused himself of having been within a hairs-breadth of murdering her, although the image of Tchaikovsky murdering anybody somehow lacks credibility. Anyway—and even if we remember that she was a nymphomaniac and grant that he was a homosexual, we cannot help but feel that there was some disproportion between the causes and the effect—he worked himself up to a real breakdown. That he could have done so in such a short time is so strange that a question arises: did his marriage drive him into a state verging on insanity or was he already in bad shape and did he react to his marriage as he did because of the state in which he was?

On 23rd September Tchaikovsky telegraphed Anatoly, asking that he should send him a telegram ostensibly signed with the name of the conductor Napravnik and summoning the composer to St Petersburg. On the 24th, Tchaikovsky left Moscow under this pretext. His family life was at an end.

5 I agree to be the guilty party

In St Petersburg Anatoly met him at the station and took him to the nearest hotel where he lost consciousness. Doctors were sent for and the composer recovered fast. On 1st October he wrote to Modest: "I am finally becoming myself again and coming back to life." On 4th October he was already in Berlin and beginning a long trip which was to take him to Austria, Switzerland, France and Italy. He came back to Russia in the beginning of April 1878.

His friends, especially Nikolai Rubinstein, stood by him and undertook to explain the situation to Mrs Tchaikovsky. She bewildered everybody by her calm. "I never would have thought that Rubinstein would come and have tea with me today," was her com-

* Cf. p. 92.

o

ment. She would agree to everything for Peter's sake, she said, even never to see him again as the doctors suggested. As we shall see, she soon changed her mind, but it is not our purpose to follow all her whims: we want to know what was becoming of the composer, and this will be relatively easy since the sources, which went under at the time of the crisis, reappear as soon as the crisis is past.

On 5th October Tchaikovsky wrote to Modest: "Do not expect from me a description of what I had to undergo during this last month. I still cannot recollect without a smarting pain the torture through which I have gone. Some day I shall tell you about it."

On the 9th, to his sister Sasha: "I expect a letter . . . from my poor wife in order to reach a decision." He meant a decision about a possible separation or divorce. It is interesting that Mrs Tchaikovsky was still at this point 'his poor wife.'

On 11th October to Mrs von Meck: "I feel that everybody must now despise me for my cowardice, my weakness, my foolishness. I am mortally afraid that a feeling akin to contempt for me will also pass through your mind. But this is because I am morbidly suspicious. In reality I know that you will instinctively understand that I am an unhappy, not a bad man. . . . I should like to tell you many things, I should like to describe my wife, to explain why we cannot live together, why all this happened and how I reached the conviction that I should never get used to her, but I still cannot find in me the quiet tone of voice necessary to tell the story." Which indicates clearly enough that either Tchaikovsky was boldly lying or he did not attribute the failure of his marriage to his own peculiar tastes.

On 17th October to Modest: "Whatever happens I shall never agree to spend be it only one day with Antonina Ivanovna! I wish her every happiness, which does not prevent me from hating her. I should accept any torture so long as I should not have to see her. So your hope to transform her into a companion for life suitable for me is vain. First, experience has shown that it is insane that I should live with a wife. Second, even if this would be possible with somebody else, with A.I. it is not, I never met a more loathsome human being. You are wrong to imagine that she is kind. This is a great mistake. But I shall not talk any longer about her. She is hateful to me." It is to be wondered what transformations Modest may have dreamed to introduce into Mrs Tchaikovsky in order to turn her into a suitable companion for a homosexual. It is to be noted that for the first time Tchaikovsky begins to criticize his wife, to find real or imaginary faults in her. The reference to her non-existent kindness is particularly interesting. There must have been something besides sexual misunderstandings to separate the couple.

On 20th October Tchaikovsky begins to give some explanations to Mrs von Meck: "Without work life has no meaning for me. To work in the presence of a person who was apparently so close but in fact so foreign was impossible. I have lived through a terrible ordeal and I deem it a miracle that my soul has not been killed by it, only severely wounded. My sister, as intelligent as she is kind, writes to me that she has . . . found my poor wife and taken her to her estate. My sister has promised me to arrange my future relations with my wife. What will help her much is that my wife has an incomprehensibly calm disposition. She who, by threatening to commit suicide, made me come to her place, has endured my flight, our separation, the news of my illness, with an indifference which I cannot understand at all. Oh! how blind, how insane I have been!"

Finally, on 25th October the composer, having apparently found a satisfactory—though somewhat tense—tone of voice, submits to Mrs von Meck a long report which has been cleverly cut into small pieces by different biographers,[14] and reproduced by them with minor mistranslations, in an unrecognizable form. Thanks to this subterfuge we are led to believe that lots of evidence is available concerning the mysterious period in September when the couple lived together. Unfortunately it is not so, and all or nearly all the information that we have comes from this report; in other words it corresponds to one mood of the composer, and, still more narrowly, to the image he cared to give of his wife and himself to one particular person, his friend and benefactress, Mrs von Meck. We do not believe that Tchaikovsky lied in his letter, but we definitely do think that jigsaw methods cannot give objective results. For once, we have a context and, long as it is, we want to keep it.

Antonina Ivanovna, wrote Tchaikovsky,

is of medium height, blonde, rather unattractively built, but with a face of the kind of beauty known as cuteness. Her eyes are of a beautiful colour but expressionless; her lips are too thin, so that her smile is rather unpleasant. Her complexion is pink. In general she looks very young: she is twenty-nine but she does not look more than twenty-three or twenty-four. Her manners are full of affectation; she never makes one simple movement, one simple gesture. However her appearance is rather attractive than the opposite. Neither in the expression of her face nor in her movements can one find that elusive grace which reflects inner, spiritual beauty, and which cannot be acquired: it is given by nature. In my wife one constantly, permanently, sees the desire to please; this artificiality spoils her appearance. Nevertheless she belongs to the category of good-looking women, i.e. those who retain the attention of men who meet them. So far it was not difficult for me to describe my wife. Now that I have to begin presenting her spiritual and intellectual sides, I find an unconquerable obstacle. In her head and in her heart there is an absolute emptiness; therefore I can particularize neither the one nor the other. I can only give you my word that not once did she express in my presence one thought or one feeling. She was demonstrative with me, that is true. But her demonstrations consisted in constant hugging, in constant caresses, even at times when I could not hide from her my—perhaps undeserved—antipathy, which grew with every hour. I felt that behind these caresses there was no real feeling. It was something conventional, something which seemed indispensable to her, an attribute of married life. Not once did she show the least desire to know what I was doing, in what consisted my profession, what were my plans, what I was reading, what I liked in intellectual and artistic domains. Among other things I was particularly astonished by the following fact. She told me that she had been in love with me for four years, and she is quite a decent musician. Can you imagine, this being so, that she did not know one note of my music, and only the day before my flight asked me what piano pieces of mine she should buy from Jurgenson. This really nonplussed me. I was not less surprised to learn from her that she never went to the concerts and quartets sponsored by the Musical Society, whereas she certainly knew that the object of her four-year love could be met at these functions, and she had the possibility to attend them. You will of course want to know how we spent our time when we stayed alone together? She is very talkative but all her talking is limited to the following subjects. All the time she told me innumerable tales about the innumerable men who entertained tender feelings for her. For the most part they were generals, nephews of famous bankers, famous artists, even members of the Imperial family. Then, just as often and with an inexplicable fascination she described to me the vices, the cruelties, the villainies, the repugnant behaviour of all her relatives: it seems she is at swords drawn with all of them, without exception. Her mother was particularly ill-treated on these occasions. My wife has two friends whom I had to meet. During the several weeks which I spent living with my wife, both these friends unceasingly fell and rose in her opinion. At the very beginning of our acquaintance she had one more friend whom she called her sister, so much she loved her. Two weeks had not elapsed when this sister of hers fell in her opinion to the lowest level of human degradation. When we went to visit her mother in the country, during the summer, they seemed on the best of terms.

When I came back from Kamenka, I learned that they had already
seriously quarrelled in Moscow, and soon I received from the mother
a letter in which she complained about the disobedience of her
daughter. The third subject of her indefatigable chattering consisted in stories about her life at school. These knew no end.

To give you an idea of the impossibility of obtaining from her
any sincere reaction of the soul, here is an example:

I wished to learn something about her maternal instincts and
I asked her once if she was fond of children. "Yes," she answered,
"when they are smart."

My flight and the news of my illness, which my brother brought
her, she took with an incredible indifference and immediately told
him about several men who had fallen in love with her; then she
asked what he liked for dinner and ran into the kitchen to take
care of it. In all fairness I have to add this: she tried to please me
as best she could, she positively abased herself before me;* not
once did she object to any desire or idea of mine, even concerning
housekeeping. She sincerely wanted to earn my love and lavished on
me a superabundance of affectionate demonstrations.

As you read all this you must wonder that I could have bound
my life to such a strange companion. At present I do not understand
it myself. A kind of insanity swept over me. I imagined that I should
surely be touched by her love for me, in which I then believed, and
that I should begin to love her in return. Now I have the inner
certitude that she never loved me. But one must be fair. She behaved honestly and sincerely. She mistook her desire to marry me
for love. And then, I repeat it, she did all she could to attach me
to her.

Alas! the more she tried, the more she drove me away. In vain
did I fight a feeling of antipathy which, as a matter of fact, she does
not deserve; but what could I do with my defiant heart! This
antipathy grew every minute and little by little became a hatred,
earnest and fierce, of a kind which I had never experienced and did
not expect from myself. I finally lost my self-control.

What happened later you know.

At the present time my wife lives temporarily with my sister.
Later she will choose a permanent residence.

Yesterday my brother received a letter from her. She presents
herself in a completely new light. The tender dove has suddenly
become a rather angry, very demanding, very untruthful person.
She makes many accusations against me, the meaning of which is
that I have wickedly deceived her. I have replied to her, explaining
categorically that I did not intend to enter any discussion with her
since that would lead us nowhere. I agree to be the guilty party.
I begged her to forgive me all the harm which I nevertheless did to
her, and I bowed in advance before any decision she might wish to

* The Russian word *presmykat'sa* suggests a reptile. See below, page 217.

reach. As to living with her, this would never be; I have told her so in the most decisive form. Then I of course undertook her expenses and asked her to accept her livelihood from me. I shall expect her reply. At present I have already taken care of her needs for some time.

That is all that I can tell you about my relations with my wife. When I look retrospectively at our short life together, I come to the conclusion that *le beau rôle** is altogether hers and not mine. I have to repeat that she behaved honestly, sincerely and coherently. With her love she was deceiving herself, not me. I think that she was really convinced that she loved me. On my side I had very clearly explained to her that I did not love her but promised to do everything to try to do so. And since I have reached a result directly opposite to that one, I have therefore deceived her. Anyway she deserves compassion. Judging by her letter of yesterday, it is apparent that offended pride has lifted its head in her and is now speaking very loudly indeed.

Speaking about coherence, this is not a very coherent letter, and it contradicts some of the scanty information we have. If Tchaikovsky and his wife had agreed on platonic relations, what does he mean by the word "attacks" in his letter to Anatoly since he says that Antonina behaved coherently? And why, if Tchaikovsky's report is a truthful one, did his wife accuse him of deceiving her? If they had not agreed on platonic relations and he refused to fulfil his duty, how can he say that he 'agrees to be the guilty party'? He could be lying, of course, but does one feel any real sense of guilt in this whole letter? Not the slightest. Shame at having fled, yes, but guilt, no. We have to assume then that Tchaikovsky told Miss Milukov that he would try to be her lover and did not succeed. But this is obviously false since when the separation became necessary and divorce was envisaged no one ever spoke of an annulment, which would have been the easy way out if the marriage had not been consummated.† In other words the situation is mysterious and will remain mysterious as long as we have no access to the real sources.

The next day Tchaikovsky wrote to Modest a letter which we know only in part and which, instead of clarifying matters, makes them even more obscure.

The last letter (from my wife) is remarkable: in it the dove who touched you so much that you contemplated the possibility of a reconciliation between us in the distant future, has suddenly be-

* The nice part.
† This point has been entirely disregarded by all biographers.

come a fierce, perfidious and astute she-cat. I was turned into a
deceiver who had married her to disguise myself. I insulted her
every day, she had much to suffer from me, she is appalled by my
awful vice, etc, etc. Oh! how disgusting! But devil take her. The
letter from Sasha is also unpleasant. From what she says I conclude
that since even Baby* knows my story and condemns me, I have
nothing better to expect from anybody else.

Now what does all that mean? That Baby had been told that
his Uncle Peter was a homosexual? This is scarcely probable. That
Antonina Tchaikovsky knew about her husband's instincts? This
could be; but then why did she never sue for divorce on such
serious grounds? And then are we to assume that Tchaikovsky
in this passage confesses to having married Antonina 'to disguise
himself'? His indignation seems to indicate the opposite: he seems
to say that this is what she accuses him of doing, but she is a perfidious she-cat, devil take her! And all the biographers who followed
suit are included in the same condemnation: they are all perfidious
he or she-cats, devil take them! Was then Tchaikovsky lying to
Modest? Or to himself? And if he really was a homosexual and
had told her so, how are we to understand that he does not seem
frightened? Surely a man who was as touchy about his reputation
as Tchaikovsky† and who knew himself guilty would have been
afraid of the disclosures that his wife could make. But Tchaikovsky
was not.

On the same day the composer wrote to Sasha who had become
Antonina's champion. "Let my wife be innocent and me guilty on
all counts: I still cannot live with her, I still dislike her in the full
meaning of the word. . . . We have not quarrelled; I do not accuse
her of anything. . . . Tell Antonina Ivanovna to forgive the harsh
tone of my last letter; it has been provoked by her unexpected and
insulting accusations." Once again, without denying Antonina's
accusations in as many words, Tchaikovsky is certainly very far
from owning up. Later the same day or more probably the next
one, after having received other news, the composer wrote to
Sasha again:

Having thought about it, I am glad that she has finally abandoned
the part of a gentle lamb which touched you so much. I have replied
to her; you will find my reply included; please give it to her and
read it with her. And then explain to her, my angel, that I understand all the extent of my guilt towards her, but let her know that

* Tchaikovsky's beloved nephew, Vladimir Davydov. He was six at the
time.
† Cf. p. 255.

I remember everything that passed before our marriage, down to the smallest detail, and that she too should remember a little better how we got on intimate terms. She seems to have forgotten everything. Fondled by you, she seems to have imagined that it was I who insisted on our marriage, that it was I who, by my passionate eloquence, touched her heart, in a word that I am guilty on all counts. But she has to be guilty too, if only a little. I cannot hide from you that the presence of Antonina Ivanovna in your midst is the most painful wound in my heart. I am glad that you treated her so affectionately, but I am not glad that now all the inhabitants of Kamenka know my story. How shall I appear among you when even Baby accuses me, when even he knows all?

The reference to Baby is again rather startling.

To Mrs von Meck Tchaikovsky wrote in more or less the same terms, expressing pity for his wife who had no friend but him, and some annoyance at Sasha, who still intended to *transmute* Antonina into an acceptable wife. This is difficult to understand if we assume that Sasha thought of her brother as a homosexual: * such a change would have been a transmutation indeed!

And the alternation of good and bad feelings towards Antonina Ivanovna goes on. To Anatoly: "When I picture to myself that you are maybe travelling with Antonina Ivanovna, the blood turns to ice in my veins from sheer horror. What can be more awful than to contemplate this revolting creation of Nature! What are such reptiles born for? And what was the point of the madness which came over me? What was the use of all this vulgar tragicomedy?" To Sasha: "I bear her no grudge. But I beg of you, when you are distressed for her, remember that forty thousand of her spiritual sufferings are nothing compared to what I experienced during that time!! From that standpoint she can consider herself satisfied. If I have done her unintended harm, she has done me a million times more of the same. . . ." "Her heart is not wounded in the least. Her vanity is most painfully insulted and I understand that she must suffer. . . ." "She has told Anatoly about her suspicions: my servant Mihailo, having lost his place as a consequence of my marriage, would have gone to see a witch and by means of her wizardry would have put hate in my heart towards my wife. You cannot want me to confirm that story. She has begun to imagine that I changed towards her after staying in Kamenka. I can only be surprised that she did not notice the progressive exhaustion which I underwent in my struggle with my own heart." The passage concerning the witch is essential: it shows that An-

* Cf. p. 198.

tonina had no clear idea of why her husband did not love her. It shows also on what intellectual level she felt and thought. Sasha must have been something of a busybody. "With wonderful zest she undertook the re-education of my wife and kept sending me letters in which she tried to convince me that my wife had many real qualities and that with time she would become an excellent helpmate for me. . . . She could not understand that my antipathy to my wife, deserved or undeserved, was a pathological state, that I should be left in peace and that it was unnecessary not only to describe the qualities of but even to mention a woman whose name and remembrance drove me to insanity." Finally Antonina and all the colonels who were supposed to have fallen in love with her were too much for Sasha herself. "Little by little she arrived to the conclusion that any man who would have been mad enough to marry my wife would have had no recourse but to run away." Antonina was politely asked to leave, and on 12th December Tchaikovsky, who had felt himself excluded from a place and a family very dear to him, was assured that all the inhabitants of Kamenka forgave and understood him.

6 The formidable avenger of my villainies and vices

Soon monetary problems took precedence over sentimental ones. Tchaikovsky gave Antonina a monthly allowance, which he raised as he became richer. When she had not pestered him with letters for some time, he rewarded her by an extra gift. With cold shrewdness he realized that exactly this type of material help, a monthly allowance which he could raise or lower at will, was necessary to hold her under control. He must be alluding to facts that we do not know when he writes to Mrs von Meck: "I do not want to acquaint you, my friend, with loathsome details proving that *a certain person** is not only hollow and a nullity but at the

* Antonina generally was "The Reptile' 'to Tchaikovsky's brothers, "A certain person" to Mrs von Meck and "The person bearing my name" to Jurgenson.

same time a being deserving utter contempt." All this was naturally pretty expensive, but Tchaikovsky did not mind: "The more the better, since it will give me more freedom and less worrying. I ought to pay for my foolishness. Only with money can I buy the right to despise as much as I hate." Since after all Tchaikovsky had undoubtedly undertaken to provide for Miss Milukov when he married her, there must be some unknown factor which allowed him to despise her for accepting his money. What this factor was is a matter of surmise.

Having once recovered from his nervous illness, Tchaikovsky showed considerable resilience. In March 1878 he was already writing to Anatoly: "There is no trace left in me of my sickly mental state. I have become again what I was before the catastrophe. I am now used to think about the catastrophe itself as about the manifestation of madness, of insanity. At the future I look without any fear." This by the way would confirm the interpretation according to which Tchaikovsky married Antonina because he was already in a slightly pathological state for reasons unknown to us. In May he was still optimistic: "Of course it will be necessary to live through several unpleasant minutes, but finally everything will turn out right. . . . Even if I did not attain the desired aim (divorce) there would be no ground for despair. Whatever happens, my conscience will remain clear. Now I have done everything to atone for my guilt concerning a certain person. I have now perfectly obvious proof that she is completely deprived of the ensemble of human qualities known as a soul. She is incapable of spiritual suffering. The only part of her which can suffer is the most despicable vanity of a female possessed by a mania consisting in imagining that all males, I included, are in love with her. She cannot acknowledge that I am really trying to obtain a separation because of a spiritual repugnance towards her." Mrs von Meck having suggested that Rubinstein could exercise his influence on Antonina in order to persuade her to ask for a divorce, Tchaikovsky replied that, according to him, Rubinstein had no such influence and that there were reasons why he did not want to have that gentleman interfere in his affairs. "As to the risk that Rubinstein and others might learn the real reasons of my rupture with a certain person, there is no reason to fear it, my friend. First they all know these reasons very well. Second, since I have recovered and become a man with normal intellectual capacities, I can afford again to pay no attention to *les qu'en dira-t-on*."* This is an in-

* Gossip.

teresting passage: if the real reasons and the gossip had to do with homosexuality, it is doubtful that Tchaikovsky would have written to Mrs von Meck about them.

In September Tchaikovsky referred to Antonina as to "that living monument of my insanity" and could even laugh at the unexpected letters which he received from the mother of that lady: "Her mother bombards me with letters full of declarations of the most tender affection, invitations to visit her and requests that I should give away her younger daughter who is getting married: my blessing, she says, will bring happiness to the girl (!!!!).'' When Modest suggested that some spying could bring out new circumstances favourable for a divorce, Tchaikovsky was disgusted and said so. It is only at the end of the year that, for a brief time, he fell back into a hysterical mood, the pretext of which was a letter in which Anatoly said that he had received the visit of an unknown gentleman empowered to act for Antonina: "Your letter . . . left me absolutely thunderstruck. Although my mind told me that it was all nonsense, all my being was shocked by this reminder of the Reptile. I never thought about her any more! Sometimes in Florence in the midst of my meditations and dreams I would remember the whole story and have trouble to convince myself that it had happened in reality and not in a nightmare. On arriving here I received one after the other two reminders of the Reptile, from Jurgenson and from you. As soon as I saw her handwriting, I felt myself unhappy and my heart fell. Such is the venom of that monster. Your letter finished me. But yesterday I was already more peaceful and today I have begun to forget." His hysterical moods seldom lasted long: three days later he was already making fun of that one: "I laugh and feel ashamed when I remember what a to-do I raised about your letter concerning Antonina Ivanovna. I become completely mad as soon as this business comes up! What did I not picture to myself! Among other things I had already imagined that she was starting a criminal suit and wanted to accuse me. I vividly saw myself in the dock, and, although I harried the prosecutor in my last speech, I was nevertheless destroyed under the light of an infamous accusation. In my letters to you I feigned courage but actually I thought myself lost. Now all this appears to me as sheer insanity."

If we were to assume that (a) Tchaikovsky was a real homosexual, (b) that he had given his wife grounds to believe that he was one, then there would have been nothing insane about such fears; on the contrary, it would have been madness on his part to insist on any public action such as a divorce. More than that.

If we assume only that Tchaikovsky married Antonina in order to re-establish his reputation and that she knew nothing about his tastes, even then we should expect him to try to keep their separation a secret. After all, what could be more convenient than a secretly separated wife, who would be there to produce when necessary, would stay elsewhere at all other times, and could be kept on a leash by means of a generous allowance? But there is little doubt that Tchaikovsky wanted a divorce and wanted it badly. He hoped that she 'would fall in love with somebody else and demand a divorce: this would be the best thing for him.' His sister, who certainly would have objected to any unseemly gossip, advised Antonina to ask for a divorce and took pains to persuade her that Tchaikovsky would never accept to live with her any more. A divorce was "so desirable" that the composer tried to bribe Antonina into suing for one: she was to receive a handsome sum of money (which Mrs von Meck would gladly have provided) for giving Tchaikovsky his legal freedom. When she refused, a year's respite was granted to her for meditation, and if she agreed, the procedure could then begin, at somewhat less advantageous conditions. In all this Antonina behaved not as a despicable mercenary creature, but as a completely unbalanced one. Now she would not hear of a divorce at any price, now she 'wanted to force Tchaikovsky to agree to the fulfilment of his dearest wish.' As for the composer, 'he was ready for a divorce at any time.'

It cannot be seriously argued that he was afraid of any disclosures she could make. He treated her with the authoritative manner of a man who had nothing to fear: "I tried to explain to her that she had no right to demand anything and that if she dared bother me or any of my relatives with her letters, she would be punished by a cut or if need be by a cancellation of her allowance. I advised her not to lead an idle life, to undertake some kind of work, to keep quiet and to try to deserve my pity and not my hatred." If she took a lawyer, so much the better. "Of what could she complain? Can I even for a minute be afraid of her efforts to harm me? The only thing she can do is to demand a divorce, which is exactly what I want and what she refused." The lawyer would have to be "a person officially empowered by her." "Nothing mysterious" was to be tolerated; 'no blackmail was possible': "I have been unquestionably honest with her and not once did I use any expression which could have compromised me." Tchaikovsky expressed satisfaction on learning that Antonina had important connections. He was indignant when Antonina declared that she was weary of the numberless insults which she had to suffer; he deduced 'that she did not understand what it was all about' from the fact that 'she spoke of being indulgent as if she had the right to demand anything from me.' To Jurgenson he said in as many words that he had nothing to fear: "From what you write I conclude that you do not entirely know the substance of my relation to her and that you are quite pointlessly afraid that she could somehow harm me. There is no such danger. The danger is that I am not sure of myself. If I were to meet her, I could very well have a fit of madness and strangle or kill her. Let me assure you that it nearly happened last year and that this is a serious risk." We would naturally be tempted to ridicule this threatening declaration from such a man, but we should not forget at least that the same theme—obviously an incident which stuck in Tchaikovsky's memory—is to be found in one of his letters to Mrs von Meck: "When I think of her, I am filled with such anger, such loathing, such criminal desires, that I am afraid of myself. It is an illness against which there is only one remedy: not to see, not to meet her, and if possible avoid contacts. Even now, when I am writing these lines to you, and the hateful image necessarily rises before my eyes, I am agitated, tormented, furious, and I hate myself not less than her. Last year, in September, there was one evening when I was very close, within one step, from that blind, crazy, sick anger which leads to crime. I assure you, I was only saved by a miracle." As to being afraid of his wife, Tchaikovsky felt so much the opposite that, at one point, he even contemplated pretending that he was, in order to persuade her to ask for a divorce: "maybe she will then become more amenable and will accept a divorce in order to do me a bad turn."

A complete ignorance of Russian laws is displayed by all biographers[15] who wonder why Tchaikovsky did not himself sue for a divorce, especially when Antonina had taken a lover and had several children by him. But this at least is easily explained. Adultery was the only ground on which divorce was granted by the Church, which was in charge of all matters having to do with matrimony. The adultery had to be proved, and the guilty party had no right to marry again: only the plaintiff could remarry. Before Antonina took a lover, Tchaikovsky could not accuse her of adultery and consequently could not ask for a divorce After she started living with the man and had children by him, it would have been particularly ugly to prosecute her for a state of things for which, after all, her husband was directly responsible through his flight. The only way for them to obtain a divorce which would have allowed the innocent party, Antonina, to marry again if she wanted, was for her to accuse Tchaikovsky of infidelity. Obviously he could not force her to do so if she refused. He could only induce her by the hope of material gain.

At first, thanks to Mrs von Meck's material help and energetic advice, the composer's hopes were high, and Antonina, after some wavering, seemed agreeable. Tchaikovsky would give her 10,000 roubles on the day when the divorce would be pronounced; he would take care of all expenses, would declare himself guilty, and would sign an I.O.U. for 2,500 roubles which Antonina demanded as a supplement. Jurgenson undertook to explain to her exactly what she would have to say and do to obtain satisfaction. But suddenly Mrs Tchaikovsky changed her mind. She declared that she would not lie for anything on earth. When Jurgenson told her that she would not have to lie, that her husband's 'guilt' would be 'proved,' she calmly replied: "And I shall prove the opposite." In fact she had come to believe that Tchaikovsky was still in love with her, but that for some inexplicable reasons, his family had arranged for a divorce even before they were married, and wrote to the priest who had performed the ceremony that it was his responsibility to persuade the composer to go back to her. Tchaikovsky was sad that his desire for complete freedom was not to be fulfilled till circumstances changed and Antonina herself wished for a divorce, but he was naturally reluctant to appear before a clerical court of justice in front of which Antonina would have declared that the proofs of her husband's guilt were false and that she asked for nothing better than to live again with him. This indeed would have been a scandal. Her insanity began to appear more and more clearly. "She suggests that I come to her in Moscow and that we go together to the people (???) to be judged and divorced by them. She undertakes to prove to the people that she is not guilty, as if I had once accused her of anything, irresponsible as she is." Irritated by the loss of his hopes, Tchaikovsky declared that 'he wanted her to behave as if she did not exist,' and again proposed to punish her by diminishing her allowance. If he did not think her guilty of the failure of their marriage, he obviously despised her for other misdeeds. He was deeply indignant when he wrote to Mrs von Meck: "She is actually taking herself for the personification of virtue, and even now, when she has been un-masked for a long time, she still wants to be the formidable avenger of my villainies and vices. If you read her last letter to me, you would be horrified to see how far can go insane oblivion of truth and facts, insolence, stupidity and outrage. . . . There is no way to free her from the idea that sooner or later I shall live with her. . . . It is impossible to start a divorce suit now. The only hope is that perhaps one day she will understand and then take the initiative." This hope never came true: Tchaikovsky remained a married man until his death.

In the meanwhile Antonina did not cease pestering him. She wrote him love letters in which she told him how painful it was for her to listen to love declarations from other men. She ambushed him in the streets, she waylaid him at his brother's. She accepted bribes to leave him in peace but still believed that he loved her, just as all other men. Maybe Modest was right in saying that 'she was not a human being but something special,' so pitiful and disgusting did she succeed in making herself. Those two adjectives belong to Tchaikovsky: they are harsh but scarcely exaggerated. In March 1879, as if by chance, she rented a room in the house in which he lived, and invited him to come and see her: "My dear little Petichka! What is happening to you? I have not seen you, I have no news from you. Maybe you are ill. . . ? Please come and visit me, my dear. I should however be sad if you came only for a cere-monious visit, in order to satisfy me. . . . Nothing on earth will ever make me cease loving you; at least have compassion on me. I belong to you body and soul, do with me what you like. . . . You are a hundred times more intelligent than I. You should seriously think about our situation, and then let us discuss it like real men and wives do. Until now God only knows what our relations were. . . . I kiss you a numberless amount of times, although you are not here. I know that you are not particularly fond of the real thing. All right, I shall try not to displease you; forgive me for last time. I am devoted to you with all the might of my soul. Antonina. I write in the dark: this is why my handwriting is so messy." When this did not succeed, she took his apartment by assault with the help of her sister and demanded a reconciliation. "After I said and repeated several times 'Never, never, not at any price' she did not resort to tears and hysterics but raised the question of her allowance. I expressed satisfaction at seeing that we could now talk figures. . . . I was injudicious enough to say that from time to time I should give her supplements to her allowance and allowed her to have recourse to me if she found herself in any special need. Finally she left. I was rather shaken, but at dinner, with Kondratiev, I ate and drank well and went back home at around nine in a perfectly quiet state of mind. Here I found a note from the Reptile: she had overspent in St Petersburg and wanted fifty roubles. I had the weakness to send her twenty-five." The conclusion of all that was that Tchaikovsky rather sensibly wanted to arrange his apartment so as not to be taken by surprise any more.

Later the tone of Antonina's letters changed. "I find no honour in corresponding with you, Sir," she wrote, "but . . . I have decided to write to you one last time." She began by accepting the idea of a divorce, then switched to nasty remarks about Tchaikovsky's relatives, and accused him and his brothers of spreading gossip about her. 'Why did you not begin with yourself?' she added. 'You should first have confessed your own awful vice and then you might have judged me." She repeated that she would not sign any "dirty and improbable" document. She concluded by entrusting the whole business to her mother. The mother in turn was not favourable to 'a scandalous divorce' and offered, maybe hinting at the possibility of blackmail, a friendly separation: Tchaikovsky would pay and Antonina would leave him in peace, the ideal solution for a man who would really have had something to hide: "You are a genius," she wrote, "your reputation is important to you. You must believe that we shall not soil it but shall remain faithful to our word of honour, as befits an honourable and genteel family." Why did the Milukovs recoil before a divorce which could only have turned to their advantage? There must be some reasons that have not reached us. Anyway there is no evidence that this attempt at blackmail—if it was one —had any particular effect on its victim.

There is no evidence either that Tchaikovsky was overjoyed when in 1881 he got from Jurgenson—who had taken upon himself all the less savoury aspects of the proceedings—'irrefutable proof' that Antonina had had a child by a Mr Bolkov, master of arts, lawyer, and "unattractive." The child was sent to an asylum; other children followed, and Tchaikovsky was more or less safe, since Antonina was now the one really guilty of adultery. At least such is the opinion of most commentators, but Tchaikovsky expressed no exultation on receiving the news: on the contrary, for the first time he began feeling seriously concerned about his wife. In 1883 he wrote to Jurgenson: "For a long time I have been worried by the idea that I may not be entirely right in abandoning to her fate the unfortunate person who is bound to me by the ties of pseudo-matrimony. More and more often this thought bothers me. If she is in need, if she has been jilted by her lover (which is very probable), if she has no home, it is fitting that I should help her." Those of her letters which reached him caused him "deep grief," but not for very long: he had an enviable aptitude for forgetting.

TCHAIKOVSKY AND HIS SECRETS

Jurgenson was in charge of the censure and whenever he sent a letter on to Tchaikovsky instead of reading and answering it himself, the composer complained in the most bitter terms. Jurgenson was not even supposed to write about Mrs Tchaikovsky: "My friend, how cruel you are towards me! Oh, it is only involuntarily that one can harm a friend as much as you have harmed me by today's letter. I beg of you, never write to me about Antonina Ivanovna unless it is absolutely necessary. Any news of her, of her new tricks, irritate and kill me without any use to anybody. This is an awful wound of mine which I implore you not to touch if it can be avoided. All day I have been like a madman, I cannot eat or work (this is the most dreadful: now for several days I shall not be able to work), or read, or walk, in one word I am deeply unhappy. Of course I am being morbid about it. What of it if a madwoman has again done something insane? Well, I am the victim of my peculiar, hysterical nature."

In 1886, Antonina wrote to express two startling wishes: why would not Tchaikovsky dedicate a piece of music to her and, even more startling, why would he not undertake to bring up her children? In 1889, she sent him a threatening letter of which, as is always the case when serious matters are in question, we are allowed to read only one small quotation. The Soviet editor tells us that this letter is very long, full of reproaches and of complaints, and that Tchaikovsky must have been shocked by Antonina's threats to publicize his hidden instincts. Unfortunately the quotation that is available contains no such reference although it does indicate that Antonina possessed or seemed to possess some information which could have been damning if it was disclosed. But then Antonina was a madwoman, and Tchaikovsky showed no special fear after receiving the letter. Here is the quotation: "My mother was a friend of a sister of the deceased N. V. Mesentsov, who was a police general. He knew about you and suggested personally to me that I should give him a report which would enable him to prosecute you. . . . (Omission in the quotation) . . . If I wished it I still could hurt you. But this will never be. What right have I to judge you?" Whether Antonina really could hurt Tchaikovsky by disclosing a mystery or just imagined that she could, she was true to her word "as befits an honourable and genteel family" and, to our knowledge, never gossiped about him.

We possess only one letter written by Tchaikovsky to his wife. He never mailed it, which is why history did not lose it. It is of

P

course an essential document; it has never been translated in any Western language; it was written on 30th January/11th February, 1890.

Antonina Ivanovna! You have lately been behaving like an unreasonable child* and I am obliged to punish you as a child, by depriving you of a material benefit. I shall reduce your allowance by one third; from now on and until I change my mind you will receive one hundred roubles. I advise you of this and at the same time I think that it may not be unnecessary to tell you a few things, although I have little hope that you will read in my letter what I shall put in it and not what you will imagine. You are again like a child in that you believe in the creations of your imagination as in real things. Will you please read attentively what I shall tell you now and, be it only for once in your life, will you be sober about a grim and sad reality. Four years ago, in a letter where you unceasingly humbled yourself, you asked me for financial help. This help you did not deserve and here is why: (1) When, in 1878, I offered you the means to which resort all unsuitable couples, you let yourself be moved by some blind whim and decisively refused a divorce which would have given freedom to you and me. (2) Once separated from me you were far richer than I, and I am not responsible if you did not keep your small property. (3) Having refused to divorce, you began to poison systematically my life, now by insulting letters full of reproaches and of threats (the meaning of which I never could understand), now by presenting yourself in my home and pursuing me from one capital to the other. (4) Having contracted an illegitimate liaison with a man with whom I am not acquainted, you discontinued your letters and requests only because of imaginary fears that I might somehow spoil your well-being (as you explained to me later, in great detail). (5) This liaison brought you three children whom you sent to an asylum!!!! (I also have a very detailed letter from you concerning that subject.) (6) At the time when you requested help from me, i.e. four years ago, you were in perfect health and apt to work. To sum up: having refused to divorce, deserved my justified indignation by persecuting me, being an independent woman, having nevertheless sent your children to an asylum and being consequently in good health, not old, and without any worries, you deserved a negative answer. However, out of pity for you, I decided to give you fifty roubles a month, and your gratitude was at that time boundless, since you vaguely understood that you had not the slightest right to demand anything from me. Soon after that, having become richer thanks to a pension granted by the Tsar, I doubled my monthly help to you. A year had not elapsed when you wished for a new raise.

* Antonina had applied for a position as a teacher at the Conservatoire and said she intended to ask money from the Tsar.

Again I said yes. Now you present absolutely fantastic demands including a position at the Conservatoire, and you quote the example of A. I. Hubert!!!!* This new mania that you have of writing requests, complaints and letters is finally becoming intolerable to me. I have not the right to prevent you from it, and although every new creation of your indefatigable pen serves only to prove again how right I am, I have not the slightest desire to spend money earned by my work on improving your well-being, when you show so much ingratitude and forgetfulness of a very recent past! I deplore the necessity of telling you so many unpleasant things. But am I responsible for the strict measures which you force me to take? On the other hand, how easy it would be for you to rouse in me nothing but a strong desire to make your joyless life a little sweeter for you. I should be very happy to eradicate for ever from my heart any bad feeling towards you, to provide you with some help, in a word to be, although from a distance, of service and assistance to you. Alas! As soon as pity for you triumphs over aversion, as soon as I feel the urge to show compassion for you and to forget the past, you, with astonishing miscalculation, with incredible tactlessness, with a levity unbelievable in a person of your age, begin again to antagonize me. I have learned from Peter Ivanovich [Jurgenson] that you had written to Rubinstein. This is really unimaginable!!! The cup of patience is overflowing. Do not answer me; otherwise I shall take even stricter measures. Good-bye. I shall not write to you for a long time. Try and understand how you ought to behave. If you do not, it is too bad for you. P. Tchaikovsky. P.S.—I advise you to get rid of your hostility towards P. I. Jurgenson, whom you praised so highly so little time ago. He has no hostility towards you and can be an excellent go-between.

It is a hard letter, even a brutal one. Tchaikovsky was not a hard or brutal man. That he lived in a patriarchal society, where marrying rich husbands and divorcing them for alimony had not yet become a sport, can explain his overbearing and sometimes pedantic tone, but not the substance of what he says. It is clear that he felt entitled to his hatred of the Reptile, that whatever he gave her he thought she did not deserve. Why? We could of course invent some explanation having to do, for instance, with Antonina's past, or with her behaviour at Kamenka, but irritating though it is we prefer to leave the question open. Maybe there is no mystery, maybe it was only Antonina's personality which brought Tchaikovsky so far out of character. What naturally should not be forgotten is that she was insane, and that mad people living among normal ones can have the strangest whims. . . . In

* Otherwise known as Batashka.

1896, three years after Tchaikovsky's death, she was confined to a lunatic asylum.* She died in 1917, and if she knew any of Tchaikovsky's secrets—which is doubtful—she took them with her.

7 My friend will hear and understand

Tchaikovsky's relationship with Désirée Artôt will probably never become clearer than it is now; the story of his marriage with and separation from Antonina Milukov could perhaps be understood a little better if primary sources were disclosed; his friendship with Mrs von Meck is well known, and—with one exception—it is only through excess of information and interpretation that it has been made to sound mysterious. Titles like "Beloved Friend" or "Florentine Idyll"†[16] are voluntarily misleading; and the amount of bad literature written about this rewarding straightforward friendship would no doubt have startled the protagonists of the real events. A summary of the facts may be useful here.

December 1876: a rich widow, Nadejda von Meck, impressed by young Tchaikovsky's music, writes to tell him so. Wishing to help the composer, she begins to commission piano music from him. Her payments are so liberal that he guesses her real intention and asks her to lend him a large sum which will enable him to pay off his creditors (May 1877). His only way of thanking her is music and he proposes to dedicate a symphony to her. She hates publicity and accepts only an anonymous dedication: "To my best friend."

---

* So much for Mr Ken Russell's apparent revelations about the *Pathétique*, which he seems to interpret as showing remorse on Tchaikovsky's part for driving his wife to the asylum. Tchaikovsky may have been a genius, but not a prophet.

† The Russian verb *lubit'* (to love) has, among a few others, two passive past participles: *lubimy* (loved, dear to one's heart) and *vozlublenny* (beloved, with amorous connotations). Mrs von Meck used often the first one, never the second one, when addressing Tchaikovsky in her letters. The impression gather by a Western reader from the title *"Beloved Friend"* is, to say the least, inaccurate.

Consequently, Tchaikovsky and Mrs von Meck refer to the Fourth Symphony as to 'our symphony.' Of course the obvious thing would be for the patron and the artist to meet. But Mrs von Meck is shy, a little deaf, neither handsome nor even feminine; at 45, she feels nearly old, whereas at 36 the composer is still a young man. Why meet? Why risk unnecessary disappointments, maybe on both sides? Very sensibly, the patron and the artist agree on a friendship by correspondence.

The composer gets married, runs away, is in dire need of money and sympathy; the patron provides both, the former being presented as the first instalment of a pension which Wealth undertakes to pay to Talent, and which Talent accepts as simply as it is offered by Wealth (October 1877). In September 1878 a close friendship has developed between them; Mrs von Meck suggests that Tchaikovsky, in her absence, visit her mansion in Moscow. In December 1878, Mrs von Meck decides to spend some time in Florence and invites Tchaikovsky to 'accompany' her there. She arranges a house for him and frequently walks past his windows; they attend the same operas, exchange daily notes, but do not meet except by chance. In May 1878, in August 1878, in May 1879, the composer is invited to the widow's princely estate, Brailov. In August 1879 he spends a very happy time at another estate, Simaki, while Mrs von Meck resides close by at Brailov. Chance meetings take place but no conversation. In November 1879 Mrs von Meck hires the whole Colonne orchestra* to perform 'our' symphony. In July 1880, Tchaikovsky goes for the last time to Brailov and Simaki. Mrs von Meck is losing money and sells Brailov. But Tchaikovsky will live again under her roof, for instance in January 1887, in Moscow. The friendship is still very deep if less passionate; contrary to what has been said[17] there are no signs of a decrease of interest on his or her part.

In October 1890, Mrs von Meck announces that she is financially ruined and will not be able to give any more money. In spite of Tchaikovsky's efforts to save their friendship from the wreck, Mrs von Meck declines to write him any more. Soon he learns that she is as wealthy as ever, but very ill. For the last time, he writes to her son-in-law Pahulsky in June 1891, and does not obtain any explanation concerning Mrs von Meck's strange attitude. He dies in 1893 and she, four months later, in 1894.

During all the time that Tchaikovsky and Mrs von Meck were on friendly terms they wrote to each other long and numerous

---

* One of the main Parisian orchestras founded in 1871 by Edward Colonne.

letters. Very few are missing from the collection. Unfortunately her last note, the one in which she so strangely lied, is one of them, but the rest are there, have been published with few omissions, and still constitute the main source of information about the way Tchaikovsky thought, felt and worked. It cannot be said that Mrs von Meck ever had any direct influence over the composer, but it certainly was her privilege to help him through one of the most difficult times of his life and to follow him to the threshold of international glory (Chart II: third period). That her name was on his lips when he died could mean much or nothing at all: a man's last moments become solemn *a posteriori*, and we can very well be delirious about unimportant things. Still the rupture hurt him deeply as we shall see, but all in all posterity ought to be thankful to the woman who for fourteen years played guardian angel to an artist who was clearly in need of one.

It will not be necessary here to give a detailed portrait of Mrs von Meck. She was a Russian gentlewoman by birth, had married a foreigner, had apparently managed his business for him and ascended from nearly sordid poverty to extravagant wealth thanks to the railway boom in nineteenth-century Russia. She did not belong to fashionable society, but lived like a maharanee, travelling with enormous retinues, worried when, having found a doctor to take abroad, she could not find a pianist for her wandering court. Modest said that she dressed funnily and her own son Nikolai proclaimed that she was 'a capricious, insufferable, old woman.' She may have suffered from a slight mania of persecution which would account for her incredible misanthropy: asked if she was Mrs von Meck she would answer no. "Everywhere I go," she wrote "I pretend not to understand the language." She had six sons and six daughters, but at the same time she gives the impression of having been an inhibited and unhappy wife. Although obviously sensual— "I love music passionately; I don't deny myself this pleasure, but I never dream meaning into it. I feel a purely physical pleasure. . . ." "Music affects me as does a glass of sherry, and I find the effect most wonderful. . . !" "Flowers intoxicate me; I breathe their aroma with a kind of fierce joy"—she also was a puritan, we should be tempted to say something of a virgin, with all her twelve children: "Falling in love is a dream, a game of the imagination, the excitement of an emotion which is not respectable at all: sensuality. . . ." "What a pity that human beings cannot be bred by artificial means, like fish for instance: then one would not have to marry and that would be such a relief. . . !" "Recently a big picture, *Les tentations de Saint-Antoine*, was exhibited here, at a gallery. You understand of course that these temptations were women surrounding him in tantalizing nakedness and teasing attitudes; he, all shrunk and trembling and pale like a deadman, seemed to me both laughable and loathsome: his own vulgarity and bad thoughts have brought about such apparitions, and here he is, wanting to be commended for his continence. In my opinion he ought to have been thrashed and not canonized for imagining such disgusting things." Important though it is, Mrs von Meck's squeamishness cannot be the key to her whole personality; it takes all its meaning only when put in the light of the woman's need for active, sometimes devouring love. "I am a person who has lived all her life with her heart; I constantly need somebody to love, to spoil, to take care of. But at the present time there is nobody to fulfil this need. My children are grown and I cannot spoil them, my attentions annoy them; I am not allowed to take care of my grand-children; therefore I have transferred my tenderness and need to love on little dogs: these enjoy my spoiling, do not object to my attentions because they fully recognize my authority, and love me very much themselves: such is the explanation of my passion for little dogs."

It could be said that, from some standpoints, Tchaikovsky himself was one of Mrs von Meck's little dogs, or it could have been said if it was not for his music, for it was with the music that she first fell in love: "For several days after hearing your *Tempest*, I was in a delirium from which I could not emerge." She never ceased to rave about what he wrote, and whoever knows anything about artists will understand how precious a tonic her constant, passionate, unlimited praise must have been for the composer. Her first letter to him contained rather elaborate compliments like: "To tell you what enthusiasm your compositions inspire in me, would, I feel, be uncalled for, since you are used to much more exalted praise, and the worship of such an insignificant person as I am, as far as music is concerned, could only seem ridiculous to you, while my delight is so dear to me that I do not want it to become a matter for amusement; therefore I shall tell you only this: that your music makes life easier and more pleasant to live—I mean it literally, please believe me." But soon she forgot her insignificance to declare: "All that is admirable in Mendelssohn, Schumann, Glinka, you have too, but with the addition of your own original, unique qualities which distinguish you so much from all other talents that have existed so far, that it is impossible even to compare you with anyone. . . . After you nobody will be able to bring anything new into Russian music; you have reconciled in yours all the aspects of learned music and folklore. Followers you may have, reformers no." If a critic dared write that Tchaikovsky had no talent for opera, Mrs von Meck flew into a rage: "You can only laugh at seeing . . . him decide with such authority that the best talent in the world is incapable of doing what he does. He himself is incapable of doing what he does, for if he cannot grasp the beauty of your music, he is clearly inapt to be a critic." What balm for Tchaikovsky who was so sensitive to opinion! And when he wondered whether he would find the courage to conduct his own work, with what tact Mrs von Meck prepared the ground for a possible retreat: "In my opinion, it is not only unnecessary, but it would even be much better not to profane your person by appearing on the stage, to be seen and judged by any audience. I consider a composer too sacred a person to be presented like this to the crowd." That anybody could presume to judge her favourite was not to be tolerated: only sheer admiration was acceptable: "Among all the reviews of your music, of which I have read so many, my dear friend, the one from Prague pleased me most. This is exactly how I told you that your music should be treated: to criticize it from a musical point of view is preposterous since it stands higher than any critic: therefore it is only possible to talk about one's own impression, one's own reaction to it. That is precisely what the author of the Prague article does: he does not criticize, he is content with admiring everything." Tchaikovsky would not have been the creator that he was if he had found any exaggeration in such appraisal of his genius, and he probably did not smile—although we may—when we read that he was "a sun irradiating miserable mankind with the light and warmth of his music."

Having fallen in love with the composer, Mrs von Meck was certainly not indifferent to the man, although it is a very far-fetched suggestion that she wanted to marry him. But she loved him and with all the passion of which she was capable: "When I enter my drawing-room and see on the table an envelope with the dear, familiar handwriting, I feel the cessation of all pain, as from breathing ether. . . ." "My love for you is a fate against which my will is powerless. . . ." "How grateful I am to you for such minutes, how much brighter and warmer life has become for me . . . how much is redeemed by such a nature as yours. . . ." "I cannot express what I feel when I listen to your compositions. I am ready to surrender my soul to you, you become godlike for me." She was the one to propose a switch from the formal *you* to the more intimate '*thou*', which Tchaikovsky declined. She was the one to put sentimental meaning in their common stay in Florence, to the point of hating the 'intruder' who, after Tchaikovsky's departure, rented the villa where he had lived, to the point of wanting 'to evict this person immediately and rent the house herself so nobody could live there.' She never did anything to prevent the few meetings that chance offered them, and freely described the occasion on which she sat in the same box as the composer, whom as yet she did not know but started 'adoring' on that day. Any mark of affection from Tchaikovsky touched her deeply: "I cannot refrain from expressing to you, my incomparable friend, the deep, indescribable feeling of gratitude which was created in me by one of your sentences: 'The thought that I could survive you is unbearable to me,' you wrote. Oh how grateful I am to you for saying this, how sweet, how unutterably dear to me is this sentence. . . . Ten times a day I reread [it] and involuntarily pressed your letter to my heart from an excess of gratefulness." A kind remark of Tchaikovsky's about her protégé Pahulsky, sent her into ecstasies: "If you were here I could not have helped throwing myself on your neck and pressing you against my heart." She even had some trouble restraining herself in the polite closings of her letters: "A moment ago I wanted to say that I embrace you with all my heart, but perhaps you would find it strange; so I will say as usual—good-bye, my sweet friend."

Mrs von Meck's passion is maybe still better expressed in the two letters she wrote to the composer about his marriage. The first one, when he informed her of it: "I congratulate you, my dearest friend, with all my heart I congratulate you on this new step, which generally is a gamble, but which in your case, can only make me happy, for a man with such a golden heart, with such a delicate sensitivity as yours, ought not to bury such treasures. You gave happiness to another person and so you will be happy yourself, and in all justice, who should be happy if not you, who afford such noble pleasures to others? In the present case you have behaved with the honour and delicacy that are characteristic of you. You are such a dear person . . . and of course you will be happy." The second, two years later, when Antonina was fading away and Tchaikovsky seemed to belong to his patroness:

I do not know if you can understand the jealousy which I feel toward you, there being no personal relations between us. Do you know that I am jealous of you in the most unpardonable way, as a woman of the man she loves? Do you know that, when you married,

I suffered a great deal, it was as if something had been torn away from my heart. I was in bitter pain, the thought of your intimacy with this woman was intolerable to me, and, do you know how despicable I am, I was glad when you were unhappy with her; I reproached myself for that feeling; I hid it from you rather successfully, I think, but I could not destroy it: our feelings are not to be controlled by us. I hated this woman because you were *unhappy* with her, but I should have hated her a hundred times more if you had been *happy*. I felt that she had robbed me of something that could only be *mine*, to which I *alone* was entitled, because I *love you* more than anyone else does and value you above everything in the world. If it is unpleasant for you to learn all this, forgive me this involuntary confession. I have betrayed myself: it is the symphony's fault. But I think that even for you it is better to know that I am not such an ideal person as you think. Moreover it cannot change anything in our relationship. I do not wish for *any* change in it; in fact I should like to be sure that *nothing* will be changed until the end of my life, that *nobody* . . . but that I have no right to say. Forgive me and forget everything I said, my mind is upset. The weather is beautiful today, the fresh air will do me good. I shall not write any more, since I am adding nonsense to nonsense. Forgive me and understand that *now* I am all right, that I need nothing more. Good-bye, my dear friend, forget this letter, but do not forget me, who love you with all my heart . . . P.S. Please do not forget to acknowledge this letter if you receive it.

What she thought herself about her passion we do not know. Tchaikovsky did not seem astonished at receiving such declarations and enjoyed being petted with small or big gifts, with little or great attentions, and, of course, with an unceasing flow of money. This was a less straightforward age than ours and many complicated relationships were still possible. Love did not necessarily mean sharing sleeping accommodation. We find Tchaikovsky, to whose advantage it probably would have been if people had gossipped about his patroness of the arts and her favourite composer, very keen on protecting her from any such unpleasantness. The one thing which we want to avoid doing is judging the past by modern standards. Not only did Tchaikovsky enjoy the relationship, he also gave her due to his generous friend: "I know well that I shall never lose your support in what I do. I do not believe I could write another line of music if I did not know that no matter what the world thinks my friend will hear my music and will understand what I have tried to say."

8 My good genius

The money Tchaikovsky accepted without qualms. In fact he was the first to ask for it, as a loan of course. "You are the only person in the world from whom I am not ashamed to ask money. First you are kind and generous. Second, you are wealthy." When the loan became a pension, he did not feel the worse for it. To his brother-in-law Lev Davydov he wrote: "It could very well be that, at first thought, you and Sasha could disapprove of my living at Mrs Meck's expense. But if you take into consideration the substance of my relationship to her, which is entirely based on her desire to afford me the opportunity of wholly giving myself to my composing; if you think that personally we are not even acquainted, I imagine that you will pardon me for not having the mental courage to refuse such means coming from a source so *simpatichny* to me." With as much simplicity Tchaikovsky refused the money which Mrs von Meck offered him to buy a house when he wanted one: "Finding myself in such a flourishing financial position it would be a positive shame to turn again to you to have my wishes fulfilled." And when in 1881 Mrs von Meck believed herself relatively ruined,* Tchaikovsky hastened to ask her to cease paying his allowance:

> If you have to live all the time in the country, it is obviously my duty to find also one place of residence. I beg you, my friend, not to forget that the doors of both Conservatoires are widely open to me and that from this standpoint I am perfectly safe. The freedom and materially luxurious life which I enjoy are precious to me. But they would immediately become painful if I knew that I benefited from them at the expense of too delicate, too generous a friend! Be perfectly open with me, I beg of you, concerning such things, and know, my best friend, that it would be a great happiness for me to give up the most precious material advantages if this were to improve be it ever so little, your situation. You have already done too much for me. Without exaggeration I consider that I owe you my life. If you had not existed, if you had not come as my guardian-angel at that fearful period of my life,† I am sure that I should not

---

* It was a false alarm. Tchaikovsky's pension continued to be paid.
† His marriage.

have had the strength to conquer the mental illness which was dragging me to destruction.

There was a genuine love for his benefactress in Tchaikovsky's heart. He depended on her: "With you I feel the way a small person feels in talking to a very tall one." He was grateful to her: "Soon, I hope, the time will come when I shall no longer require the material assistance which you have afforded me with such wonderful delicacy of feeling, with such fabulous generosity, but I stand in even greater need of the moral assistance which you are affording me now." He knew exactly what he owed to her: "I owe you everything: my life, the possibility of going forward to distant goals, freedom, and that complete happiness which formerly I believed unattainable." He had the deepest confidence in her: "You are the only person in the world who can make me deeply, profoundly happy. I am infinitely grateful, and hope only that what inspires your feeling for me will never end or alter, because such a loss would be unendurable." And how did she, whom he never really met, make him happy? By her sympathy: "Never has anyone, except perhaps my brothers, made me as happy as you with your sympathy. If you only knew how precious that sympathy is to me, and how little I am spoiled by it!" And just by being herself: "What wonderful, kind souls live in the world! Meeting such people as you on the thorny road of life, one becomes convinced that mankind is not as hard and selfish as pessimists represent it. There are admirable exceptions, *admirable* in the full sense of the word. If a person like you appears among a million others, it is enough to prevent one from despairing of men. . . ." "Before knowing you I did not know that people with such a tender, such a noble soul existed. I am as astonished by what you do for me as by how you do it."

This of course reminds us of Mrs von Meck's expression "How much is redeemed by such a nature as yours." This should not surprise us. The artist and his patroness felt very much alike on many subjects and were conscious of it. She wrote: "I have been impressed a long time ago and am still amazed by this extraordinary empathy, by this supernatural similarity of thoughts and feelings." And he: "Between you and me there is a spiritual kinship manifesting itself decidedly in everything; in numberless cases you and I may seem strange or eccentric to other people, while perfectly understanding each other."

It is true that he liked things as they were and never encouraged any attempt at familiarity: "My relationship to you, as it is now, is my greatest happiness and an indispensable condition for my well-being. I should not want it to change by one iota." But he loved her enough to ask frankly favours from her, like allowing him to live in her house in her absence. He was touched by her attentions: "All the little objects Nadejda had put on [his desk in Florence], he had brought home to Russia: penknife, eraser, inkstand and the little bell."[18] He was sensitive to her love for him: "In your album, among the [pictures] of your closest friends I came upon my photograph—twice. It touched me to discover myself the only person in the book who is not a member of your family." He felt a real tenderness for her: "I shall write at your table which I have moved a little forward in order to have more light. It is very pleasant for me, when I sit at that table, to think that not more than four days ago you were sitting in my place." He was himself full of attentions for her, trying to prevent her from writing to him at night since her eyesight was poor and giving her wholesome advice about her health: he had the same heart trouble as she and knew very well what she ought to do to feel better: walk instead of lying down and drink a big glass of wine, preferably Spanish.

"I cannot and will not write anything untrue to you," declared the composer and we have proof that he was faithful to his word, for we have his letters to his brothers, in which he speaks very freely about his benefactress, expresses a few reservations about the whole situation but never says one word which could have shamed him or her.

Sometimes he was tired of accepting money from her: "I do not know why, but this time I find it painful to exploit the astonishing generosity of this woman. . . ." "Maybe for the first time I experienced some difficulty in writing to her. Whether from embarrassment or because it is awkward to thank and thank all the time, I had really some trouble writing that letter." Sometimes he was under the impression that she was bored with their relationship and then he became conscious of its unnatural quality. Sometimes he reproached himself for not being grateful enough: "Ah! how spoilt I have become! I get used to all that I owe to this wonderful woman and forget to value it."

He always felt self-conscious at the idea of living close to her: "I know that this is foolish, and that my solitude will not be broken into, but I am so used to thinking of Nadejda F. as a kind of far-away, invisible angel that the consciousness of her near and mortal presence is disturbing. . . ." "Although we shall be separated by four versts* people will say the devil knows what. Her own children will look askance at our relationship and spread out lots of nonsense, as it happened for Kotek. . . ."† "How can I help being angry with that wonderful, intelligent woman when she obstinately refuses to understand, in spite of all my hints, that I do not feel like living so close to her and playing the mysterious stranger?"

There were other reasons to get angry with the insistent lady. "I was incensed against . . . N.F. Yes! Against her. Long hair, short mind, nothing could be more true. Among all women is she not intelligent and perceptive? Have I not described myself at length to her?‡ And in her last letter she asks me why I do not call on Turgenev!" Not unfrequently the composer felt that his benefactress was infringing on his freedom by her constant invitations: "With all her delicacy, with all her tenderness, N.F. still interferes a little with my liberty. I should happily give up the apartments she rents for me if I could do so, for the money that she gives me is perfectly sufficient for my well-being. O Lord, forgive me my sins. That I should complain of N.F., what base wickedness!"

And that is all. On the other hand the expressions of his devotion to her knew no end. His gratitude was genuine and deep: "What should I do without Mrs von Meck? May this woman be blessed a thousand times. . . !" "How grateful I am to this wonderful woman and how afraid I am of beginning to consider as my due all that she does for me. . . !" "All that she offers to me is presented with such astonishing tact, with such kindness, that I am scarcely embarrassed to accept. Oh, how kind, generous and tactful is this woman! She is also amazingly clever, for, while she renders me such enormous services, she does it in such a way that I cannot doubt for a minute that she finds joy in doing it." Having once confessed to Nikolai Rubinstein that he received money from her, Tchaikovsky always felt remorse for this indiscretion and was at great pains to explain to him what was the substance of their friendship. "Concerning Mme Meck, first you are completely wrong about her relationship to me, in which you play no part at all, and second, even if it was true, I should consider your mentioning the fact that I get an allowance from her at your initiative completely uncalled for. I cannot tell you the whole history of my

---

* Approximately three miles.
† Kotek had been Mrs von Meck's private musician. She had dismissed him for indiscretion.
‡ Allusion to Tchaikovsky's misanthropy.

relations with Mme Meck because it would be too long and anyway unnecessary. I only beg you to arrange things so that no one, except you and Karlusha [Albrecht] should suspect anything. It would be extremely unpleasant for me if she were to learn that anybody besides me knows about our relationship. . . . [Omission] . . . I must tell you that your hints at Mme Meck, in spite of your friendly motives for which I am very grateful, could only spoil my relationship to her and disturbed her very much, since she deduced from what you said that you knew about our former relationship, which she desired to keep absolutely secret.* Concerning this woman I have to say that never were kindness, delicacy of feelings, generosity, boundless magnanimity united in one person as fully as in her. I owe her not only my life but also my ability to go on working which is dearer than life to me. I was offended for her, that you should understand her as little as me. She is not whimsical at all. For me, she is like Providence's inexhaustible hand. One must know her as I do now to be sure that there still are people so incredibly kind and trusting. As for my part in relation to her, it is not to be envied. I am simply exploiting her kindness, and this would torment me if she did not know how to soothe and deafen the reproaches of my conscience."

The fear that people would gossip about Mrs von Meck and him seldom left the composer, which is somewhat unexpected coming from a self-conscious homosexual. "Although nothing can be more innocent than this relationship, people will undoubtedly make something despicable of it, and although it is completely indifferent to me, it could be unpleasant to her. It is essential that this should not be known by the public, especially of Moscow, whose tongues have already wagged a lot about me as well as about her."

True, the composer definitely did not wish to meet the lady. Here is how he describes their sojourn in Florence: "The presence of N.F. has ceased to embarrass me. I am even used to our daily correspondence, although one has to be fair to this woman, who is not only wonderful but also intelligent: she arranges everything so that I never lack material for letter-writing. Every morning I receive a huge letter from her, sometimes even on five sheets, and at the same time the Russian papers and *Italie*. I reply in the evening. Exactly at half past eleven in the morning, she strolls by my house and stares into my windows, trying to see me but not

* Rubinstein's letter has been lost. The 'former' relationship is probably a reference to the time when Mrs von Meck commissioned Tchaikovsky to write music for her.

succeeding for she is short-sighted. I on my part see her very well. We have also seen each other once at the theatre. There are no hints as to any desire of getting acquainted, so that I am at peace in this respect. In general things are pleasant here, and there is nothing to clash with my misanthropy." At the theatre, Tchaikovsky not only examined Mrs von Meck with the help of his eyeglasses and felt a mixture of "curiosity, tenderness and surprise;" he also found that her face, when talking to her favourite daughter Milochka, "expressed so much tenderness and love . . . that he even liked her appearance, not handsome but full of character." And when she left Florence, he did not expect to be sad, but he was. "I feel quite lonesome without her. With tears on my eyes I walk by her deserted villa, and the Viale dei Colli has become gloomy and boring. I was so used to commune with her every day, to see her walk by every morning, followed by her numerous retinue. What embarrassed and disconcerted me in the beginning I now very sincerely regret. But oh, what a wonderful, marvellous woman! How touching was her care of me, entering into details but on the whole making my life here extremely pleasant. . . ." "So recently I felt embarrassed by her presence so near to me, and now I miss it!" To summarize: "One person plays the chief part in the story of the last ten years of my life: she is my good genius; to her I owe all my prosperity and the power to devote myself to my beloved work."

Being the artist that he was, we ought not to think that he stayed in her debt. She gave him money, and a much more valuable gift: sympathy; he gave her music. The Fourth Symphony is dedicated to her, and if not directly inspired by her, at least completed thanks to her: "Dear Nadejda Filaretovna, I may be making a mistake, but it seems to me this Symphony is not a mediocre work, but the best I have done so far. How glad I am that it is *ours*, and that, hearing it, you will know how much I thought of you with every bar. Would it ever have been finished but for you? When I was still in Moscow and believed my end to be imminent, I made the following note upon the first sketch, which I had quite forgotten until I came upon it just now: 'In case of my death I desire this book to be given to N. F. von Meck.'" The First Suite is also dedicated to Mrs von Meck, although even more secretly than the Symphony, which had been inscribed "To my best friend": "The suite is dedicated to you but, for this time, let the dedication be known only to you and to me. I made no inscription on the title-page as I had done for our symphony. Was I right? I did not want to use the same words 'To my best friend,' so that idle people would not start inquiries as to who this best friend could be." Finally it can be said that all the music Tchaikovsky composed during the von Meck period is dedicated to his patroness, since he wrote her as much on 25th October 1877: "I doubt that circumstances will ever allow me to prove to you that I am ready to make any sacrifice for you; I do not think that you could ever have to turn to me and ask me to do you a real friend's service, so that I can only try to serve and please you with my music. From now on . . . every note that comes from my pen will be dedicated to you."

All of which makes only more pitiful the sordid ending of this noble friendship.

9 Ashamed and sick

The letter in which a deceived or a deceiving Nadejda von Meck wrote that she had lost her fortune and could not help Tchaikovsky any more has been accidentally—or maybe not quite accidentally— lost. We have to deduce what it was from the composer's moving and obviously heartfelt reply.

Most dear friend, the piece of news contained in your letter which I have just received makes me deeply sad, *but for you and not for me.*

This is not an empty phrase. Of course I should be lying, if I told you that such a radical reduction of my budget will not influence at all my material well-being. But it will do so much less than you probably think. The fact is that, during the past years, my income has considerably grown, and there is no reason to doubt that it will continue to grow in fast progression. Therefore, if among the number-less circumstances which bother you, you have special worries for me, for God's sake rest assured that I did not feel the slightest, the shortest moment of sadness on learning about my material losses. You must believe that all this is the perfect truth: I am no good at putting on airs and making speeches. So then, it is un-important that I shall have to reduce my expenses for some time. What is important is that you, with your habits, with the scope of your normal life, will now have to endure privations! That is awfully offensive and irritating; I should like to find a guilty party for all that happened (since, in any case, you cannot be guilty), but I do not know who is the real culprit. However, this anger is pointless and valueless, and moreover I have no right to try to penetrate your family affairs. It will be better if I ask Vladislav Albertovich to write me at his convenience how you intend to settle down, where you will live, to what extent you will have to suffer privations. I cannot tell you the pity and fear I feel for you. I cannot imagine you without wealth! . . . .

The last words in your letter have slightly offended me, but I think that you cannot seriously imagine what you write. Do you really think that I can remember you only as long as I make use of your money! How could I, even for one second, forget all that you did for me and how much I owe you! Without the least exaggeration, let me say that you have saved me, and that I should certainly have become insane and have perished if you had not come to my rescue and had not sustained me with your friendship, sympathy and material help (then it was my anchor of salvation) at a time when my energy and my desire to climb my destined path were nearly dead! No, my dearest friend, be sure that I shall remember that and bless you till my last breath. I am happy to be able to tell you, precisely now when you cannot any longer share your means with me, the full extent of my boundless, warm, unutterable thankfulness. You yourself may not imagine how immeasurable your beneficence has been! Otherwise you could never have thought that now that you are poor I should think about you *sometimes*!!!! Without any exaggeration I can say that I have never forgotten and shall never forget you for one minute, for whenever I think about myself, I cannot help thinking about you.

I warmly kiss your hands and beg you to know for all times that no one has more sympathy and compassion for your sorrows. . . .

Some other time I shall write you about myself and what I am doing. Kindly forgive my hasty and ugly writing: I am too upset to write clearly.

Here it is necessary to open a parenthesis. Vladislav Pahulsky has been cast by many biographers in the part of the villain of the play, and although no proof exists of his villainy, the least one can say is that his influence must not have been exerted in Tchaikovsky's favour. A poor Polish violinist, he was employed by Mrs von Meck as a house musician, but also as an exalted errand-boy. To live at the lady's constant beck and call must have been tiresome enough, but, more than that, she used him as a go-between for her secret relationship with Tchaikovsky and, since he wanted to be a composer, asked the great man to give the younger one lessons in harmony and composition. Pahulsky played his role to a marvel, shamelessly flattered all and sundry, and, in particular, professed himself an ardent admirer of Tchaikovsky's music. He would have been less than human if he had not come to hate a man to whom he had to be continuously subservient. Anyway he succeeded brilliantly: although he did not become a composer, he won a much more difficult wager, which Claude Debussy had lost: he, the poor foreigner about whom Mrs von Meck could not write two words without putting him 'in his place,' managed to marry his employer's daughter and to become at the same time her family and business factotum. We can only guess at his feelings for the composer whom he must have felt he had magnificently beaten at the finish, but we know Tchaikovsky's opinion of him, and it was consistently negative. Couched in reserved terms and even sand-wiched between compliments for Mrs von Meck's use, frankly rude if shared with his brothers, the composer's estimate of Pahulsky and of his music can hardly be termed admiring: "I shall tell you openly that I have had students with more brilliant germs of talent," he wrote to their common patroness; "I had to spend all evening over Pahulsky's indigestible musical trash" he wrote to Modest. He even complained to Mrs von Meck's son about the situation, but Nikolai begged him to go on seriously discussing Pahulsky's com-positions so as not to offend his mother. What Pahulsky's music was like we do not know, but since we have never found Tchaikov-sky unfair to anyone, we may assume with a certain degree of probability that a man about whom he wrote for instance "Now that Pahulsky has gone the sun shines again" and other remarks of the same vein, was at least not very *simpatichny*. And what we know of Pahulsky's hyperbolic flatteries ("That is music!" he used to say after hearing a Tchaikovsky piece. "What is Wagner now, and why do we all exist on earth?") tends to confirm our feeling. If he could do anything to forget the day when Mrs von Meck sent him to bribe Colonne into performing Tchai-kovsky's music, he would not miss the opportunity. Parenthesis closed.

A few days after having replied to Mrs von Meck, Tchaikovsky wrote in a different tone to Jurgenson. The little phrase "Do not forget and think of me sometimes" which had 'offended him a little' at first reading had had time to sink down. He understood now that it was the end, that 'his best friend' did not want to have anything to do with him any more.

> I have to tell you a thing which is very unpleasant for me. I shall have six thousand less a year. . . . I received this shock philo-sophically, but nevertheless I was unpleasantly impressed and

surprised. [Mrs von Meck] wrote so often that this allowance would never cease till my last breath that I believed her. . . . Now I shall have to lead a completely different kind of life, on another scale, and even probably to look for some kind of employment in St Petersburg with a good salary attached. I am deeply, deeply, deeply hurt, yes, hurt. My relationship to N. F. v. M. was such that her generous bounty was never burdensome to me. Now I retrospectively find it oppressive; my pride is offended; my faith in her boundless readiness to help me materially and to sacrifice herself for me is deceived. Now I should like her to lose all her money and need my help. For I know perfectly well that from our point of view she is still awfully wealthy. In other words everything has been turned into a silly, vulgar farce, so that I feel ashamed and sick.

Jurgenson understood the composer's feelings. "I remember how in 1881, in Paris, after you had given up your allowance because she was in a difficult situation, she wrote to tell you that your pension could never suffer from it, etc. The devil knows her, I do not know what happened at the von Meck's, a real bankrupt or some kind of mix-up, but I am very much hurt for you. I have got tears in my throat and I would like to howl, but I cannot."

Modest, also informed of the catastrophe, shared his brother's grief: "It is not the six thousand that I regret (if you stop paying a few allowances like mine you will find yourself in nearly the same position as you were before). It is the offence to your pride which I find painful."

Aleksei Sofronov was the first to raise the main question: why. And he answered it with a simple fellow's assurance of being right, and maybe with a simple fellow's natural flair: "Do you know, my dear benefactor, I think that N.F. has not lost as much money as she writes she has. I think that this is the work of your Pole Pahulsky, as the Riazan Railway stocks* stand much higher than last year (395 roubles instead of 365). Therefore I think that the main part has been played here by Pahulsky. During the summer he envied your good means all the time."

On one point at least Aleksei was right. Mrs von Meck was far from bankrupt and could very well go on paying Tchaikovsky's allowance.

The correspondence did not altogether cease. Mrs von Meck was ill and could not write herself but Pahulsky announced that he was going to take her place. He wrote from time to time and gave meaningless messages which may, and again may not, have

* The Riazan Railway belonged to the von Meck family.

come from his mother-in-law: "Nadejda Filaretovna sends hearty greetings and deep gratitude for your interest," etc. Tchaikovsky replied; he desired to know if he had offended his patroness in any way. Pahulsky retorted: "I gave her your letter to read, and she ordered me to tell you that 'it is an impossible thing that she should ever be angry with you and that her feelings towards you cannot change.' " Given the circumstances, this sounds as heavy irony. This situation lasted for eight months. Finally Tchaikovsky had enough of it and said so:

I have just received your letter. It is true that Nadejda Filaretovna is ill, weak, nervously upset and cannot write as she used to. I certainly should not want her to suffer through me. I am saddened, embarrassed, and, to speak sincerely, profoundly insulted not by the fact that she does not write to me but by the fact that she has lost all interest in me. If she wanted me to correspond with her regularly as in the past, it would be quite feasible, would it not, since you and Julia Karlovna* could be our constant intermediaries. But not once did she ask you or her to tell me that she would like to receive information about my life and what is happening to me. I tried to arrange for a regular correspondence with N.F. through you, but each of your letters was nothing but a courteous acknowledgment of my attempts to preserve even in the slightest degree the shadow of the past. Obviously you must know that in September of last year, N.F. informed me that, having lost her fortune, she could not help me materially any longer. You probably also are acquainted with my reply. I *wanted and craved* that my relationship to N.F. change not because I did not receive any more money from her. Unfortunately this was impossible due to a perfectly obvious coolness on N.F.'s part toward me. The result is that I ceased writing to N.F., ceased practically any contact with her, *after being deprived of her money.* Such a situation humiliates me in my own eyes, makes insufferable the memory of the bounties which I accepted from her, constantly tortures and torments me unbearably. During the autumn, in the country, I reread N.F.'s former letters. No illness, no sorrow, no material trouble, would have seemed to be able to alter the feelings which she expressed in those letters. But they are altered. Perhaps for the very reason that I never met N.F. *personally*, she seemed to me to an ideal person; I could not imagine inconstancy in such a demi-goddess; I thought that it would be easier for the whole earth to explode in little pieces than for N.F. to change toward me. But it has happened, and my whole conception of mankind, my faith in the best of men, are upside down: my peace is troubled, that part of happiness which Fate has allotted me is poisoned. Without wanting to do so of course, N.F. has dealt cruelly with me. I have never

* Mrs von Meck's daughter, Vladislav Pahulsky's wife.

felt so humbled, so offended in my pride as I do now. And the most
painful is that, since N.F.'s health is so seriously affected, I cannot
express to her all that torments me, for fear of hurting and up-
setting her. I cannot express what I feel, and only that would help
me. But enough of that. I may regret that I wrote what I wrote, but
I gave way to the urge of pouring out at least some of the bitterness accumulated in my soul. Of course, not a word of all that
to N.F. If she wishes to know what I am doing, tell her that I am
safely returned from America, that I live in Maidanovo and work.
I am in good health. Do not answer this letter.

Pahulsky's reply amounted to a dead end: nothing had happened,
nothing had changed, Tchaikovsky was imagining things. His letter
would be returned to him. Mrs von Meck's health was the only
cause for the misunderstanding.

For a long time historians have thought that Tchaikovsky did not
insist: Mrs von Meck had kicked out her little dog and that was
that. It appears now, according to the testimony of Anna von
Meck,* that the composer asked her to intervene, and that she
did so. She saw her mother-in-law in October 1893, persuaded her
to break her long silence—Nadejda Filaretovna was dying from
tuberculosis and practically could not speak—and obtained a painfully whispered explanation: "I knew I was no longer necessary
to him, that I could no longer give him anything he wanted. Our
correspondence was still a joy to me but I didn't feel I had any
right to please myself alone if it had become a burden to him. It
is true I refused to give him any further material assistance but
could that really have been important to him? If he didn't understand why I had done it and he still felt that I was necessary to
him, why didn't he write again?"

If Anna von Meck is to be believed, it clearly appears that
Pahulsky did not tell his mother-in-law about Tchaikovsky's letters.
On the other hand Anna never expressed any criticism of Pahulsky's attitude, on the contrary. Besides, her testimony does sound a
little contrived, especially as she goes on in a happy-ending style:
she told her uncle about the result of her investigations, and 'she
would like to believe that the little she did say was partly the
cause of the particularly brilliant mood of his last days, a mood
noticed by everyone who met him.' For our part we have not found
such unanimity about his mood and anyway there was little to re-

---

* Tchaikovsky's niece, daughter of Sasha and Lev Davydov, wife of
Nikolai von Meck, Nadejda von Meck's son. The marriage of a von Meck
with a relative of Tchaikovsky was one of the dearest and most obstinate
wishes of Nadejda von Meck.

joice about in learning that a friendship of fourteen years had ended in a ridiculous misunderstanding.

A short time before asking Anna to investigate, Tchaikovsky had once again written to Jurgenson about the rupture. In connection with his poor finances, he exclaimed with somewhat bitter humour: "O! Nadejda Filaretovna, wherefore, old and perfidious female, hast thou betrayed me!!!" And he added more seriously: "I have recently been rereading N.F. v. Meck's letters and I am astonished at the fickleness of feminine infatuations. When one reads these letters, one would sooner believe that fire could be turned into water than that her allowance could cease; one wonders also at the insignificant sum with which I am satisfied when she is ready to give me nearly everything. And suddenly—fare you well! And I did believe that she had lost her fortune. It appears that she had not. Just a woman's caprice. Devil take it, it hurts."

Whether he did learn something from Anna or not, it would seem that the wound inflicted on his feelings or at least on his pride was never cured. According to Modest's oral declarations, his last words would have been to curse the faithless friend.

The question raised by Aleksei is still not solved. Even the nefarious Pahulsky had to have a pretext in order to obtain the dismissal of the composer. The following explanations have been proposed.

The most popular one is that Mrs von Meck finally discovered Tchaikovsky's homosexuality, was horrified by it, and deliberately put an end to the friendship. The only evidence in favour of this solution is that twelve years earlier, Tchaikovsky, in a letter to Anatoly expressed fear at the idea that Mrs von Meck might have learned about "that." "That" may of course have meant homosexuality; it could also have meant the fact that Tchaikovsky had told Rubinstein about the secret allowance: this is unclear since the whole letter is not available. Anyway nothing in Tchaikovsky's own reaction, in the reaction of his servant, brothers, friends, indicates any possibility of such a motive. Either the motive had never existed or it did not exist any more. If Tchaikovsky had felt like an unmasked villain it is scarcely probable that he would have gone on writing to his ex-friend's son-in-law and implicated his own niece into the bargain. And Jurgenson, who seldom minced words and who must have known about his friend's singularities would scarcely have expressed himself in the following terms: "My dear friend. I enclose your account. You see that I owe you more than one thousand. It is a pity that you lost money through the old woman, but, to be truthful, you never were in need after it happened. Undoubtedly it was pleasant to have golden eggs laid for you. . . . I do not think that this is just a whim on the part of the old biddy: there must have been some calumny coming from a he or a she-Iago. But that she should have believed it without investigation is really typical of a petticoat! "

Mrs von Meck's illness has also been put forward. It was partly a nervous disease, and insane people are unpredictable. . . . This is hardly satisfactory.

Some consider that, being ill and not feeling able to correspond any more, Mrs von Meck preferred to discontinue all relationship. This would not explain why she ceased to pay the allowance.

Some have tried to find in the correspondence indications of a lagging interest: according to them, Tchaikovsky would have lost his fascination for the ageing woman, and she saw no reason for paying him when he could not afford her any more pleasure. This, the most insulting explanation, is not improbable in itself: but there is no evidence to support it: Mrs von Meck's last letters are just as affectionate as the preceding ones and she did ask Tchaikovsky "to remember her sometimes." Neither does anything indicate that, as Anna has it, Mrs von Meck imagined herself to be a burden to the composer. Even if she had, why would she have discontinued the allowance which was still a bond between them?

A psychological explanation has been propounded. Tchaikovsky's protestations of affection had been insincere: "scarcely one reference to his feeling for her, gratitude apart, had been completely genuine throughout a whole decade of the correspondence. Now, it seemed, she had found him out."[19] But there is no evidence that the composer was such a hypocrite—on the contrary we have found him to be a rather truthful person—and no evidence that he was found out.

The influence of Mrs von Meck's children, who found it annoying and maybe ridiculous that their sixtyish mother should entertain a composer who was earning a very comfortable life for himself, may well have played its part in the drama. They could have persuaded her, ill as she was, that she had no more money to give away and she would have been too proud to continue a friendship in which she would not have appeared any more as the benefactress. This is possible, and Pahulsky may have worked in the same direction.

But there is a more romantic and at the same time more rational explanation at which Anna herself has hinted. Mrs von Meck's "sorest trial was the disease of her eldest, her beloved son. He died before her eyes after a protracted and agonizing illness and it seemed to her . . . that her friendship with Peter Ilich had taken her thoughts away from her family and home and that perhaps she was even guilty of the horrible death of her gifted son. 'I must atone for my sin,' she said. She went back to her Faith, began to pray once more and asked me to order prayers for her in church. Such a frame of mind naturally affected the correspondence with Peter Ilich; she did not feel it to be such a vital necessity as formerly." A curious understatement, this. Vladimir von Meck died in 1892, but he fell ill in 1890, the year of the rupture. According to Anna, Mrs von Meck had 'gone back to her Faith' before the rupture. Now we know that she was a passionate woman, and if she became religious, she had to be religious with a vengeance. If she imagined that her friendship with Tchaikovsky was a sin, what would have been more natural for her than to offer it in sacrifice for the life of her son? And the sacrifice would have to be complete: she could not cheat God and explain to her friend why she was forsaking him: it had to be done brutally, without looking back. The allowance would have to go also, not because it was expensive, but because the sacrifice would have no value if any bond were to be preserved. She allowed herself one weakness. She could not refrain from writing the pitiful little phrase: "Do not forget" because her friend was as dear to her as ever.

Besides Anna's hints there is no support for this last explanation, but we find it in character. That Mrs von Meck was a tyrant is fairly certain, but she was not cruel, foolish, vulgar, mentally ill, childishly vain, or easy to influence, as other explanations make her to be. And Tchaikovsky himself wrote that she was not whimsical. She was passionate, proud, uncompromising. There is no reason to suppose that her motives were stupid or debased. If a noble motive can be found, all evidence being equal, it should be received as more probable than any other. And sacrifice is the noblest of motives, or was thought to be so by our ancestors. Lovers, wives, mothers sacrificing themselves, the literature of the eighteenth and nineteenth centuries is full of them, and if any nation is particularly fond of self-sacrifice, it is undoubtedly Russia. Maybe further investigation of the von Meck archives, if they still exist, would confirm what we are now content to leave as a hypothesis, not the least absurd of all those which have been suggested.

10 Amours of another kind

The last of Tchaikovsky's secrets is not a pleasant one. It has already been mentioned several times in this study and no new material can be provided about it at the present time.

Gossip about Tchaikovsky's homosexuality started long ago. Proofs, if they exist, are locked in the Tchaikovsky Archives. What will mainly concern us here is: first, a brief survey of existing theories; second, a listing of facts related to this question, both positive and negative.

Any sexual abnormality is such an appealing subject that biographers have obviously had a good time with Tchaikovsky's supposed one. Since "Proof is lacking," since "no documents reveal such transactions," since "the most revealing documents *appear* to have been destroyed," since "no records survive," "nor are there any hints that he was giving in to the urgings of the hidden side of his nature in any overt way," we are exposed to the most formidable array of expressions of probability ever found: "It is more than possible," "it is also possible," "there is no doubt," "possible causes," "obviously," "there is reason to believe," "it may be assumed," "perhaps," "there is but one answer to that question" are just a few examples.[20] At least they reveal a kind of formal honesty (or caution) even if what follows these expressions is surmise or high fantasy. There is worse. Some statements are presented as verified although there is no evidence to support them: "It is established that he was a homosexual" when technically it is not established;[21] "he was [his wife's] husband in name only"[22] when the contrary is very probable;* "he told her the facts about his sexual nature"[23] when nothing is less certain; "he claimed that he wanted to save his family and friends from the disgrace of having him publicly branded as a homosexual"[24] when he never claimed anything of the kind.

It is particularly curious to read what biographers have to say about homosexuality in Russia: "Imperial Russia accepted homosexuality with the same shrug of the shoulders with which a small, highly sophisticated society has accepted it everywhere in all ages

* Cf. p. 205.

of history."[25] "The thing being very strongly objected to in Russia."[26] "Homosexuality was far from uncommon in Russia, particularly among the upper and military classes."[27] "This anomaly was exceedingly rare among the Russians, who are a rustic people in everything that concerns the science of love and despise all unnecessary refinements. . . ."[28] The truth is that we know very little about what anomaly was and was not practised in Russia in the 1870s, although testimonies personally gathered by the author among survivors of old Russia concord fairly well: homosexuality, it seems, was not unheard of but seldom found.

Now for the enlightened opinions of our commentators.

The most popular one is that of the 'Oedipists.' Tchaikovsky "was homosexual and unhappy about it."[29] He "never wanted a wife; he had wanted, in company with all homosexuals, a mother."[30] "Neither the passing years nor the awful experience of Antonina Ivanovna . . . destroyed [his] intense need for a woman to replace his long-lost mother."[31] Oedipists generally agree between themselves although they do not seem to be able to make up their mind which of the composer's works best expresses his predicament: for Havelock Ellis and Herbert Weinstock the Sixth Symphony is "The Homosexual Tragedy", for Edward Lockspeiser the Fourth (the one dedicated to Mrs von Meck) expresses the composer's fear "lest his perversion be exposed. . . . The wretched man was riddled with guilt."

A merrier version of the situation is presented by Kurt von Wolfurt. Homosexuality, yes; guilt, not at all. Tchaikovsky was a real Greek of the time of Pericles. Men being by essence nobler than women, it was natural for a man with his noble instincts to be attracted to his peers. Common people can love women and children, nothing but bodies, whereas a great man adores the spirit, which he can find only among those of his own sex. Of course Tchaikovsky realized that it is not always simple to be a homosexual, and suffered from the uncomfortable situation, but "there was no moral problem as such for him." He was a deliberate worshipper of the Greek Eros. Although this is a somewhat bizarre rendition of Tchaikovsky's plight and certainly does not fit the conventional image of the composer, on one point at least Kurt von Wolfurt is right: the sense of guilt about which we hear so much has come out hugely exaggerated from under several layers of biographies.

Other specialists repudiate the homosexuality and keep the guilt. Tchaikovsky would have felt frank disgust towards women but no particular attraction to men, and the famous "The" or "That" which can be found in his letters to Modest and is supposed to have meant homosexuality would have referred to solitary bad habits "so natural for a man who deified women in his music and never got anything but kicking from them."[32] This is not quite so absurd as it seems at first sight. Tolstoi's *Kreutzer Sonata* is there to show that practices which are now taken for granted by most psychologists were dramatized in nineteenth-century Russia. It may be added that Tchaikovsky's consternation at recognizing Rousseau's secrets as his own would confirm this theory, since Rousseau was not a homosexual but described with gusto his solitary experiences.

Other writers grant that Tchaikovsky was a homosexual, but maintain that it was through an excessive idealization of women.[33] Having worshipped his mother, he transferred this worship on all women and could not bear the idea of desecrating them. This is ingenuous; still, we cannot help finding a little childish the evidence presented by the supporters of this theory: it is, quite simply, *Romeo and Juliet* and *Francesca da Rimini*.

Finally one of the most recent theories is that "the tragedy of Tchaikovsky was not that he was homosexual but that he was a reluctant one."[34] This could well be, but in spite of the numerous assumptions the authors make whenever necessary, it still remains unclear what forced Tchaikovsky into what was unnatural to him.

Starting from such contradictory postulates, it is not surprising that biographers arrive at most contradictory conclusions. For instance the question "Did Mrs von Meck know about Tchaikovsky's instincts?" gets two opposite answers: "Plainly, the widow knew nothing about *The*. Even in face of the gossip that had raged around Moscow since his marriage and flight, Nadejda apparently had remained ignorant. Nobody, in short, had dared whisper it to her."[35]—"Several of Tchaikovsky's letters to her reveal his homosexuality so plainly that a woman of her intelligence could not have been deceived. She was besides, very well informed about everything to do with the musical circles in Moscow and could not have avoided hearing what everybody knew."[36] Incidentally this last remark reveals not only a strange ignorance of what Victorian education was in Russia (as a matter of fact Nadejda von Meck may very well have been ignorant that such a thing as homosexuality even existed) but also a negligent reading of her letters. If she had heard any gossip of that kind—and she did admit "having taken 'every opportunity' of hearing what was said of him: 'I stored up every remark, every fragment of criticism [and] I must confess that just those things for which others blamed you were charms in my eyes"—would she have written him the following lines (unless the charm to which she was alluding was precisely homosexuality): "I have heard of your antipathy for teaching young girls and I approve of your attitude and like you for it, because it proves that nothing can corrupt you in art, not even girls. One hears that some of the professors court them. Disgusting! In general, the morals of the Conservatoire are such that not only should I not send a daughter there: I should not send my son." The last part is to be interpreted in its Victorian context: if boys and girls were kissing behind the pianos, the Conservatoire was no place for any son of Mrs von Meck's.

And now for facts. For those facts which are firmly established by written evidence.

First of all let us investigate the infamous passages of Tchaikovsky's diaries, where 'Sensation Z' is mentioned, and also a mysterious feeling, which finally becomes less mysterious. We are told by the translator that Z "was the secret symbol that Tchaikovsky employed to refer to his homosexuality."[37]

23rd April 1884: "A letter to Emma* in answer to her confession. Supper. Vera Vasilievna† and the Stals. The Butakov oppression during whist. Whist twice. There was much Z. Oh what a monster of a person I am."

12th May: "Was terribly angry during whist but not on account of cards but just generally so at something indefinite which may be called Z. Yes, Z is less tormenting and perhaps more steady than X, nonetheless it is also disagreeable."

13th May: "A disagreement took place about who was to be in the game and I left for my room and started to study English but Lev‡ soon came for me. Played with fairly good luck but made many blunders in the last rubber with Roman Efimovitch and, even now, cannot forgive myself, that instead of spades I led with hearts!!!! Z tortures me unusually today. God spare me such a bad feeling."

14th May: "Whist. I was extremely irritable and angry, not on account of the game, but Z was torturing me and what was even more amazing was that it had subsided in the morning."

25th May: "I got a headache so that I played whist with difficulty. Had terrible luck and I was awfully sorry for Sasha. Was

---

* Emma Genton.
† Vera Vasilievna Butakov *née* Davydov.
‡ Lev Davydov, Tchaikovsky's brother-in-law.

very tortured not by the sensation Z itself, but by the fact that it is in me."

And now comes the "feeling." 29th May: "A trip by landau. . . . It would have been very enjoyable were it not for the 'feeling' which appeared to pass at first but then returned with added strength. During the supper at home, the strange behaviour of the hostess* of the house, openly arousing her children against their close ones or, in any case, against their revered relatives. Oh, why, why all this. . . ?"

30th May: "Since morning, the 'feeling.' "

Now the explanation of the "feeling." 2nd June: "Whist. No luck; was not angry, but kept breaking out in a cold perspiration. There was a little 'feeling' but now I am not afraid of the enemy as I know him; it is still the same thing—my stomach."

Back to Z, 3rd June: "Supper and whist with Kern at home. Frightfully intense sensation Z. Oh, my God! Forgive and appease me! The 'feeling' has passed completely."

Last mention of Z, 4th June: "Whist. I had bad luck. On account of that, but principally because of a thousand other reasons which constitute what I call Z, I was as angry as a venomous snake. Came home under a melancholy, heavy pressure of this Z."

That is all. How homosexuality can be deduced with such assurance from these quotations is another mystery. At best we can say that Z is a sensation of which Tchaikovsky disapproves and that it might be anything, including homosexuality.

More serious is the only published passage where Tchaikovsky hints at something of that kind so clearly that it cannot even be called a hint. We know that he was terribly nervous about public opinion and hated being discussed by the press, even if the press was favourable. But to Jurgenson he wrote repeatedly that 'he was very much afraid of a scandal and insinuations from the press, for he had one sensitive and vulnerable spot.' When Nikolai Rubinstein was violently attacked for the despotic way in which he ruled the Conservatoire, Tchaikovsky would have liked very much to defend his friend by means "of a thundering article; and I should do it willingly and well, but there is a reason which makes me for ever unable to indulge in polemics against anonymous journalists. You know the tactics of these reptiles. They gossip and hit their opponent with insinuations. And you know how unfortunately vulnerable I am from that side." He was indeed. And maybe on more than one count. On one hand, to quote

---

* Sasha Davydov, Tchaikovsky's sister Aleksandra.

from Hanson, "he saw possible disgrace, his life broken, his family humiliated, if he should be dismissed from the Conservatoire for perpetual insobriety." On the other hand an article that he once read dismayed him completely, and his reaction to it seems to be, if we understand the word 'amours' right, the only published confession of some sexual guilt.

The *Novoe Vremia* of 26th August 1878, No. 895, contained a violent criticism of the Conservatoire in general and of Rubinstein in particular. Certain teachers were also criticized. The author finally mentioned "the amours of the music teachers which put miserable girl-students into ambiguous and difficult positions. . . . There are also other amours at the Conservatoire, about which, for reasons easy to understand, I am not going to speak at all." Such was the conclusion of the masterpiece.

Tchaikovsky was thunderstruck, and he wrote to Modest: "I have found an article containing a dirty, cowardly, disgusting and slanderous attack against the Conservatoire. Personally I am scarcely mentioned: they even say that my only occupation is music and that I do not participate in the intrigues and plots. But at one point there is a remark about the amours of the teachers with young ladies and at the end an addition: 'there are also at the Conservatoire amours of another kind, but about them, for a reason very easy to understand, I shall not talk' etc. There is no doubt about the hint. So, the sword of Damocles in the shape of an insinuation in the press, which I fear more than anything else in the world, has again fallen on my neck. True, for this time the insinuation does not concern me personally. But that is even worse. My reputation reflects on all the Conservatoire, and that makes my shame and my pain worse."

So we might consider the question as closed, if everything else was to fall into place as soon as the postulate of active homosexuality was accepted. But many points still remain obscure, and some become even more so. To begin with this article, Tchaikovsky should obviously have kept quiet about his reactions to it. Why did he discuss them at length with Mrs von Meck? Why did he carefully extract from the paper whatever he thought was good in it and coolly analyse the qualities and faults of Rubinstein, when he should have pooh-poohed the whole thing, or, on the contrary, emphasized the good that was said of him? The passage is worth quoting:

> I took a newspaper in which I found an article about the Moscow Conservatoire, an article full of dirty insinuations, calumny and all kind of filth, in which my name and personality are mentioned. I

cannot describe to you the impression which this article produced on me: it was as if I had been knocked on the head with a log. . . ! It is unfortunate that newspapers do not keep to the artistic activity of a man: they like to penetrate further, in his private life, and to touch on the intimate aspects of his life. Whether that is done with sympathy or with the obvious desire of causing harm, I find it equally unpleasant to be made the object of attention. Many times have I had to suffer at the hands of invisible friends, who presented me in the press as a man deserving all sorts of sympathy, or of invisible enemies, who threw mud at me by means of insinuations in the press, but formerly I was capable of enduring these favours with patience. . . . Now, having spent a whole year far from the centres of our public life, I have become unbearably sensitive to this form of popularity. Nevertheless, though there is a lot of calumny in this article, which plunged me in an ocean of public, vulgar intrigues, at heart I cannot deny that its main thought is not deprived of justice. One has to admit that Rubinstein's rough despotism, his arbitrary rule which knows no bounds, cannot be endured without protest. The Conservatoire is slowly becoming a pantry-full of flunkeys. Only those who have voluntarily enlisted as flunkeys breathe freely there. Highly as I esteem many good aspects of Rubinstein's energetic character, much as he has done for Moscow and for Russian music, it is indisputable that he has no more tolerance for anyone who dares hesitate to obey his every word. I told you that there had been some unpleasantness between us. There will be more. We do not feel at ease with each other. Rubinstein sees in me a man at whom he cannot shout, whom he cannot order about, who is not ready to submit unconditionally to all his sayings as if they were absolute truth. In a word, I am very indignant when his despotism provokes in the press undeserved onslaughts, when he is accused of vile and dirty traits and characteristics which he has not, but, at the same time, I have to admit that, little by little, he is becoming an awful and eccentric despot, and that he unceasingly violates legality.

The two letters just quoted were written in 1878, one year after Tchaikovsky's scandalous marriage. If gossip about his peculiarities was all over Moscow, why did the unknown journalist spare the composer who must have been such a tempting target? How did Modest, who is supposed to have destroyed all proof of his brother's homosexuality, let the letter about the 'amours' reach posterity? Is it that he read some different meaning in the incriminating words "other amours," for instance, amours between teachers? Or was he just remiss about it? Why did the same Modest, if he was bent on discouraging all suspicion of the composer, tell stories as the following one, maybe perfectly innocent, but still suspicious for a man about whom everybody, as we are led to believe, had already gossiped? 'While travelling to France by sea, Tchaikovsky made the acquaintance of an extraordinarily gifted boy, the son of Professor Sklifasovsky, accompanied by a student. "I shall miss them very much," Tchaikovsky wrote Modest of the two boys, and Modest adds that he went to his cabin and cried bitterly, as if he knew in advance that he would never again meet this lovable and highly gifted boy on earth. Volodia Sklifasovsky died in January 1890. Tchaikovsky was deeply affected by his loss, and dedicated to his memory the *Chant Elégiaque*, op. 72.'

How is it that no friend of Tchaikovsky seems to have attributed Mrs von Meck's betrayal to some indiscretion, but only to calumny?

Tchaikovsky is supposed to have become a homosexual at the School of Law: all biographies concord on this point. If Kurt von Wolfurt is wrong, and Tchaikovsky was not happy about his sexual nature, how could he advise his sister to send her two boys to the same school, and he did so, very strongly indeed.

And then, of course, arises the question of lovers.

With commendable modesty, Catherine Bowen declares that she does "not desire to record the names of his inamorata nor any incidents connected with these affairs." Maybe a little more frankly Rostislav Hofmann writes: "Our investigations among people who had closely known the composer and his intimate friends did not produce one name deserving consideration." We do not know what intimate friends of Tchaikovsky's Rostislav Hofmann may have met, but we have to grant that most of the names which are generally quoted do not seem to fit the picture.

There is the servant, Aleksei Sofronov. But why did Tchaikovsky encourage his marriage and weep at the death of his wife?

There is Vladimir Shilovsky. But Tchaikovsky wrote quite coolly to Modest about Shilovsky's love affairs.

There is Kotek. But Tchaikovsky did not mind at all his running after girls. And then would a man like Tchaikovsky have asked his lover to be a witness at his marriage?

There is Siloti. But how strange that a man so anxious about his reputation should have himself photographed with his lover, and not by chance, but on a posed photograph, where the younger man appears to be leaning on the shoulder of the older one?

There is Bob Davydov, the nephew. But if the composer had had special designs on the boy, would he have written words as these: "Admirable as is his younger brother, Volodia* neverthe-

* Volodia, Bob: diminutives for Vladimir.

R

less occupies the warmest nook in my heart. In general, flowers, music and children are the best ornaments of life. Is it not strange that fate should have refused children of his own to a man who loves them as much as I do?"

We are not saying that all these gentlemen could not have been Tchaikovsky's lovers, but that there is no published evidence that they were, and that, Tchaikovsky being the man that he was, presumptions are against it.

Things are slightly different in four other cases.

First here is, hitherto unpublished in the West, the only available text which seems to reveal an exaggerated sensitivity to masculine charm. Having been to a French play, Tchaikovsky wrote, in a humorous mood, to Modest: "What should I not give to receive a hundred daily cuffs on the ear from the hand which insults Got! * This hand belongs to the divine being whom we admired during a memorable show in 1876. His name is Boucher. Do you remember him? What a charming personality! And what an excellent actor he turns out to be!"

Second, during Tchaikovsky's stay at Anatoly's house in Tiflis, he met a young officer called Ivan Verinovsky, about whom there are several ambiguous entries in the diary. Some relationship seems to have existed between Tchaikovsky's sister-in-law and the officer. It is not clear if the composer objected to it on personal or on brotherly grounds. Here are the most significant of these entries:

6th April 1886: "Korganov and Verinovsky, an officer. Whist. Experienced a feeling . . . of an unusual sort." Stomach again?

14th April: "Over display of love on the part of I." This I. could be Ivan Verinovsky or anybody else.

15th April: "Pania† in a cotillion with Verinovsky."

26th April: "A quarrel with Pania on account of Verinovsky during lunch."

27th April: "Infinitely sorry for Verinovsky and am angry at that hussy."

That is all.

A third track seems a little more promising. We know that in the sixties, Tchaikovsky was a close friend of Prince Aleksei Golitsin. This gentleman he met again in 1879 and he speaks about him with a panic which may simply have been motivated by a fit of misanthropy but which may also indicate unpleasant reminiscences. This Golitsin appears both in the correspondence and, later, in the diaries, and is generally accompanied by 'young gentlemen friends.'

---

* A French actor.
† Praskovia, Anatoly's wife. Cf. p. 182.

He is also present at a curious little scene, or a scene which seems curious due to the diary's telegraphic style and where morphine, that plague of the Davydov family, plays a part: "Brandukov. With him to Golitsin. There was another good-looking (flat-chested) young man; an elegant gentleman and a doctor. Morphine injection. All went to dinner to the Maire restaurant. It was delicious and merry. I paid after a little struggle." Granted that Tchaikovsky did not criticize Golitsin for having flat-chested good-looking friends, but again there is nothing to connect prince and composer in any disreputable fashion.

Finally the only serious track to be found in Tchaikovsky's writings leads nowhere since, at least to our knowledge, the person to whom the composer refers, Edward Zak, was never identified. Here are the only two diary entries in which his name is quoted:

4th September 1887: "Before going to sleep, thought much and long about Edward. Wept much. Is it possible he is not here now at all??? Don't believe it."

5th September: "Was recalling and thinking about Zak again. How amazingly lifelike my memory of him is: the sound of his voice, his motions, but, in particular, the rarely beautiful expression of his face at times. I cannot realize that he is not here at all now. Death, i.e. his complete nonexistence is beyond my understanding. It seems to me that I never loved anyone so intensely. God! what they did not say to me then; and no matter how I console myself, my guilt is terrible regarding him! And in the meantime, I loved him, or I should say I still love him,* and his memory is sacred to me!"

It may be worth noting that although Kotek's real Christian name was Iosif (Joseph), his mother used to call him Edward, that Tchaikovsky did not dedicate his violin concerto to him "to avoid talking," and that Kotek died in 1885. But, on the other hand, his last name was not Zak, and Tchaikovsky disapproved of his being called Edward. So again this is at best inconclusive, and Edward Zak remains a mystery.

Although it is not a feeling of which an historian should be proud, let us confess that we are glad. About the unknown Edward, Tchaikovsky speaks with such an earnest tone of voice, with such a tremulous feeling, that, whether he was his lover or his friend, their secret ought to be respected, since they wanted it so. Whatever their relation was, it was clearly not frivolous, not sordid, not vulgar. Besides, since no information about it has

---

* Wladimir Lakond's muddled translation: "I loved him, i.e. did not love and also love him now."

reached us, this friendship or this affair cannot have lasted very long and if it was in need of purification, Edward's death must have purified it long ago.

NOTES TO PART IV

1 Rostislav Hofmann.
2 Hanson.
3 Weinstock.
4 Hanson.
5 Weinstock.
6 Michel Hofmann.
7 Hanson.
8 Weinstock.
9 Hanson.
10 Weinstock, Hanson.
11 Weinstock.
12 Especially Weinstock.
13 Weinstock.
14 Especially Hanson.
15 For instance, dear Herbert Weinstock.
16 Bowen.
17 Michel Hofmann.
18 Bowen.
19 Hanson.
20 Borrowed from relevant chapters by Bowen, E. Lockspeiser in G. Abraham, Hanson and mainly Weinstock.
21 Weinstock.
22 Hanson.
23 Hanson.
24 Hanson.
25 Bowen.
26 Michel Hofmann.
27 Weinstock.
28 Rostislav Hofmann.
29 Weinstock.
30 Bowen.
31 Weinstock.
32 Rostislav Hofmann.
33 Michel Hofmann.
34 Hanson.
35 Bowen.
36 Hanson.
37 Lakond.

PART FIVE

TCHAIKOVSKY AND HIS WORK

1 *More fatigue than pleasure*

An artist, we said, is a demi-god. So far we have dealt with the mortal part of Tchaikovsky. The immortal one is to be found in concert halls, on records and in scores, not in books. But there is a borderland where the mortal and immortal are mixed, where they reacted on each other, and to this region we are coming now. No cheap sensations to be got out of it, but the more refined, nearly mystic delight of catching a creator creating, a hobgoblin at work.

Art is impossible without three things: inspiration, taste and work. We tend to think that romantic artists gave more importance to inspiration than to the other two ingredients. This is undoubtedly true of some writers, and it is a lamentable but scarcely disputable fact that good taste was not the main virtue of most romantic artists. Tchaikovsky, for one, has the reputation of ignoring it completely. But was it really so? Or are we, maybe, superimposing narrow twentieth-century values on nineteenth-century realities? Would it not be true to say, contrary to the generally accepted opinion, that Tchaikovsky was an artist in whom the three ingredients were closely blended, that he considered them as equally important, but that his values were different from ours? For instance, that his art was still of the human, humane, humanist variety, whereas we are getting more and more used to intellectual games taking the place of a more robust though less sophisticated approach to art? Surely this is worth investigating.

Often an artist reveals himself more in his reactions to arts other than his, because he knows less about them and so is naturally more spontaneous, less on his guard. Balzac's appreciation of music ("Mozart, Beethoven, drop on your knees before Rossini!" he ordered) has much to teach us, not about music, of course, but about Balzac. The same, we feel, might be true of Tchaikovsky and painting, Tchaikovsky and literature; only after catching him, so to speak, unawares, shall we investigate his relationship to music.

Slavs are seldom endowed with a very strong or very refined feeling for plastic arts. Dostoievsky's considerations about the moral value of painting, for instance, are worth reading as an example of utter nonsense written by a genius, and we should not be surprised to find under Tchaikovsky's pen notations like 'Julius Caesar looks like a government clerk'—'Who would think that Trajan, with this general impression of vacancy, was a great man?'—'I can walk for hours outdoors, but the minute I get in a museum I am exhausted.' Or monstrous remarks like: "Florence is all right for tourists for a few days. In fact the city is dead and presents no interest at all. . . . Maybe it is precisely because the city is so poor in resources that I succeeded in writing an opera in an incredibly short time." Or at the end of his life, frank confessions like: "In spite of my efforts, I cannot acquire any appreciation of painting, especially of the old masters – they leave me cold."

But efforts he did make, all his life. In the Naples museum, he had a favourite *Antinous*; he found French portraits 'very interesting and quite in his taste'; he experienced pleasure from Murillo's *St Anthony* and altogether tried his best to be pleased: "I notice that I am making great progress in my appreciation of painting. I take the greatest delight in many things, especially in the Flemish school. Teniers, Wouvermans, and Ruysdael please me far more than the renowned Rubens, who represents even Christ as healthily robust, with unnaturally pink cheeks. One fact makes me begin to see myself as *a great* connoisseur. I recognize Correggio's brush before I see his name in the catalogue! But then Correggio has his own manner and all his male figures and heads resemble the Christ in the Vatican, and his women the Danae in the Borghese Palace."

All this remained rather laborious and Tchaikovsky was the first to be surprised if painting really produced any impression on him. "This last period has been made significant by the fact that I have experienced pleasure from visiting a few museums. At the Vatican, certain paintings, Rafael's *Transfiguration* and Domennicchino's *Communion of St Hieronymos*, have impressed me. Michelangelo's frescoes in the Sistine have ceased to be hieroglyphics for me and I am beginning to be impregnated with astonishment at his original and powerful beauty. . . ." "Today I went on foot to the Vatican and sat a long while in the Sistine Chapel. Here a miracle was worked. I felt—almost for the first time in my life*—an artistic ecstasy for painting. What it means to become gradually accustomed to the painter's art! I remember the time when all this seemed to me absurd and meaningless." During the

* Tchaikovsky was 40.

same period of astounding revelations, Tchaikovsky wrote to Mrs von Meck: "The frescoes of Michelangelo have ceased being incomprehensible to me, although I am still very far from the enthusiasm with which they fill Modest. The athletic musculature of Michelangelo's figures, the sombre grandeur of his painting are not enigmas any more; they interest and even impress me, although I feel no admiration, no emotion, no response. My favourite is still Rafael, this Mozart of painting. I also find very *simpatichny* Guercino's paintings . . . ; some of his Madonnas are so angelically beautiful that they fill my soul with a silent fervour. But I must confess that I am naturally deprived of sensitivity to plastic arts and very few paintings and statues make any real impression on me. In museums I find more fatigue than pleasure. In general I think that museums are the worst place in which to get acquainted with art, because they give much more food than a man can absorb at one time. To seriously study the artistic treasures of Rome, for instance, it would not be enough of a whole life. Each painting requires at least a day. Not later than today did I experience how important it is to examine a painting attentively and for a long time. I was sitting in front of Rafael's *Transfiguration*, and at first I did not find anything special in this painting, but little by little I began to understand the facial expressions of the disciples and other characters, and the more I looked, the more I was penetrated by the charm of the ensemble and details. But I had scarcely begun to feel delight when Modest reminded me that it would soon be three o'clock and that we still had to go to the Sistine."

This psychological way of enjoying art we find again in Tchaikovsky's reaction to Michelangelo: "The more I look at Michelangelo's works the more wonderful they seem to me. Just now I was contemplating his 'Moses.' The church was empty, and there was nothing to disturb my meditations. I assure you I was filled with terror. You will remember that Moses is standing with his head slightly turned towards the sacrifice which is to be offered to Baal. His expression is angry and menacing; his figure majestic and commanding. One feels he has only to speak a word, for erring mortals to fall on their knees before him. It is impossible to conceive anything more perfect than this great statue. With this genius the form expresses his entire thought, there is nothing forced, no pose, such as we see, for instance, in Bernini's statues, of which Rome unfortunately possesses so many examples.

"I am so pleased with a book that has come into my hands, I cannot put it down. It is nothing less than an excellent rendering of Tacitus into French. He is a great artist."

Is not this last remark typical? How much effort spent on admiring, for psychological reasons, a plastic masterpiece! And at the same time what a natural reaction to the non-plastic, but not less great, beauties of Tacitus! Still, even from his slightly grudging admiration for the sculptor we can learn much about the composer. Throughout his life Tchaikovsky had a difficult relationship with Michelangelo. At one point he wrote: ". . . Of all that I have seen here the chapel of the Medici in San Lorenzo has made the most profound impression upon me. It is grandiose and beautiful. Here, for the first time, I realized the greatness of Michelangelo in its fullest significance. I think he has a spiritual affinity with Beethoven. The same breadth and power, the same daring courage, which sometimes almost oversteps the limits of the beautiful, the same dark and troubled moods." The comparison with Beethoven is, of course, important, but more important still is the phrase "which sometimes almost oversteps the limits of the beautiful." This concern with beauty—we should say with good taste—was in fact one of Tchaikovsky's main preoccupations, and this ought not to surprise us after all we have learned about the man. It is a fact that he did not consider himself as a romantic, but rather as a classical artist. In another passage, he ridicules excessive preoccupation with good taste, but only because he was himself on the brink of it. "What a monumental work is Michelanglo's 'Moses'. Several times I have already scrutinized this statue, and every time with greater veneration. This indeed has been conceived and executed by a first rate genius. They say it has a few irregularities! Which reminds me of old Fetis who looked for irregularities in Beethoven and triumphantly announced that he had found in the *Eroica* Symphony—an inverted chord which good taste does not allow. And is it not true that there is a deep kinship between Beethoven and Michelangelo?"

2 *That feeling for beauty which exists in us all*

To literature, on the contrary, Tchaikovsky was very sensitive, and made a few attempts at it himself. At school, he was the editor of the students' magazine; later he wrote many articles about music; his letters show real literary qualities, and he even composed a few poems. One of them, "Lilies of the Valley," is indeed a charming piece of which he was immoderately, though humorously, proud. He wrote to Modest: "For the first time in my life I have succeeded in writing a decent and deeply heartfelt poem. I assure you that, although it cost me great effort, I worked at it with as much pleasure as if it had been music. Please publicize my creation widely: read it to Lola,* Laroche, the Davydovs, Sasha and Tania, Alina Ivanovna,† Jedrinsky and Tola‡ etc. I want very-body to be astounded and to admire. . . ." "Proud as I am of 'Lilies of the Valley,' I still do not think they are fit to be published and therefore refuse your offer. . . . No. Spread my poetical fame, proclaim it, trumpet it, but do not let it fall in the hands of printers." Tchaikovsky also participated in the concoction of his own librettos and produced conventional but rather elegant texts, like the aria of the prince, in *The Queen of Spades*. This he did with tremendous difficulty, as he had trouble not only with the psychology of his characters but also with the mechanics of poetry. Concerning *The Maid of Orleans* he dramatically confessed:

"I am very well pleased with my musical work. As regards the literary side of it, I believe it will cost me some days of my life. I cannot describe how it exhausts me. How many penholders I gnaw to pieces before a few lines grow perfect! How often I jump up in sheer despair because I cannot find a rhyme, or the metre goes wrong, or because I have absolutely no notion what this or that character would say at a particular moment! As regards rhyme, I think it would be a blessing if someone would publish a rhyming dictionary."

As far as we know, he never attempted to write a story, but once he composed the synopsis of one, more or less taken from life. Here it is, for curiosity's sake: It is sweet and cruel, some-what in Tchekhov's manner.

The tale should be told in the form of a diary, or letters, to a friend in England. Miss L. comes to Russia. Everything appears to her strange and ridiculous. The family into which she has fallen please her—especially the children—but she cannot understand why the whole foundation of family life lacks the discipline, the sense of Christian duty, and the good bringing-up which prevail in English

* The poet Apuhtin, Tchaikovsky's friend.
† A. I. Konradi, better known as A. I. Brullov, mother of Nikolai Konradi, Modest's pupil.
‡ Anatoly.

homes. She respects this family, but regards them as belonging to a different race, and the gulf between herself and them seems to grow wider. She draws into herself and remains there. Weariness and oppression possess her. The sense of duty, and the need of working for her family, keep her from despair. She is religious, in the English way, and finds the Russian Church, with its ritual, absurd and repugnant. Some of the family and their relations with her must be described in detail.

A new footman appears upon the scene. At first, she does not notice him at all. One day, however, she becomes aware that he has looked at her in particular—and love steals into her heart. At first, she does not understand what has come over her. Why does she sympathize with him when he is working—others have to work too? Why does she feel so ill at ease when he waits on her? Then the footman begins to make love to the laundrymaid. In her feeling of hatred for this girl, she realizes she is jealous, and discovers her love. She gives the man all the money she has saved to go on a journey for his health, etc. She begins to love everything Russian. . . . She changes her creed. The footman is dismissed for some fault. She struggles with herself—but finally goes with him. One fine day he says to her: "Go to the devil and take your ugly face with you! What do you want from me?" I really do not know how it all ends. . . .

Tchaikovsky knew that he was not a writer and never seriously strayed in that direction. The more revealing his tastes, since they were completely disinterested.

He liked serious reading. Travels in India, ants, bees and wasps, but especially historical books, mainly about the eighteenth century, fascinated him. For instance, he was particularly taken with Catherine the Great's correspondence with Grimm. He also read philosophy, in particular Spinoza, whose personality he admired, and Schopenhauer, who displeased him because "his final deductions contain something hurtful to human dignity, something dry and egotistical which is not warmed by any love towards mankind." Having finished the works of this philosopher, he gave his impressions to Mrs von Meck.

Schopenhauer seems to me particularly inconsistent in his final conclusions. While he demonstrates that it is better not to live than to live, one waits and wonders: maybe he is right, but what should I do about it? His answer to that question is weak. As a matter of fact, his theory very logically leads to suicide. But, frightened by such a dangerous way of getting rid of a painful life and not daring recommend suicide as a universal means of putting his philosophy into practice, he embarks on very bizarre sophisms, and tries to prove that a man who commits suicide does not deny but on the contrary confirms his love for life. This is neither logical nor brilliant. His theory of love is extraordinarily original and new, although some details in the factual demonstrations are twisted and far-fetched. You are perfectly right when you say that it is impossible to believe in the sincerity of a philosopher who teaches us not to acknowledge any of life's joys and to mortify our body to the last extremity, and at the same time enjoys the advantages of being alive till the very last day, and, quite un-abashed, takes good care indeed of his interests.

Already in this passage we find the humanist point of view which was Tchaikovsky's predominant characteristic in his judgements of intellectual activities.

He read much and was well acquainted with Russian, French and English literature. Although Goethe's *Wilhelm Meister* was "a revelation" to him, we seldom find him reading Goethe for his pleasure: on the contrary, Thackeray, George Eliot, and Dickens were on his reading table most of the time, and he finally even learned English to be able to read them in the original. He was particularly fond of *Scenes from Clerical Life*. For a time he seri-ously contemplated founding the libretto of his next opera upon *The Sad Fortunes of the Rev. Amos Barton*. He "laughed heartily" over *The Pickwick Papers*, cried over *Bleak House*, enjoyed *David Copperfield* in the original; as to *Little Dorritt*, it sent him into ecstasies: To Modest: "Supper is just finished; I write this letter and then I shall resume the reading of *Dorritt*. My goodness, what a wonderful book! If you have not read it, buy it immediately and read." To Anatoly: "Have you read this production of an arch genius? Dickens and Thackeray are the only men whom I forgive their being English. I should also add Shakespeare, but he lived at a time when that paganation [*sic*] was not so obnoxious." Doubtless, the crime of being English was not to be held against Byron, either, since in the great romantic's poems Tchaikovsky recognized his own *'profession de foi.'*

With French literature the composer was familiar. His mixed feelings about Bourget, his condemnation of Loti, his amusement at 'Meilhac et Halévy' are commendable though not revealing. But his admiration for Maupassant by whom he was "utterly charmed" is already more indicative: Maupassant is a very delicate, but also a very cruel, writer, with an unflinching interest for Man and his sufferings: sometimes this interest borders on sadism, but most of the time on sympathy; his realism is never an end in itself, but a means of assimilation to other human beings and also of attaining a very personal, very intimate blend of poetry. It is typical that Tchaikovsky should also have felt deep admiration for Maupassant's master, Flaubert: "I think there is no more *simpatichny* personality in all the world of literature. A hero and martyr to his art. And so wise! I have found some astonishing answers to my questionings as to God and religion in his book."[*] But who was Flaubert? A born romantic, who spent his whole life trying to become a sober realist and became, in fact, the father of that whole movement. It is not surprising that Tchaikovsky, who oscillated between *Swan Lake* and *Eugene Onegin*, should have felt a kind of kinship with the author of *Salammbo* and *Madame Bovary*. Musset was, of course, one of Tchaikovsky's favourites: the romance of *Les Caprices de Marianne* was bound to arouse sympathy in the composer, and also Musset's split personality. But the immortal classics of the seventeenth century were also an essential part of Tchaikovsky's regime: after seeing Corneille's *Polyeucte* and Molière's *Les Femmes Savantes* at the *Comèdie Française*, the composer wrote to Modest: "Every time, one leaves that theatre with a feeling of repletion: it is as if one had been hungry for a long time and had finally satisfied oneself to the necessary extent." This, by the way, is a very apt way of summarizing what the classics stand for, and should be pondered by those of our contemporaries whose literary menus are perhaps more sophisticated but certainly less nourishing.

Still, Tchaikovsky's two main antipathies are even more revealing than his preferences. One was Hugo, the other Zola, and it is certainly not to the composer's discredit that he objected to these two writers' taste. He wrote to Modest:

Thanks (in an ironical sense) for your suggestion that I should read *L'homme qui rit*. Do you not know the story of my relations to Victor Hugo? Anyhow, I will tell you what came of them. I took up *Les Travailleurs de la mer*; I read, and read, and grew more and more irritated by his grimaces and buffoonery. Finally, after a whole series of short, unmeaning phrases, consisting of exclamations, antitheses and asterisks, I lost my temper, spat upon the book, tore it to pieces, stamped upon it, and wound up by throwing it out of the window. From that moment I cannot bear the mention of Victor Hugo! Believe me, your Zola is just such another mountebank, but more modern in spirit. I do not dislike him quite so much as Hugo, but very nearly. He disgusts me, as a girl would disgust me who pretended to be simple and natural, while all the time she was essentially a flirt and coquette.

* Flaubert's correspondence.

In fact, Tchaikovsky had a complicated relationship with Zola. He admired "the beast's" talent. *Germinal* moved him to palpitations and insomnia. In the character of Lazare (*La Joie de Vivre*) he found sheer genius and an incredibly true description 'of certain details which he himself had experienced.' He was always, and rightly, moved by Zola's realism, but he strongly objected to any unartistic exploitation of it. After seeing a play based on *L'Assommoir*, Tchaikovsky wrote to Mrs von Meck:

> It is interesting to sit through this piece, for it is highly entertaining to see washerwomen getting up linen in the second scene, all the characters dead drunk in the sixth, and in the eighth, the death of a confirmed toper in an attack of *delirium tremens*. The play deals a double blow at that feeling for beauty which exists in us all. First, it is adapted from a novel written by a talented, but cynical, man who chooses to wallow in human filth, moral and physical. Secondly, to make it more effective and pander to the taste of the Boulevard public, a melodramatic element has been brought into the play which is not in keeping with the rest of it. In this way *L'Assommoir* loses on the stage its chief merit—the wonderfully realistic presentment of everyday life.
>
> But what do you think of Monsieur Zola, the high priest of the realistic cult, the austere critic who recognizes no literary art but his own, when he allows perfectly unreal and improbable episodes and characters to be tacked on to his play—all for the sake of a royalty?

The passage is important because on one hand it shows Tchaikovsky's obsession with "that feeling for beauty which exists in us all"; on the other hand it demonstrates how he tended to assimilate the artist's sincerity and the truth of the work of art. For him the second was unthinkable without the first. His violent antipathy for Zola the man Tchaikovsky expressed to Anatoly: "I had already disliked Zola for a long time. But now that his photograph stares at me from all the stores, and that I see what an extraordinarily repugnant, impudent, conceited physiognomy he has, now also that I have seen the play in which this priest of realism has allowed completely unrealistic additions to his subject in order to create a greater effect, I simply loathe him."

This loathing was the origin of one of Tchaikovsky's most curious productions: a brilliant pastiche the zest and gusto of which reminds us that there was a rich comical streak to Tchaikovsky's talent. Here he describes his own supper in Zola's style.

Une serviette de table négligemment attachée à son cou, il dégustait. Tout autour des mouches, avides, grouillantes, d'un noir

inquiétant volaient. Nul bruit sinon un claquement de machoirs (sic)
*énervant. Une odeur moite fétide, écœurante, lourde, répandait un
je ne sais quoi d'animal, de carnacier* (sic) *dans l'air. Point de
lumière. Un rayon de soleil couchant, pénétrant comme par hasard
dans la chambre nue et basse, éclairait par-ci, par-là tantôt la figure
blême du maître engurgitant sa soupe, tantôt celle du valet,
moustachue, à traits kalmouks, stupide et rampante. On devinait un
idiot servi par un idiot. 9 heures. Un morne silence régnait. Les
mouches fatiguées somnolentes, devenues moins agitées, se dis-
persaient. Et là-bas, dans le lointain, par la fenêtre, on voyait une
lune, grimaçante, énorme, rouge, surgir sur l'horizon embrasé. Il
mangeait, il mangeait toujours. Puis l'estomac bourré, la face
écarlate, l'oeil hagard, il se leva et sortit. . . .*

It is a pity to translate such a piece. However, let us see what
we can do.

A napkin negligently hanging from his neck, he gourmandized.
Around him hovered greedy, swarming flies, disquietingly black. No
noise but the irritating clashing of his teeth. A damp, nauseous,
sickening, heavy odour tinted the air with some bestial, carnivor-
ous, touch. No light. One ray of the setting sun entering as if by
accident into the naked and low-ceilinged room, lit up, here and there,
now the ashen face of the master gulping down his soup, now the
moustached, kalmouk-featured, obtuse and servile countenance of
the valet. An idiot served by an idiot: one guessed that. Nine o'clock.
A gloomy silence reigned. The sleepy, tired flies, less excited now,
were disbanding. And lo, far away, through the window, one could
see a grimacing, enormous, red moon emerging from the horizon, all
aflame. He ate and still he ate. Finally, his stomach stuffed, his face
crimson, his eyes haggard, he got up and went out.

Russian literature constituted Tchaikovsky's daily fare, and
there his likes and dislikes have even more to tell us about him.

There is nothing surprising in the fact that he adored Pushkin
(all Russians do) or in his partiality for the sweeter Russian poets,
like Fet, Homiakov, Count Aleksei Tolstoi; if they were religious,
nationalists or slavophiles into the bargain, so much the better.
His rather cold admiration for Turgenev, certainly an adept of
beauty, but not a very sincere or *simpatichny* writer, was also to
be expected. His enthusiasm for Aksakov's *Family Chronicle* is
typical and interesting, for it shows how sensitive Tchaikovsky was
to the most simple, to the most *intimiste* art that can be found
in any literature: "What a beautiful original work and how I like
books of that kind! To penetrate down to the most intimate depths
of strange lives and in addition into the remote past—that is an
immense satisfaction to me." As typical is the composer's admira-

tion for Melnikov-Pechersky's *On the Hills*. "What an astonishing insight into Russian life, and what a calm objective attitude the author assumes to the numerous characters he has drawn in this novel! Dissenters of various kinds, merchants, moujiks, aristocrats, monks and nuns—all seem actually living as one reads. Each character acts and speaks, not in accordance with the author's views and convictions, but just as they would do in real life. In our day it is rare to meet with a book so free from 'purpose.'"

Thus we begin to see how deeply Tchaikovsky was attached to the ideal of 'Art for Art's sake;' indeed this was one of the main differences which separated him from his contemporaries of the Powerful Handful.

We have seen* Tchaikovsky deeply moved by Dostoievsky, but this does not indicate that he admired or understood him. As a matter of fact it has to be confessed that Tchaikovsky missed altogether the prophetic significance of Dostoievsky's works. "Read the sequel of the *Karamazovs*. It begins to be intolerable. All characters without exception are insane. In general, Dostoievsky can be endured only during the first parts of his novels. Afterwards it is always a madhouse. . . ." "I am reading the *Karamazovs*, and I am anxious to have done with it. Dostoievsky is a genius but an unpleasant writer. The more I read him, the more painful it is." Although he was not blind to the beauty of Dostoievsky's world, in which he found "incredible revelations of artistic analysis," Tchaikovsky was never really fair to it: obviously Dostoievsky belongs to the modern school, for whom ugliness can be turned into beauty by the magic of art. Whereas Tchaikovsky was a conservative, practically a man of his dear eighteenth century; beauty for him was made out of beauty and of nothing else.

Tchekhov on the contrary appealed to him. He must have liked the delicate humanism, the humour, the modesty of the storyteller's tone, and he recommended him to all his friends, foretelling that he would be one of the main pillars of Russian literature.

His feelings about Nekrasov, the liberal poet who made a fortune out of rhyming the sufferings of the poor, deserve to be examined in detail. They are characteristic of the man, of the gentleman, and of the artist that Tchaikovsky was.

> I cannot forget that Nekrasov, this protector of the weak and of the oppressed, this democrat, this indignant avenger of all the manifestations of gentility, lived like a real squire, i.e. won and lost hundreds of thousands of roubles at cards, managed very smartly

---

* Cf. p. 171.

s

his literary business, knew how to enrich himself at other people's expense . . . etc. . . . I have often been told that it is wicked and unfair for a critic to mix up the literary and the human qualities of an artist. Conclusion: I am a bad critic, since I have never been able to distinguish these two aspects of an artist. But independently from Nekrasov's qualities as a man . . . I am annoyed by something vaguely spurious in his poetry and I remember several of his pieces which have left me for ever with an unpleasant impression because of their affected whimpering, their unnaturalness, their lack of the straightforwardness which characterizes real artists, not deformed and distorted by a biased purpose.

A few days later:

I have reread many of Nekrasov's works and . . . I am still of the same opinion, or rather my impression has become worse. Long ago, when I was young, I liked the poems of his first period: *The Troika*, *The Gardener*, etc. Now even these pieces have lost all their charm for me. Nekrasov was undoubtedly a gifted man, but not an artist. In every piece I read between the lines and find them fussing about popularity, obstinately trying to attain recognition as a protector and a friend of the people. In the last poems written before his death, he touches me not by the might of his art but by his suffering. But he indulges still in the same hobby. He unceasingly accuses himself of having been useless to the people, of never having done anything to better their lives. He whimpers because common people do not recognize him as their defender, but all that is expressed in the tone of a flirt simpering about her unattractiveness in order to be convinced of the opposite by her beau. Some of his last pieces are simply intolerably boring, so mediocre, vulgar and indifferent are the objects of his satire. . . . As for *Russian Women**
I should have preferred the detailed story in prose of the trip to Siberia made by these really wonderful women, rather than Nekrasov's rhymed production, which remains bad poetry in spite of its attractive heroines. What was the use of verse here? Say what you like, the Governor of Irkutsk addressing Princess Volkonsky in verse to inform her that the Emperor has forbidden her to proceed with her trip is rather funny. Even in the choice of his heroines Nekrasov has again given in to his weakness: earn the reputation of a liberal. There is no straightforward art here. If he wanted to sing feminine altruism, why go so far for examples? There have been virtuous women besides Decembrists' wives. But then Decembrists . . . they are so interesting, they will give a poem the valiant tone of a protest against political oppression!

All this is an honest display of good common sense, human and artistic. And in art, common sense is not a very common quality.

* Cf. p. 173, footnote.

But Tchaikovsky's reactions to Tolstoi are even more significant from that point of view: to use his own words, 'the less he liked him as a philosopher and preacher,* the more he admired the powerful genius of the writer.'

"I am convinced that the greatest of all artistic writers who ever lived is L. N. Tolstoi. He alone is sufficient, so that a Russian should not bow his head in shame when he hears enumerated all the great contributions that Europe has given to mankind. And in my conviction of the eternally great, almost divine, significance of Tolstoi, patriotism does not play any part at all." It would be difficult to express oneself more clearly and Tchaikovsky repeated these same words or other similar ones more than once. He also made clear what was, according to him, Tolstoi's main quality, showing once again that art and artist were for him inseparable:

As regards Tolstoi, I have read and re-read him, and consider him the greatest writer in the world, past and present. His writings awake in me—apart from any powerful artistic impression—a peculiar emotion. I do not feel so deeply touched when he describes anything really emotional, such as death, suffering, separation, etc., so much as by the most ordinary, prosaic events. For instance, I remember that when reading the chapter in which Dolokhov plays cards with Rostov and wins, I burst into tears. Why should a scene in which two characters are acting in an unworthy manner affect me in this degree? The reason is simple enough. Tolstoi surveys the people he describes from such a height that they seem to him poor, insignificant pygmies who, in their blindness, injure each other in an aimless, purposeless way—and he pities them. Tolstoi has no malice; he loves and pities all his characters equally, and all their actions are the result of their own limitations and naïve egotism, their helplessness and insignificance. Therefore he never punishes his heroes for their ill-doings, as Dickens does (who is a great favourite of mine), because he never depicts anyone as absolutely bad, only blind people, as it were. His humanity is far above the sentimental humanity of Dickens; it almost attains to that view of human wickedness which is expressed in the words of Christ: 'they know not what they do.'

It is characteristic of Tchaikovsky that his dislike for the thinker Tolstoi did not prevent him from enjoying the writer and vice versa.

The main feature, or rather the main note which resounds through every page of Tolstoi, even the seemingly unimportant ones, is love,

* The reader no doubt remembers that the last decades of Tolstoi's life were dedicated to the creation and fostering of a new religion based on chastity, non-violence, anarchy and systematic opposition to the Church.

compassion for Man in general (and not only for the humiliated and the offended), pity of some sort for his weakness, his insignificance, the shortness of his life, the vanity of his desires. . . . Yes, Tolstoi is for me the dearest, the deepest, the greatest of all artists. But this concerns the Tolstoi of yesterday, who has nothing in common with the exasperating moralist and theorizer of today. In all that he writes now, I can find craftsmanship, but no source of deep delights and enthusiasms, nothing resembling the mysterious, irresistible charm of his previous works. . . . I have read *The Power of Darkness*, Tolstoi's drama. I can see in it only one great quality: the mastery of the language. All the rest, if you think about it, is extremely artificial and strange and at times revolting. It is enough to say that such hardened villains as Matrona belong in popular melodramas, and not in a serious play. And this disgusting and contrived character was created by Tolstoi! ! ! ! Unconceivable! ! ! . . . There are of course a few scenes which produce a touching impression. . . . In general, *The Power of Darkness* seems to me the production of a great master but not of a great artist. An artist's absolute truth is not to be found in banal, formal meaning, but in a higher meaning, which discloses to us unknown horizons, unattainable spheres, which music only can reach, and towards which no writer went so far as the Tolstoi of the past.

The only work of Tolstoi about which Tchaikovsky appears to have changed his mind is *Anna Karenina*: at first he was indignant. "Shame on you!" he wrote to Modest. "How can you admire such revoltingly vulgar gibberish, hiding under the pretence of a deep psychological analysis. Devil take it, all this psychological analysis, when the result appears fatuous and insignificant!" We have seen that later he expressed completely different feelings: he re-read the book "with enthusiasm bordering on fanaticism."* But this is an exception. In general, he was much more faithful to his ideal than Tolstoi himself.

When we read the autobiographies or memoirs of great men, we frequently find that their thoughts and impressions—and more especially their artistic sentiments—are such as we ourselves have experienced and can therefore fully understand. There is only one who is incomprehensible, who stands alone and aloof in his greatness—Leo Tolstoi. Yet often I feel angry with him: I almost hate him. Why, I ask myself, should this man, who more than all his predecessors has power to depict the human soul with such wonderful harmony, who can fathom our poor intellect and follow the most secret and tortuous windings of our moral nature—why must he needs appear as a preacher and set up to be our teacher and guardian? Hitherto he has succeeded in making a profound impres-

* Cf. p. 185.

sion by the recital of simple, everyday events. We might read between the lines his noble love of mankind, his compassion for our helplessness, our mortality and pettiness. How often have I wept over his words without knowing why! . . . Perhaps because for a moment I was brought into contact—through his medium—with the Ideal, with absolute happiness, and with humanity. Now he appears as a commentator of texts, who claims a monopoly in the solution of all questions of faith and ethics. But through all his recent writings blows a chilling wind. We feel a tremor of fear at the consciousness that he, too, is a mere man; a creature as much puffed up as ourselves about 'The End and Aim of Life,' 'The Destiny of Man,' 'God,' and 'Religion;' and as madly presumptuous, as ineffectual as some ephemera born on a summer's day to perish at eventide. Once Tolstoi was a Demigod. Now he is only a Priest. . . . Tolstoi says that formerly, knowing nothing, he was mad enough to aspire to teach men out of his ignorance. He regrets this. Yet here he is beginning to teach us again. Then we must conclude he is no longer ignorant. Whence this self-confidence? Is it not foolish presumption? The true sage knows only that he knows nothing.

'Once a demigod, now a priest': the phrase is well-coined and well-deserved. At a time when Tolstoi was fancying himself as a somewhat improved Jesus Christ and when the hysterical adoration of some and the blind hatred of others helped him to delude himself more and more, Tchaikovsky, with the good sense and the good taste, the feeling for measure and for proportion, with which he is seldom credited but which we have learned to associate with him, coolly noted in his diary: "Read *What I believe* in the evenings, and am astonished by its combination of wisdom and childish naïveté "

3 *Rays extinguished by Mozart's sun*

We know enough now about Tchaikovsky's taste in general not to be astonished at his preferences and antipathies in music, and maybe to understand them a little better than if we had begun with them.

Mozart he idolized and called 'the Christ of music!'* At times,

* "To hear his music is to feel one has accomplished some good action."

when he played Mozart, it seemed to him that he was living in the eighteenth century and that after Mozart there was nothing.' He had a particular tenderness for the pianoforte *Fantasia* from which he arranged the vocal quartet *Night*, for the adagio of the D minor string quintet ("No one else in music has ever known as well how to interpret so exquisitely the sense of resigned and inconsolable sorrow"), for *The Marriage of Figaro*: "How much majesty and beauty in this unpretentious music." He loved the *Requiem* and pitied whoever was incapable of appreciating it. But his greatest admiration went to *Don Giovanni*, which had haunted him since childhood. He was less than eight years old when he could reproduce at the piano arias from *Don Giovanni* which he had heard played on an 'orchestrion.' 'He found such delight in playing,' says Modest, 'that it was frequently necessary to drag him by force from the instrument. Afterwards, as the next best substitute, he would take to drumming tunes upon the windowpanes. One day, while thus engaged, he was so entirely carried away by this dumb-show that he broke the glass and cut his hand severely.' He was ten when he heard the whole opera sung, and he never forgot his impression of it: "The music of *Don Giovanni* was the first to make a deep impression upon me. It awoke a spiritual ecstasy which was afterwards to bear fruit. By its help I penetrated into that world of artistic beauty where only great genius abides. It is due to Mozart that I devoted my life to music. He gave the first impulse to my efforts, and made me love it above all else in the world."

He was 38 when he described what he had felt, or what he now thought he had felt then.

True, Mozart reaches neither the depths nor heights of Beethoven. And since in life, too, he remained to the end of his days a careless child, his music has not that subjectively tragic quality which is so powerfully expressed in that of Beethoven. But this did not prevent him from creating an objectively tragic type, the most superb and wonderful human presentment ever depicted in music. I mean Donna Anna, in *Don Giovanni*. Ah, how difficult it is to make anyone else see and feel in music what we see and feel ourselves! I am quite incapable of describing to you what I felt on hearing *Don Giovanni*, especially in the scene where the noble figure of the beautiful, proud, revengeful woman appears on the stage. Nothing in any opera ever impressed me so profoundly. And afterwards, when Donna Anna recognizes in Don Giovanni the man who has wounded her pride and killed her father, and her wrath breaks out like a rushing torrent in that wonderful recitative, or in that later aria, in which every note in the orchestra seems to speak of her wrath and pride and

actually to quiver with horror—I could cry out and weep under
the overwhelming stress of the emotional impression. And her lament
over her father's corpse, the duet with Don Ottavio, in which she
vows vengeance, her arioso in the great sextet in the churchyard—
these are inimitable, colossal operatic scenes!

He was always ready to acknowledge his debt towards Mozart:
"Fortunately, fate decreed that I should grow up in an unmusical
family, so that in childhood I was not nourished on the poisonous
food of the post-Beethoven music. The same kind fate brought me
early in life in contact with Mozart, early impressions can never
be effaced. Do you know that when I play Mozart, I feel brighter
and younger, almost a youth again?" And if anybody dared insult
his darling, he gallantly rushed to the defence. "Having just remembered that you had expressed such a negative opinion of my
ideal, Mozart, I went to the piano and played through the whole
first act of Don Giovanni. Oh how I pity you! How I pity people
sensitive to music but who nonetheless have lost the ability to
delight in this divine beauty and simplicity! I should like to die
hearing extracts from Don Giovanni or the andante of the G-flat
quintet!"

Some misunderstandings were bound to arise, and Mrs von Meck,
who disliked Mozart, expressed astonishment that such a dramatic
and emotional composer as Tchaikovsky should worship one who
seemed to her dry and unfeeling. "You say," he answered, "that my
worship for him is in contradiction with my musical nature, but
maybe it is precisely because, as a child of my century, I am shattered and morally ill, that I love to look for rest and consolation
in Mozart's music, which, for the most part, expresses the joy of
life belonging to a healthy, wholesome, temperament, not yet
corroded by reflection."

As passionately as he adored Mozart, Tchaikovsky hated his
antithesis, Wagner. There is no doubt that in his hatred Tchaikovsky was unjust, unfair, obstinate, blind, deaf. Our intention has
never been to idealize him but to present him as he was. And the
deafness itself seems to us very typical of him: how could the man
and the artist that he was understand the overbearing Teuton
Richard Wagner? Wellington said of Napoleon that he was no
gentleman: Tchaikovsky's reaction to Wagner is of the same vein.

At his most indulgent, Tchaikovsky admitted that "in Parsifal
one deals with a great master, with a genius, although the artist
in him has gone astray;" that "Das Rheingold is an incredible
chaos through which extremely beautiful and remarkable details
twinkle from time to time;" that 'Die Niebelungen may be a

masterpiece, but there never was a longer or a more boring one,'
and even that "if the *Ring* bores one in places, if much in it is at
first incomprehensible and vague, if Wagner's harmonies are at times
open to objection, as being too complicated and artificial, and his
theories are false, even if the results of his immense work should
eventually fall into oblivion, and the Bayreuth Theatre drop into an
eternal slumber, yet the *Niebelungen Ring* is an event of the greatest
importance to the world, an epoch-making work of art."

In a word: "Formerly music was supposed to excite admiration
in people; now, torment and fatigue. Of course, there are marvellous details, but everything put together is boring to death!!! The
ballet *Sylvia** is thousands of times dearer to me!!!"

Maybe Tchaikovsky erred most when he tried to find reasons
for admiring his enemy:

> The principle of Wagnerism is not congenial to me, and Wagner
> as a person inspires me with antipathy, but I have to acknowledge
> his huge musical gifts. These gifts, in my opinion, never shone more
> brightly than in *Lohengrin*. This opera is the crown of Wagner's
> creations; after *Lohengrin* began the decadence of his talent,
> destroyed by the satanic pride of the man. He lost his sense of
> measure, started to work without observing necessary proportions,
> and everything which he composed after *Lohengrin* is an example
> of music incomprehensible, impossible, and without any future. . . .
> Wagner's orchestra is too much of a *symphony* orchestra, it is *too
> full and too heavy* for vocal music, while I, the older I grow, the
> more convinced I become that these two genres, i.e. symphony and
> opera, are irreconcilable extremes.

Still, foolish as his strictures may now seem to us, he knew how
to press his point. And his idea that Wagner was more a symphonist than a composer for the human voice is anything but absurd:

> In my opinion, Wagner is by nature a symphonist. This man has
> received an enormous talent, but his intentions spoil it, his inspira-
> tion is paralysed by the theory which he has invented and which he
> wants to put into practice, no matter what the result is. In pursuit
> of *realism, truth and rationalism* in opera, he has forgotten all about
> music . . . for I cannot give the name of music to those kaleido-
> scopic, variegated little pieces which unceasingly follow each other
> without ever leading anywhere or letting you rest on a comprehensible
> musical form. Not one broad, finished melody, not once is the singer
> given free space. All the time he must run after the orchestra and
> take care not to miss his one little note which has no more import-
> ance in the score than a note written for the fourth *Waldhorn*. . . .

---

* By Léo Delibes.

Let me prove to you with an example how much the symphonist in him predominates over the vocal and opera composer in general. You must have heard in concerts his famous *Walkürenritt*. What an heroic, magnificent picture! You can see the wild giants thundering on their fabulous horses in the clouds. In concert, the impression is always tremendous. In a theatre, among cardboard rocks, clouds made of rags, and soldiers clumsily galloping up stage . . . the music loses all its imagery.

So far, we have selected passages where Tchaikovsky dealt gently with his foe. He could be much more fierce, much more incensed against a style in which he saw the death of music: "If music is really to find in Wagner its main and greatest champion, then despair is in order. Is this really the last word of music? Will future generations make their delight of this pretentious, ponderous and graceless balderdash* as we do of the Ninth Symphony, which, in its time, was also considered as nonsense? If so, it is awful. . . ." "The operas of the last period . . . are false in principle: they renounce artistic simplicity and veracity and can only live in Germany, where Wagner's name has become the watchword of German patriotism." As to *Tristan und Isolde*, "which is so intolerably wearisome on the stage" and which could not charm the Parisians if it were not for their snobbishness, it was too much even for Germans:

The work does not give me any pleasure, although I am glad to have heard it, for it has done much to strengthen my previous views of Wagner, which—until I had seen all his works performed—I felt might not be well-grounded. Briefly summed up, this is my opinion. In spite of his great creative gifts, in spite of his talents as a poet, and his extensive culture, Wagner's services to art—and to opera in particular—have only been of a negative kind. He has proved that the older forms of opera are lacking in all logical and aestheic *raison d'être*. But if we may no longer write opera on the old lines, are we obliged to write as Wagner does? I reply, *Certainly not.* To compel people to listen for four hours at a stretch to an endless symphony which, however rich in orchestral colour, is wanting in clearness and directness of thought; to keep singers all these hours singing melodies which have no independent existence, but are merely notes that belong to this symphonic music (in spite of lying very high these notes are often lost in the thunder of the orchestra), this is certainly not the ideal at which contemporary musicians should aim. Wagner has transferred the centre of gravity from the stage to the orchestra, but this is an obvious absurdity, therefore his famous operatic reform—viewed apart from its negative results

* Written—O sacrilege! —about *Die Walküre*.

—amounts to nothing. As regards the dramatic interest of his operas, I find them very poor, often childishly naïve. But I have never been quite so bored as with *Tristan und Isolde*. It is an endless void, without movement, without life, which cannot hold the spectator, or awaken in him any true sympathy for the characters on the stage. It was evident that the audience—even though Germans—were bored. . . .

As to *Parsifal*, its

wealth of harmony is so luxuriant, so vast, that at length it becomes fatiguing, even to a specialist. . . . To my mind Wagner has killed his colossal creative genius with theories. . . . If the singer may not sing, but—amid the deafening clamour of the orchestra—is expected to declaim a series of set and colourless phrases, to the accompaniment of a gorgeous, but disconnected and formless symphony, is that opera? What really astounds me, however, is the seriousness with which this philosophizing German sets the most inane subjects to music. Who can be touched, for instance, by *Parsifal*, in which, instead of having to deal with men and women similar in temperament and feeling to ourselves, we find legendary beings, suitable perhaps for a ballet, but not for a music drama? I cannot understand how anyone can listen without laughter, or without being bored, to those endless monologues in which Parsifal, or Kundry, and the rest bewail their misfortunes. Can we sympathize with them? Can we love or hate them? Certainly not; we remain aloof from their passions, sentiments, triumphs, and misfortunes. . . . That which is unfamiliar to the human heart should never be the source of musical inspiration. . . .

We may, nay we must, be appalled by such abominable conservatism, by such narrow fidelity to the classic ideal. But we must also acknowledge that Tchaikovsky committed his worst artistic crimes through an excess, not through a lack, of what is generally known as taste. Indeed, modern Bayreuth productions seem to comply with some of Tchaikovsky's wishes: Wieland Wagner has disposed of the more questionable properties and theatrical gimmicks so that music could reign alone. And we should inscribe to Tchaikovsky's credit his preference for *Die Meistersinger* where "the subject is human and the music pleasant." It is also impossible to disagree entirely with his remarks about Wagner's librettos: "wake beautiful ladies with kisses, chat with little birds, fight monsters, all this is silly because it is impossible." Finally, there may have been some sense in his opposition to Wagner's systematic *recitative*: "if characters must speak and not sing, what is the opera for?"

It is most reassuring, however, to abandon Wagner and to see what Tchaikovsky had to say about Beethoven. Not only did he find the Scherzo of the Ninth Symphony "divinely beautiful, strong, original and significant," not only did he give ample justice to Beethoven's absence of 'padding': he went so far as to compare him to the incomparable Mozart, not always, it is true, to his advantage:

> To begin with Beethoven, whom I praise unconditionally, and to whom I bend as to a god. But what is Beethoven to me? I bow down before the grandeur of some of his creations, but I do not love Beethoven. My relationship to him reminds me of that which I felt in my childhood to the God Jehovah. I feel for him—for my sentiments are still unchanged—great veneration, but also fear. He has created the heaven and the earth, and although I fall down before him, I do not love him. Christ, on the contrary, calls forth exclusively the feeling of love. He is God, but also Man. He has suffered like ourselves. We pity Him and love in Him the ideal side of man's nature. If Beethoven holds an analogous place in my heart to the God Jehovah, I love Mozart as the musical Christ. I do not think this comparison is blasphemous. Mozart was as pure as an angel, and his music is full of divine beauty.
>
> While speaking of Beethoven I touch on Mozart. To my mind, Mozart is the culminating point of all beauty in the sphere of music. He alone can make me weep and tremble with delight at the consciousness of the approach of that which we call the ideal. Beethoven makes me tremble too, but rather from a sense of fear and yearning anguish. I do not understand how to analyse music, and cannot go into detail. . . . Still I must mention two facts. I love Beethoven's middle period, and sometimes his first; but I really hate his last, especially the latest quartets. They have only brilliancy, nothing more. The rest is chaos, over which floats, veiled in mist, the spirit of this musical Jehovah.

The last words are dreadfully unfair and Tchaikovsky, in spite of his eighteenth-century ear, soon recognized it himself: "In the last quartets, which were long regarded as the productions of an insane and deaf man, there seems to be some padding until we have studied them thoroughly. But ask someone who is well-acquainted with these works . . . he would be horrified at the idea of abbreviating or cutting any portion of them." And he added: "It is astonishing how all that this giant among musicians ever wrote is equally full of significance and might, and also how he managed to control the incredible pressure of his colossal inspiration and never neglected balance and perfection of form. . . . [This was a sore spot with Tchaikovsky.] . . . This genius who liked to express himself broadly, majestically, strongly and even harshly, had much in common with Michelangelo. . . . Is Brahms anything but the caricature of Beethoven?''

Not everybody likes Brahms and Tchaikovsky decidedly did not. To read what he said of his German contemporary, one would think that it is Cesar Cui writing about Tchaikovsky himself: "Brahms' creative gift is meagre, unworthy of his aspirations. . . ." "We played Brahms, the villain. What a talentless s——! It angers me that that presumptuous mediocrity is recognized as a genius." In 1878, when some of his friends would have liked him to go 'the round of all the European capitals, calling upon the big-wigs and displaying his wares to them,' he even imagined an encounter between 'Brahms, the celebrity, and himself, the unknown composer.' "I may tell you, however, without false modesty, that I place myself a good deal higher than Brahms. What could I say to him? If I were an honourable and sincere man I should have to say something of this kind: 'Herr Brahms, I regard you as an uninspired and pretentious composer, without any creative genius whatever. I do not rate you very highly, and look down upon you with disdain. But you could be of some use to me, so I have come to call upon you.' "

A real meeting took place ten years later; the two men had a good drink together and sympathized on the spot. "Brahms' personality as a man and an artist, his purity and loftiness of aim and his earnestness of purpose won [Tchaikovsky's] sympathy."[1] He had already expressed respect and admiration for the German and after that he tried to get the Russian Musical Society to invite him to Moscow, but his feelings for the musician never changed. "[Brahms'] music is not warmed by genuine emotion. It lacks poetry, but has great pretentions to profundity. . . . He never expresses anything, or, when he does, he fails to express it fully. His music is made up of fragments of some indefinable *something*, skilfully welded together. . . ." Tchaikovsky must have felt the great qualities of the German, but they were absolutely foreign to him:

In the music of this master (it is impossible to deny his mastery) there is something dry and cold which repulses me. He has very little melodic invention. He never speaks out his musical ideas to the end. Scarcely do we hear an enjoyable melody, than it is engulfed in a whirlpool of unimportant harmonic progressions and modulations, as though the special aim of the composer was to be unintelligible. He excites and irritates our musical senses without wishing to satisfy them, and seems ashamed to speak the language

which goes straight to the heart. His depth is not real: *c'est voulu.**
He has set before himself, once and for all, the aim of trying to be
profound, but he has only attained to an appearance of profundity.
The gulf is void. It is impossible to say that the music of Brahms is
weak and insignificant. His style is invariably lofty. He does not
strive after mere external effects. He is never trivial. All he does is
serious and noble, but he lacks the chief thing—beauty. Brahms
commands our respect. We must bow before the original purity of
his aspirations. We must admire his firm and proud attitude in the
face of triumphant Wagnerism; but to love him is impossible.

And where he could not love, Tchaikovsky could not admire. There
may have been aesthetic or moral reasons for this antipathy. On
the other hand, Brahms does irritate many of his auditors for
motives that can scarcely be grasped and analysed. "I must simply
confess," wrote Tchaikovsky, "that, independent of any definite
accusation, Brahms, as a musical personality, is antipathetic to
me. I cannot abide him. Whatever he does—I remain unmoved and
cold. It is a purely instinctive feeling."

German music, in general, did not appeal to Tchaikovsky. He
liked Weber, admired Mendelssohn, loved the sweet Schumann,
although he found the latter's means of expression lacking force.
"Liszt's compositions leave me cold; they show more poetic colouring than true creative power, more paint than drawing. In brief,
what he writes though dazzling, is devoid of inward structure."
Schubert's prolixity he found disappointing. He naturally had
strong feelings about Richard Strauss: "To my mind such an
astounding lack of talent, united to such pretentiousness, never
before existed." With typical diffidence, though, he added that
maybe it was his fault, maybe there was something there that he
did not understand. And it should not be deduced that he was
deaf to so-called modern harmonies. All the Germans without
exception were simply eclipsed by Mozart; he said so himself:
"I like to play Bach, because it is interesting to play a good fugue;
but I do not regard him, in common with many others, as a great
genius. Handel is only fourth-rate, he is not even interesting. I
sympathize with Glück in spite of his poor creative gift. I also
like some things of Haydn. These four great masters have been
surpassed by Mozart. They are rays which are extinguished by
Mozart's sun."

The same was, to a lesser extent, true of Italians and their
"semi-music" [sic]. Tchaikovsky was 'fascinated' by Bellini,
enthusiastic about Cherubini, sympathetic to Mascagni, dubious

---

* It is assumed.

about Rossini, sometimes bored by Verdi: nothing here is very important to him, and if we add that he found Grieg 'very highly gifted' and that according to Modest, he cherished for Chopin "a sentiment of instinctive and unconquerable antipathy," we shall have made the round of most Western musicians about whom he expressed an opinion, except the French, who deserve a study apart.

4 That element of freshness

Tchaikovsky said that he loved the music of contemporary France in proportion as he loathed her literature. It can even be maintained that he was sometimes a little indiscriminate in his passion for it. We cannot help being surprised on learning that he dearly loved Ambroise Thomas' *Hamlet*, that Lalo's *Le Roi d'Ys* 'pleased him very much,' and that he wrote to Mrs von Meck "My *Swan Lake* is simply trash in comparison with *Sylvia*."* Writing to Kashkin, he even used a stronger word than trash. On the other hand, it is to his credit that he expressed sympathy for Fauré, and that he was one of the first to recognize the importance of Bizet:

> Yesterday evening—to take a rest from my own work—I played through Bizet's *Carmen* from cover to cover. I consider it a *chef-d'oeuvre* in the fullest sense of the word: one of those rare compositions which seems to reflect most strongly in itself the musical tendencies of a whole generation. It seems to me that our own period differs from earlier ones in this one characteristic: that contemporary composers *are engaged in the pursuit of charming and piquant effects*, unlike Mozart, Beethoven, Schubert and Schumann. What is the so-called New Russian School but the cult of varied and pungent harmonies, of original orchestral combinations and every kind of purely external effect? Musical ideas give place to this or that union of sounds. Formerly there was *composition, creation*; now (with few exceptions) there is only research and invention. This development of musical thought is naturally purely intellectual, consequently contemporary music is clever, piquant and eccentric; but cold and lacking the glow of true emotion. And behold, a Frenchman comes on the scene, in whom these qualities of piquancy

* By Léo Delibes.

and pungency are not the outcome of effort and reflection, but flow from his pen as in a free stream, flattering the ear, but touching us also. It is as though he said to us: 'You ask nothing great, superb, or grandiose—you want something *pretty*, here is a *pretty opera*;' and truly I know of nothing in music which is more representative of that element which I call *the pretty* [*le joli*]. . . . I cannot play the last scene without tears in my eyes; the gross rejoicings of the crowd who look on at the bull-fight, and, side by side with this, the poignant tragedy and death of the two principal characters, pursued by an evil fate, who come to their inevitable end through a long series of sufferings.

I am convinced that ten years hence *Carmen* will be the most popular opera in the world. But no one is a prophet in his own land. In Paris *Carmen* has had no real success.

Most of the time, in fact, Tchaikovsky analysed his preferences clearly enough. He found some qualities but no inspiration in Halévy's *The Jewess*; Auber's *Fra Diavolo* pleased him only as an antidote to 'Italian pomposity;' and, although Modest tells us that "Tchaikovsky used to say that Saint-Saëns knew how to combine the grace and charm of the French school with the depth and earnestness of the great German masters," this enthusiasm is to be ascribed either to Modest's imagination or to Tchaikovsky's courtesy for a foreigner, since we know that he accused the Frenchman of ingratiating himself with the public by means of excessive simplicity, and, for instance, found *Etienne Marcel* 'insignificant, inept, flat, dry, boring, without style or character.'

It is true that Tchaikovsky was wont to change his mind fairly easily, especially when his opinions were not very well founded. At one time he wrote: "I consider Gounod as a first class master, if not a first class creative genius. Except Wagner, there is no composer of operas now alive who could safely compete with Gounod. As for me I should be the happiest of men if I could write an opera half as beautiful as *Faust*." And after hearing *Roméo et Juliette* 'with much pleasure': "Gounod is one of the few contemporaries who compose not according to prefabricated theories, but moved by feeling. Moreover he is a devotee of Mozart, which proves the wholeness, the wholesomeness of his musical nature." At another time, Tchaikovsky found the same opera 'mediocre,' declared that Gounod's Symphony is "the charming prattle of a classically disposed babe," and as to *Polyeucte*, he "had never heard anything worse."

Massenet is a good example of Tchaikovsky's changing opinions. "I place Massenet lower than Bizet, Delibes, or even Saint-Saëns, but he, too, has—like all our French contemporaries—that element of freshness which is lacking in the Germans." This was Tchaikovsky's general feeling, but confronted with a particular work, he could react differently. The first time he heard *Manon*, he found it "very graceful, quite polished, but without one touching, captivating, impressing passage." Two years later:

1st August: "Played *Manon* at home. It pleased me better than I expected."

2nd August: "Played *Manon*. Today Masseret seems to cloy with sweetness."

4th August: "Played *Manon* at home. Oh! how nauseating is Massenet!!! But what is most aggravating is that my music has a certain affinity with his."

This is a harsh judgement, and unfortunately a true one. But Tchaikovsky could also feel "enthusiastic about Massenet. I found his oratorio, *Marie Madeleine*, at N.F.'s. After I had read the text, which treats not only of the relations between Christ, the Magdalene, and Judas, but also of Golgotha and the Resurrection, I felt a certain prejudice against the work, because it seemed too audacious. When I began to play it, however, I was soon convinced that it was no commonplace composition. The duet between Christ and the Magdalene is a masterpiece. I was so touched by the emotionalism of the music, in which Massenet has reflected the eternal compassion of Christ, that I shed many tears. Wonderful tears! All praise to the Frenchman who had the art of calling them forth. . . . The French are really first in contemporary music. All day long this duet has been running in my head, and under its influence I have written a song, the melody of which is very reminiscent of Massenet."

Tchaikovsky's most interesting opinions concern Berlioz. In *Les Francs-Juges* he recognized "the hand of the master who was to create *La Damnation de Faust, Roméo et Juliette* and *La Symphonie Fantastique*." But the *Symphonie* itself he found full of "anti-artistic effects, such as the representation of the thunder." *Les Troyens à Carthage* appeared to him "a weak, tedious piece, revealing the principal defects of its composer; namely, poverty of melody, over-harmonization and an imagination too rich for its owner's musical invention. Berlioz was a high-minded man who conceived beautiful things, but lacked the power to fulfil his conceptions." *La Damnation de Faust* was Tchaikovsky's favourite: "The devil only knows what a strange man was this Berlioz. In general I find his musical nature rather antipathetic, and I cannot reconcile myself to the ugliness of his harmonies and modulations. But sometimes he attains incredible heights. . . ." "You know, my friend, that I am definitely not an unconditional admirer of Berlioz. His musical organization was not complete; he lacked something in the art of delicately choosing harmonies and modulations. There is in him an element of sycophancy which I cannot abide. But this did not prevent him from having the soul of a great and refined artist. . . . Certain passages of *Faust* and in particular the marvellous scene on the banks of the Elbe, are among the pearls of his creation. Yesterday, during that scene, I restrained my sobs with difficulty. How wonderful is Mephistopheles' *recitative* before Faust goes to sleep, and the chorus of the spirits and dance of the sylphs which follows! Listening to that music, one feels how its composer was seized by poetical inspiration, how deeply swayed he was by his plan." Here we hold one of the keys to Tchaikovsky's aesthetics: "to be deeply swayed by one's plan" was, for him, the necessary condition of any worthwhile artistic creation. Its validity can be debated, but it is interesting to find it so strongly expressed by one who appears as the extreme antithesis of all that our century holds to be true in the world of art.

5 *I do not belong to any party*

Among the Russians, Tchaikovsky's place was a difficult one. There were two main tendencies: one was centred around the Mighty Handful and the critic Stasov: it stood for Panslavism, folklore, nationalism and freedom from all musical rules; the other one, centred around the Conservatoire, stood for the classics, for harmony, for 'beauty.' Unfortunately this second tendency never produced one interesting work besides Tchaikovsky's, whereas the modernists created such unorthodox but admirable masterpieces as *Boris Godunov* or *Prince Igor*. All his life, Tchaikovsky tried to show that he did not really belong to any group, that good music was welcome from wherever it came, and that he would not be tied either to Balakirev or to Rubinstein. Still his sympathies went mostly to the serious, professional musicians of the Moscow tendency, serving under Rubinstein; and although he entertained courteous and sometimes even friendly relations with the St

T

Petersburg group and its 'generalissimus' Stasov, their unconventional, amateurish techniques were always distasteful to him.

Borodin he found "greatly talented, but . . . blind fate brought him a Chair of Chemistry in the Academy of Medicine rather than an active musical career. He cannot write a line without somebody's help. . . ." Cui's music is "elegant, coquettish and meticulous, but what can one expect of a Professor of Fortification. . . ?" "Balakirev is the greatest personality of the entire circle. But he relapsed into silence before he had accomplished much. . . . He spends all his time in church, fasts, kisses the relics—and does very little else." Musorgsky was the worst: his 'vulgar and villainous parody of music' Tchaikovsky happily sent to the devil; *Hovanshtchina* was characterized by pseudo-realism, poor technique, weak invention, some talented episodes, but drowned in confused and affected harmony, as is usual among the circle of musicians to whom Musorgsky belonged." And still Tchaikovsky was not entirely obdurate. He admitted that Musorgsky's "gifts are perhaps the most remarkable of all, but his nature is narrow and he has no aspirations towards self-perfection. He has been too easily led away by the absurd theories of his set and the belief in his own genius. Besides which, his nature is not of the first quality: he likes what is coarse, unpolished and ugly. . . . Musorgsky plays with his lack of polish—and even seems proud of his want of skill, writing just as it comes to him, believing blindly in the infallibility of his genius. As a matter of fact, his very original talent flashes forth now and again."

Rimsky-Korsakov was the only member of the Five for whom Tchaikovsky had any sympathy, because the former Navy officer accepted to go back to school after already having started to compose, which showed proper modesty and a respect for his art. In spite of Rimsky-Korsakov's contrapuntal tricks and 'dry pedantry,' of 'an excessive wealth of graceful details' which did not hide 'the lack of inspiration and impulse,' of a 'preference given to technique over the quality of the thought,' Tchaikovsky did not spare his compliments to the younger man: "Your *Spanish Capriccio* is a colossal masterpiece of instrumentation and . . . you can consider yourself the greatest of all contemporary masters. . . ." "I am but a craftsman whereas you are going to become a creative artist." And, highest praise of all: "The first movement (of your quartet) is a model of virginal purity of style. It has something of Mozart's beauty and unaffectedness."

There may have been some deliberate exaggeration in these compliments: Tchaikovsky was 'very happy to prove publicly that he did not belong to any party and that he found it flattering to be present at a function where Rimsky-Korsakov was the main character.' Let us not forget, however, that Tchaikovsky's first published article was precisely in defence of the only man whom he considered as a possible rival: Rimsky-Korsakov.

To Glinka, the father of Russian music, Tchaikovsky turned with more than admiration, with awe. Glinka was a paradox, and although Tchaikovsky was one himself, he never could reconcile Glinka's genius with his lack of musical training on one hand and his mediocrity as a man on the other. Again and again, Tchaikovsky came back to this insoluble problem, and the very fact that he could not solve it has much to tell us about his own fastidiousness and naïveté.

From his diary:

Glinka. An unheard-of and astonishing apparition in the world of art. A dilettante who played the violin and the piano a little; who concocted a few insipid quadrilles and fantasias upon Italian airs; who tried his hand at more serious musical forms (songs, quartets, sextets, etc.), but accomplished nothing which rose superior to the jejune taste of the thirties; suddenly, in his thirty-fourth year, creates an opera, which for inspiration, originality, and irreproachable technique, is worthy to stand beside all that is loftiest and most profound in musical art! We are still more astonished when we reflect that the composer of this work is the author of the *Memoirs* published some twenty years later. The latter give one the impression of a nice, kind, commonplace man, with not much to say for himself. Like a nightmare, the questions continually haunt me: How could such colossal artistic force be united to such emptiness? and how came this average amateur to catch up in a single stride such men as Mozart and Beethoven? Yes, for he *has* overtaken them. One may say this without exaggeration of the composer of the 'Slavsa.'* This question may be answered by those who are better fitted than myself to penetrate the mysteries of the artistic spirit which makes its habitation in such fragile and apparently unpromising shrines. I can only say no one loves and appreciates Glinka more than I do. I am no indiscriminate worshipper of *Russlan*; on the contrary, I am disposed to prefer *A Life for the Tsar*, although *Russlan* may perhaps be of greater musical worth. But the elemental force is more perceptible in his earlier opera; the 'Slavsa' is overwhelming and gigantic. For this he employed no model. Neither Gluck nor Mozart composed anything similar. Astounding, inconceivable! *Kamarinskaia* is also a work of remarkable inspiration. Without intending to compose anything beyond a simple, humorous

* Final chorus in *A Life for the Tsar*.

trifle, he has left us a little masterpiece, every bar of which is the outcome of enormous creative power. Half a century has passed since then, and many Russian symphonic works have been composed; we may even speak of a symphonic school. Well? The germ of all this lies in *Kamarinskaia*, as the oak lies in the acorn. For long years to come Russian composers will drink at this source, for it will need much time and much strength to exhaust its wealth of inspiration. Yes! Glinka was a true creative genius!

From his correspondence:

What an exceptional phenomenon is Glinka! When one reads his memoirs, one finds a kind and nice, but empty and even vulgar personality; when one plays his small pieces, one cannot believe that some of them have been composed by the same man who created, for instance, *Slavsa*,* *that production of an arch-genius, equal to the highest creations of the noblest artists!* And how many other astounding beauties in his operas, in his overtures! What a strikingly original piece is *Kamarinskaia*, from which all subsequent Russian composers (I, of course, included), are still borrowing quite freely contrapuntal and harmonic designs as soon as they are working on a Russian dance tune. . . . And here is the same man, in full maturity, composing such a trivial, vulgar piece of nonsense as the *Coronation Polonaise* (written a year before his death), or the Children's *Polka*, which he mentions in his memoirs with such complacency and in such detail as if they were masterpieces. Mozart in his letters to his father and in all his life also reveals a certain naïveté, but of a completely different kind. Mozart is a genius, pure as a child, gentle as a dove, modest as a virgin; he does not belong to this world. There is never any complacency, never any conceit in him; he does not seem to suspect the grandeur of his genius. *Glinka*, on the contrary, is full of self-adoration; he tells in detail the story of the most insignificant circumstance of his life or the composition of the slightest piece, and thinks that he is writing history. . . . In his memoirs Glinka writes at one point that he had a bulldog who *did not behave properly*, so that the servant had to clean up after him. Kukolnik, on reading the manuscript, made a note in the margin: *"Why tell this?"* To which Glinka immediately answered in pencil: *"And why not?"* It is very characteristic, is it not?

And yet he wrote *Slavsa*!

* The finale of *A Life for the Tsar*.

6 *Never untrue to myself*

Tchaikovsky is generally considered as a musician of the romantic school, and this may be true. But all he ever had to say about aesthetics shows that he was a classic at heart. It is true that he considered 'a pleasant nervous shiver as a certain sign of real artistic power' on the part of the artist, but the classics also aspired to create terror, pity, admiration and what not among their readers or spectators; it is true that his communion with Nature, his already mentioned 'ability to hear, in the absence of all noise, amidst the silence of night, I know not what sound, as if the earth, flying through space, were emitting a mysterious bass note,' was somewhat on the romantic side, but surely the romantics did not invent the music of the spheres! In fact, all Tchaikovsky's preferences and dislikes were characterized by a strictly classical taste.

He hated effect for the sake of effect, long words for the sake of long words, fantasy for the sake of fantasy. He hated affectation in all its forms—he even reproached Modest for writing 'in a too curly style'—and not least affectation of simplicity. He hated violence in art and ridiculed all kinds of excesses: "This un-happy African, what she endures!" he wrote about Meyerbeer's *L'Africaine*. "Slavery, imprisonment, death under a poisoned tree, in her last moment the sight of her rival's triumph—and yet I never once pitied her!" He hated petty motivations in art and said so with all a classic's belief in the superiority of 'great' over 'effective' art. "I feel that the composers of our period are not attracted by the lofty and the great, but by the pretty and the piquant. The idea is not the purpose any more but the means. . . . The last heirs of the golden age of music were Mendelssohn, Chopin, Schumann, Glinka, Meyerbeer, but, along with Berlioz, they already represent the transition towards 'savoury' music instead of 'good' music. Now only savoury pieces are written; Wagner and Liszt themselves are nothing but priests of savoury music. . . . [Bizet] compromises with the decadence of our age, but he still remains an artist and does not become, as our Messrs Cui and Co a kind of musical cook."

He strongly believed in classical unities. "Either my characters will sing or they will mime. That they should do both is absolutely unthinkable." He was attached to authenticity in all its forms, in particular for church and folklore music. His admiration for old Russian church modes and his antipathy for the modifications brought about in the seventeenth and eighteenth centuries are typical: whereas in the early ones he rightly found 'originality, majesty and beauty,' the others reminded him of "a hand accordion which possesses no harmonies beyond the tonic and dominant." His courteous, though somewhat flippant reply to Tolstoi who had sent him a few popular songs for his use as a composer, is typical in that respect:

Count, I am sincerely grateful to you for sending me the songs. I must tell you frankly that they have been taken down by an unskilled hand and retain no more than a trace of their original beauty. The greatest defect is that they have been arbitrarily and artificially forced into a regular rhythm. Only dancing Russian songs have a regularly accented rhythm, and epic poems have nothing in common with dancing, have they? Moreover the majority of these songs have been noted in the solemn D major key, once again artificially or so it seems, since Russian songs in their natural state have no definite tonality, resembling in that the ancient church modes. In general, the songs you sent cannot be treated regularly and systematically, i.e. they cannot be published as a collection, for in that case it would be necessary to have each song written the way it is executed by the people, as far as that would be possible. This is an extremely difficult task and requires the most delicate musical feeling as well as profound knowledge of the history of music. Besides Balakirev and maybe Prokunin, I know no one who could do justice to the work. But your songs may serve as material for symphonic treatment, and very good material indeed: I shall certainly make use of them one way or the other.

No wonder Musorgsky, of the 'savoury' school, made fun of him, complaining that every time he met Sadyk-Pasha (Tchaikovsky's nickname), he heard the same refrain: "Our aim in music must be beauty, nothing but beauty." Yes, Tchaikovsky was obstinate in his defence of beauty as the only purpose of art. But what did he mean by beauty? His concept of it was harmonious, complete, perfectly balanced, in a word: classic.

"The purpose of art is to delight not only the ear but also the soul and the heart," he declared. But at the same time he cannot be suspected of over-emphasizing the sentimental aspects of artistic creation: when he was asked what were his musical ideals, he answered: "Is it absolutely necessary to have ideals in music? I have never given a thought to them," and even "I never possessed

any ideals," or better still: "My ideal is to become a good composer." Bach or Mozart could have said as much. And they would
no doubt have sympathized with other Tchaikovskian declarations, as for instance: "Nothing is so pointless as looking for
originality and independence. Geniuses never give a thought to such
problems. They look for beauty. Whether it is original or borrowed
from someone appears only later." Just as they would have sub-
scribed to this profession of faith: "The question how one should
write operas I have always decided, do decide and shall decide
extraordinarily simply. One should write them (just like everything else, for that matter) as God has put it into your soul to
write them. . . . If I am confident of anything it is that in my
writings I have shown myself as God created me and as I have
been formed by education, circumstances and the nature of the age
and land in which I live and work. I have never been untrue to
myself."

Even this insistence on self cannot be called romantic, for, where
romantic artists complacently pamper their disconsolate ego, Tchaikovsky maintains that "self-control, strength of character, faith
in oneself" are indispensable to an artist.

It is true that he did not consider music as a pure world of
sounds. He liked to quote Heine: "music begins where words leave
off," and dissonance seemed to him essential because "without it
music would be eternal bliss—lost to us would be the privilege of
telling in music all our passion and our pain." He even thought
that great poetry, for instance Pushkin's, is closer to music than to
literature: "over and above his literal meaning, the verse itself
possesses something that pierces to the depths of one's soul. And
that something is Music." Pisarev's joke, that loving music was
the same as loving salted cucumbers and that Beethoven was no
better than a good cook, angered him no less than Mrs von Meck's
serious declaration that music intoxicated her as wine would. He
replied somewhat hotly: "Man has recourse to wine to deceive
himself. . . . Music is not deception but *revelation*. Her victorious
strength consists precisely of the fact that she reveals to us
elements of *beauty* which are inaccessible otherwise and the
contemplation of which reconciles us to life not temporarily but
for ever. Music creates light and joy." He went further and argued
that music could express love, that only music could express love,
and if he had our modern weakness for generalizations, he might
have added that the main purpose of music was to express love.
Did he not write that "where the heart is not touched, there cannot be any music" and also: "I cannot write music with love

and enthusiasm for any subject, however effective, if the characters
do not compel my lively sympathy, if I do not love them, pity
them, as living people love and pity."

But this should not be interpreted as shallow romantic expres-
sionism. In fact, we should be tempted to say that at this point
Tchaikovsky laid his finger on one of the greatest mysteries of
creation: mediation through art. Proust was to assert a few years
later that it takes a kind man to be a great artist, because art
is nothing without sympathy, and Proust, of all men, can never be
suspected of romanticism. Tchaikovsky himself refused subjects
for librettos because they made expressionistic demands which he
thought music unable to satisfy. For instance, Pushkin's *Captain's
Daughter* and Turgenev's *Yesterday* were both unsuitable because
of the politics involved. He stated many times his dislike for 'grand'
subjects, because he wanted to stay close to nature, as a classic
would: "If *Aida* is effective," he wrote, "I can tell you I wouldn't
compose an opera on such a subject if you gave me a fortune. I want
to create human beings, not puppets." And what appealed to him
in *Eugene Onegin* was not its realism, but, on the contrary, "the
poetry, the humanity of it all, the simplicity of the story united
to an admirable text." Later, he grew a little sick even of stylized
realism and looked for "subjects from another world, without cook-
ing of preserves, hanging of people, dancing of mazurkas, filing of
applications, etc." So were written *Iolanthe* and *The Sorceress*,
about which Tchaikovsky harried his librettist with very unromantic
recommendations: "Too many words. Please be as short and laconic
as possible. I shall leave out a few things."

It can still be rightfully objected that Tchaikovsky was a writer
of *programme music*, and that, as such, his ideals, whatever they
were, could not have been classic ones. This cannot be disputed
but serves once more to show that Tchaikovsky's nature was
basically paradoxical. Modest tells us that his brother "was always
an impassioned lover of programme music." This, to say the least,
is a simplified statement. After making up his mind to compose
Manfred and to follow very closely the programme proposed by
Balakirev (full of precise indications like "The customs of the
Alpine hunters . . . Manfred sees an Alpine fairy in the rainbow
above a waterfall. . . . A wild Allegro representing the caves of
Ariman . . ."), Tchaikovsky felt "very discontented. No! It is a
thousand times pleasanter to compose without any programme.
When I write a programme symphony I always feel I am not paying
in sterling coin, but in worthless paper money." How could he
then confess that his Fourth Symphony had a programme but

refuse to see that this was a fault? "On the contrary," he wrote,
"I should be deeply sorry if meaningless symphonies, consisting
solely of progressive harmonies, rhythms and modulations, were
flowing from my pen." How could he explain the programme of the
Fourth in great detail,* decline to disclose the programme of the
Sixth,† and declare, for instance, that he wanted to describe in
the introduction to *Romeo and Juliet* "a solitary soul striving to
reach heaven?"

All this is not as absurd as it seems at first sight. The composer
himself wrote to Mrs von Meck in order to explain his point of
view, and although it differs naturally enough, from the doctrine
of the eighteenth-century classics, it contains a classicism of its
own. "What is programme music? Since you and I do not recognize music which would consist of a purposeless game of sounds,
from our broad standpoint all music has a programme. But, in a
narrow sense, this expression means symphonic and in general
instrumental music supposed to illustrate a certain subject which
the public will find in their programme, and bearing the title of
this subject. The inventor of programme music was Beethoven,
partly in the *Eroica* but still more in the Sixth or *Pastorale*. But
its real founder was Berlioz, whose compositions not only have all
a title, but are also equipped with detailed explanations which the
auditor should have in hand during the performance. . . . For my
part, I consider that the inspiration of a symphonic composer can
be double—subjective and objective. In the first case, he expresses
his own joys and pains in his music, in other terms he pours out,
so to speak, his soul, as a lyric poet. In this case a programme is
not only unnecessary: it is impossible. The situation is different,
when a musician, reading a poem or impressed by a landscape,
wants to treat musically the subject which has lit up his inspiration. Here a programme is indispensable. . . . In any case, I consider that both forms have a right to exist and I do not understand
those gentlemen who accept only one of the two. It is obvious that
all subjects are not fit for a symphony, just as they are not all fit
for operas, but programme music is possible and necessary, just as
the epic element is necessary in literature, which cannot live by
lyricism alone."

In other words, Tchaikovsky denied the possibility of writing
what we call 'pure' music. All music, as far as he was concerned,
was a language, and he felt that, for most appropriate subjects,

* Cf. p. 317*ff*.
† Cf. p. 325.

this language was self-sufficient. It is only when the composer wanted to treat a non-musical subject that a written programme became necessary. And although he recognized the validity of both forms, he felt that genuine music, 'sterling coin' music, was of the non-descriptive kind. Tchaikovsky's system of differences seems somewhat difficult to comprehend now, because we have become used to judge art in non-humanistic values—indeed that is the meaning of the great artistic revolution of the twentieth century—but, for him, non-humanistic, we would say 'pure,' art was just pure rubbish.

Another example of his characteristic attitude concerning the main purpose of art is the contrast which he found between fundamental truth and contingent reality, betwen art dedicated to 'beauty' and 'realistic' art. The fact that he objected to Tatiana's aria of the letter being performed without the following scene with the nurse, would seem to range him among the realists: the letter he considered part of an action and not a separate number in an opera of the Italian style. Once he even confessed himself a realist: "It seems to me that I am really gifted with the aptitude of expressing in music, truthfully, sincerely and simply, the feelings, moods and images suggested by a text. In that respect I am a realist and a true Russian. As to the artistic value, as to the quality of creative power with which I have been endowed, that is another question. I do not in the least take myself for a genius." But in most instances Tchaikovsky repudiated realism and maintained—rightly in our opinion—that artistic truth can be obtained only at the expense of apparent, transient, superficial realism. The question was particularly acute in the composer's time since Dargomyjsky in Russia, Wagner in Germany, Debussy in France, were abandoning the traditional aria and desperately looking for a more 'realistic' musical declamation. About Dargomyjsky, Tchaikovsky expressed himself tersely and to the point: "If the quest for realism in opera is carried to its ultimate conclusion, then you will inevitably arrive at a complete negation of opera." And elsewhere: "I have never come in contact with anything more antipathetic and false than this unsuccessful attempt to drag *truth* [he meant realism] into the sphere of art, in which everything is based upon falsehood, and 'truth' in the everyday sense of the word, is not required at all." We should here stress the fact that in Tchaikovsky's time—which was the time of the Victorian novel, of French naturalism, of the very beginning of Impressionism—the idea that there are two truths, one common and 'not required at all' in art, the other of a higher essence, was absolutely new. That such an old-fashioned man as Tchaikovsky should have caught it and lived by it speaks highly for his artistic intuition and lack of prejudice. "Of course," he wrote, "I am the child of my generation, and I have no wish to return to the worn-out traditions of opera; at the same time, I am not disposed to submit to the despotic requirements of realistic theories." Indeed he was not. He was far in advance of his time in that respect.

Our musical critics, often losing sight of the fact that the essential in vocal music is truthful reproduction of emotion and state of mind, look primarily for defective accentuations and for all kinds of small declamatory oversights in general. . . . Absolute accuracy of musical declamation is a negative quality, and its importance should not be exaggerated. What does the repetition of words, even of whole sentences matter? There are cases where such repetitions are completely natural and in harmony with reality. Under the influence of strong emotion a person repeats one and the same exclamation and sentence very often. I do not find anything out of accordance with the truth when an old, dull-witted governess (in *The Queen of Spades*) repeats at every appropriate opportunity during her admonition her eternal 'refrain' about decency. But even if that never happened in real life, I should feel no embarrassment in impudently turning my back on 'real' truth in favour of 'artistic' truth. The two are completely different. . . .

7 Just as a cobbler makes a pair of boots

At the beginning of this book we pledged not to discuss Tchaikovsky's music and have not changed our mind. Discussing the musician is another matter: how did the man appraise his own work? What did he mean when he claimed that he wanted 'to become a good composer'? What did he expect from himself and from us his auditors? That is indeed the heart of our subject.

Tchaikovsky considered himself as a craftsman; this should be strongly emphasized. We have seen already passages where he referred to his productions as to his *wares*. We are familiar with his regular way of life, with his insistence on the proper techniques (after all, he did publish a harmony textbook which is still considered excellent by specialists), with the conscientiousness with which he treated his calling. We know his quaint mixture of modesty and pride typical of a craftsman. If on one point Tchaikovsky was not a paradox and did not contradict himself twenty times a day,* it was in his art and in the way he regarded it.

He was a good pianist—his ability "to reproduce music on a first hearing was startling"[2]—he sang well; he played the flute satisfactorily, could use an organ, was excellent with cymbals and much appreciated as a kettle-drummer because of his 'firm rhythm.'[3] As a composer, his technique was more than correct; it was brilliant even in his student days. As we have already seen, when Anton Rubinstein asked him to write a dozen contrapuntal variations on a given theme, "Tchaikovsky turned up the next class day with more than two hundred."[4] He hated arranging symphonic music for piano but adored orchestration: "It is difficult to express the happiness which one feels when an abstract musical thought takes on a real form after being entrusted to an instrument or a group of instruments. It is, if not the most delightful, one of the most delightful moments of composition." At times he went even further and declared that he never composed in the abstract: "never does the musical idea come to me except with suitable exterior form. So I find the musical thought simultaneously with the orchestration. When I wrote the Scherzo of our symphony,† I imagined it just as you heard it. It is impossible if not performed *pizzicato*. If played with the bow it would lose everything. It would be a soul without a body and all its charm would disappear."

Nevertheless he had, all his life, difficulties with form and was deeply, even pathetically, conscious of it. As a young man he still had a few illusions. About his Second Symphony he wrote in 1872: "It seems to me to be my best work, at least as regards correctness of form, a quality for which I have not so far distinguished myself." But in 1888, in the midst of his European glory, he confessed to Grand Duke Konstantin: "I have suffered all my life from my incapacity to grasp form in general. I have fought against this innate weakness, not—I am proud to say—without good results; yet I shall go to my grave without having produced anything really perfect in form. There is frequently *padding* in my works; to an experienced eye the stitches show in my seams, but I cannot help it."

The proportion of inspiration and application which goes into a work of art would be an interesting factor by which to judge it

---

* But only occasionally. Cf. end of next paragraph.
† Number Four.

if only such a factor could be determined. With our post-romantic upbringing, we, of the twentieth century, would tend to say that inspiration has to come foremost and that artists for whom work counted most were no artists at all. As the typical 'inspired' artist, we could be tempted to quote Tchaikovsky himself. With his begging to be set free from the tyranny of music, with his drumming so hard on window panes that the glass broke and seriously wounded him, with darkness 'brightening his imagination,' with his crying over the calamities happening to the heroes of his operas, with his 'gnawing his nails to the quick, smoking any number of cigarettes and pacing up and down his room,' with the careful distinction he drew between 'a musician studying composition and a composer,' Tchaikovsky may appear as a likely candidate for a part among The Inspired Variety of Artists. What a disappointment when we discover that in his most exalted view of those composers whom he admired more than others, he compared them to . . . cobblers!

> Ever since I began to compose I have endeavoured to be in my work just what the great masters of music—Mozart, Beethoven, and Schubert—were in theirs; not necessarily to be as great as they were, but to work as they did—as the cobbler works at his trade; not in a gentlemanly way, like Glinka, whose genius, however, I by no means deny. Mozart, Beethoven, Schubert, Mendelssohn, Schumann, composed their immortal works just as a cobbler makes a pair of boots—by daily work; and more often than not because they were ordered. The result was something colossal. Had Glinka been a cobbler, rather than a gentleman, besides his two (very beautiful) operas, he would have given us perhaps fifteen others, and ten fine symphonies into the bargain I could cry with vexation when I think what Glinka might have left us, if he had not been born into an aristocratic family before the days of the Emancipation. He showed us what was in him to do.

This does not mean, of course, that Tchaikovsky denied the power of inspiration; on the contrary, he distinguished "two kinds of inspiration: one comes from the heart freely, for some creative reason, the other comes to order. For the latter one needs a definite plot or text, a time limit, and a promise of several hundred rouble notes."*

This sounds a little cynical but should not surprise us coming from a 'cobbler' anxious to sell his 'wares.' Far from seeing any

---

* Catherine Bowen translates more nobly: "and the future advent of many Great Catherines." She probably does not know that a "catherine" was the familiar name for a hundred-rouble note watermarked with a portrait of the Empress.

antinomy between work and inspiration, Tchaikovsky invariably found the second after attending to the first and saw in the process what could be called the modest grandeur of art.

Work he enjoyed: "Work is for me the greatest possible good; it cannot be compared to anything; without it, I feel that sadness and melancholy would become extremely oppressive." We have already seen that he arranged his day in consequence. For instance, in 1883, he got up at 8, lit up his own fire, washed, breakfasted and read the paper. At 9.30, he sat to work and worked till lunch. He lunched at a restaurant, took a long walk, and, at 2.30 was back at work till 6. He had the evenings off for the theatre or strolling through the city. This means a minimum of six hours of creative work every day. And although he did write that "for ten weeks to sit down every day at fixed hours and squeeze music out of one's brain . . . is no simple matter" and expected to 'luxuriate in his earned rest,' he had no sooner finished one work than he undertook another: "For about a month and a half I worked in all haste on the instrumentation of *The Queen of Spades*, and have successfully completed it. The score has been shipped off long ago. I felt utter exhaustion, dreamed about taking a long rest, resuming my correspondence with my friends. But on the very next day I felt an incredible depression, langour and regret concerning the work which had entirely occupied me for several months and which I had now finished. And what do you think I did? I immediately began a large and technically very difficult composition (a sextet for strings) which instantly absorbed me, and once again I forgot everything and everybody in order to satisfy my selfish need of immersing myself into my work. I am terribly nervous and apt to become melancholic; the older I get, the more this tendency threatens me. But I know of a radical remedy against it: work." When he did not feel like working, the composer wondered what was happening to him: "I worked without enthusiasm, I had to force myself. I do not know, I cannot understand why, in spite of so many favourable circumstances, I am not disposed to work. Am I finished? I have to squeeze out from me puny, washy little ideas and reflect about each bar. But I shall get what I want; I hope that finally inspiration will come to me."

This obstinacy, this belief in the power of will, maybe not over inspiration but over the forces which prevent inspiration, is one of the main characteristics of Tchaikovsky the classic, Tchaikovsky the craftsman. To an amateur writer, he said: "You will reply that it is impossible to write when one does not feel like it, but I know by experience that one never does anything if one submits to one's reluctance to work. Any artist, writer, musician, is at the same time a craftsman. Only dilettanti, weaklings and sluggards wait for inspiration: it does not come if you relax." Tchaikovsky found inspiration so important that he thought any means good enough to create it: coaxing, seducing, insisting, and occasionally sheer violence. "Do not believe those who tried to convince you that musical creation is a cold and rational occupation. Only the music that poured out of the depth of an artistic soul visited by inspiration can touch, affect and impress; there is no doubt that even the greatest musical artists sometimes worked without being warmed up by inspiration. It is a guest that does not always come on first invitation. But *work* is necessary always, and a really honest artist cannot sit with his hands crossed under the pretext that he is not in the right mood. If one waits for *moods* instead of trying to meet them half-way, it is easy to fall into *laziness and apathy*. One must endure and believe, and inspiration is bound to come to the man who conquered his *negative mood*."

An honest artist: the words are essential. It is exactly in those terms that Tchaikovsky thought of himself. His aim: the work of art. His method: inspiration. His means to obtain it: work. Art may be the only domain where the end does justify the means. Tchaikovsky thought so. Any means was good enough for him: "the majority of my fellow-workers, for instance, do not like working to order; I, on the other hand, never feel more inspired than when I am requested to compose something, when a term is fixed and I know that my work is being impatiently awaited." He even liked to work in haste; he liked to be rushed; and he felt that excessive speed did not impair the quality of his work. Always ready to conform to the commissioner's desire (for instance, they could chose between opera by arias and modern continuous music), he was not above composing a military march for a cousin's regiment: "The orchestration will have to be done by your conductor, as I do not know the make-up of the orchestra he conducts." "Besmearing a few sheets of music paper for six hundred roubles" appealed very much to him, and having decided to compose twelve pieces corresponding to the twelve months of the year, he coolly ordered his servant to remind him of his promise two or three days before each deadline. Servant and master were true to their word; all twelve pieces arrived on time. When there was nobody to impose deadlines on him, he did so himself. For instance, he decided he would compose one piano piece a day, for thirty days. The fifteenth day found him three "musical pancakes" ahead of schedule and he figured out that if he could stay a whole year in the country and if his publisher were willing to print all he would have composed with that system, he would make thirty-six thousand five hundred roubles a year.

Once, when Mrs von Meck asked him about his methods of composing, he replied at length, and his answer was so detailed, so much to the point, and in several respects so original, that it is definitely worthwhile to quote it at length.

I shall try to tell you in a general way how I work.

First of all I must make a difference between my two kinds of work, which is very important for the understanding of the process of creation.

(1) Compositions which I write on my own initiative because of immediate inclination and unconquerable inner urge.

(2) Compositions which I write under outside influence, such as the request of a friend or publisher or a *commission*, as for instance the Cantata that was ordered from me for the Polytechnical Exhibition or the Serbian-Russian march* for the Red Cross, by the board of directors of the Musical Society, etc.

I hasten to explain that I already know from experience that the quality of the composition does not depend from its belonging to one category or the other. It has very often happened that a piece belonging to the *second* category . . . was a success, whereas a piece conceived by me alone, due to secondary circumstances, was not so good. Absolute calm is necessary for an artist at the moment of creation. In that sense, artistic creation is always *objective*, even in music. Those who think that the creating artist is able to express, by the means of his art, what he feels at the time when he feels it, are wrong. Both sad and joyful feelings are always expressed *retrospectively*, so to speak. Without having any particular reason to be happy, I can impregnate myself with a cheerful creative mood, and on the contrary, among happy circumstances, create a piece full of despair and gloom. In a word, the artist leads a double life: the man's life and the artist's one, which are not always parallel to each other. . . .

For compositions belonging to the first category not the slightest effort of the will is necessary. One submits to one's inner voice, and if the first life does not oppress the other one with its unpleasant incidents, the work proceeds with unimaginable ease. One forgets everything, one's soul quivers with a sweet, incomprehensible, unutterable excitement, one wants to fly *somewhere* faster than one can, time goes by unperceived. There is something *somnambulistic* in this state, you do not hear yourself living.† It is

* Known as the *Slavonic March* or *Marche Slave*.
† In French in the original.

impossible to tell you about those minutes. What is written or composed in the head . . . in that state is always good. . . .

For compositions of the second category one has *sometimes* to put oneself in the *right mood*. Very often one has to conquer laziness, lethargy. . . . Sometimes the victory is easy. Sometimes inspiration resists, escapes. But I consider it the *duty* of an artist never to submit, because *laziness* is very strong in men. There is nothing worse for an artist than to submit to it. . . . Inspiration is a guest who does not like to visit the lazy. She comes only to those who call upon her. . . .

I can say that the force which I have called a capricious guest has been on intimate terms with me for so long a time that we live inseparably together, and that she leaves me only when the circumstances which oppress my human life make her feel useless. But as soon as the cloud is dispersed, there she is. Therefore, when I am in a normal state of mind, I can say that I compose all the time, every minute, in any situation. Sometimes I observe with curiosity the unceasing work which goes on in that part of my head which belongs to music, independently from what I am talking about, or from the people with whom I am. Sometimes it is preparatory work, i.e. elaboration in detail of an already conceived project; at other times, an entirely new and independent musical thought appears, and I try to retain it in my memory. Where all that comes from is an impenetrable mystery. . . .

I write my sketches on any sheet of paper. . . . The melody cannot appear without the corresponding harmony. In general these two elements of music, together with rhythm, cannot be separated from each other, i.e. every melodic idea carries an implicit harmony and comes with a rhythmic structure. . . . If I am composing for orchestra, the musical idea appears already coloured with orchestration, although the first intention can change when the whole work is orchestrated. . . . The sketching period is very pleasant, interesting, affords sometimes the most indescribable delights, but is accompanied with restlessness, with a certain nervous excitability. One sleeps badly, sometimes one forgets to eat. On the other hand, the completion of the project is quiet and peaceful. It is great fun to orchestrate a composition which has already matured in the mind down to the last detail. . . .

I have not explained clearly enough that phase of the work when the sketch is transformed into the finished product. This phase is essential. Things written in haste have to be critically verified, corrected, extended and mainly condensed to fit the requirements of form. Sometimes one has to force oneself to do it, to treat oneself mercilessly and cruelly, i.e. to cut out entirely passages conceived with love and inspiration. If I cannot complain of poor invention and imagination, I have always suffered from inaptitude to polish form. Only by obstinate work have I achieved the fact that now the form of my compositions corresponds more or less to their content. Previously I was too negligent, I was not conscious enough of the importance of a critical verification of one's sketches. This is why one could always sense the *seams*, the different episodes were not blended together as they should have been. That was a substantial defect, and it is only with years that I began to correct it, although I cannot radically change the essential properties of my musical organization: my compositions will never be *models of form*.

So the main point was to create music, and emotions had to be excited somehow, so that music would flow.* But once the music was written, it could be used practically for any purpose. Although Tchaikovsky did not systematically make use of folk themes, his production is permeated with them: "As to the Russian element in my music, i.e. melodic and harmonic trends akin to folk songs, this happens because I grew up in the country: from my earliest childhood I was made sensitive to the unutterable beauty of the characteristic traits of Russian folk music; I passionately love the Russian element in all its expressions; in short, I am *Russian* through and through." The main theme of the famous Andante Cantabile of the First Quartet was a folksong beginning with the words "Vania sat on the divan and smoked a pipe of tobacco." Tchaikovsky's own music also could serve where it was most needed. The great scene between Mazepa and Maria in *Mazepa* had first been composed for *Vanka the Steward* (which was never completed). The folksong *The Nightingale* was incorporated into *The Voivode* and then transferred into *The Oprichnik*. The original Andante of the Violin Concerto was replaced by another one, but not discarded: two other pieces were to be added in order to create a separate opus. The first theme of the fourth movement of the Third Symphony served also for the apparition of the Countess's ghost in *The Queen of Spades*. When Tchaikovsky was asked to write incidental music for *Hamlet*, he used, in addition to his original *Hamlet* overture, the strangest ingredients: his *alla Tedesca* movement from the Third Symphony, the intermezzo from *Snegurochka*, an Elegy written seven years before for the birthday of an actor, plus a new funeral march composed on purpose. From his unsuccessful opera *Undine*, Tchaikovsky borrowed the prelude, which became the overture of *Snegurochka*, a whole aria of *Tempest*, *My Sister* which is heard as one of Lel's songs in *Snegurochka*, a nuptial march, later the Andantino Marziale of the Second

---

* Compare Renoir's penetrating remark: *"Le modèle n'est là que pour allumer le peintre."* The only use of the model is to excite the painter.

Symphony, and the main duet of Undine and Hildebrand, which we know as the great pas de deux of the *Swan Lake*. Of the 62 pages of Act I in the vocal score of *The Oprichnik* only 13 are new music: all the rest was stolen from *The Voivode* including a conversation between two young heroes which became the plotting of a villain and his accomplice. Whenever anybody objected to this borrowing, Tchaikovsky was furious: "having learned by accident that in my opera (*The Maid of Orleans*) I had at one point transferred a melody from the part of Joan to the part of Agnes for stage and vocal reasons, [the Director of the Repertoire of Imperial Theatres] declared that I had no right to do it, that I had to beg permission for it from somebody or other!!! ... Scandalous, revolting! I should like to run away from this city where reigns the arbitrariness of officialdom."

It would be a great mistake to interpret all these permutations as a sign of indifference to music on the artist's part. On the contrary, they show that all his motives were always musical and only musical. Such were his preferences for the 'bold, bright'[5] key of D major; his partiality to orchestration ("orchestration, I feel, is not work; it is a pleasant and perfectly peaceful occupation"); his wariness as regards librettos ("words often spoil music and degrade it from its highest level"); his hatred of teaching harmony ("a hatred which partly springs from a consciousness that our present theories are untenable, while at the same time it is impossible to build up new ones. ... For ten years I taught harmony, and during that time I loathed my classes, my pupils, my text-book, and myself"), his reluctance to transpose pieces from one key to another, his unwillingness to write anything for the harp ("it is not an independent instrument, because it has no melodic quality"). His aversion to chamber music for strings and piano is an interesting example: he found it 'very difficult and unappealing;' he wrote Mrs von Meck a long letter to explain why he could never compose a trio:

> My auditory organs cannot endure the combination of a violin or a cello *solo*. These *timbres* seem to me to exclude each other, and I assure you that it is sheer torture for me to have to listen to a trio or a sonata with violin or cello. I can only state this physiological fact, not explain it. Piano with orchestra is completely different: here also there is no consonance of the *timbres*—besides the piano is incapable of merging with anything, since its sound is elastic and rebounds from any other mass of sound, but you have two forces with equal rights, i.e. the orchestra, powerful, inexhaustibly rich in colour, fought against and conquered by ... its

small, plain but spirited rival. In this struggle there is much poetry and innumerable combinations tempting to a composer. But what is this unnatural combination of such three individuals as a violin, a cello and a piano? Their proper merits are lost. The wonderful singing, warm sound of the violin and cello appears to be one-sided when compared to the *king* of instruments, who, in turn, tries to prove that he can *sing*, as his rivals do. In my opinion the piano can only appear (1) alone, (2) in its struggle with the orchestra, (3) as accompaniment, i.e. as background for a picture. A trio, however, presupposes equality and similarity, which can never be achieved between bow instruments played *solo* on one side and the piano on the other. . . . I pay due homage to such composers as Beethoven, Schumann or Mendelssohn, whose art and genius prevailed against these difficulties. I know that there are lots of excellent trios, but, as a form, I do not like the *trio* and cannot write for this combination anything that would have the warmth of sincere feeling.

Having thus made his point, Tchaikovsky composed his own trio dedicated to the memory of N. Rubinstein! "At the beginning it was a real effort to reconcile myself to this combination of instruments, but now the work interests and intrigues me."

Conservative as he was in other fields, Tchaikovsky was always on the lookout for new possibilities in the more technical aspects of music. He was the first composer to use a piano and an organ within an orchestra (in *Undine* and *Manfred* respectively). In his symphonies he took advantage of a primitive Russian instrument of the psaltery type, the *gusli*. For *1812* he wanted a piece of artillery. For the Second Suite he needed four accordions with ten keys, playing in E major. In *The Nutcracker* he introduced children's drums, rabbits' drums, a child's trumpet in C, a rattle, and various devices to imitate cuckoos, quails, etc. He also was the first Russian to use a *celesta** which he ordered from Paris in deep secret: "I am afraid Rimsky-Korsakov and Glazunov might hear of it and make use of the new effect before I could." This partiality for special effects was an old habit of his: as a student he had been reprimanded by Anton Rubinstein for orchestrating Beethoven's D minor sonata with the help of "an English horn and all manner of unusual accessories."

Nowadays we tend to forget that, in his time, Tchaikovsky was regarded, in Germany, for instance, "as a notorious revolutionary." Although his innovations are not as obvious as those of, for instance, Musorgsky, they can be considered, in the long run, as more basic and more universal at the same time. This is not the

* In *The Nutcracker* and the symphonic poem *The Voivode*.

place to discuss them in detail, but two points may be mentioned. One: Tchaikovsky can be considered as the inventor of modern ballet, for in his time choreographic music was looked down upon. He was the first to declare that there was nothing inferior about it, and to put as much talent and care in his ballets as in his symphonies. Two: when he wrote *Eugene Onegin* he practically invented a new kind of opera, the possibilities of which have not yet been entirely exploited. This deserves a few explanations.

Whereas his contemporaries started from the concept of theatrical effects, Tchaikovsky wanted to "see in opera the musical interpretation of simple human feelings, far removed from the theatrical and dramatic." As for effects, 'he spat upon them.' The consequences were twofold. On one hand, much of the emotional intensity of the opera was to be entrusted to the orchestra which would have to be directed by "a conductor who is not a machine or even a musician à la Napravnik, concerned only with the fact that a C sharp must not be played as a C, but a real leader of the orchestra." On the other hand, the singers would have to become artists 'who could act simply and well,' and the setting, instead of being unnecessarily sumptuous, would have to correspond faithfully to its period. The chorus ought not to resemble 'a flock of sheep like in the Imperial Opera, but be composed of real people participating in the plot.' For the first presentation of *Eugene Onegin*, Tchaikovsky even preferred non-professional singers, in fact students from the Conservatoire. 'So and So,' he wrote, 'is not an ideal Lensky, but, being young, he will still be better, I think, than D. of the big belly, the shopkeeper O., or old K, who has no voice. . . . Mainly the Conservatoire presentation will be free from the vulgar, deadly commonplaces, the loud anachronisms and all the inevitable trash of an official production.' All this, of course reminds us of Stanislavsky, the drama director, who reinvented modern theatre from scratch along the same lines. It is also significant that, in *The Queen of Spades*, Tchaikovsky wrote an aria on a text in prose. This was unheard of audacity in his time, and he declared himself very satisfied with the effect: "Pushkin's text has remained almost unchanged, but there is rhythm." The object of these reforms was not realism, but, on the contrary, a more artistic approach to the musical expression of human feelings.

Above all, Tchaikovsky took his work in earnest and was more conscientious about it than any cobbler. "I live on music. Apart from this I am good for nothing. I must hurry because I am afraid of dying before being able to pass on to others what I have in me to give. This feeling was ever-present in him. He wrote music as he would have *served* in another capacity. And all the time he oscillated between opposite anguishes: would he have time enough to say what he had to say? had he not already said it long ago? did he know how to say it right? At 36, displeased with his Third Quartet, he wrote: "I am afraid that . . . I am beginning to repeat myself and cannot invent anything new. Is it possible that my song is already sung and that I can go no further? It is very sad!" At 50, he was once again in the same mood: "Sometimes I feel an insane anguish, but not that kind of anguish which is the herald of a new tide of love for life; rather something hopeless, final, and—like every *finale*—a little commonplace. Simultaneously a passionate desire to create. The devil knows what it is! In fact, sometimes I feel my song is sung, and then again an unconquerable impulse, either to give it fresh life, or to start a new song."

He was always concerned with the quality of his work. He had, more than any other artist, moods of doubt and despair, alternating with moods of confidence and strength: "Now there is before me such an infinite line of various proposed or promised works that I am even afraid of peering into the future. How short is our life! At the present time, when I have probably reached the highest level of perfection which I can attain, I already have to turn back and, seeing how many years I have spent, I throw timid looks at the road before me and ask myself: 'shall I have the time? is it worth while. . . ?' On the other hand it is only now perhaps that I can write so as not to doubt myself, so as to believe in my own power and skill. . . ." "In my work I am always in a hurry. My productions suffer from it, but such is my nature. I am always afraid of not having time to finish. And I have so many plans!" He felt it his duty to progress in his craft: "During the last ten years, I do not seem to have made much progress. . . . I have not written one piece, however short, of which I might say: 'This is perfect.' Not one is on the level of what I could do. Perhaps this is good stimulation: if I were pleased with myself, maybe I should not work any more." The discrepancy between what he thought himself called upon to produce and what he was in fact producing left him no peace: "All false modesty aside, everything I have written up to now seems weak, unfinished, in comparison with what I can and must do. And I will do it." But he was always ready to profit by his errors. After *The Voivode* (the opera), he remarked: "To reach perfection, a whole series of trial-and-error is necessary, therefore I am not ashamed of my failures. They served their purpose as

lessons and as signposts to further effort." We have seen that, as
a man, Tchaikovsky was always underestimating his qualities,
judging himself more severely than he deserved: this severity did
not leave him when he spoke about his works and especially about
his whole career as a composer: "I have written much that is
beautiful, but how weak, how lacking in mastery. . . !" "I shall
soon be 44. How much I have been through, and—without false
modesty—how little I have accomplished! In my actual vocation
I must say—hand on heart—I have achieved nothing perfect, nothing which can serve as a model. I am still seeking, vacillating."
And, even more pathetic: "And so, in all probability, I shall strive
for mastery until my last breath, without ever attaining it. Something is lacking in me—I can feel it—but there is nothing to be
done."

The huge amount of work Tchaikovsky put into his compositions
is only one among many indications of the composer's conscientiousness. He practically could not do without working: "As soon
as I am not considering a piece, I get bored. Too bad! I ought to
refresh a little my creative powers. . . ." "Nothing could be more
sensible than your advice to rest more and use one's creative
powers less. But how can I? As soon as the sketch is written, I cannot rest until I have completed it, and the moment the composition is finished, I feel an irresistible desire to start a new one. For
me, work (that work) is as necessary as air. If I am idle, I become
unhappy, I doubt that life will afford me the opportunity of bring-
ing my talents to their perfection, whatever that is, I am dissatis-
fied with myself, I even begin to hate myself."

Everything concurds to show what a serious worker he was. He
made a rule of never beginning a new composition before finishing an old one, and broke it but seldom. He was always ready to do
research on a subject if he was not familiar enough with it, which
happened when he decided to write church music: "I am
swallowed up in this sea of Graduals, Hymns, Canticles, Tropaires,
Exapostelaires, etc., etc. I asked our priest how his assistant
managed, and how he knew how, when and where to sing or
read. . . . He replied: 'I do not know; before every service he has
to look out something for himself.' If the initiated do not know,
what can a poor sinner like myself expect?"

True, some people have accused Tchaikovsky of an anachronism
in The Queen of Spades: the old countess remembers a song
which, she says, used to be sung in her youth. Now the period in
which the opera takes place is anterior to the composition of that
song (an aria, from Grétry's Richard Coeur de Lion). But it would

be just as appropriate to reproach Shakespeare with Caesar's clock or Cleopatra's billiards: Tchaikovsky was haunted by the eighteenth century; Pushkin's story, from which the libretto is derived, takes place in the nineteenth; and so nothing could be more natural than this reminiscence of an old melody, much more in keeping with the style of the whole work than would have been some piece borrowed from an earlier epoch. And as to the accuracy of the historical reconstruction, critics have said that the Pastorale—which forms a play in the play in the middle of *The Queen of Spades*—"is neither an evocation nor a vision of history: it has been composed by a man who lived in the eighteenth century." *

Tchaikovsky's tender love for his music did not extend only to the sounds that he created. Everything about it was dear to his heart. He was childish enough to have his first song, *Mezza Notte*, privately printed; he was proud of his musical penmanship, suffering "no erasure, corrections or inkstains" on the completed manuscript, and he saw in an orchestral score "not only the promise of future pleasure for the ear, but instant pleasure for the eye."

When Rimsky-Korsakov composed an opera on *Snegurochka*, a play for which Tchaikovsky had formerly written incidental music, he was hurt as if Snegurochka had been unfaithful to him: "Do you not like me resent," he wrote to Jurgenson, "that our subject has been stolen from us, that Lel is to sing the same words to another musical setting, that I have been deprived as if by violence of something which was dear and precious to me, and which will now be presented to the public in a new and brilliant attire. I am ready to weep."

Not only with the scores that he loved, but also with the proofs that he hated, Tchaikovsky was careful. He, who was always losing cigar-cases and walking-sticks, never lost one of his own works. The proofs he always read very carefully, did not allow any work to be published which had not been reviewed by him, nor any publication to be sold until the mistakes had been corrected. Mis-

---

* For some reason this Pastorale does not agree with biographers. Rostislav Hofmann calls it *The Unfaithful Shepherdess*, whereas the Russian title is *The Sincerity of the Shepherdess*. Catherine Bowen goes into raptures about a 'duet of ladies imploring a handsome shepherd who strolls unheeding away,' but in reality there is only one lady (another woman sings the part of one of the two men, hence the error) and the story is completely different: a shepherdess is courted by a possessor of gold mountains, but gives her heart to a poor shepherd.

takes made by a professional corrector he found particularly annoying: "The main fault is that wherever a harmony seems strange to him, he corrects it in his own way!!!!! On the very last page of the opera he has made such a correction that if he were here I think I should hit him."

Tchaikovsky's works were to be printed right and performed right. He, for his part, went so far as to include metronome markings on his scores, and did not hesitate to surrender the baton to a native conductor if he thought that a translated libretto would confuse his own directions to singers and orchestra. The music came first.

Logically enough, he could be impatient with negligent interpreters. Rubinstein having declared that the First Suite was too difficult to be performed, Tchaikovsky fumed: two high E's could not spoil forever the precious little lips of the oboist, from which his wife had already plucked so many kisses, and if they could, too bad; music was music. Testimonies do not concord as to the composer's attitude during rehearsals. According to Ella Eichenwald, the singer, he would sit in a corner, just watching, and at the end he would say that everything had been wonderful. According to O. O. Polyechek, assistant to the conductor Napravnik, Tchaikovsky "had something to say about everything that went on. He literally cavilled at every phrase that was played or sung. . . . Assisted by Napravnik and me, he worked out every move on stage with the singers, every note they sang, every gesture they made. He insisted that we study the character of the music as he had written it before allowing it to be played or sung. . . . And I must admit that his directions were so very much to the point that it would be true to say that he alone was the real producer of the opera." So we have one paradox more, and we are not going to shove it under the rug. That Tchaikovsky was courteous to everyone is probable; that he demanded perfection from all is probable, too. As a director he would not have been more lenient than as a teacher, and some of his students thought he was less than patient in the classroom. One of them had written some music and forgotten to add the tails to the thirty-second notes. He "slashed the page across with a red pencil: 'You'd better try to master the art of making tails before you try to master harmony,' he said coldly and moved on to the next student."[6]

8   From my inmost being

A complete enumeration of Tchaikovsky's sayings about his own works is definitely not intended here, but a sampling of the most typical ones will add much to our knowledge of the composer; and what he thought and wrote about his main works will bear a more detailed analysis.

His partiality for *The Queen of Spades* has already been noted, and he founded it on the fact that his hero, Hermann, "was not a pretext for music, but a living man who deserved sympathy." His judgement on *The Maid of Orleans*, which was never successful, throws some light on what he meant by the word *emotional*: something like 'in close harmony with the composer's subconscious' and not at all what we generally mean by it, since, according to our interpretation of the word, *The Maid of Orleans* is certainly not lacking in emotionalism. "I have just been playing the first act of *The Maid of Orleans*, which is now ready for the printer," he wrote to Mrs von Meck. "Either I am mistaken, or it is not in vain, dear friend, that you have had the watch you gave me decorated with the figure of my latest operatic heroine. I do not think *The Maid of Orleans* my finest, or the most emotional, of my works, but it seems to me to be the one most likely to make my name popular. I believe *Onegin* and one or two of my instrumental works are far more closely allied to my individual temperament. I was less absorbed in *The Maid of Orleans* than in our Symphony, for instance, or the second Quartet; but I gave more consideration to the scenic and musical effects—and these are the most important things in opera." The reference to the Second Quartet should not surprise us: "I consider it as the best of my compositions," said the composer in 1874. "Not one of my productions has flown so easily and simply. I wrote it almost at one sitting." *Vakula the Smith* was also one of his favourites, 'his beloved child' as he put it; he even rewrote it under a new title, *Cherevichki*, because he found it wanting in operatic qualities: "Operatic style should be broad, simple and somewhat picturesque. The style of *Vakula* does not belong to opera but rather to symphony or even to chamber music. One should be surprised that this opera was not a complete failure, but is still performed and attracts large audiences. Finally it may even become a success. As to my own feelings towards *Vakula*, I can tell you that, although I fully realize its *operatic* defects, I nevertheless place it in the front row of my compositions. I wrote that music with love, with delight, just as *Onegin*, the Fourth Symphony, or the Second Quartet."

Sometimes the composer's opinion about what he had written changed brutally. *Manfred* is a good example. At one time, we find Tchaikovsky declaring: "The composition of the *Manfred* Symphony—a work highly tragic in character—is so difficult and complicated that at times I myself become a Manfred." At another: "*Manfred* is a work which I loathe; I sincerely hate everything in it but the first movement. I intend to destroy very soon the three last movements which are, from a musical standpoint, absolutely vulgar, especially the finale, which is impossible. So, from a piece which is much too long for a symphony, I shall make a symphonic poem. Only then am I sure that my *Manfred* will please. I wrote the first movement with infinite pleasure; the rest with so much effort that I was ill for some time afterwards." We are fortunate in that Tchaikovsky did not execute his threat, which we cannot suspect of having been idle, since *Undine*, *Fatum*, and the symphonic poem *The Voivode* were pitilessly annihilated by their creator. "The Direction of Imperial Theatres refused my *Undine* in 1870," wrote the composer. "At the time I was hurt and accused them of injustice. Later I was deeply disappointed in my opera and very happy that it had never been performed on an official scene." *The Oprichnik* survived, but at the time of its creation Tchaikovsky coldly wrote to his pupil and friend Taneiev: "If you really intend to come to St Petersburg (from Moscow) to hear my opera, I beg you not to. Frankly there is nothing good in *The Oprichnik*, and I should hate for you to bother to come and see it." When the performance of the same *Oprichnik* was forbidden, because the subject was considered too revolutionary in that moment of political agitation: "So much the better," wrote the composer on receiving the news, "for I am glad of any hindrance to the performance of this ill-starred opera." For the opera *The Voivode*, Tchaikovsky was not less severe: "To remember this opera and also *The Oprichnik* is like remembering two nefarious crimes which I might have committed."

Especially characteristic is Tchaikovsky's opinion about *1812* on one hand, the Serenade for Strings on the other: "The overture will be very loud and noisy, but I wrote it without the warm emotion of love; consequently there will probably be no artistic qualities in it. On the contrary, I composed the Serenade because I was inspired from within. This piece I felt through and through; therefore I dare think that it is not devoid of real qualities."

Eugene Onegin had a special place in Tchaikovsky's heart. Before writing the music, before even having a libretto, the composer was already enthusiastic: "You have no notion how crazy I am upon this subject. How delightful to avoid the commonplace Pharaohs, Ethiopian princesses, poisoned cups, and all the rest of these dolls' tales! *Eugene Onegin* is full of poetry. I am not blind to its defects. I know well enough the work gives little scope for treatment, and will be deficient in stage effects; but the wealth of poetry, the human quality and simplicity of the subject, joined to Pushkin's inspired verses, will compensate for what it lacks in other respects." Having completed the first act, he sent it to Nikolai Rubinstein and trembled lest "Jupiter" should not like it: "I am agitated by uncertainty as to whether the first act will please you or not. Pray do not give it up on your first impressions: they are often so deceptive. I wrote that music with such love and delight! The following numbers were specially dear to me: (1) the first duet behind the scenes, which afterwards becomes the quartet; (2) Lensky's Arioso; (3) the scene in Tatiana's room; (4) the chorus of maidens." When Taneiev expressed doubts about the fittingness of Pushkin's poem as a subject for an opera, Tchaikovsky replied: "*Onegin* is the outcome of an invincible inward impulse. I assure you one should only compose opera under such conditions. It is only necessary to think of stage effects to a certain extent. If my enthusiasm for *Eugene Onegin* is evidence of my limitations, my stupidity and ignorance of the requirements of the stage, I am very sorry; but I can at least affirm that the music proceeds in the most literal sense from my inmost being. It is not manufactured and forced." And later: "Let *Onegin* be a very boring production with warmly written music: I ask for no more. . . . I was melting and trembling from an inexpressible delight when I composed it."

To the Fourth Symphony also Tchaikovsky remained faithful: to use his own terms, it was his child; he loved it greatly and was not afraid of its ever disappointing him. The first movement, he found himself very complicated and long, but thought that it was the best; the other three were 'great fun to orchestrate.' To Mrs von Meck, the 'best friend' in the dedication, he wrote:

As for the music, I knew beforehand that you *could not help* loving it: it could not have been otherwise. When I wrote that music, I was thinking constantly of you. My relationship to you, at that time, was not at all as close as it is now, but even then I felt, though vaguely, that the whole world does not hold one soul better able to react to the deepest and most secret movements of my own soul, than yours. Never did the *dedication* of a musical composition have a more serious and actual meaning than in this case. I expressed myself, I poured myself out in it not only on my part but also on yours; it is indeed not my but *our* symphony. You alone can feel and understand all that I felt and understood when writing it. It will always remain my favourite work, because it is the *monument* of a time when, after a long-growing spiritual illness and a whole series of unbearable tortures, anguish and despair which very nearly brought me to complete insanity and ruin, suddenly the dawn of regeneration and happiness shone for me, embodied in the person to whom the symphony was dedicated.

When Mrs von Meck desired to know 'what the symphony meant,' Tchaikovsky answered by a most curious literary transposition of a musical work. We are no longer accustomed to search orchestral music for a hidden literary meaning; for us, music is not a cryptogram, and the only feeling that we like to find in a score is feeling for music. For Tchaikovsky and his contemporaries, it was obviously different, as it still is for simpler minds (and maybe purer hearts) than ours. For them music is a kind of language in which the composer can and must communicate his own emotions to the listener. Tolstoi, in *The Kreutzer Sonata*, goes even further: he is convinced that the mood in which the composer was when writing a piece is automatically transmitted to the listener; Tolstoi even expresses doubts as to whether music should not be forbidden altogether, since it allows one man to reign over many others by suggesting to them his own impulses and thoughts. So there is nothing surprising in Tchaikovsky's very seriously explaining to his patroness the intellectual and sentimental content of 'their' symphony.

You ask me if this symphony has a definite programme. Generally, when I am asked that question about a symphonic work, I reply: *none*. As a matter of fact it is a difficult question. How can one describe the indefinite sensations that come to one when one writes a composition for instruments, without any given subject? It is a purely lyrical process. It is the musical confession of a soul which has been through many experiences and whose nature is to pour itself out by means of sounds, just as the lyrical poet expresses himself in verse. The difference lies only in this, that music possesses much more powerful means and a more delicate language to express the thousand different moments of the mind's moods. Most of the time it is quite suddenly and unexpectedly that the *seed* of a future composition appears. If the soil is fertile, i.e. if the composer is in the mood for work, this seed takes root with amazing strength and

speed, shows itself above ground, grows a stalk, leaves, branches,
and finally flowers. I cannot define the creative process without use
of this metaphor. The only problem is the apparition of the seed
and its falling into a favourable situation. All the rest comes of
itself. I could only try in vain to describe to you the boundless bliss
which seizes me when the main idea has appeared and begins to
grow into definite forms. . . . If that state of mind of the artist
which is known as *inspiration* . . . were to last constantly, it would
be impossible to live even one day: the strings would break and
the instrument would fly to pieces. . . . But I am digressing from your
question. In *our* symphony there *is* a programme, i.e. it is possible
to express in words what it is trying to say, and to you, to you only,
I am able and willing to indicate the meaning of the whole and of
the different parts. Of course I can do it only in general terms.

The introduction is the *seed* of the whole symphony, without a
doubt its main idea:

This is *Fatum*, the fateful force which prevents our urge for happiness
from achieving its end, enviously watches lest our welfare and peace
should become full and unclouded, hangs over our head like Damocles' sword, and constantly, unceasingly, poisons our soul. It is
unconquerable, invincible. One has to resign oneself and to languish
aimlessly.

Discontent and despair grow stronger, become more scathing. Would
it not be better to turn one's back upon reality and plunge into
dreams:

O joy! At least one sweet and tender dream has appeared. Some
beatific, luminous human image flies by, beckoning us on:

What bliss! How far away seems now the obsessive first theme of
the allegro. The dreams have, little by little, entirely overpowered

the soul. All that was gloomy and joyless has disappeared. Happiness is here, it has come. . . !

No! They were only dreams, and *Fatum* awakes us:

So life itself is the incessant alternation of painful reality and evanescent dreams of happiness. . . . No haven. . . . Sail on that sea until it encompass and drown you in its depth. Such, approximately, is the programme of the first movement.

The second part of the symphony expresses a different aspect of human anguish. It is the melancholy feeling which appears in the evening, when you are sitting alone, you are tired of working, you take a book but it falls from your hand. Memories swarm around you. You feel sad about *what was and is no more*, but also you find it sweet to remember your youth. You regret the past, but you have no wish to start life all over again. You are tired of it. It is pleasant to rest a little and to have a look around. There are many things you remember. You have had joyful minutes, when your young blood ran hot and life satisfied you. You have had hard times too, you have made irreparable losses. All that is far away already. It is sad and somehow sweet to sink into the past.

The third part expresses no definite sensation. It is made of the capricious arabesques, of the intangible images which pass through the mind when one has drunk a little wine and feels the first phase of intoxication. The soul is neither merry nor sad. One does not think of anything; one leaves free rein to the imagination, and, for some reason, it begins to draw strange designs. . . . Among them comes to mind the picture of tipsy peasants and a street song. . . . Far off somewhere a military parade goes by. These are the disconnected pictures which pass through the head when one goes to sleep. They have nothing in common with reality: they are bizarre, strange, incoherent.

Fourth movement. If you do not find cause for joy in yourself, look at others. Go to the people. Look how smartly they make merry and surrender wholeheartedly to joyful feelings. Picture of a popular festival. Scarcely have you forgotten yourself and become interested in the spectacle of other people's joy, when the tireless Fatum appears again and reminds you of his existence. The others are indifferent to you. They have not even turned their heads towards you, they have not noticed that you were solitary and sad. Oh! how merry they are! how happy they are, because their feelings are all natural and simple. Your troubles are nobody's fault but your own. Do not say that everything is sad in the world. There exist simple but deep joys. Let the good cheer of others be your good cheer. Life can still be lived.

320 TCHAIKOVSKY: A SELF PORTRAIT

This, my dear friend, is all I can tell you about the symphony. Of course it is unclear and incomplete, but this is in the nature of instrumental music, which does not lend itself to detailed analysis. As Heine said: "Where words end, there music begins."

Taneiev did not like the Fourth: the first movement was too long; it gave the impression of a symphonic poem; the folktune was neither important nor interesting; everything reminded Mr Taneiev of ballet music. Tchaikovsky retorted:

I do not understand in the least what you call ballet music and why you cannot reconcile yourself to it. Do you mean by ballet music any gay melody with a dancing rhythm? If so you cannot be reconciled to most Beethoven's symphonies in which such melodies are found at every step. . . . In general I cannot understand how the expression *ballet music* could be in any way *pejorative*. All ballet music is not bad: it can be good (for instance, Delibes' *Sylvia*). . . . I must conclude that the *ballet* passages in the symphony displease you not because they sound like ballet but because they are bad. You may be right, but I still do not understand why a symphony could not contain occasional dance tunes, even with an intentional, coarse, popular, comical aspect. . . . As to your remark that my symphony is programmatic, I agree with it entirely. Only I fail to see why you consider this to be a defect. I fear just the reverse: i.e. I should not like to see streaming forth from my pen symphonic compositions which would not express anything and would merely consist of an empty game of chords, rhythms and modulations. Of course my symphony is programmatic, but its programme is such that it is impossible to express it in words. . . . Is that not exactly what a symphony ought to be, since it is the most lyrical of all musical forms? Must it not express that for which there are no words. . . ? Furthermore, I shall confess to you that, in my naïveté I imagined that the idea behind the symphony was obvious, and that in its general lines it could be understood without a programme. Please, do not think that I am trying to impress you with the depth of my feelings and the grandeur of a thought too great for utterance. I did not try to express anything new. As a matter of fact my symphony is an imitation of Beethoven's Fifth, i.e. I did not imitate his musical thoughts but his basic idea. What do you think, is there a programme to the Fifth? Not only is there one, but there is no question as to what it is supposed to mean. It is approximately the same as mine, and if you did not understand it, the only conclusion is that I am not Beethoven, which I never doubted anyway.

Such elaborate explanations have not reached us concerning Tchaikovsky's Fifth. Here are the only notes that we have about it:

Programme of the First Movement of the Symphony: Introduction. Complete resignation before Fate, or, which is the same, before the inscrutable predestination of Providence.

(Allegro I) Murmurs, doubts, plaints, reproaches against XXX (three crosses in the original)

(II) Shall I throw myself into the embraces of Faith???

In the corner of the notebook leaf is written: "A wonderful programme, if I could only carry it out."

Tchaikovsky never really thought that he could. He always lacked sympathy for this work, which, to our ear, is perhaps the most beautiful of the last three. ". . . After two performances of my new Symphony in Petersburg, and one in Prague, I have come to the conclusion that it is a failure. There is something repellent, something superfluous, patchy and insincere, which the public instinctively recognizes. It was obvious to me that the ovations I received were prompted more by my earlier work, and that the Symphony itself did not really please the audience. The consciousness of this brings me a sharp twinge of self-dissatisfaction. Am I really played out, as they say? Can I merely repeat and ring the changes on my earlier idiom? Last night I looked through *our* Symphony (No. 4). What a difference! How immeasurably superior it is! It is very, very sad!"

Taneiev's opinion, favourable this time, did not change his own gloomy one. "Every time I am more and more convinced that my last symphony is an unsuccessful production, and this feeling of an accidental failure (or maybe of a deterioration of my capacities) hurts me very much. The Symphony appears too colourful, too heavy, insincere, drawn out, in general very un-*simpatichny*. With the exception of Taneiev, who insists that the Fifth Symphony is my best composition, all my honest and sincere friends have a poor opinion of it. Am I then, so to speak, finished? Has *le commencement de la fin**already begun? If so, it is awful. The future will show if I am mistaken in my fears, but, in any case, it is a pity that a symphony written in 1888 should be worse than one written in 1877. As to *our* symphony's being infinitely better than the last one, I am utterly convinced of it." This is the place to observe that although Tchaikovsky was desirous of pleasing his audience, no ovations would persuade him that a piece which he did not like could in fact be good. He had to be satisfied first; only then could he find pleasure in success. A rare example of exacting conscientiousness on the part of a so-called 'popular' artist.

* The beginning of the end.

X

The Sixth is apart, if only because more nonsense was written about it than about any other symphony, including probably Berlioz's *Fantastique*. For once, it is, partly at least, Tchaikovsky's fault. He told Rimsky-Korsakov that the Symphony had a programme but that he did not feel like disclosing it. This, added to the fact that three weeks later he was dead, was enough to kindle imaginations. Here are a few examples of the resulting extravaganza.

For Modest, the Sixth "was like an act of exorcism by which Peter Ilich cast out all the black spirits that had possessed him for so long." For Kurt von Wolfurt, it is "a funeral dirge which the poet sounds for himself." Kurt Pahlen explains all the programme in detail, on five pages: it is complete, with invasion of the earth by inhabitants of another planet in the third movement.

We have already seen that Havelock Ellis found in the Sixth the confessions of a homosexual. Michel Hofmann calls it the "musical confession of a nihilist who would like to get rid of whatever is bad in him;" he also finds, in the second movement, a representation of "the indifference of men seized in the evil whirlpool of social balls (Mrs von Meck and her set?)" as if he did not know that Mrs von Meck, far from attending balls, lived like a hermit in her palaces and estates, refusing to see not only friends but even her children's in-laws.

Hugo Riemann saw resemblances between Tchaikovsky's *Pathétique* and Beethoven's *Pathétique Sonata*. Other commentators read a whole autobiography of the composer in his score. Finally, James Huneker and Edwin Evans may deserve a prize for the most ludicrous programme from us who know that a little before writing the *Pathétique*, Tchaikovsky considered crowning his career with a symphony expressing his attachment to tsarism in general and to Alexander III personally.* According to these two critics, the nature of the secret programme "was mainly political, in the democratic sense. . . ." "The most profound truths, the most blasphemous things, the most terrible ideas, may be incorporated within the walls of a symphony, and the police be none the wiser."

Rostislav Hofmann had a better suggestion. Noting that there are many technical resemblances between the Sixth and the Fourth, and that Tchaikovsky was re-reading Mrs von Meck's letters at the time when he was composing the *Pathétique*, he observed: "The Sixth looks to us like a response to the Fourth, and its cancellation,

* Cf. p. 160.

unless it is simply *The Reproach* which the 'benefactress' had ordered from Tchaikovsky at the beginning of their relationship."

The idea cannot be verified, but it is appealing enough. In May 1877, Mrs von Meck, who was then in the habit of ordering music from Tchaikovsky, wrote him the following letter:

> Will you kindly fulfil this most humble request: write me a composition which would express, and be entitled, *Reproach* (for violin and piano). I have a small composition by Kohne, which is called "Le Reproche," also for violin and piano. I like it very much but it does not express what I want; moreover it is, I believe, addressed to a person. My reproach must be impersonal, it must be addressed to nature, Fate, oneself and to no one else. My reproach must express an unbearable state of mind, the one to which corresponds the French phrase: *je n'en peux plus.** In it one must find a broken heart, a trampled faith, principles insulted, happiness torn away, all that is dear and precious to man pitilessly torn away from him. If you ever lost what you loved and valued, you will understand that state. In that reproach one must hear the despairing movement of anguish, the impossibility to endure such suffering any longer, exhaustion, and, if possible, death, so that at least in music one could find the appeasement that life does not always procure when you want it. Oh! yes, in the reproach, one must also hear the *remembrance* of the happiness that was taken away. Nothing can express such a state of mind better than music, and nobody could understand it in another being better than you. So I bravely give over into your hands my feelings, my thoughts, my desires, and I am sure that this time I am not mistaken, that it is really into clean hands that I place my most valued possession.

Whom did Mrs von Meck want to reproach? This is a mystery,† but it is quite clear that she, like Tolstoi, believed that music could express feelings and thoughts. Tchaikovsky, independent as usual but willing to oblige, replied: "As always, I shall of course be very glad to fulfil your wish and to express as closely as possible all that you would like to hear in this future piece. But this time I shall have to make you wait longer than on previous similar occasions. I am very busy at present and I do not know when I can find time and the appropriate mood." A little later, he had second thoughts about it, and did not hesitate to express them frankly: "On receiving your former musical orders, I already had the idea

---

* Literally: 'I cannot any more.'

† Unless, of course, the von Meck gossip is true, and Mrs von Meck did have a lover in the person of her husband's secretary, Aleksandr Elshin, who would also have been the real father of Mrs von Meck's youngest daughter, Milochka. The last lines of the quoted passage do suggest a former, very bitter, mistake.

that you were guided by two motives: on the one hand you really wanted to have a certain composition of mine in a certain form; on the other, having heard about my constant financial troubles, you were trying to help me. The over-generous payment with which you rewarded my insignificant work convinced me of that. This time, for some reason, I am sure that you were *exclusively* or nearly exclusively guided by the second reason. This is why, having read your letter, in which, between the lines, I read all your kindness and delicacy of feeling, as well as your touching sympathy for me, I felt, in the depth of my heart, an unconquerable distaste for be-ginning the work at once, and hastened to postpone, in my answer-ing note, the fulfilment of my promise. I do not want in my re-lationship to you the sham and lies which would necessarily appear if, without listening to my inner voice, without impregnating myself with the mood that you require, I were to fabricate *some-thing* in all haste, to send that *something* to you and to receive from you an undeserved payment." At the end of this letter he added a post-scriptum: "Nevertheless I shall positively write *The Reproach*, but I cannot tell you when. When I am sure about my summer plans, I shall write you. Kindly send me the Kohne piece." This was in the midst of his matrimonial project, and he obviously felt little enthusiasm for the order. Yet when Mrs von Meck had sent 'the Kohne piece', he expressed his dislike of it and declared that he 'hoped to do better than Kohne had'. Still later, without refusing to fulfil his commission, he acknowledged his failure to do so. In July, he wrote: "If I cannot always satisfy your wishes as to the composition of one or another piece, because I cannot always be in the mood that is needed for composition, I can always do any other type of musical work." And that was the end of *The Reproach*: Mrs von Meck did not insist.

Now if we re-read the programme she had suggested, listen to some passages from the *Pathétique*, and recall the fact that Tchai-kovsky died a few weeks after finishing the symphony, with Mrs von Meck's name on his lips, we may well grant that Hofmann was right and that the sixteen-year-old order was finally executed. But this, of course, will have to remain a matter of personal opinion.

What do we really know about the *Pathétique*?

In 1892, Tchaikovsky was working on a new symphony which he never finished. He destroyed whatever he wrote of it, or in-corporated it into the Sixth that we know. Its programme has been found among his papers for 1891, and, as far as we, who do not believe in expression through music, can judge, fits the spirit of the *Pathétique* rather well. "The ultimate essence of the plan of the symphony is Life. First part—all impulsive passion, confidence, thirst for activity. Must be short. (Finale Death—result of collapse.) Second part love; third disappointment; fourth ends dying away (also short)." In February 1893, the composer wrote to Vladimir Davydov, to whom the Sixth is dedicated:

> I must tell you how happy I am about my work. As you know, I destroyed a Symphony which I had partly composed and orchestrated in the autumn. I did wisely, for it contained little that was really fine—an empty pattern of sounds without any inspiration. Just as I was starting on my journey (the visit to Paris in December, 1892) the idea came to me for a new Symphony. This time with a programme; but a programme of a kind which remains an enigma to all—let them guess it who can. The work will be entitled "A Programme Symphony" [No. 6]. This programme is penetrated by subjective sentiment. During my journey, while composing it in my mind, I frequently shed tears. Now I am home again I have settled down to sketch out the work, and it goes with such ardour that in less than four days I have completed the first movement, while the rest of the Symphony is clearly outlined in my head. There will be much that is novel as regards form in this work. For instance, the Finale will not be a great Allegro, but an Adagio of considerable dimensions. You cannot imagine what joy I feel at the conviction that my day is not yet over, and that I may still accomplish much. Perhaps I may be mistaken, but it does not seem likely. Do not speak of this to anyone but Modeste.

In May, he lifted just one little corner of the veil: "Yesterday I suffered so much that I could neither sleep nor eat, which is very unusual for me. I suffer not only from torments which cannot be put into words (there is one place in my new Symphony—the Sixth—where they seem to me adequately expressed) but from a dislike to strangers, and an indefinable terror—though of what the devil only knows."

In July, he was 'up to his eyes in the Symphony': "The further I go, the more difficult the orchestration becomes. Twenty years ago, I should have rushed it through without a second thought, and it would have turned out all right. Now I am turning coward, and have lost my self-confidence. I have been sitting all day over two pages, yet they will not come out as I wish. In spite of this, the work makes progress, and I should not have done so much anywhere else but at home."

In August, he teased Vladimir Davydov who did not write him as much as he was expected to: "The Symphony which I intended to dedicate to you—although I have now changed my mind—is progressing. I am very well pleased with its contents, but not quite so satisfied with the orchestration. It does not realize my dreams. To me, it will seem quite natural, and not in the least astonishing, if this Symphony meets with abuse, or scant appreciation at first. I certainly regard it as quite the best—and especially the 'most sincere'—of all my works. I love it as I never loved any one of my musical offspring before." Two weeks later he announced to Jurgenson: "Dear friend, I have finished the orchestration of the new Symphony. I have made the arrangement for four hands myself, and must play it through, so I have asked the youngest Konus to come here, that we may try it together. As regards the score and parts, I cannot put them in order before the first performance, which takes place in St Petersburg on 16th [28th] October. . . . On my word of honour, I have never felt such self-satisfaction, such pride, such happiness, as in the consciousness that I am really the creator of this beautiful work."

He had scarcely completed his work when he learned that one of his oldest friends, the poet Apuhtin, had died in St Petersburg. The composer mentioned it to his nephew: "While I write this, funeral services are being held for Lola Apuhtin!! Although his death was not unexpected, it is nevertheless fearful and painful. He was at one time my closest friend!" In September he wrote to Grand Duke Konstantin about his new Symphony: "Without exaggeration I have put my whole soul into this work." But when the Grand Duke suggested that he compose a setting of Apuhtin's *Requiem*, he declined in the following terms: "For the music to be worthy of the poem you like, that poem would have to warm my creative feelings, to touch and agitate my heart, to awaken my imagination. The general mood of this piece does, of course, call for musical reproduction, and my last symphony (particularly the Finale) is permeated with a similar mood. But if one turns to the details, there is a great deal in this poem of Apuhtin's that, though expressed in excellent verse, does not call for music—is, in fact, even antimusical." He was, also, he said, "afraid of repeating himself if he took up so quickly a composition akin in spirit and character to the one he had just completed."

"At rehearsals, the new symphony seemed to make no impression on the orchestra players," which disturbed Tchaikovsky. Nevertheless, according to Kashkin, he declared himself satisfied with the first three movements, but wondered whether he should not destroy and rewrite the last one. The first performance was not very successful, and the composer wrote to Vladimir Davydov: "Something strange is happening to this symphony. It is not that it did not please, but it seemed to puzzle the audience. As to me, I am prouder of it than of any other of my compositions."

The Symphony had still no title, since the first one, *Symphonie à Programme* had been abandoned. Why Modest affects a certain coyness to tell us about its christening is not clear. Anyway, here is his version of the event.

The morning after the concert I found my brother sitting at the breakfast-table with the score of the Symphony before him. He had agreed to send it to Jurgenson in Moscow that very day, and could not decide upon a title. He did not wish to designate it merely by a number, and had abandoned his original intention of calling it "a programme Symphony." "Why programme," he said, "since I do not intend to expound any meaning?" I suggested "tragic Symphony" as an appropriate title. But this did not please him either. I left the room while Peter Ilich was still in a state of indecision. Suddenly the word "pathetic" occurred to me, and I returned to suggest it. I remember, as though it were yesterday, how my brother exclaimed: "Bravo, Modest, splendid! *Pathetic!*" Then and there, in my presence, he added to the score the title by which the Symphony has always been known. There was no other witness of this incident but myself. But it is clear from the programme of the concert of 16th [28th] October that this title had not been given to the work. Moreover, anyone can see by a glance at the title-page that this name was written later than the rest.

The only conclusions that may safely be drawn from this passage are that, according to Modest: (*a*) Tchaikovsky wanted to give a place apart to the *Sixth*, which is not surprising, since he was so happy with it; (*b*) it was Modest who first suggested the term "Pathétique," and not the composer, so that too much meaning should not be read into the title. That is all.

9 *The happiest moments of my life*

And now only one story remains to be told, the story of Peter Ilich Tchaikovsky's relationship to us, his listeners. Did he think about us? What did he expect of us? Would our opinion have been important to him, or did he pretend that he wrote for himself alone?

Although Tchaikovsky lived at a time when artists were expected to create and not, as nowadays, to philosophize about what they could have created but did not, he expressed himself on all these points in his correspondence. Of course, he contradicted himself from time to time, but we know now enough about him to realize that it is precisely among his contradictions that his most intimate truth is to be found.

Some of the contradictions, by the way, are only apparent. In 1879, when he heard his own *Tempest* in Paris, he was ill twenty-four hours before the concert, distressed by the apologetic expression which he imagined on one of the 'cellists' faces, insulted by the hissing, grateful for the exclamations of protest against the hissing, and altogether very unhappy. But this changed with the years. Around 1885, a great transformation came over him: just as he decided not to fight against his misanthropy any more and at once became much more sociable, just as he grew into a very successful conductor, he began to enjoy his own music, especially if nobody suspected that he was in the concert hall. This he found "very merry," although he was sometimes annoyed with the perpetual repetition of the Andante cantabile from the First Quartet.

That he wrote for the general public cannot be doubted. He even accused himself of being partial to opera, "because opera has the privilege of influencing the musical feeling of the masses, whereas a symphonic composer deals with a few selected auditors." He realized that "in composing an opera, the author must constantly think of the stage, i.e. not forget that the theatre needs not only melodies and harmonies but action to hold the attention of the theatre-goer who has come to hear *and see*,—finally, that the style of theatre music must correspond to the style of scene-painting: simple, clear and colourful." He felt remorseful when, as in *Vakula the Smith* for instance, he had 'wearied his listeners with a superfluity of details, and made his harmony too complicated, so that there was no moderation in his orchestral effects; besides, he had given the audience no repose, he had set too many heavy dishes before them.'

On the other hand, he refused to be subservient to the taste of the public, whether composed of 'the masses' or 'the experts,' with nevertheless a little preference for the latter: "It seems to me that some of the *elect*, listening to my music, will maybe experience the feelings which were mine when I wrote it. I do not mean to say that my music is so beautiful that it cannot be understood by the *despicable crowd*. As a matter of fact, I do not understand how it is possible to write intentionally for the crowd or for the elect; in my opinion, one must write in submission to one's own inclination, without ever intending to please this or that part of mankind." He went even so far as to say about *The Sorceress*: "According to me it is an opera seriously and conscientiously composed; if the public does not like it, too bad for them. The public should rise to our level; we, the authors, should not emulate their unintelligence. Experience has taught me that trying to please the public brings no good results." He summarized all this in a revealing passage, which shows how important it was for him to communicate with an audience, but at the level of his choice: "I have always written, and always shall write, with feeling and sincerity, never troubling myself as to what the public would think of my work. At the moment of composing, when I am aglow with emotion, it flashes across my mind that all who will hear the music will experience some reflection of what I am feeling myself. Then I think of someone whose interest I value—like yourself, for instance—but I have never deliberately tried to lower myself to the vulgar requirements of the crowd."

More than a means of communication, music was for Tchaikovsky a means of communion. Starting with the fate of his heroes if he was writing an opera, and in general with the happiness and unhappiness of Man; using the artist's sensibility for mediation, the artist's talent for resonance; the ultimate aim of art, as far as he was concerned, was to create in the public the appropriate response to the original emotion. This is definitely not a vulgar conception of art; in fact, it has metaphysical and religious overtones, and it is useless to try and excuse Tchaikovsky for it, as has been done only too often. His insistence on love as the main ingredient of his work is typical: not only the love of Romeo for Juliet, but the love of man for man, in the boundless geometry of universal communion. Love of Tchaikovsky for his hero, love of the audience for Tchaikovsky's music, and through it, for Tchaikovsky's heroes, for Tchaikovsky the man, and so on. The following passages leave little doubt about this melting-pot of love and art which Tchaikovsky attempted to create: About the *Queen of Spades*: "I cried terribly when Hermann died. It may be the result of fatigue, or then really it is good. . . ." "At one place in the fourth scene, which I was arranging today, I felt such horror, such gruesome thrills, that surely the listeners cannot escape the same impressions." And, more generally, to Mrs von Meck: "Of course I am no judge of my own works, but I can truthfully say that—with very few exceptions—they have all been *felt* and *lived* by me, and have come straight from my heart. It is the greatest happiness to know that there is another kindred soul in the world who has such a true and delicate appreciation of my music. The thought that she will discern all that I have felt, while writing this or that work, invariably warms and inspires me."

Criticism, if expressed in friendly terms, he used to receive gratefully and could even be persuaded—although with tears in his eyes, says Kashkin—to abandon a project which did not meet with the favour of his friends. He wrote in a very understanding tone to Glazunov: "You say your friends did not approve of the work, but did not express their disapproval at the right time—at a moment when you could agree with them. It was wrong of them to oppose the enthusiasm of the author for his work, before it had had time to cool. But it is better that they had the courage to speak frankly, instead of giving you that meaningless, perfunctory praise some friends consider it their duty to bestow, to which we listen, and which we accept, because we are only too glad to believe."

But harshness hurt him deeply. Laroche 'enraged him' by 'the general tone of his remarks and the insinuation that he had borrowed everything from other composers and had nothing of his own.' He observed sadly that 'he had no luck with critics' and was not surprisingly offended by Hanslick's polite declaration that his music stank. He objected to "the cold and inimical note which pervades Cui's criticisms" and Ivanov's "cold and hostile manner, although in Moscow I taught him theory for three years, and did not in the least deserve his enmity." Critics were violent in these days, and we should not be surprised if a 25-year-old musician's head began to spin on reading that his first opera* was "poor in ideas, nearly entirely mediocre, without one remarkable passage, without one happy inspiration." Indeed it is remarkable that eight years later, he was able to write: "Cruel as Cui's review is, and though his verdict is monstrously partial, his evaluation of the musical and dramatic qualities of my work is in substance fair enough." When Laroche, who was supposed to be his friend, wrote that, in *The Voivode*, the composer displayed a limited capacity of adapting himself to the theatre, ignored the Russian setting of his opera, and refused to discard virtuosity for the sake of poetry, Tchaikovsky expressed a strong, but by no means excessive, displeasure:

* *The Oprichnik.*

Laroche: Did you receive my article, Peter Ilich?

Tchaikovsky: Yes, I did, I tore it in pieces and threw it into the fire, as you deserve.

We cannot either accuse Tchaikovsky of over-reacting when, after hearing from Nikolai Rubinstein, also a friend, that his First Piano Concerto* was 'worthless, impossible to play, that its themes had been used before, were clumsy, awkward and beyond possibility of correction, that the composition was poor, that various passages had been stolen from other works, that only two or three pages could be salvaged and the rest had to be thrown away or changed completely,' the composer replied: "I shall not change a single note and shall print it exactly as it is now."

In 1879, Tchaikovsky was still diffident enough to be surprised by his own reaction to *The Tempest*'s failure in Paris: "I was hurt. I had thought myself capable of more courage, namely of complete indifference to public failure." But soon he was to adopt a more philosophical attitude and systematically avoid useless pain. When he learned that *Mazepa* had also been a failure, although Modest had telegraphed him at the time of the creation that it was a success, he thanked the liar: "I can imagine how painful it must have been for you to lie about the great success of *Mazepa* in St Petersburg. But you did well: truth might have killed me." Also, "the circle of those to whom he communicated the fruits of his inspiration became ever smaller, and when he played any of his compositions, he begged his hearers to keep their opinions to themselves. From 1885, he ceased to show his works to anyone. The first to make acquaintance with them was the engraver at Jurgenson's publishing house." For instance he wrote to Taneiev: "When you see me, do not tell me anything about *Iolanthe*, neither praise, nor—God forbid!—criticism. Once the opera has been produced, then you may criticize it to your heart's content." In 1891, the Tsar's opinion could still bother him, even when it had not been expressed: he nearly refused to compose for the Imperial theatres, because he imagined that Alexander III had become indifferent to his music: "If the Tsar does not approve of my production for the theatre, how can I work successfully, well and with love for an institution in which he is the master?" The misunderstanding was soon cleared, and Tchaikovsky stopped sulking.

Maybe more acutely than any other musician, Tchaikovsky felt the basic paradox which every artist has to solve somehow: create

* Cf. p. 118.

for the public, but according to one's own standards; aim for success, but acknowledge no judge of one's work besides oneself. This, to say the least, is not a comfortable situation, and Tchaikovsky was deeply conscious of it. His personal need of sympathy, which, on the artist's plane, became need for admiration and encouragement, did not facilitate matters.

He could afford to look down on the verdicts of the press: "Please, my dear fellow," he wrote to Jurgenson, "do not bother to send me articles in praise of my music, for if there is something I spit upon, it is precisely press reviews, whether favourable or insulting. Both kinds, most of the time, mean nothing, and in fact always irritate me a little: their commendation and their deprecation are mostly unfounded. From which does not follow that I have no regard for the reactions of my friends or the opinion of such authorities as Rubinstein." But his need for approval extended further than a narrow circle of authorities and friends, and he expressed it now with poise and logic, now in the most pitiful tones. "I compose, i.e. through the means of the musical language, I pour out my moods and feelings, and naturally, as any man who speaks and has, or has the pretension of having, something to say, I want to be listened to. And the more I am listened to, the more pleased I am. In that respect, I obviously love fame and aim for it with all my soul." Such was his confession to Taneiev. To his friend Klimenko, he complained: "My overture, *Romeo and Juliet*, has hardly any success here, and has remained quite unnoticed. . . . After the concert we supped, a large party, at Gurin's [a famous restaurant]. No one said a single word about the overture during the evening. And yet I yearned so for appreciation and kindness!" After the creation of the First Suite, which he did not attend, he confided in Jurgenson: "I feel a little hurt that none of my friends telegraphed me after the performance. I am forgotten. The one interest which binds me to life is centred in my compositions. Every first performance marks an epoch for me. Can no one realize that it would have been a joy to receive a few words of appreciation, by which I should have known that my new work had been performed and had given pleasure to my friends?" A similar—and very cruel—silence followed the performance of the Fourth Symphony; then the poor composer poured out his heart to Mrs von Meck:

I am deeply pained, offended and amazed by the incomprehensible silence of all my friends in Moscow concerning the symphony. The only news I have had about it so far comes from you, and also indirectly from Kotek, who informed me that one of his friends . . . had liked it very much. I expected this symphony at least to interest my musical friends, if not to stir and move them. I expected them to understand with what avidity and impatience I waited for sympathetic reactions from them, every one of them describing his own impressions, and not only after some reflection, but also his first and fresh ones, just as you did, my dearest friend. I needed this very much. And imagine, not one word, except a telegram mentioning that the symphony had been *performed* perfectly, an assurance, as I see from your last letter, that was not true. How can I help being offended and pained? Admittedly, I am perfectly satisfied with your warm response and I can do without their enthusiasm, but it is not their enthusiasm I want, it is their friendly attention.

It was also to Mrs von Meck that he wrote on the same subject some of the most pathetic words that ever escaped a great artist in need of a little understanding: "You cannot imagine what an effect your praise has upon me; if you only knew how rarely I hear praise!" Thirsting for understanding, for receptivity perhaps more than for praise as such, he went on to add: "A famous actor said that he always selected one *simpatichny* person from the audience and played for him. I write music for you."

Such being the man, such being the lack of attentiveness which surrounded him, it is not surprising that, to quote Modest: "Tchaikovsky only conducted his works well when he knew they appealed to the players. To obtain delicate *nuances* and a good balance of tone he needed his surroundings to be sympathetic and appreciative. A look of indifference, a coolness on the part of any of the band, seemed to paralyse him; he lost his head, went through the work perfunctorily, and cut the rehearsal as short as possible, so as to release the musicians from a wearisome task."

This exaggerated delicacy of feelings, this almost morbid respect for other people, made Tchaikovsky wary even when he met with approval. He often thought that the audience applauded only to please him, and comments like the following one come frequently under his pen: "The performance was excellent, but it seemed to me the public were unintelligent and cold, although they gave me quite an ovation at the end." But this does not change the fact that when he believed in the sincerity of the public's approval, he was gratified and grateful; he felt that his very existence was then justified.

His reactions varied from amusement to deep emotion. He thought it funny when 'a critic, speaking of the variations in the Third Suite, said that one described a sitting of the Holy Synod and another a dynamite explosion,' or when another one declared that "the variations of the Trio figure a representation of the episodes of Nikolai Grigorievich's [Rubinstein's] life. . . . How amusing! To compose music without the slightest desire to represent something and suddenly to discover that it represents this or that, it is what Molière's Bourgeois Gentilhomme must have felt when he learnt that he had been speaking in prose all his life." He answered most conscientiously requests for autographs coming from every part of America, although he would occasionally ask a friend to sign his name for him on a photograph if the recipient of the gift was not acquainted with his handwriting and would be reached faster this way. He was sensitive to the strangest homages as, for instance "an ice served in some kind of small boxes to which were attached small slates, with pencils and sponges, on which excerpts from my works were finely written in pencil. Then I had to write my autograph on these slates." He was particularly flattered to be honoured in Prague, the first city to recognize the genius of Mozart. And he never played blasé about his successes: "I should gladly say that your praise is equally justified," he wrote to Taneiev after agreeing with him about some criticism, "but modesty forbids me to confirm the fairness of your estimation. Therefore I shall not say that I agree with you, but that your praise makes me very happy. I enjoy very much being praised by you."

Towards the end of his life, he certainly could not complain about the coldness of his audiences. He was applauded, cheered, blessed; he received silver wreaths and precious gifts; he—the first Russian to be acclaimed in Europe—became in Russia a kind of national hero. In Odessa, for instance, "not knowing how to better express their sincere enthusiasm, the people carried Peter Ilich onto the stage when he was called, and that several times. But even that seemed too little to the musicians of the orchestra who were completely under his charm. Understanding what great talent the man had who stood before them, they snatched at his hands to kiss them, and it was not done on impulse, but in conscious worship of him."

Comparable fame Tchaikovsky knew for the last eight years of his life, and it is a pleasure to state that he enjoyed it thoroughly. Already in 1866—the composer was 26—an overture of his, in F major, met with approval: "My overture was performed on Friday, and had a good success. I was unanimously recalled, and— to be grandiloquent—received with applause that made the welkin ring. More flattering still was the ovation I met with at the supper which Rubinstein gave after the concert. . . . After supper he proposed my health amid renewed applause. I go into these details because it is my first public success, and consequently very gratifying." But it was nothing to what began in 1885. The Third Suite created a sensation: "A secret presentiment told me that my Suite would please and move the public. I was glad and at the same time afraid of it. But actual facts left my expectation far behind. I have never experienced such a triumph; I saw that all the mass of the public was impressed and grateful to me. Such moments are the finest ornaments of an artist's life. They make it worthwhile to live and toil." In 1886, at a concert of chamber music "the enthusiasm was sincere, and I went out melting with tender thankfulness. For two days I have even been ill from so much excitement. . . . From everybody, at every step, I found in St Petersburg so many expressions of sympathy and love, that I often found myself weeping from emotion." In 1887: "Received a telegram . . . before supper about the success and packed house of *Cherevichki.* Am awfully gratified. For I, as usual, was imagining just the opposite: emptiness, etc. Even saw distinctly in my sleep an empty theatre." And it went on, and on, till Tchaikovsky's death, and after it, and it is still going on in all the world, so that if the composer is in any position to know what is happening, he must be jubilating in his self-made, artist's paradise.

"The happiest moments of my life come when I see that my music enters deeply into the hearts of those I love, and whose sympathy is dearer to me than fame." So wrote the man who had also said: "The one interest which binds me to life is centred in my compositions." There is no doubt that for him, fame appeared as a kind of synthesis, some would say of beauty and love, but we prefer more modest terms: sympathy and music. That this eminently *simpatichny* man had practically no private life, no all-involving personal attachments, no family, no house, no money, none of those things which tie an artist to his surroundings; that, in a word, he had more or less deliberately given up his life in order to attain immortality, comes out as one of the very few indisputable statements which can be made about this paradoxical and elusive character. All his loyalty was to music, and through music he achieved love: *our* love, the only one, maybe, which he was equipped to get.

As a child, he wrote one of his quaint little French poems on the subject of Joan of Arc. The four last lines went as follows:

> *Tu étais si célèbre*
> *Que l'ange Michel t'apparut.*
> *Les célèbres on pense à eux*
> *Les mechants on les oublie!*

(You were so glorious
That the angel Michael appeared to you.
The glorious, one thinks about them—
The mean are forgotten.)

This could serve as a fitting epitaph for a man who certainly was not mean, who felt throughout his life that glory, present or future, would be his, and whom angels visited frequently under the disguise of inspiration. But Mrs von Meck unwittingly composed a better one. She had sensed that Tchaikovsky was much more musician than man, that this unimportant, though handsome, body, this commonplace, though rather pleasant, life of his, had been given to him only so that his music could flow to us. After all, it is easy to imagine some of the greatest musicians in other parts: Bach could have been a preacher, Chopin an actor, Beethoven a painter, Wagner a soldier, and maybe Mozart a diplomat, but what could Tchaikovsky have been if not what he was: 'a musical cobbler'?

In a great movement of the heart which speaks well for her understanding of the man, she wrote: "Peter Ilich, you are nothing but your music, while your music is nothing but you, your very self."

NOTES TO PART V

1   Modest.
2   Hanson.
3   Hanson.
4   Hanson.
5   Bowen.
6   Hanson.

Bibliography

DOCUMENTS IN RUSSIAN
Literary Works and *Correspondence*. Moscow. Publication begun 1944; 8 vols. published by 1973. Total of 13 expected.

Correspondence with P. I. Jurgenson. Ed. Zhdanov & Zhegin. Moscow.

Correspondence with N. F. von Meck. Ed. Zhdanov & Zhegin. 3 vols. Moscow. 1934–1936.

Letters to Relatives. Ed. Zhdanov. Moscow. 1940.

Letters to Intimates. Moscow. 1955.

Taneiev S. I. *Archives and Documents.* Moscow. 1952.

DOCUMENTS AVAILABLE IN ENGLISH
Diaries of Tchaikovsky—Tr. Wladimir Lakond. New York. 1945. Norton.

ANNALS IN RUSSIAN
Days and Years of P. I. Tchaikovsky—Ed. V. Yakovlev. Moscow–Leningrad. 1945.

BIOGRAPHIES AND ESSAYS IN ENGLISH
Modest Tchaikovsky, *Life and Letters of P. I. Tchaikovsky.* Eng. trans. abridged by Rosa Newmarch. 1906. John Lane.

Rosa Newmarch, *Tchaikovsky: His Life and Works.* London. 1907. Reprinted 1969 by Haskell House.

C. Drinker Bowen & B. von Meck, *Beloved Friend.* New York. 1937. Random House.

H. Weinstock, *Tchaikovsky.* New York. 1943. Knopf.

L. & E. Hanson, *Tchaikovsky: The Man Behind the Music.* New York. 1965. Dodd, Mead & Co.

E. Evans, *Tchaikovsky.* London. 1966. J. M. Dent & Sons.

G. Abraham, *The Music of Tchaikovsky.* Port Washington. 1969. Kennikat.

J. Warrack, *Tchaikovsky.* New York. 1973. Charles Scribner & Sons.

Y

BIOGRAPHIES IN FRENCH
Rostislav Hofmann, *La vie passionnée de Tchaïkovski*. Paris. 1947.
Editions du Chêne.
Michel Hofmann, *Tchaïkovski*. Paris. 1959. Le Seuil.

BIOGRAPHIES IN GERMAN
K. von Wolfurt, *Peter Ilyitsch Tschaikowski*. Zurich. 1952. Atlantis.
K. Pahlen, *Tschaikowsky*. Stuttgart. 1959. Hans E. Günther.

Index

The first date after the title of a work is the date of composition; the second is the date of the first performance.